Winterthur Portfolio 13

American Furniture and Its Makers

Winterthur Portfolio 13

Edited by Ian M. G. Quimby

Published for

The Henry Francis du Pont Winterthur Museum

by the University of Chicago Press

Chicago and London

Statement of Editorial Policy

The objective of The Henry Francis du Pont
Winterthur Museum in publishing *Winterthur Portfolio*
is to make available to the serious student an
authoritative reference for the investigation and
documentation of early American culture.

The publication presents articles about many aspects
of American life. Included are studies that extend
current information about objects used in America in
the seventeenth, eighteenth, and nineteenth centuries;
or about the makers, the manufacture, the distribution,
the use, and the settings of such objects. Scholarly
articles contributing to the knowledge of America's
social, cultural, political, military, and religious
heritage, as well as those offering new approaches or
interpretations concerning research and conservation
of art objects, are welcome.

Ian M. G. Quimby, *Editor*
Catherine E. Hutchins, *Associate Editor*
Catherine H. Maxwell, *Editorial Assistant*

To Charles F. Montgomery
1910–1978

Contents

Introduction   vii

Style and Structure in the Joinery of Dedham
and Medfield, Massachusetts, 1635–1685
Robert Blair St. George   1

Wallace Nutting: Collector and Entrepreneur
William L. Dulaney   47

Furniture in Philadelphia: The First Fifty Years
Cathryn J. McElroy   61

Cabinetmaking in Philadelphia, 1820–1840:
Transition from Craft to Industry
Kathleen M. Catalano   81

Furnishing an Eighteenth-Century Tavern for
Twentieth-Century Use
Constance V. Hershey   139

Wares and Chairs: A Reappraisal of the
Documents
Deborah Dependahl Waters   161

A Cabinetmaker's Price Book
Martin Eli Weil   175

A Methodological Study in the Identification of
Some Important Philadelphia Chippendale
Furniture
Philip D. Zimmerman   193

Mitchell and Rammelsberg, Cincinnati
Furniture Manufacturers, 1847–1881
Donald C. Peirce   209

Notes on Contributors   231

Index   233

Introduction

THE PRACTICE OF COLLECTING American furniture and other antiquities was stimulated by the Centennial Exposition in Philadelphia. Celebration of the nation's one-hundredth birthday called attention to the great men and great deeds of an earlier time while contrasting sharply with the problems of 1876—political corruption, burgeoning industrialism, and the lingering trauma of the Civil War. Filiopietism thus became the dominant motive for preservationists and collectors alike. George Washington's Mount Vernon and many another national shrine would not otherwise have survived.

The perceived evils of industrialism, especially the massive quantities of cheap consumer goods, were another factor that stimulated the collecting of antiquities. Efforts to save or revive handcrafts by such figures as John Ruskin, Charles Eastlake, and William Morris lent a romantic aura to the handmade object while the craftsman himself was elevated to a status seldom found in preindustrial societies. Handcrafted furniture was more "honest" and, hence, more "moral" than the products of the factories of Grand Rapids and Cincinnati.

Filiopietism and the reaction to industrialism combined to create a compelling motive for Americans to collect the furnishings of their ancestors. Furniture and silver in particular became symbols of a happy past when, supposedly, contented craftsmen lavished time and attention on the morally superior task of making elegant furnishings for their well-heeled patrons. Being well heeled themselves, collectors bought not only a piece of the past but identification with their social peers of a golden age.

Whatever the initial motivation to collect, the process of collecting calls forth the desire to know more about what is being collected. The study of

American furniture began with the amateur efforts of collectors and dealers to learn such basic information as When was it made? Where was it made? and Who made it? Gradually, a body of literature was created that provided the broad outlines for classifying furniture made in early America according to period and place of origin. The scarcity of furniture marked with the names of makers led to the practice of attributing many unmarked examples to the relatively few known makers in a few cities. Great emphasis was placed on high-quality workmanship and design, and it often happened that these qualities were equated with age. The view that good design gave way to bad design about 1840, a view that prevailed among collectors of Americana until recently, was at least partly responsible for the common tendency to equate good design and workmanship with the "right" degree of antiquity and bad design and workmanship with a post-1840 date of manufacture. It is a curious fact that for many years antiquarians and modernists shared a common revulsion for much of the furniture and architecture made in America after 1840. In spite of such crippling prejudices, much useful work was done, and many attributions have withstood more recent rigorous investigation.

In the past fifteen years, a marked change has occurred in the way furniture is studied. Fundamentally, the new methodology combines minute examination of the furniture itself with extensive documentary research. Questions pertaining to the quality of workmanship and design, while still important, have given way to questions of technique. The new trend in object examination is based on the assumption that the traditional craftsman held to successful techniques of fabrication however much he might vary the exterior to please a customer. Scribe marks, saw marks, chisel marks, dovetails, methods of joining wood, repeated pattern shapes, and many other criteria, when properly interpreted, can provide the basis for defining the work of an individual craftsman or a local or regional group of craftsmen. Supplemented by exhaustive research in probate records, tax lists, and other records, the furniture craftsmen in a given community can not only be identified but classified according to their status and productivity. No longer is it considered necessary to relate an unmarked piece of furniture to a famous cabinetmaker. Young scholars now find it even more exciting to discover a previously unknown furniture craftsman.

Still another component of the new methodology is the application of scientific techniques to the study of old furniture. Microscopic examination of wood samples taken from furniture has become an indispensable tool. The growing ability to distinguish between European and American woods of the same species has sometimes had dramatic consequences. The secondary woods in chairs and case furniture—the wood the craftsmen thought no one would look at—have been found to be rather important as determinants of regional or even national origin. X-radiographs, long used in the study of old paintings, now reveal joining techniques that are often the key to dating furniture. Previously the only way to be sure was to disassemble the joint, something most curators were reluctant to do.

All these aspects of the new methodology have brought to the study of furniture not only rigor

the seventeenth century and the William and Mary period. When Montgomery left Winterthur for Yale, Forman assumed his teaching duties. Now Forman's students are producing pioneering studies of their own. First there was Robert Trent's *Hearts and Crowns,* written under the auspices of the New Haven Colony Historical Society, and now there is the sophisticated essay in this collection by Robert Blair St. George. Forman's own brilliant work, as yet unpublished, is known best to his students, and they are in the fortunate position of being able to build on a base of information unavailable to others. Finally, it should be observed that all authors represented in this volume, save one, were students of either Montgomery or Forman.

American Furniture and Its Makers opens with St. George's study of a group of chests made in Dedham and Medfield, Massachusetts, during the third quarter of the seventeenth century. Most of the residents of the towns had migrated from a small region in Suffolk, England. Using the analogy of linguistics, St. George hypothesizes a transfer of visual as well as linguistic vocabularies. He finds that design motifs on the Massachusetts chests resemble their English counterparts. While the results may not seem startling, this kind of comparative study has always been very difficult to carry off successfully. Working from two documented carved pieces from the altar of the meeting house and known to have been made by John Houghton, St. George has been able to identify

ture is being produced that is gradually but profoundly changing the way we study artifacts. While many people share the credit for the advances made in this field, one figure towers over the rest. Charles F. Montgomery (1910–78) during his years as a teacher at the Winterthur Museum and Yale University was instrumental in transforming the field. For twenty-six years he urged, cajoled, and inspired his students—both graduate and undergraduate—to try anything that would result in new information about or a new perspective on the artifact of his choice. Above all he tried to teach everyone how to look and, through looking and background study, how to read the object. One of his students, Benno M. Forman, teaching associate at the Winterthur Museum, carries on the Montgomery tradition. For ten years Forman has been researching and writing a major study of American furniture of

A similarly structured analysis by Philip D. Zimmerman examines the construction and the documentable histories of two groups of unusual Chippendale-style chairs. The methodology demonstrates the advantages of combining history and measurable data when making attributions to a single chairmaker or his shop. Zimmerman's study seriously weakens the Randolph sample-chair theory and questions the validity of attributions based on inference or external similarity of decoration on dissimilar furniture forms.

Not all furniture historians focus on attributing surviving pieces to individual craftsmen. Many are more interested in determining the relationships between the furniture available and the culture that used it. Their approach is particularly valuable for identifying forms that did not survive decades or generations of continued use. Cathryn J. McElroy's survey of Philadelphia wills and inventories filed between 1682 and 1730 delineates the wide variety of furniture forms, both new and inherited, available during the early years of settlement.

By 1750 Philadelphia had become the leading city in the colonies. In the ensuing decades, however, the continued expansion was not without its pitfalls. Martin E. Weil recently discovered a manuscript pricebook, dated 1772, which reveals that Philadelphia cabinetmakers consciously sought to stabilize the furniture trade by setting prices. Its entries detail costs per piece based on wood (mahogany or walnut), style, and carved embellishment. That the cost of the journeyman's labor is also listed suggests the master craftsmen attempted to regulate wages in addition to prices. Internal evidence suggests that the manuscript was copied from an unknown printed source that would have predated any known English or American examples.

Until well into the nineteenth century Philadelphia maintained a dominant position in the furniture trade, but the nature of the trade itself was changing. Between 1800 and 1840 a better than fivefold increase in the number of furniture craftsmen and the simultaneous expansion of the export market stimulated the development of wholesale merchandising. Kathleen M. Catalano analyzes this transformation and traces its impact on the already weakened apprenticeship system, the strained employer-journeymen relations, and the continued market demand for large quantities of up-to-date Philadelphia-made furniture.

Meanwhile, across the river in lower New Jersey, an indigenous familial tradition of part-time chairmaking endured. Throughout the nineteenth century and into the twentieth, four generations of the Ware family produced rush- or cane-seat ladderback chairs with few variations—so few that without corroborative evidence it is difficult to distinguish between the chairs made by individuals of different generations. Deborah D. Waters's study of the Ware family chairmakers chronicles the persistence of techniques and local markets despite the availability of products made by Philadelphia craftsmen and, later, from Philadelphia furniture factories.

Although the Ware's cottage industry remained relatively static, this was not true of much of the nineteenth-century furniture industry. Population growth, fueled by a high birth rate and increased migration from Europe, encour-aged westward expansion. Cincinnati was one of the first of several western cities to develop a burgeoning industry that capitalized on the middle-class demand for furniture. Donald C. Peirce discusses the transition of one Cincinnati shop from a two-man partnership to a large factory which supplied its own warerooms in Cincinnati, Memphis, St. Louis, and New Orleans.

As furniture factories produced vast quantities of imitation high-style furniture for the middle class, some people developed an interest in the furniture of their colonial forebears. During the first four decades of the twentieth century the popularity of American antiques soared, and no one capitalized on this trend more vigorously than Wallace Nutting, collector, reproduction-furniture manufacturer, and author of several books on early American furniture. Nutting's aggressive collecting policies earned him notoriety but few friends among sellers and buyers alike. William L. Dulaney examines the career of this controversial self-proclaimed authority and his repeatedly unsuccessful attempts to gain acceptance in the world of the wealthy collectors with whom he dealt.

In no small measure Wallace Nutting contributed to the middle-class interest in colonial America which persists to this day. The strength of the continued interest in the past is demonstrated by the decision of the National Park Service to reconstruct a popular eighteenth-century tavern in Independence National Historical Park in Philadelphia. The reconstruction is unusual because the tavern, operating under Park Service guidelines, is now open for business and serves drinks and eighteenth-century dinners daily. Constance V. Hershey, former curator in charge of furnishing the tavern, recounts the successes, failures, and compromises.

Winterthur Portfolio has been published since 1964 as an annual collection of essays on American art, decorative arts, and related historical subjects. *American Furniture and Its Makers* is volume 13 in the series. With volume 14 this publication becomes a quarterly journal published by the University of Chicago Press. To better reflect its scope, it will be called *Winterthur Portfolio: A Journal of American Material Culture.*

Style and Structure in the Joinery of Dedham and Medfield, Massachusetts, 1635–1685

Robert Blair St. George

IN 1898 HARRIET A. FOWLE presented to the historical society of Medfield, Massachusetts, various relics of the town's early history that had passed to her as a descendant of the Reverend Joseph Baxter, minister at Medfield from 1697 until his death in 1745. Included in the gift were two carved oak panels said to have been part of the original 1655 pulpit of the first meetinghouse. The lozenge-shaped panel (figs. 1, 2) was described in the society's records as "A piece of carved oak from the first church Date 1656 cut on the back." The rectangular panel was not described (fig. 3).[1]

Local antiquarians knew of the panels prior to their acquisition by the historical society. Twelve years earlier, William S. Tilden, in *History of the Town of Medfield*, described the lozenge-shaped panel: "A piece of rudely carved oak is still preserved, which was taken from the front of the gallery when the meeting house of 1706 was pulled down. It bears the date 1656, the year the first pulpit was made. This ornament was probably a part of that piece of furniture, and was put into the second house as a memento."[2] The panels had been rescued from the first meetinghouse when it was torn down sometime between 1703 and 1706 to make room for a larger structure that could accommodate the town's increasing population. The builders of the second house, carpenters Robert Pond and Comfort Starr, were allowed to "have the old one and what appertains to it toward the building and furnishing the new."[3] According to Tilden, the lozenge-shaped panel was originally applied to the pulpit and later nailed to a grooved section of the gallery framing of the 1706 structure (it still bears the remains of a protruding tenon on each end). In 1789, when the second meetinghouse was demolished, the panels were given to the surviving children of Joseph Baxter, during whose ministry the structure had been built. The two pieces subsequently passed through the Baxter family to Mary Baxter Fowle, whose daughter Harriet donated them to the historical society in 1898 (fig. 4).

The two panels are the only remaining clues to the appearance of seventeenth-century furniture in Medfield, and, by extension, its parent town, Dedham. The artifactual evidence from early Dedham, which by 1648 was the fourth largest town in Suffolk County, Massachusetts, is

I am grateful for the generous assistance of Frank Thurston of Libertyville, Illinois, Thurston family genealogist, for information concerning John Thurston's English heritage, and Laura Smith of the Medfield Historical Society for providing access to the two panels from the Medfield 1655 pulpit. Muriel Peters, librarian of the Dedham Historical Society, and Robert Hanson of the Dedham Town Office assisted in researching the Farrington and Metcalf chairs and the genealogy of John Houghton. I am also indebted to John Walton and Douglas Wright for permission to examine objects in their possession and to Alice Gray Read of the Department of Architecture, Graduate School of Fine Arts, University of Pennsylvania, for her patience and skill in preparing the drawings which accompany the text. Special thanks are due Jonathan L. Fairbanks, curator of the Department of American Decorative Arts, Museum of Fine Arts, Boston, who first rediscovered the Medfield panels and recognized their importance, and to Benno M. Forman, teaching associate and research fellow of the Henry Francis du Pont Winterthur Museum, for the constant advice and encouragement he gave as my thesis advisor. Finally, I am most indebted to Robert F. Trent, research associate in the Department of American Decorative Arts, Museum of Fine Arts, Boston, for his many helpful suggestions, constant enthusiasm, and careful reading of the manuscript.

[1] Catalogue of the collection of the Medfield Historical Society, bound manuscript, Medfield Historical Society, pp. 411–12.

[2] William S. Tilden, *History of the Town of Medfield, Massachusetts, 1650–1886* (Boston: George H. Ellis, 1887), p. 115.

[3] Medfield Town Records as cited in Tilden, p. 113.

Fig. 1. John Houghton, Medfield pulpit panel. Dedham, Massachusetts, 1655. Oak with traces of verdigris coloring; H. 12″ (30.5 cm), W. 8″ (20.3 cm), D. 1″ (2.54 cm). (Medfield Historical Society: Photo, Robert F. Trent.)

Fig. 2. Detail of reverse side of figure 1. Because 1656 is cut into the attached section of the 1706 gallery, it was probably added sometime between 1706 and 1887.

Fig. 3. John Houghton, Medfield pulpit panel. Dedham, Massachusetts, 1655. Oak; H. 6⅝″ (16.8 cm), W. 14″ (35.5 cm), D. ½″ (1.3 cm). (Medfield Historical Society: Photo, Robert F. Trent.)

Fig. 4. The Harriet A. Fowle gift to the Medfield Historical Society. From *Proceedings at the Celebration of the Two-Hundred-and-fiftieth Anniversary of the Incorporation of the Town, June 6, 1901* (Boston: George H. Ellis Co., 1902), p. 107.

puzzling in its scarcity.[4] The Fairbanks house is a singular survival of the town's early architecture for which no equally documentable counterpart in furniture has yet been found. And, although collectors have long referred to a group of chests of drawers as "Dedham chests" because one was discovered there in the 1920s, recent research has shown that they were actually made in Boston.[5]

The General Court of the Massachusetts Bay Colony established Dedham in 1636 as a large tract of wilderness bounded on the north by the Charles River, on the east by Roxbury and Dorchester, and extending as far south as the Providence Plantations. The land was well suited to English husbandry, and an economy developed that fostered the raising and processing of grain crops and livestock for the Boston market. In 1660, the observant Samuel Maverick noted that

on Charles River stands the Towne of Dedham about 8 miles either from Boston or Roxberry, a very pleasant place, and the River affoords plenty of good ffish In this Towne leiveth many Bisquett makers and Butchers and have Vent enough for their Commodities in Boston.[6]

Yet, despite the town's apparent success, its vast size soon proved too unwieldy for the selectmen seated in its extreme northeast corner. A steady rise in population from about 410 in 1648 to about 750 by 1700 was accompanied by a rise in land prices and increasing competition for land close to the village center. Inevitably, young farmers became more and more willing to settle in outlying districts. Continued over time, the decentralization pattern effected a pervasive shift from the common field/nucleated-village plan

implemented by the town fathers to a system of individually owned farms in the expanses of available land southwest of town. By 1720, four new towns had been carved out of the original Dedham grant.[7]

Medfield, the first town to split away, petitioned the General Court in 1649 and was allowed to incorporate two years later. Settled as a "village" of an established town, Medfield was made up of people who were from the same cultural background as their Dedham neighbors; in all but four cases, Medfield families had been members of the Dedham community. Indeed, it may be said that Dedham and Medfield formed a single cultural unit within the larger sphere of seventeenth-century New England life. Recent head counts of English emigrants have shown that the two towns were predominantly East Anglian, with a few settlers from the northern counties of Yorkshire and Lincolnshire.[8]

On a more specific level, available evidence suggests that the majority of East Anglians in Dedham came from a small area in eastern Suffolk and southeastern Norfolk bounded by Ipswich on the south, the textile towns of Norwich and Great Yarmouth on the north, and New Buckenham on the west.[9] In particular, many Dedham yeomen came from the Suffolk towns of Syleham, Fressingfield, Ringsfield, and Wrentham. This Suffolk group included Dedham elders Nathan Aldis, George Barber, Henry Brock,

[4]Don Gleason Hill, ed., *Early Records of the Town of Dedham*, 6 vols. (Dedham, Mass.: Transcript Press, 1886–1936), vol. 3, *Town and Selectmen, 1636–59* (1892), p. 153 (hereafter *Dedham Town and Selectmen, 1636–59*). In the rate of October 19, 1648, Dedham was fourth in total funds levied. Above Dedham were Boston, Dorchester, and Roxbury; below Dedham were Braintree and Weymouth. Hingham and Hill were not rated. It should be mentioned that the Seth Clark House (ca. 1678), or Peak House, also survives in Medfield, but it has been heavily restored.

[5]Benno M. Forman, "Urban Aspects of Massachusetts Furniture in the Seventeenth Century," in *Country Cabinetwork and Simple City Furniture*, Winterthur Conference Report 1969, ed. John D. Morse (Charlottesville: University Press of Virginia, 1969), pp. 8–10. Forman notes that a chest of drawers formerly in the Fairbanks house in Dedham is now at the Shelburne Museum; a second example, found by Hollis French, is now in the Museum of Fine Arts, Boston; a third example descended in the Pierce family of Dorchester.

[6]The Dedham grant covered nearly two hundred square miles; see Samuel Maverick, "A Briefe Discription of New England and the Severall Townes Therein; Together with the Present Government Thereof," *Proceedings of the Massachusetts Historical Society*, 2d ser. 1 (October 1884): 238.

[7]Kenneth A. Lockridge, "The Population of Dedham, Massachusetts, 1636–1736," *Economic History Review*, 2d ser. 19, no. 2 (August 1966): 327. The four new towns were Medfield (1651), Wrentham (1673), Needham (1711), and Bellingham (1719). For the only study that treats the implications of land ownership patterns in Dedham in the seventeenth century, see Kenneth A. Lockridge, *A New England Town: The First Hundred Years* (New York: W. W. Norton, 1970), pp. 93–118.

[8]David Grayson Allen, "In English Ways: The Movement of Societies and the Transferal of English Local Law and Custom to Massachusetts Bay, 1600–1690" (Ph.D. diss., University of Wisconsin, 1974), p. 423n., presents the most recent information available regarding the English background of Dedham settlers. Allen maintains that 37.5 percent of all pre-1660 selectmen can be traced to towns in East Anglia.

[9]A cursory survey of the emigrants from the three eastern counties of England listed as settling in Dedham in Charles Edward Banks, *Topographical Dictionary of 2885 English Immigrants to New England, 1620–1650* (Baltimore: Genealogical Publishing Co., 1969), pp. 39–54, 115–24, 149–66, shows that of the thirty-nine heads of household mentioned, twenty-one (53.1 percent) came from eight towns in eastern Suffolk, eleven (28 percent) came from nine towns in southeastern Norfolk, and seven (17 percent) came from five towns in Essex. For specific information on Dedham settlers from Fressingfield, Suffolk, see J. Gardner Bartlett, "Edmund Dana Barbour," *New England Historical and Genealogical Register* 79, no. 316 (October 1925): 339.

Eleazer Lusher, Robert Ware, John Thurston, Francis and Henry Chickering, and Anthony, Cornelius, and Joshua Fisher. Nonconformists all, they may have first met while congregating at Wrentham to hear the sermons of the Reverend John Phillips, who himself migrated to New England in 1638.

The geographical proximity of these Suffolk villages suggests that the early settlers of Dedham and Medfield were a culturally homogeneous group, particularly since the Suffolk area was not a borderline zone between regional subcultures. In fact, recent research in English dialectal linguistics indicates that the particular Suffolk subculture dominating Dedham society coincided with a linguistic subculture that still exists in eastern Suffolk and southeastern Norfolk.[10] If one recognizes that all communication systems are

simultaneous manifestations of shared mental structures, one may tentatively assume that there would exist a dialect of artifactual language that parallels the eccentricities of local verbal language. Theoretically, the peculiarities of speech used by the dominant culture in Dedham, Massachusetts, would have been accompanied by similar localisms in their artifactual expression.

In converting the concept of an "artifactual dialect" from linguistic to art historical terminology, one could expect to find certain similarities in the "regional styles" of artifacts made in the Suffolk subculture and those made in Dedham and Medfield. The continuity of artifactual language should be quite apparent in the woodworking trades; of nine first-generation craftsmen whose regional origins are known, only Jonathan Fairbanks had not emigrated from the Suffolk

[10]See Hans Kurath and Guy S. Lowman, Jr., *The Dialectal Structure of Southern England: Phonological Evidence* (University: University of Alabama Press, 1976); and Harold Orton and Phillip M. Tilling, *The East Midland Counties and East Anglia*, vol. 3, *The Survey of English Dialects: (B) The Basic Materials*

(Leeds: E. J. Arnold & Sons, 1971), pp. i–ii, passim. Kurath and Lowman's analysis of the eastern Suffolk–southeastern Norfolk area as a distinct linguistic subculture is confirmed by the phonetic similarities in Orton and Tilling's returns from Norfolk locations 10, 12, and 13 and Suffolk locations 2 and 3.

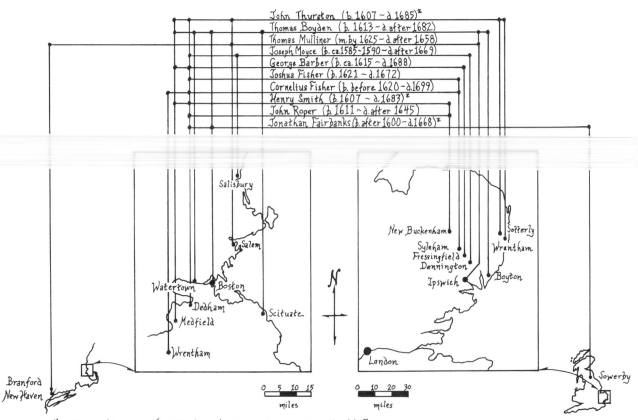

* Craftsman had son(s) who followed in his trade and was working by 1685.

Fig. 5. The English origins of Dedham and Medfield craftsmen (to be used with Appendix). (Drawing, Robert B. St. George.)

area (see fig. 5 and Appendix, p. 37). Because Suffolk craftsmen so dominated the woodworking trades, their apprentices would have been trained in the Suffolk regional dialect, thus perpetuating to a certain degree the same style and structure transferred from England to New England by the first generation. By examining the style and structure, or the "how" and "why" that lie both on and under the phenomenological surface of the artifact, it may be possible to glimpse how the mid-seventeenth-century New Englander reacted to his rapid movement from the rarified culture of the rural English village to the relative cultural pluralism of New England. If there was change, the corresponding patterns of stylistic-linguistic variation evident in the decorative and structural details of the handmade object should serve as a reliable indicator of its intensity.

The two Medfield panels provide the basis for the first steps in reconstructing the artifactual language of early Dedham and Medfield, although they must be tentative. In its broadest sense, the study of the material culture of the seventeenth century in New England is primarily an archaeological pursuit, limited by a relatively low survival rate of artifacts. The diversity of the surviving objects is only a slight sampling of the variety available in the period. As a discipline fraught with the difficulty of connecting object with document, it quickly becomes a species of diffusionist ethnography, concerned with the appearance, distribution, and relationships of types of artifacts. Only through precise genealogical research can an object be associated with a known craftsman, so the relationship between a New England object and its English regional precedent usually must remain generic at best. Thus far, only the connections between objects produced by craftsmen of the William Searle–Thomas Dennis school of Boston and Ipswich, Massachusetts, and craftsmen in Searle's birthplace of Ottery St. Mary, Devonshire, and the similarity of Hadley carving to that found on Lancashire area objects have been noted.[11] The lack of specific documentation usually renders the study of a specific town, ideally the unit upon which re-

gional studies should be based, a difficult task at best. The two Medfield panels are fortunately one of two known instances when the name of a maker whose artifacts survive was entered in seventeenth-century town records.[12]

Work on the first meetinghouse of Medfield probably began immediately following the incorporation of the town in 1651. Within four years, the interior was ready to be finished. On January 14, 1655, the selectmen noted that there was

Due to John hoton for ye Deske & pilers
imp. for ye Deske	7-11-00
it. ye tabel	0-11
Balisters 48 at 7d p[er] piler	1- 8
2 gred [great] pilers	0- 2

sum [£] 9-12-00

paid to John hoton
imps. paid ———— 28 Bushle wheat at 4s [per] Bushel [£] 5-11-00
(by John Dwite 1-0-00[13]

The "Deske," as a pulpit was called in the seventeenth century, was the source of the two surviving panels. John "hoton," or Houghton, of Dedham was the maker. Houghton had arrived at Dedham at the age of eleven in 1635, probably in the company of his father. He had to have apprenticed with a working Suffolk craftsman sometime after arriving in Dedham and before reaching his majority in 1645. For twenty years he worked in Dedham, and in 1665 he moved to Lancaster. When that town was threatened by Indians in 1675, he sought refuge in Charlestown, where he died in 1684 (see Appendix, pp. 41–42).

At first glance, the designs on the two meetinghouse panels are such that they appear to

---

[11]Patricia E. Kane, "The Seventeenth-Century Furniture of the Connecticut Valley: The Hadley Chest Reappraised," in *Arts of the Anglo-American Community in the Seventeenth Century*, Winterthur Conference Report 1974, ed. Ian M. G. Quimby (Charlottesville: University Press of Virginia, 1974), pp. 81–86, 92. Kane states that the pattern on group 2 Hadley chests relates most closely to Lancashire prototypes.

[12]The other instance is the surviving pieces of the original seating of the first meetinghouse of Marblehead, Mass., which were made by carpenter John Norman; see "Marblehead Town Records," *Essex Institute Historical Collections*, n.s. 69, nos. 3–4 (July-October 1933): 226. Another fragment which survives is a pew door from the first meetinghouse of Bristol, R.I., built ca. 1685. However, information about its maker has not yet come to light. The door is illustrated in Marian Card Donnelly, "New England Meeting Houses in the Seventeenth Century," *Old-Time New England* 47, no. 4 (April-June 1957): 90, fig. 3. The author is indebted to Robert F. Trent for the information about John Norman and the Marblehead seats and for giving him access to the extant seats, which are in the collections of the First Church of Christ, Congregational (Old North) in Marblehead, the Marblehead Historical Society, and Robert F. Trent.

[13]All dates prior to 1752 are old style in compliance with the Julian calendar, in which the new year began March 25; therefore, July 1655 came before January 1655. Meeting of January 14, 1655, Medfield Town Records, Town Office, Medfield, Mass.

Fig. 6. Chest, vicinity of Milford, Connecticut, 1640–80. Oak with traces of vermilion coloring; H. 26½″ (67.3 cm), W. 48″ (121.9 cm), D. 20⅜″ (51.8 cm). (New Haven Colony Historical Society: Photo, Robert B. St. George.)

Fig. 7. Chest, probably vicinity of Milford, Connecticut, 1640–80. Oak; H. 27″ (68.6 cm), W. 54½″ (138.4 cm), D. 19″ (48.3 cm). (Metropolitan Museum of Art, gift of Mrs. Russell Sage, 1909.)

have been carved by two different hands. The "spiky-flower" motif used on the lozenge-shaped panel bears little likeness to the S-scrolls cut into the rectangular panel. However, a chest which uses these same motifs simultaneously does survive, demonstrating that both were active in at least one craftsman's vocabulary of ornament and that both were accepted as "going together" by his clientele (fig. 6). This chest is said to have originally belonged to a member of the Merwin family of Milford, Connecticut. Another chest which lacks a provenance (fig. 7) also bears the lozenge-shaped spiky-flower motif (fig. 31*f*). Instead of an S-scroll pattern across the top rail there is a row of carved lunettes which introduces the possibility that the vocabulary of carved decoration included a third type of ornament. The choice of elaborate S-scrolls or simplified lunettes may have depended on the time and money expended on the chest. The construction techniques used on both chests indicate they were the work of a craftsman trained in the Suffolk tradition.[14]

The presence of the two carved motifs on the pulpit Houghton made for the Medfield congregation suggests that the Puritans continued using the embellished pulpit form they had known in the English parish church. A surviving seventeenth-century pulpit in the Church of the Holy Trinity at Blythborough (fig. 8; detail, fig. 30*a*), a town in the Suffolk subcultural area, and the two surviving Houghton panels have provided sufficient data for a conjectural reconstruction of the Medfield pulpit (fig. 9). Like the Blythborough pulpit, it was of joined construction with decorated panels; perhaps lozenges applied to open oak fields would have decorated two levels of the Medfield pulpit and a row of the rectangular panels would have encircled the top. In all probability, the Medfield pulpit was free-standing, supported by the "2 gred pilers" that Houghton supplied. No mention is made, however, of the Medfield pulpit having been "covered" by a sounding board, like that which Job Lane made in 1658 for the first meetinghouse of Malden, Massachusetts. The forty-eight balusters either supported a handrail for the steps to the speaking platform commonly found in most post-Reformation church pulpits or they may have been used on the stair to the gallery.[15]

Marian Card Donnelly has rightly criticized the commonly held view of a "plain style" in Puritan meetinghouse design, noting that the many instances of ornament stipulated in building contracts of the period indicate that clergy and congregation alike were anxious to embellish their structures with carvings and decorative turnings.[16] Whereas Puritans abhorred a sacrificial interpretation of the Eucharist, and thus rejected the communion rail and marble altar of the Anglican church, they continued to view the sermon as the principal means of grace and thus saw no reason to change the form of the pulpit. If the Puritans were iconoclasts, they were selectively iconoclastic.

The location and meaning of the communion table were central concerns of Puritans in seventeenth-century New England. It would have been placed directly in front of the pulpit. The Medfield table probably had turned legs (Houghton had already used a lathe to produce the forty-eight balusters and the two pillars), like the communion table made for the first meetinghouse of Sudbury between 1642 and 1685. Because eleven shillings was a relatively high fee in the mid-seventeenth century, the decoration on the Medfield communion table was probably comparable to the guilloches on a communion table found in Salisbury, Massachusetts.[17]

[14]A similar instance of lunettes and S-scrolls being used on the top rails of two chests appear on two examples attributed to the hand or shop of Thomas Mulliner of New Haven. The chests are illustrated in Patricia E. Kane, *Furniture of the New Haven Colony: The Seventeenth-Century Style* (New Haven, Conn.: New Haven Colony Historical Society, 1973), pl. 1; and Dean F. Failey, *Long Island Is My Nation* (Setauket, N.Y.: Society for the Preservation of Long Island Antiquities, 1977), p. 33. The Merwin family chest was illustrated in "Museum Accessions," *Antiques* 113, no. 5 (May 1978): 978, wherein it was misattributed to Thomas Mulliner of New Haven and Bradford, Conn., or one of his apprentices. Instead it is probably the work of another first-generation Suffolk craftsman who was Mulliner's contemporary.

[15]Contract of November 11, 1658, between the town of Malden and Job Lane, carpenter; called for "the pulpitt and cover to be of wainscott to conteyne ffive or six persons" (Marian Card Donnelly, *The New England Meeting Houses of the Seventeenth Century* [Middletown, Conn.: Wesleyan University Press, 1968], p. 138); Hugh Braun, *Parish Churches* (London: Faber & Faber, 1970), p. 207.

[16]Donnelly, *New England Meeting Houses*, p. 107. Donnelly's conclusions concerning the definition of a Puritan plain style differ with those of other scholars, such as those expressed in Anthony N. B. Garvan, "The Protestant Plain Style before 1630," *Journal of the Society of Architectural Historians* 9, no. 3 (October 1950): 5–13.

[17]The Sudbury table is illustrated and discussed in Robert F. Trent, "The Joiners and Joinery of Middlesex County, Massachusetts, 1630–1730," in Quimby, ed., pp. 140, 142. The Salisbury example, which may have been made by Joseph Moyce, a joiner who lived in Dedham in the late 1630s, is discussed in Phillip Johnston, *Art in 17th-Century New England* (Hartford, Conn.: Wadsworth Atheneum, 1977), p. 33.

Fig. 8. Pulpit at Holy Trinity, Blythborough, Suffolk, ca. 1630–40. Oak. From J. Charles Cox, *Pulpits, Lecterns, & Organs in English Churches* (London: Oxford University Press, 1915), p. 111.

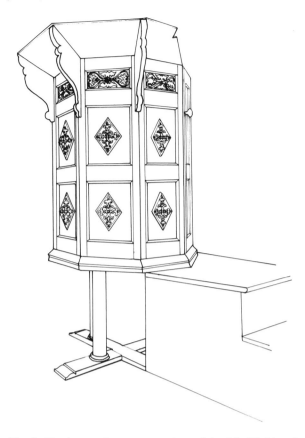

Fig. 9. Conjectural reconstruction of the Medfield pulpit made by John Houghton in Dedham in 1655. (Drawing, Alice Gray Read.)

On the basis of the two panels from the Medfield pulpit, it is possible to attribute two chests and one joined armchair to the hand or shop of John Houghton. The origin of one chest, now in the Museum of Fine Arts, Boston, is unknown (fig. 10). The other tentatively may be associated with Houghton's stay in Dedham between 1645 and 1665; in 1898 it was identified as the "Oak Chest in Store Room 2d Story" of the Fairbanks house in Dedham (fig. 11). If the chest actually descended in the Fairbanks family, it may be the one mentioned in Jonathan Fairbanks's 1668 inventory.[18] Because Houghton plied his trade in Dedham, Lancaster, and Charlestown between 1645 and 1684, in theory the objects could have been made at any point in any of the towns.

The two chests share basic structural similarities that suggest they were made by the same craftsman. Their overall dimensions are almost identical after one compensates for some loss in height due to wear on the corner posts and a decrease in width due to shrinkage of vertical framing members across the grain. The arrangement of panels on the chests is also the same. Each chest has three panels across the front and back and one large panel on each end. The profile and location of the moldings on the two chests are identical. Finally, the two chests also share an unusual construction detail involving the bottom boards. The bottom boards of the Museum of Fine Arts chest are placed with their grain running from front to back. While the boards are nailed onto the bottom edge of the lower rear rail, they are inserted into grooves cut into the inside of the lower side and front rails. The joiner had feathered the edges of the oak planks with a drawknife until they were thin enough to fit into the groove; tool marks left by the drawknife are still visible. Similar grooves in the Fairbanks chest indicate that its bottom

[18]Because only two of the Dedham-Medfield objects retain their original lids, all measurements given in captions do not include the lid. The two examples which retain their original lids are the chest in the Winterthur Museum collection and the box owned by the Metropolitan Museum of Art. William Rotch Ware, ed., *The Georgian Period, Being Measured Drawings of Colonial Work,* 7 vols. (Boston: American Architect & Building News Co., 1898), 1:pl. 26. The chest was later illustrated in Marta K. Sironen, *A History of American Furniture* (East Stroudsburg, Pa.: Towse Publishing Co., 1936), p. 3, and described as "the chest now in Pilgrim Hall Having Modest Decorations." A check into the loan and accession records at Pilgrim Hall, Plymouth, has proved this statement to be in error. The author is indebted to Bert and Ellen Denker for bringing the present location of the chest to his attention. Suffolk County Probate Records, Suffolk County Court of Probate, Boston, 5:112–14.

Fig. 10. Chest, attributed to John Houghton. Dedham, Lancaster, or Charlestown, Massachusetts, 1645–84. Oak and pine with traces of verdigris coloring; H. 26½″ (67.3 cm), W. 41¾″ (106 cm), D. 18″ (45.7 cm). (Museum of Fine Arts, Boston: Photo, Robert B. St. George.)

Fig. 11. Chest, attributed to John Houghton. Probably Dedham, Massachusetts, 1645–65. Oak and pine with traces of verdigris coloring; H. 26″ (66 cm), W. 41¾″ (106 cm), D. 17¾″ (45.1 cm). (Joseph E. Seagram & Sons: Photo, Robert B. St. George.)

Fig. 12. Joined armchair, attributed to John Houghton. Dedham, Massachusetts, 1645–64. Oak; H. 47″ (119.4 cm), W. at seat front 23½″ (59.7 cm), D. at seat 18″ (45.7 cm). (Dedham Historical Society: Photo, Robert B. St. George.)

boards were chamfered in the same way, although the boards have since been replaced. Indeed, the failure of its original bottom boards reveals a structural flaw inherent in cutting a long, deep groove in the lower front rail. Because the slot runs with the grain, any sudden great weight placed, or dropped, on the bottom of the chest weakens the rail. Eventually the wood below the groove breaks off and the bottom boards fall to the floor beneath.

The decoration used on the two chests also points to Houghton as the probable maker. The carved S-scrolls on the Museum of Fine Arts chest bear the closest resemblance to those on the rectangular pulpit panel (details, figs. 30*t, u*). Although the more complex panels on the chest undoubtedly demanded more time to execute, they share many characteristics with the pulpit panel. First, they are set into the field similarly—the field simply follows the curves of the scrolls. Second, the separate lobes in each leaf are inscribed identically. The carver began by outlining the profile of the entire leaf on the wood. Then, using a V-shaped gouge, he articulated each lobe by running a line from the stem outward, stopping just short of the edge of the leaf. As a result, the sections of the leaf are connected by a small strip of wood. Finally, he used a carver's chisel with a slightly curved one-half-inch-wide blade to demarcate the lower corners of the design (visible at the lower corners of fig. 3). The curvature of the blade marks the curving edges of many of the lobes, perhaps indicating that Houghton also used the same tool to cut the basic design into the wood. He also used the chisel to mark the joints on the sides of the chest during construction and used a scribe to differentiate the front and back joints.

Economic circumstances may be responsible for two minor differences in the two Houghton chests. Except for its lid, which is a replacement, the Museum of Fine Arts chest is made entirely of oak, while the Fairbanks chest is oak with pine end panels. The introduction of water-powered sawmills had made pine much cheaper and easier to work with as well. Another difference is in the hinges used on the two chests. The lid of the Fairbanks chest was attached with snipebill hinges that were simply and quickly drawn through small holes and, like cotter pins, spread apart. The Museum of Fine Arts chest originally had a pintel hinge, which required fitting carefully cut cleats to the edges of the lid, drilling holes

through the cleats into the sides of the rear posts, and inserting carefully trimmed oak pins. In short, what may seem a fundamental change in Houghton's technique may have been a faster means of producing a less expensive product.

Despite many overall consistencies, however, there are variations present in the decorations of the two chests which suggest a change in Houghton's visual language as much as they do differing levels of economic intent. Notably, on the Fairbanks chest, Houghton used an extremely complicated variant of the spiky-flower motif in the center panel—the extended floral patterns radiate from a central point (detail, fig. 30*r*). Unlike the lozenge-shaped panel from the meetinghouse, the motifs curve freely. On the side panels of the Fairbanks chest, Houghton grafted a single floral motif onto the central axis of the anthemion frond (details, figs. 30*q, s*). Because the two chests cannot be set into a chronological framework, it would be inaccurate to describe these differences as a "drift" in Houghton's visual language; drift occurs predictably over time, and the intervals of time at which Houghton made these chests cannot be determined.[19]

The similarity of the center panel on the Fairbanks example to those found on chests in the Hatfield area of the Connecticut Valley suggests that it may be more fruitful to search for the sources of Connecticut Valley decoration in those parts of eastern Massachusetts from which the majority of settlers in the Hadley-Deerfield area came rather than to attempt to relate the twice-removed motifs to sources in England. The motifs, so often repeated, may have lost all vestiges of iconographic significance.[20]

The joined armchair attributed to Houghton probably belonged to John Farrington of Dedham, who died in 1678 (fig. 12). It descended through seven generations of the Farrington family until Jessie Farrington (1868–1941) gave it to the Dedham Historical Society. The chair is made entirely of oak. The carved lozenge in the center

[19]George A. Kubler, *The Shape of Time* (New Haven, Conn.: Yale University Press, 1962), pp. 60–61.

[20]Upper Connecticut River Valley objects with carving similar to that on the Fairbanks chest are illustrated in: John T. Kirk, *Connecticut Furniture: Seventeenth and Eighteenth Centuries* (Hartford, Conn.: Wadsworth Atheneum, 1967), figs. 20, 21, 22; Kane, in Quimby, ed., figs. 1, 2, 13; and Dean A. Fales, Jr., *The Furniture of Historic Deerfield* (New York: E. P. Dutton, 1977), fig. 362. All of these examples are of what Kane identifies as group 2 design. Kane suggests the relationship of the Hadley decorations to those used by the joiners of the Searle-Dennis group of Boston and Ipswich. Highly

of the back panel resembles the lozenge-shaped pulpit panel, except that in this case the small trefoil flowers lie outside the points of the diamond rather than within them (detail, fig. 31*b*). The turnings on the front posts of the chair attest to Houghton's skill as a turner. He combined well-articulated balusters above the seat with a Mannerist treatment of an interrupted columnar form below the seat. Structurally, the chair is similar to the two chests in the size of the oak stock used for its frame. Houghton used riven oak planed to a working size of 1¾ inches by 3¾ inches and 2 inches by 4 inches. And as with the sides of the chests, he used a single large panel when framing its back.

The three objects attributed to Houghton and the two panels he carved for the Medfield pulpit raise a major question: If he arrived in Dedham in 1635 at age eleven, from whom did he learn the skills of joining, carving, and turning? Apprenticeships normally began between the ages of thirteen and fifteen and lasted until age twenty-one, so any craftsman working in Dedham between 1637 and 1645 could have been Houghton's master. An examination of the known craftsmen working there during this period has shown that four carpenter-joiners were eligible: George Barber, John Roper, Henry Smith, and John Thurston (see Appendix, pp. 38, 39, 41–42). All other craftsmen were either too young, dead, or living elsewhere. Barber had trained in Fressingfield, Suffolk. Thurston probably trained in Sotterly or Wrentham, both of which are also in Suffolk. And Roper and Smith emigrated from New Buckenham, a small Norfolk village near the Suffolk border. Consequently, Houghton must have been trained in the Suffolk visual dialect that dominated Dedham.

On the basis of what little information can be gleaned from the Dedham and Medfield town records, the craftsman most often called on to do

joiner's work was John Thurston. Thurston had arrived in Dedham from Salem in late 1639, when Houghton was fifteen years old. Assuming that Houghton trained with Thurston, he would have been under his tutelage for the six years between 1639 and 1645. In 1649, Thurston cast his lot with the Medfield petitioners, while Houghton remained in Dedham and married soon thereafter. Of course, Houghton's residence in Dedham explains why the town of Medfield paid Samuel Bullen 2*s*. 6*d*.—a day's wages—for "bringing up the Deske" from Houghton's shop in Dedham.[21] The twenty-mile round trip from Medfield would have taken a day's cart ride on roads muddied by spring rains.

Prior to the 1651 incorporation of Medfield, Thurston had undertaken two large contracts in Dedham. On January 8, 1646, that town

Agreed wth Joh Thurston to make the seats in ye Meetinghouse: all that shall be placed in the new house & on the East side of the midle Alley in the old house—he to finde all the worke about them. carriag excepted, and to haue timber for that vse of the Towne. & to receaue of ye Town for the said worke [£]13 10s: to be payed [£]5 in Ceader boarde at 4s p cent.[hundred] 20s in Indian at 3s p bushell. the rest in wheat at 4s p bushell. all to be deliuered in Towne.[22]

By seats, the contract meant pews of joined construction, possibly with large vertical panels arranged below narrow horizontal panels. A balustrade of small turned spindles may have run along the top of the stalls.[23] In making the seats, Thurston would have used a plow plane fitted with a fence to cut deep grooves in the stock to hold the dressed edges of the panels securely in place.

Thurston's second major job in Dedham was the construction of the town's first schoolhouse in 1648, for which he received a partial payment of £11.0.3 on December 2, 1650. References in the contract to laying floorboards, making doors, and fitting the interior with "featheredged and rabbited" boarding indicate that it may have been Thurston who taught Houghton how to fit the feather-edged bottom boards of a chest into grooves in its rails.[24] Not surprisingly, Thurston continued to work as a carpenter-joiner after ar-

---

questionable attempts to relate ritual and royal emblemata like the lily and the Tudor rose have been made in Richard Lawrence Green, "Fertility Symbols on the Hadley Chests," *Antiques* 112, no. 2 (August 1977): 250–57; and John T. Kirk, "Sources of Some American Regional Furniture: Part I," *Antiques* 88, no. 6 (December 1965): 790–98. The latter is especially inaccurate in its claim that the folk artist has no alternative to copying high-style images; the former is an absurd attempt to read latent folk religious undercurrents from artifacts which the author assumes to be decorated with abstract depictions of fertility rituals. Among other faults, Green has not confronted the problems of iconographic meaning changing over time and has mistakenly perpetuated the misattribution of one Hadley chest to Phineas Pratt.

[21]Meeting of June 10, 1657, Medfield Town Records.
[22]*Dedham Town and Selectmen, 1636–59*, p. 115.
[23]The first meetinghouse in Marblehead had such stalls with spindles, only two of which survive; see n. 12 above.
[24]*Dedham Town and Selectmen, 1639–59*, pp. 131–32, 156–57. Similar feather-edged boards surviving in the Fairbanks house, Dedham, are noted in Norman M. Isham and Albert F. Brown, *Early Connecticut Houses* (1900; reprint ed., New York: Dover Publications, 1965), p. 257.

riving in Medfield. In June 1657, he was paid £13.5.1 for the seating in the Medfield meeting-house. Eighteen months later, Medfield "Agreed with brother thurston to make the seate aboute the tabell in the meeting house and to seat the galiry."[25] The "seate aboute the tabell," or dea-con's seat, was the one piece of freestanding fur-niture that Houghton did not supply for the Medfield meetinghouse. The gallery seats may have been boxed pews similar to those on the floor of the house or less expensive board benches.

Working backward from Houghton's work, it is possible to attribute one chest with one drawer, five chests without drawers, and two boxes to Thurston on the basis of their design, di-mensions, decoration, and workmanship. But, as with the objects attributed to Houghton, it is im-possible to arrange the master's work into any evolutionary sequence. It must be assumed that they all could have been made within a short period of time.

According to family tradition the chest with one drawer illustrated in figure 13 descended to

the present owner from ancestors who lived in Salem, Massachusetts.[26] Because Thurston lived in Salem between 1637 and 1639, it is tempting to think that the chest with one drawer could have been made that early. However, marks left by the steady up-and-down movement of the mill saw on the pine boards of the drawer bottom suggest otherwise. No sawmill was operating in Salem at that time, so the chest must have been made while Thurston lived in the Dedham-Medfield area. The chest probably does not predate 1660, the year Dedham's first sawmill was built; a date after 1660 is consistent with contemporary references to the chest-with-one-drawer form.[27] The chest passed into the present owner's family by mar-

---

[25]Meetings of June 10, 1657, and December 15, 1658, Medfield Town Records.

[26]The chest with one drawer was illustrated and tentatively attributed to Rowley, Mass., in Benno M. Forman, "The Seventeenth-Century Case Furniture of Essex County, Mas-sachusetts and Its Makers" (M.A. thesis, University of Dela-ware, 1968), pp. 98–102.

[27]Benno M. Forman, in "Mill Sawing in Seventeenth-Century Massachusetts," *Old-Time New England* 60, no. 4 (April-June 1970): 125–26, notes that Salem did not have its own sawmill in operation until 1670, although possibly milled wood in Salem was available from other area mills such as those operating at Portsmouth (1634), Rowley (1642), Salis-bury (1650), and Ipswich (1656). For early references to the chest-with-one-drawer form, see Irving W. Lyon, *The Colonial Furniture of New England* (1891; reprint ed., intro. Dean A. Fales, Jr., New York: E. P. Dutton, 1977), p. 8.

Fig. 13. Chest with one drawer, attributed to John Thurston. Medfield, Mas-sachusetts, 1660–85. Red oak by microanalysis and hard pine with traces of vermil-ion and verdigris coloring; H. 31⅜″ (79.7 cm), W. 47¾″ (121.3 cm), D. 21″ (53.3 cm). (Privately owned: Photo, Robert B. St. George.)

riage with a Dedham-Medfield family in the 1750s.

As one would expect, the chest with one drawer attributed to Thurston shares many of the construction quirks present in the work of his probable apprentice. The bottom boards of the chest portion are also feather-edged and fit into grooves cut into the side and front rails. Similarly, the drawer bottom is tapered along its front edge and fits a narrow groove on the inside of the drawer front. Unlike the bottom of the chest, the drawer bottom is comprised of one large pine board and a smaller one placed with their grain parallel to the front. The bottom boards, while feather-edged and fitted into the front rail, are nailed to the sides and back. The similar treatment of the bottom boards suggests that the maker resorted to a single means of solving what appeared to him as two instances of the same conceptual problem; in other words, he addressed the problem of "bottom" consistently.

The drawer front is rabbeted to receive the sides, which are fastened by two nails countersunk above and below the slide (fig. 14). The rear of the drawer is held between the sides with a straight butted joint and secured by a single nail driven flush into the slide. Because all of the carpenters working in Dedham and Medfield were from the Suffolk subculture, this drawer can be relied upon to be an example of that region's construction methods. Ultimately, it may help to identify the wares of other Suffolk joiners working in New England.

An additional noteworthy detail on the front of the chest is the presence of mitered tenons (fig. 15) that give each panel a uniformly beveled surround; thus the carving looks more like a framed picture. Mitered tenons were also used on chests made in the Hadley area and are related to similar detailing on the regional furniture of Lancashire and Yorkshire. The use here by a Suffolk-trained craftsman proves that the technique was

Fig. 14. Side view of drawer from chest shown in figure 13. Note the feather-edged bottom board. (Photo, Robert B. St. George.)

Fig. 15. Detail of mitered tenon joint on chest shown in figure 13. Joint is at junction of the front rail under the drawer and the front right corner post. (Photo, Robert B. St. George.)

Fig. 16. Chest, attributed to John Thurston. Dedham or Medfield, Massachusetts, 1639–85. Oak; H. 26″ (66 cm), W. 46″ (116.8 cm), D. 20″ (50.8 cm). (Hampton Gallery: Photo, courtesy Benno M. Forman.)

not confined to craftsmen trained in the northern counties. And the fact that in all known instances it is used only on the front of an object suggests that it is not a regional trait but rather an economic detail.[28] It further suggests a direct relationship between the working techniques of Dedham and Hadley area craftsmen, thus fundamentally weakening an argument linking Hadley joinery to Lancashire, a county in England from which few documented New England woodworkers actually emigrated. Cutting a mitered tenon and beveling the mortised post required extra work and increased the cost. Such a conspicuous display of workmanship was intended for equally conspicuous consumers.

The overt display of extra workmanship and purposeful variety is most apparent in the decorative details. On the front of the chest with one drawer in figure 13, complex moldings embellish the framing members. The framing members surrounding the panels are chamfered, a technique traceable to medieval carpentry still extant in East Anglian parish churches.[29] The elaborately carved panels (details, fig. 30c, d, e) at first appear to be identical. Closer inspection reveals many deliberate differences, especially in the designs of the central flower. Far from being the uncalculated bumblings of a primitive craftsman, these panels vary because variety—not uniformity—was the desired effect. The carved motif on the drawer front (detail, fig. 30b) added a final variation. (Its S-scroll design resembles the upper panels of the Holy Trinity Church pulpit [detail, fig. 30a]. This is not coincidental. Blythborough is only ten miles from Wrentham, the town from which Thurston emigrated.) Once the carving was finished and the chest with one drawer assembled, it was painted with vermilion and verdigris coloring. The combination of surface textures, motif, contrasting colors, and complex form dazzled the eye.[30]

[28]Kane, in Quimby, ed., p. 92; Christopher G. Gilbert, "Regional Traditions in English Vernacular Furniture," in Quimby, ed., pp. 53, 75n.; Gilbert notes that the mitered tenon detail was first observed by Benno M. Forman and subsequently published as a note in *Country Life* 152, no. 3924 (August 31, 1972): 519. Other examples of probable East Anglian craftsmanship in New England joined furniture which have the mitered tenon are the chest shown in fig. 6 above and a chest which descended in the Hedges family of East Hampton, Long Island, illustrated in Failey, p. 33 (see n. 14 above).

[29]Braun, p. 188, fig. 25 (see n. 15 above). Although some scholars argue that chamfers used on the panel surrounds of seventeenth-century joined furniture are related to mason's moldings, Braun demonstrates that in East Anglia they derive ultimately from medieval carpentry that predates stone construction.
[30]Paint colors used throughout this essay are in the terminology taken from the 1684 inventory of Daniel George, painter of Boston, reprinted in Abbott Lowell Cummings, "Decorative Painters and House Painting in Massachusetts Bay, 1630–1725," in *American Painting to 1776: A Reappraisal*, Winterthur Conference Report 1971, ed. Ian M. G. Quimby (Charlottesville: University Press of Virginia, 1971), pp. 118–19.

The five carved chests without drawers attributed to Thurston are difficult to date because they contain no clues as definite as the use of milled pine. Three chests are related to the chest with one drawer. The chest illustrated as figure 16 was advertised for sale in May 1969, and its present owner and location are unknown.[31] The chest appears to have retained much of its original paint, but it has lost several inches of its height and has subsequently been placed on a stand. This chest is the only other member of the Dedham-Medfield group that uses the mitered tenon in its joinery. As with the chest with one drawer, the mitered tenons appear only on the front, a readily visible indication of the fine craftsmanship the owner could afford. Another chest (fig. 17), formerly owned by the late Philip L. Spalding, was sold at auction in 1974.[32] It is now in a private collection. The third chest (fig. 18), now in the collection of the Delaware Art

Museum, has a traditional history of being owned by the Brandywine School artist Howard Pyle. Although the lid of this example has been replaced, the original one was connected with pintel hinges. In addition, new feet have been added to the corner posts of this chest. The sharp contrast between the rectangular field and the relief in the carved panels of these chests again illustrates the variations of surface texture applauded by devotees of Mannerist taste. Like those of the chest with one drawer, the panels of these chests are arranged axially; the center panel on each differs slightly from the side ones (details, fig. 30*f, g, h, i, m, n*).

Two remaining chests may be attributed to Thurston on the basis of the cumulative evidence. The chest (fig. 19), now in the Wadsworth Atheneum, was formerly owned by Wallace Nutting and appeared in both *Furniture of the Pilgrim Century* and *Furniture Treasury*. In the latter publication, Nutting stated that the three panels were of identical design, but close inspection reveals that here again the center panel differs from the side panels (details, fig. 30*j, k*). The top and bottom boards of this chest are replacements, but evidence indicates that this chest too had the feather-edged bottom boards that fit into grooves

---

[31]Advertisement of Hampton Gallery, *Antiques* 95, no. 5 (May 1969): 642.

[32]*Americana*, Sotheby Parke Bernet sale catalogue no. 3596 (January 24–26, 1974), lot 781, "Pilgrim Century Carved Oak Blanket Chest." Because of repairs made to the corner posts of this chest, it is impossible to tell whether or not it originally had a drawer, as the present proportions would seem to indicate.

Fig. 17. Chest, attributed to John Thurston. Dedham or Medfield, Massachusetts, 1639–85. Oak; H. 27″ (68.6 cm), W. 40½″ (102.9 cm), D. 16¾″ (42.4 cm). (Collection of Douglas Wright: Photo, courtesy Sotheby Parke Bernet.)

Fig. 18. Chest, attributed to John Thurston. Dedham or Medfield, Massachusetts, 1639–85. Oak with traces of vermilion coloring under modern black enamel; H. 26¾″ (67.9 cm) not including pieced section of posts, W. 40″ (101 cm), D. 17¾″ (45.1 cm). (Delaware Art Museum: Photo, William Pugh.)

Fig. 19. Chest, attributed to John Thurston. Dedham or Medfield, Massachusetts, 1639–85. Red and white oaks by microanalysis; H. 26⅝″ (67.5 cm), W. 43″ (109.2 cm), D. 18″ (45.7 cm). (Wadsworth Atheneum: Photo, E. Irving Blomstrann.)

Fig. 20. Chest, attributed to John Thurston. Dedham or Medfield, Massachusetts, 1639–85. Red and white oaks and white pine by microanalysis; H. 26½″ (67.3 cm), W. 42″ (106.7 cm), D. 17½″ (44.5 cm). (Winterthur Museum.)

Fig. 21. Box, attributed to John Thurston. Dedham or Medfield, Massachusetts, 1639–85. Oak and pine; H. 9⅝″ (24.4 cm), W. 25⅜″ (64.4 cm), D. 15″ (38.1 cm). (Metropolitan Museum of Art, gift of Mrs. Russell Sage, 1909.)

Fig. 22. Box, attributed to John Thurston. Dedham or Medfield, Massachusetts, 1639–85. Oak and pine; H. 9¾″ (24.7 cm), W. 26⅛″ (66.3 cm), D. 16¾″ (42.4 cm). (Art Institute of Chicago, Wirt D. Walker Fund.)

in the framing and pintel hinges to attach the lid. Traces of vermilion coloring are still visible. Henry Francis du Pont acquired the other chest (fig. 20) for his collection at Winterthur from the collection of Herbert Lawton of Boston in 1928.[33] Although the chest lacks a provenance, the ɫS carved into the center of the top front rail and the backside of the rear left panel suggests that it originally belonged to John Smith (Smythe) of Dedham, the only member of the Dedham-Medfield community in the seventeenth century with those initials. The Winterthur Museum chest is the only member of the Thurston group whose panels are all exactly the same (detail, fig. 30*l*). Quite possibly, the three identical panels cost less than three panels with subtly deliberate variations in design.

The chests belonging to the Wadsworth Atheneum and to Winterthur Museum share a detail not found on other members of the group. Instead of using a molding plane to decorate the framing members, the maker employed used a V-shaped gouge to quickly run straight lines into the stock. The Wadsworth Atheneum chest is the only member of the group whose side framing members are also treated. Three explanations may account for the use of the gouge on either chest: (1) it was the least expensive means of satisfying a frugal customer, (2) the craftsman did not own a molding plane when he made the chest, and (3) the craftsman did not know how to use a molding plane. The last suggestion is easily refuted as the Winterthur Museum chest has bottom boards butted with V-groove joints the feathered into grooves. Both techniques demanded prowess with the plow plane and fence, and any craftsman capable of controlling the plow plane would have found the molding plane no challenge. Whatever the actual reason, it would be simplistic to maintain that such a detail is earlier because it appears more technically crude.

The two boxes attributed to Thurston demonstrate that basic board construction was part of this joiner's technical language. Similar to drawers in design, the boxes were made by nailing the side boards into rabbets cut in the front and rear boards. However, the drawer bottom was nailed

to all four sides rather than fit into grooves. The top was attached with pintel hinges, even though the thinness of the rear board prevented the attachment of an independent dowel. Instead, each end of the board was cut so that a small piece running with the grain extended to act as a pin. The cleats were then slipped over these protruding pieces and the hinge completed. This detail differs from the design of the pintel hinge used on chests, where the vertical orientation of the heavy corner posts permitted the use of a separate dowel as a pin.

One box now in the Bolles Collection of the Metropolitan Museum of Art still retains its original cleats, lid, and rear board with the small extension pins intact (fig. 21). A related box now in the Art Institute of Chicago came from the collection of B. A. Behrend of Wellesley Hills, Massachusetts (fig. 22). It has had its top and cleats replaced, but it still retains its original complementary color scheme. The AH box supposedly belonged to Adam Howe of Sudbury, the proprietor of the Wayside Inn in the late eighteenth century. Research into the Howe genealogy suggests that if the box descended to Adam from his forebears, it may once have been the property of Abraham Howe of Watertown and Marlborough (married 1658, died 1695).[34] Yet the layout and execution of the carved decoration are markedly similar to those found on the chests Thurston was making in Dedham and Medfield. In addition, it is highly unlikely that Howe would have chosen a joiner not from Watertown or Marlborough to make a box. Therefore it is more probable that this box and the one with the initials MH shown in figure 21 belonged to members of the Holmes, Hawes, Harding, or Hinsdale families of Dedham and Medfield. The AH box may have been made for Abraham Harding of Dedham and Medfield.

The decoration on the two boxes (details, fig. 30*o, p*) closely parallels that found on the central panel of the Delaware Art Museum chest, all the panels on the Winterthur Museum chest, and the rectangular meetinghouse panel by Houghton, perhaps indicating that all were made within a short time of one another or that they all fell into the same level of workmanship. However, any attempt to assign a chronological sequence to such a

[33]Nutting, *Furniture of the Pilgrim Century*, rev. ed. (Framingham, Mass.: Old America Co., 1924), no. 29; and Nutting, *Furniture Treasury*, 2 vols. (Framingham, Mass.: Old America Co., 1928), 1:no. 19. Accession no. 57.539, Object File, Registrar's Office, Winterthur Museum. The chest was illustrated in Anderson Gallery sale catalogue no. 2214 (January 6–7, 1928), p. 96.

[34]"Antiques in Domestic Settings: An Early Colonial Home in Massachusetts," *Antiques* 40, no. 5 (November 1941): 289; James Savage, *A Genealogical Dictionary of the First Settlers of New England . . .*, 4 vols. (1860–62; reprint ed., Baltimore: Genealogical Publishing Co., 1965), 2:475.

small body of undocumentable objects on the basis of these details, which may well have been economically determined, would be solely an exercise in modern subjective judgment.

The products of John Thurston and his apprentice, John Houghton, are similar. They are alike in their overall dimensions, the arrangement of panels, and the type of decoration used. Yet Houghton's carving is distinct in the way the S-scrolls are set into the field. Whereas the master invariably delineated the boundaries of the rectangular field around each S-scroll motif, his apprentice was generally satisfied to allow the field to follow the curves of the scrolls. Only on the central panel of the Fairbanks chest did Houghton define the corners of the rectangular field. The similarities between the work of Thurston and Houghton illustrate the fundamental master-apprentice relationship which, by definition, involves the transmission of ideas regarding the conceptualization and propriety of form, construction technology, and the decoration of the finished product.

In practical terms, the experienced joiner taught the would-be craftsman how to choose woods correctly, use woodworking tools properly, lay out the parts of a given form to the correct dimensions, and paint the object after it was assembled in the shop.[35] In theory, the master provided his student with a conceptual model already proved by his clientele to be aesthetically, functionally, and economically acceptable. On the most basic level, a new apprentice probably began by making chests that were devoid of any embellishments and concentrated his efforts on perfecting joinery skills. He first learned the language of form and only secondarily refined his decorative rhetoric with the molding plane and carver's gouge. As Henry Glassie has explained, objects may be disjuncted into primary and secondary components analogous to their structure and decoration, and the secondary aspects may be thought away without altering the existing structure.[36] Because structure is the basic unit of an artifactual language, it is the substance of the first lessons taught by the master to the apprentice. While decoration may vary less predictably from

hand to hand, structure will remain a more reliable index of interrelationships in the joiner's trade. Therefore, any considerations of the structures explicit and implicit in the artifactual language of the seventeenth century should move from the most abstract levels of geometry to the most particularized aspects of decoration.

Glassie has described the conceptualization and construction of housing as a series of moves working from the "selection of the geometric entity," through the "transformation of the geometric entity," to the massing and piercing of the three-dimensionalized product.[37] The beauty of this sequence is that it may be extended to the analysis of almost any handmade object, and, because joinery and carpentry are so intimately related, it is possible to apply these same steps to the design and production of furniture. The maker of the Dedham-Medfield chest illustrated in figure 19 had four similar decisions to make prior to beginning work: (1) what the dimensions of the "plan" would be, (2) how high the corner posts would be, (3) where the vertical muntins would be placed to subdivide the front and rear "walls," and (4) how the decoration would be laid out on the panels.

The joiner began by establishing the plan of the chest. His measuring tool was the twelve-inch carpenter's rule, which, when divided into its simplest fractions of one-half, one-fourth, and multiples of one inch, provided working units two, three, and four inches in length. The maker first laid out his basic geometric shape, an eighteen-inch square (fig. 23a), by adding six inches to the length of his rule. Since the trades of the joiner and the carpenter were virtually indistinct from one another in rural villages in the seventeenth century, the use of the eighteen-inch square by Thurston bears thoughtful comparison with the frequent use of the same linear unit (also known as the cubit) by housewrights of English descent working in rural Virginia.[38] He then extended this square into the final plan by doubling its length and then arbitrarily adding seven inches (fig. 23b), as in the case of the chest in the Wadsworth Atheneum. It should be noted that the length, which varied from 41¾ inches to 48 inches on the Thurston-Houghton chests, may

[35]"[The] nature of apprenticeship—for artist and artisan alike—made it axiomatic that the apprentice learn from his master not only technique but substance" (Benno M. Forman, "Continental Furniture Craftsmen in London: 1511–1625," *Furniture History* 7 [1971]: 95).

[36]Henry Glassie, "Structure and Function, Folklore and the Artifact," *Semiotica* 7 (1973): 327.

[37]Henry Glassie, *Folk Housing in Middle Virginia* (Knoxville: University of Tennessee Press, 1975), pp. 21–28. For a similar structural examination of the turned chair form, see Robert F. Trent, *Hearts and Crowns* (New Haven, Conn.: New Haven Colony Historical Society, 1977), pp. 24–29.

[38]Glassie, *Folk Housing in Middle Virginia*, pp. 22–24.

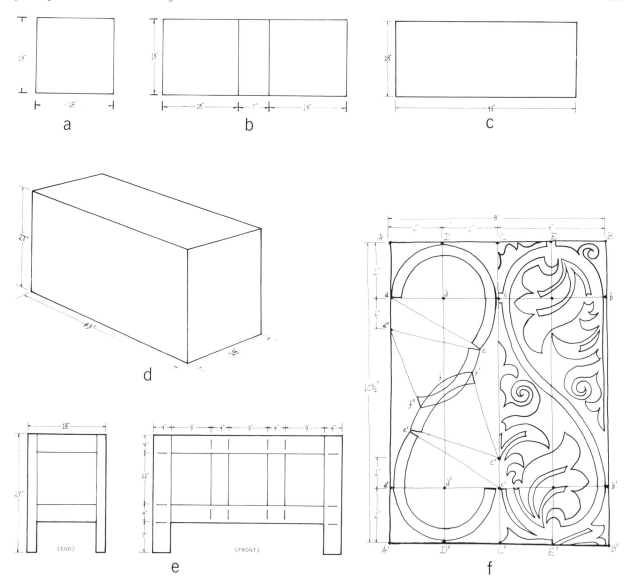

Fig. 23. Structural analysis of a Thurston chest. *a*, The geometric unit selected: the square. *b*, The geometric unit transformed. *c*, The plan defined. *d*, The definition of mass. *e*, "Piercing" the mass. *f*, The decorated surface defined. (Drawings, Alice Gray Read.)

have been a function of cost as well as design. In fact, an increase of length—provided decoration (a second variable of cost) remained constant—would have corresponded directly with an increase in cost, as material and labor in the seventeenth century were measured and appraised in linear feet. In this case the rectangular plan had overall dimensions of eighteen by forty-three inches (fig. 23c). The next step was to extend this plan into a three-dimensional mass. Pulling it up through the space, he decided on a height of 27 inches (now worn down to 26⅝ inches) for the corner posts, thus giving the mass a height-to-depth ratio of exactly three to two (fig. 23d). His next decision was how to arrange the muntins and panels, analogous to the bents and bays of a heavy-timber framed house. Fortunately, all of the chests of the Thurston-Houghton group retain the scribed lines which originally served to align the framing members conceptually and determined the locations of all needed mortises during the preparation of the stock prior to assembly.

The carefully scribed lines on the rails and posts show that the maker continued using a rational system of design, positioning the members at even intervals to call cadences of 4 inches/ 9 inches/4 inches/9 inches/4 inches/9 inches/ 4 inches along the front, 4 inches/ 12 inches/ 4 inches/ 7 inches down the corner post, and 2 inches/ 14 inches (7+7)/2 inches along the side (fig. 23e).

Finally, the craftsman laid out the decoration on the panel. Each "pierced" opening in the chest was nine by twelve inches, or a width-to-height ratio of three to four. After selecting a piece of oak larger than this void, he nailed it to his bench to be carved (the nail holes are still visible at edges of fig. 30c). So the panel could be nailed squarely down to the bench, he did not feather its edges until after the carving was completed. Working with the nine-by-twelve-inch area that would remain exposed, he established a ½-inch margin at the top and bottom and ¾-inch margin at either side and scribed the rectangle shown as *ABB'A'* in figure 23f. The rectangle provided an area 8 inches by 10½ inches for the carved surface. He divided it in half by scribing the vertical line *CC'*, leaving the two sections four inches in width. He again divided these by scribing segments *DD'* and *EE'*, leaving four strips each 2 inches by 10½ inches. Next he marked out segments *ab* and *a'b'*, which produced four two-inch squares at the top and bottom of the panel.

At this point he took a compass in hand to begin laying out the curves of the S-scrolls. Unlike the makers of the Hadley chests, who used templates in order to ensure decorative consistency, Thurston and Houghton laid out their carved designs with the compass and completed them freehand. With one foot of the compass at point *d*, the maker swung the arc *aDc*, and repeated the procedure at point *d'* to make arc *a'D'c'*. Using the four inches from the length of segment *ac* or *a'c'* as a radius, he described arcs *ce* and *a'e'*, only to find himself confronted by an unconnected area in the middle. To eliminate this, he fixed points *c''* and *a''* by extending segments *Aa* and *C'c'* by half their original length. Again setting the compass at a radius of four inches, he placed the foot at points *c''* and *a''* to make arcs *ef''* and *e'f'*, respectively. Yet the arcs still did not intersect exactly at point *f*. His only solution was to complete the design by hand, which he did in every case.[39] If so, why did he bother with the compass at all?

The tool must have represented a means of guaranteeing an essential regularization in workmanship, despite its limitations. Thurston distrusted his own hand to repeat the basic structure of the S-scroll design. In clinging to the mechanical predictability of the compass, he recognized the element of risk implicit in the unguided hand and tried to minimize it. The tool was not a crutch. More precisely, it was a jig with which the joiner could insure his clientele a high-quality product with a high degree of compositional consistency over a long period of time. Furthermore, the ease of working with the compass allowed him to make more objects in less time. Simply put, Thurston recognized that risky workmanship was risky business.[40] The joiner was dependent on his ability to demonstrate skill for his livelihood. He was aware of aesthetic criteria, and having arrived at a system of artifactual communication which "spoke" to his townsmen, he repeated it until he did it by rote.

Like the walls of a house, those of the chest were assembled on the ground prior to being connected with one another in the three-dimensional form. The Dedham-Medfield chests

[39] I am indebted to Benno M. Forman for confirming this explanation of the layout of the carved panel on the chest in the Winterthur Museum collection (fig. 30l below).

[40] For additional information on theories of good and bad workmanship in relation to risk and certainty, see David Pye, *The Nature and Art of Workmanship* (Cambridge: At the University Press, 1968), pp. 13–27.

are remarkable in that the backs and fronts of each chest are in theory conceptually identical, as are the ends. The joiner's marks which survive on the one Houghton chest (figs. 24, 25) indicate, however, that for practical purposes the separate pieces were differentiated from the very beginning of construction. The use of premolded rails, muntions, and posts on the front differentiated it from the back, whose stock was not molded. The joiner's marks shown in figure 25 were used on the front and back alike solely to make the individual parts of each section distinct from one another so that the hand-fitted joints of the two muntins on the rear could not be confused by their apparent interchangeability. Naturally, each tenon was trimmed to fit only its corresponding mortise, so no parts could be interchanged. On both the front and back, mere habit dictated that he proceed from left to right as he numbered the joints. Similarly, the ends of the chest are conceptually the same, but are marked with either single or double chisel marks, as in figure 24, to keep them differentiated during construction. It is impossible to tell exactly in what order the craftsman put up the "walls" of the chest; he may have made the completed sides (with corner posts) first and then attached the front assembly to them, or, conversely, he may have completed the front and back (with corner posts) first and then completed the chest by simply inserting the side members. As in house construction, the order of assembly may have been traditionally—although not necessarily log-

Fig. 24. Detail of figure 10 showing chiseled joiner's marks at junction of top rail on right side and front right corner post. (Photo, Robert B. St. George.)

Fig. 25. Detail of figure 10 showing scribed joiner's marks at junctions of rear muntins and inside of top rear rail. (Photo, Robert B. St. George.)

ically—related to the conceptual layout and construction of each unit part of the whole.

Such was the structure of the artifactual language that Thurston taught Houghton. The joiner's marks on the one Houghton chest do not appear on any of the master's chests, suggesting that the syntactic order, while new to Houghton, was fully understood by Thurston. The constant repetition of an idea—in artifactual terms, a structural matrix—moves it from the external activity of the craftsman's hand to the internalized patterns of the mind. In similar manner, Houghton observed the carving style of his master. In a sequence of panels arranged according to the complexity of design attained (fig. 30*b* through 30*u*), the apprentice's panels show equal workmanship although perhaps less concern with purposeful intricacy. Houghton's carvings are set further within the field, not seeking to dominate the surface by crowding it with line. Those by Thurston tend more toward the *horror vacui* associated with the late Medieval–Mannerist style.

The dimensions and layout of the chests attributed to Houghton are exactly the same as those attributed to Thurston. Yet, while the base structure allowed no variation, the vagaries of personalized decoration were enforced less strictly. That is, drift was not tolerated in the primary component but was allowed in the secondary. Seventeenth-century furniture was strictly ordered. In laying out and constructing his wares, the joiner followed a rational orderly system of compositional logic that he used over and over. All of the chests share the same basic qualities. Only economic considerations and the fleeting whims of the customer caused minor variations.

In the seventeenth century, the intrinsic quality of a completed object was judged according to standards of acceptability defined and reinforced by members of the craftsman's community. The measure of a master craftsman was his ability to make what was referred to as a workmanlike product, whether it was a house, a chest, or a pulpit. The word "workmanlike" was used frequently in many seventeenth-century contracts and meant having an acceptable degree of control over material through an acceptable degree of control over process. For example, in a contract for the construction of the first King's Chapel in Boston, dated July 21, 1688, the building committee directed carpenters John Holebrook, Stephen French, and Jacob Nash to build the church "of good sound timber well and workmanlike

wrought."[41] Thirty years earlier, the town of Malden retained Job Lane to build its first meetinghouse. The contract uses language even more specific concerning the requisite control of material through regularized workmanship: "The said Job Lane doth hereby covenant, promiss and agree to build, erect, and finish upp a good strong, Artificial meeting House, of Thirty-three foot Square, sixteen foot stud between joints, with dores, windows, pulpitt, seats, and all other things whatsoever in all respects belonging thereto."[42] When the town of Boston agreed with carpenters Thomas Joy and Bartholomew Bernard to build the first townhouse in 1657, it asked them to find "things necisarie and meet for the said Building viz: Timber in everie respect & of everie sort, substantial & meet according to Proportion & Art."[43] The use of such words in seventeenth-century New England as "workmanlike," "artificial," "proportion," and "art" proves that a craftsman's ability to control material, process, and formal composition were intimately related to the success he enjoyed in his own community. Like verbal language, artifactual interaction was ordered by the particular style and structure in which the maker and user were fluent.

The final analysis of the Dedham-Medfield artifactual language must take the components of structure and style—material, technique, compositional logic, construction, and decoration—into account in approaching a more sophisticated concept of the standards of craftsmanship and craft organization active in seventeenth-century New England. The emphasis placed on maintaining standards of workmanlike and artificial competence by the joiner's trade is indicative of a need to assert and perpetuate one artifactual language—one order—that was acceptable to the immediate community. By establishing standards of order, first-generation New Englanders could cope with the lack of order which faced them in the wilderness. In the wilderness that surrounded

[41]Contract quoted in Walter Kendall Watkins, "Three Contracts for Seventeenth Century Building Construction in Massachusetts," *Old-Time New England* 12, no. 1 (July 1921): 31.

[42]Contract quoted in Watkins, "Three Contracts," p. 27.

[43]Contract quoted in Helen Bourne Joy Lee, *The Joy Genealogy* (Essex, Conn.: Pequot Press, 1968), p. 22. A reconstruction of the 1657 townhouse drawn by Charles A. Lawrence in 1930 is now in the collections of the Bostonian Society and may be consulted in Bernard Bailyn, *The New England Merchants in the Seventeenth Century* (New York: Harper & Row, 1964), facing p. 130.

them, the Dedham settlers saw a void, not necessarily chaos. Hence, the encounter of the yeoman
and the New England wastes may be characterized as a fundamental psychological conflict
between man and lack of man.[44] This dichotomy
may be rephrased as the opposition of culture
and lack of culture or one culture and any other
foreign or threatening culture. Joiners in
seventeenth-century Dedham and Medfield
needed to show their power to imprint their own
Old England order on the New England void, to
contain their new universe by marking its bounds
with their own work.

In this light, the joinery of Dedham and
Medfield can pierce deep into the subjective reality of the yeoman. The ever-present molding
that marks the corner of an oak chest was a pro-
found reaction to lack of order; the unworked
edge was a small bit of chaos subdued with the
blade of the plane. In similar fashion, a serrated
edge marked the front of boxes. Colors made to
catch the eye covered up the wrought object, thus
adding a final level of artificial order. Each time
the craftsman added a level of artificiality, the
artifactual language became more particularized.
Viewed in this manner the highly worked and
highly specialized vocabulary and syntax of the
Dedham-Medfield chests confirm the tenacity of
the Suffolk tradition among local craftsmen.

The dominance of the Suffolk style in Dedham and Medfield is confirmed by the fact that it
had more than one exponent in the first generation. One of the few surviving pieces of
seventeenth-century furniture which demonstrates certain similarities to the work of
Thurston and Houghton is a joined armchair
with an enclosed bottom, now owned by the Dedham Historical Society (fig. 26). The chair bears
the carved inscription "M 1652 M" and is said to
have descended from Michael Metcalf, a weaver
who emigrated from Norwich in 1637 and died in
Dedham in 1664. This chair, the earliest known
example of dated American furniture, is one of
two known examples of seating furniture with a

Fig. 26. Joined armchair with enclosed bottom, Dedham, Massachusetts, 1652. White oak by microanalysis;
H. 46¼″ (117.5 cm), W. at seat front 22½″ (57.2 cm), D.
at seat 17½″ (44.5 cm). (Dedham Historical Society:
Photo, Robert B. St. George.)

---

[44]Glassie, *Folk Housing in Middle Virginia*, pp. 122–36. Glassie argues that the basic dichotomy active in an artifactual
language is, as Lévi-Strauss has described it, one between nature and culture. However, the concept of nature implicit in
his dualism is a romantic contrivance of the eighteenth-
century Enlightenment, perhaps best outlined in Jean-Jacques
Rousseau's *Les Rêveries du promeneur solitaire* (1777). The
seventeenth-century yeoman had no concept of nature per se;
hence, the applicable dichotomy is one between culture and
lack of culture or the preestablished order and either lack of
order or a different order.

storage cupboard beneath the seat.[45] A door that opened into the bottom has disappeared, but remnants of its original leather hinges survive (fig. 27). Five structural aspects of the chair suggest that it was made by a Suffolk craftsman: (1) like the Farrington family chair (see fig. 12), it has a single large panel in the back; (2) its lozenge (detail, fig. 31*c*) and crest also resemble those of the Farrington chair (detail, fig. 31*b*); (3) the manner in which the carved leaflets on its rear posts are conjoined corresponds exactly to the technique used on the panels by Thurston and Houghton; (4) the framing members are gouged rather than molded, as on the chests at Win-

terthur and the Wadsworth Atheneum; and (5) the appearance of frond motifs on the rear stiles of the chair has a stylistic precedent in the carvings on the corner posts of the Blythborough pulpit.

A chest traditionally associated with the 1644 marriage of Jonathan Rudd of Norwich and Saybrook, Connecticut, may also have been made by the same Suffolk craftsman responsible for the Metcalf chair (fig. 28). The chest shares many characteristics of the joined chests by Thurston and Houghton. It has three panels on the front and back and one large panel on each end; it retains all of the scribe marks originally intended to mark the location of mortises; it also uses stock of the same size as that used on objects in the Thurston-Houghton group. The lozenges on this chest (detail, fig. 31*d*) are exactly like that on the Metcalf chair.[46]

[45]The Michael Metcalf chair was described by Irving Whitall Lyon in his *Colonial Furniture of New England* (Boston: Houghton Mifflin & Co., 1891), p. 147. In discussing joined chairs, Lyon noted "In some of these chairs the space below the seat is enclosed by means of panels let into the framework, and panels also fill the space between the seat and the arm on each side. An example of this kind, dated 1652, is now preserved in the Old South Church of Boston." The Metcalf chair was presented to the Dedham Historical Society by Louisa Harris in 1909, who must have received it from Luther Metcalf Harris, family genealogist (see n. 46 below). The other known example of the enclosed bottom seating form is a chair-table with a cupboard beneath the seat now in the collection of the Old Saybrook Historical Society, Old Saybrook, Conn., which descended in the Jones family of Saybrook.

[46]Although the chest is traditionally associated with the 1644 marriage of Jonathan Rudd, genealogical research suggests that it actually descended in the Metcalf family of Dedham and was taken to Connecticut when Mary Metcalf, a fifth-generation direct descendant of Michael, married a John Rudd of New Lebanon in the late 1720s. At that time the initials IR/MM were cut into the center panel. The chest passed to their son William Rudd, who married Eunice Bingham of Windham on December 23, 1771. Eunice survived her husband, and after her death the chest passed to her brother,

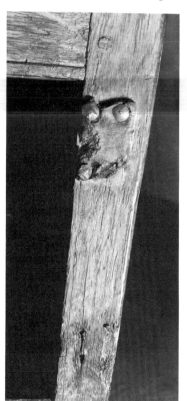

Fig. 27. Detail of figure 26 showing leather hinges on rear right post. (Photo, Robert B. St. George.)

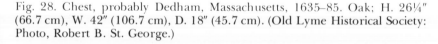

Fig. 28. Chest, probably Dedham, Massachusetts, 1635–85. Oak; H. 26¼″ (66.7 cm), W. 42″ (106.7 cm), D. 18″ (45.7 cm). (Old Lyme Historical Society: Photo, Robert B. St. George.)

The close resemblance between these two objects and those of the Thurston-Houghton group shows that the Suffolk visual dialect of Dedham and Medfield was consistent in its various parts. While the decoration of these two objects differs in details, the underlying structures do not.

Kenneth A. Lockridge has called Dedham a "Christian Utopian Closed Corporate Community" similar to other New England towns of its size in its conscious and unconscious need to preserve English tradition by maintaining social, political, and economic stability.[47] Explicit in his thesis is the concept that the 1635 Dedham Covenant, in its overt concern for establishing an exclusivist Christian order, called for a fine balance of permitted individual growth and mandatory group stasis. In short, Dedham depended on control for survival while still permitting individuals to engage in social intercourse. The artifacts show the same tendency toward control. They reveal no structural changes and only slight stylistic variation in the first and second generations. When compared to Lockridge's theory that the Dedham socioreligious experiment had failed by the 1660s, the artifacts show that cultural patterns held firm. Through the repetition of motif and structure, the artifact can act upon man's subjective reality as a mechanism of restraint and perhaps even of the stasis suggested by Lockridge. In their high degree of internal and external consistency, the Dedham-Medfield objects betray the microcosmic environment responsible for their conception, production, and use. They tell a collective story of marked conservativeness, a characteristic which had been observed as typical of folk communities in general.[48]

Ultimately one must attempt to comprehend how conservative tendencies are in fact perpetuated and manifest in the object. The answer to this lies in two parts which, when taken together, illuminate both the introspection of village life and the larger problem of the dissemination of style types in early New England.

Yet before generalizations about New England may be made, one must look at the unit of culture at the base of the region: the town. In Dedham and Medfield, the perpetuation of the Suffolk dialect in the woodworking trades was aided by apprenticeship patterns, the high rate of intermarriage between members of Suffolk carpenters' families, and the frequent instance when a son would continue in his father's trade. In short, carpentry and joinery—like many trades—became genealogically and technically cohesive unto themselves.

Because all of the first-generation carpenters and joiners in the two towns worked in the Suffolk tradition, the mechanics of supply and demand dictated that the Suffolk visual dialect would dominate the local citizenry irrespective of their cultural backgrounds. For instance, when John Farrington, a yeoman from Lincolnshire, needed a joined chair (fig. 12), he went to Houghton, a second-generation craftsman trained by a Suffolk carpenter-joiner. Similarly, when Jonathan Fairbanks, a turner from Yorkshire, needed a house, he had to retain a Suffolk carpenter such as Thomas Fisher or John Roper to do the job; indeed, the Fairbanks house is built in an East Anglian manner.[49]

As spokesmen who articulated in visual terms their common cultural language, the Suffolk craftsmen in Dedham and Medfield played a dynamic role in the acculturation of their non-Suffolk neighbors. Farrington, Fairbanks, and, no doubt, other emigrants from the north of England owned furniture which spoke the old Suffolk language; Houghton's pulpit, too, was an artifactual sign that quietly preached the dominance of the Suffolk subculture in the community. In their domestic interactions, the townsmen of Dedham and Medfield ordered function, movement, and space with Suffolk artifacts. The same motifs watched over them in the meetinghouse, where their religious and social lives met

Zacheus Bingham. Josephine Bingham, who presented the chest to the Old Lyme Historical Society, Old Lyme, Conn., sometime after 1926, was a direct descendant of Zacheus. See Thomas M. Bingham, comp., *The Bingham Family in the United States*, 3 vols. (Easton, Pa.: Bingham Assn., 1926), 1:229, 295, 470, 2:114, 3:573, illustration; and Waldo Lincoln, *Genealogy of the Waldo Family*, 3 vols. (Worcester, Mass.: Charles Hamilton, 1902), 1:246; Luther Metcalf Harris, comp., "Metcalf Family," *New England Historical and Genealogical Register* 6, no. 2 (April 1852): 176, no. 90. The chest has been published with its traditional "Bride's Brook" history in Minor Myers, Jr., and Edgar de N. Mayhew, *New London County Furniture 1640–1840* (New London, Conn.: Lyman Allyn Museum, 1974), pp. 4, 14.

[47]Lockridge, *New England Town*, pp. 16–17, 167–80 (see n. 7 above).

[48]Roger D. Abrahams, "Personal Power and Social Restraint in the Definition of Folklore," in *Towards New Perspectives in Folklore*, ed. Américo Paredes and Richard Bauman (Austin: University of Texas, for the American Folklore Society, 1975), p. 17; Glassie, *Folk Housing in Middle Virginia*, pp. 178–79.

[49]The author is indebted to Abbott Lowell Cummings, executive director of the Society for the Preservation of New England Antiquities, for confirming that the Fairbanks house is an East Anglian structure.

in a single artifactual context. Viewed in this light, the artifacts were the tangible manifestations of a movement toward cultural unity in private and public life, while the craftsmen gained new power as individuals whose peculiar role it was to make objects accepted by all.

The identification of what may be a pure Suffolk style in Dedham and Medfield sheds new light on how the dissemination of a "regional style" actually worked. Certainly the migration of craftsmen and their apprentices accounted for a great deal of the similarities among the artifacts made in different parts of New England. The master-apprentice relationship, as a mechanism developed intentionally to perpetuate high standards of communicative behavior, was responsible for spelling out to would-be craftsmen of the next generation the established standards of acceptable workmanship. The master's role was that of the exacting grammarian who placed articulate speech and memorization of rules above all else. Maintaining established standards of performance and discipline in the trades was crucial to the continued efficacy of the built environment as the real and ideal embodiment of the old order. In short, the established order depended on control for survival.

In other instances regional similarities in New England joinery resulted from craftsmen who migrated from the same area in England and settled in different villages in the new world, where their work developed in varied ways from a common root. For instance, the carved S-scrolls attributed to Thurston bear a generic relationship to those on the front posts of a chest probably made by Thomas Mulliner of New Haven, Connecticut. The similarity may be explained by the fact that Wrentham, Suffolk, where Thurston last worked, is only twenty-five miles from Mulliner's hometown of Ipswich, Suffolk, and both craftsmen were trained prior to emigrating to New England.[50] Similarly, the S-scrolls and carvings on the Merwin family chest (details, figs. 30*v*, 31*e*) and the S-scrolls found on a desk box originally owned by William Wells of Southold, Long Island (fig. 29; detail, fig. 30*w*)

suggest that East Anglian craftsmen were active throughout the New Haven colony.

More than just decorative details attests to the presence of East Anglian craftsmen. Five surviving New Haven area chests and the nine Dedham-Medfield chests share the same arrangement of panels, and two of the New Haven chests also have a V-groove in the joinery of their bottom boards.[51] The products of the New Haven craftsmen differ from the Dedham-Medfield objects because isolation from a homogeneous Suffolk subculture rapidly produced deviation in their products. In Dedham and Medfield, the high percentage of Suffolk settlers provided a relatively stable culture that demanded little change in the artifactual language. John Thurston, John Roper, Thomas Fisher, Henry Smith, and George Barber could continue making joined furniture in the same style they had known in England without worrying about its acceptability in Dedham and Medfield. Yet imagine a Suffolk joiner forced by economic circumstance to accommodate the tastes of New Haven's predominantly London culture.[52] He would have had to modify his language to suit that of the local dominant culture. Because the "mixture" of a pluralist culture is variable in space and in time, it is important that objects must not be judged outside of their respective frames of reference; as Henri Focillon suggested, the milieu is a flexible order.[53]

Indeed, the contextual fluidity which characterized life in seventeenth-century New England since the first day of settlement demands sensitivity of the scholar seeking an understanding of the material remains of the period. By closely observing interrelationships among extant objects, the historian may effectively describe and classify the

---

[50]Kane, *Furniture of the New Haven Colony,* pp. 11, 78–80 (see n. 14 above), contains the most complete biography of Mulliner published. For additional notes on Mulliner not included in Kane's sketch, see Henry F. Waters, "Genealogical Gleanings in England," *New England Historical and Genealogical Register* 51, no. 203 (July 1897): 421; and Richard Brigham Johnson, "Swampscott, Massachusetts, in the Seventeenth Century," *Essex Institute Historical Collections,* n.s. 109, no. 4 (October 1973): 251.

[51]The four examples with single end panels are illustrated in Kane, *Furniture of the New Haven Colony,* pls. 1, 20, figs. 4, 5. A fifth, owned by the Society for the Preservation of Long Island Antiquities, is illustrated in Failey, p. 33 (see n. 14 above). The two New Haven Colony chests with V-grooved bottom boards are both attributed to the Guilford area on the basis of their carved decorations and are illustrated in Kane, *Furniture of the New Haven Colony,* pls. 19, 20.

[52]Kane, *Furniture of the New Haven Colony,* p. 5, quotes Floyd M. Shumway, "New Haven and Its First Settlers," *New Haven Colony Historical Society Journal* 21, no. 2 (September 1972): 51, in estimating that 51.8 percent of the New Haven settlers came from London and the home counties, with the next largest group (16.4 percent) coming from the Midlands. By contrast, Shumway notes that only 19.3 percent of the Bay Colony's residents were from London and environs, while 61.4 percent were from Suffolk, Norfolk, and Essex.

[53]Henri Focillon, "Introduction to *Art Populaire,*" trans. Robert F. Trent, in *Hearts and Crowns,* p. 17 (see n. 37 above).

Fig. 29. Desk box, Southold, Long Island, before 1665. Post oak by microanalysis; H. at back 10″ (25.4 cm), W. 25¾″ (65.4 cm), D. 21″ (53.3 cm). (Long Island Historical Society: Photo, Joseph Adams.)

products of craftsmen from a certain region. Yet the function and meaning of the historic artifact, whether it be a chest, a gravestone, or a shard of pottery, must not be abused by scholars who employ the object in order to demonstrate the validity of a conclusion they have reached by other means. In treating artifacts within an ethnographic framework, the diffusion of style types must not be used merely as a tool for proving or disproving demographic patterns, whether they be from Old England to New England, from Suffolk to Dedham, or from Dedham to the upper Connecticut River Valley. Fortunately, such methodological tricks are quickly discovered, because artifacts are ideas in motion, not people; cultural patterns do not necessarily parallel social patterns. For example, while Lockridge argues that Medfield split away from Dedham because of disagreements over land and paying ministerial support for a cleric in a distant meetinghouse, the artifacts from the two towns suggest that beneath a surface of social and political unrest ran a steady current of cultural solidarity. Claude Lévi-Strauss has eloquently summarized these two distinct, although by no means mutually exclusive, avenues of historical intent: "Social facts do not reduce themselves to scattered fragments. They are lived by men, and subjective consciousness is as

much a form of their reality as their objective characteristics."[54] The cultural historian's burden is to respond to both paths of inquiry and to recover both the objective (demographic) and subjective (psychological) sides of the past. This essay is intended to augment the works of other scholars who are reconstructing the cumulative reality of New England in the seventeenth century.

The analysis of seventeenth-century New England material order not only offers insight into what was made where and when, but it also provides compelling information about how people viewed themselves, their neighbors, and their world. Therefore, it is imperative that students of material culture use artifacts as something more than reflections or illustrations of historical and art historical circumstances. Artifacts function as a language, and each artifact—every artifact that survives—is vitally important as a necessary segment of the language system. For this reason, social historians who pick and choose which objects they will deal with according to an arbitrary, exclusivist "Rule of Least and Best" do a gross injustice to the culture they presume to be interested in.[55] The least-and-best point of view reflects above all a lack of theoretical perspective and a lack of patience to sit down and carefully work out how the artifactual language system was structured. All surviving artifacts made by a culture must be included in a definitive material culture study, because all artifacts are equal and simultaneous manifestations of the culture's communicative structures. Viewed in such a way, the Dedham-Medfield artifacts are the psychological reality of the seventeenth-century New England yeoman embodied in physical form; by treating the so-called mute object as part of a lost language, it is possible to make the culture speak. And, by carefully examining what the artifacts say to us, we may begin to find out what people in the seventeenth century were saying to one another.

---

[54] Claude Lévi-Strauss, *The Scope of Anthropology,* trans. Sherry Ortner Paul and Robert A. Paul (London: Jonathan Cape, 1967), p. 14.

[55] For a discussion of the Rule of Least and Best, see Cary Carson, "Doing History with Material Culture," in *Material Culture and the Study of American Life,* ed. Ian M. G. Quimby (New York: W. W. Norton, 1978), p. 45.

Fig. 30. Carved S-scroll panels. *English: a,* Panel of pulpit, Holy Trinity, Blythborough, Suffolk. (Photo, Anthony Wells-Cole.) *Thurston: b–e,* Drawer front and left, center, and right panels of figure 13. (Photos,

e   *f*

g   *h*

Robert B. St. George.) *f, g,* Center and right panels of figure 16. (Hampton Gallery: Photos, courtesy Benno M. Forman.) *h,* Center panel of figure 17. (Photo, Robert B. St. George.)

i   *j*

k   *l*

Fig. 30 (*continued*). *i*, right panel of figure 17. (Photo, Robert B. St. George.) *j*, *k*, center and left panels of figure 19. (Wadsworth Atheneum: Photos, E. Irving Blomstrann.) *l*, Center panel of figure 20. (Photo, Winterthur Museum.) *m*, *n*, Center and right panels of figure 18. (Delaware Art Museum: Photo,

m

n

o

p

William Pugh.) *o*, Left side of front of figure 21. (Metropolitan Museum of Art, gift of Mrs. Russell Sage, 1909.) *p*, Right side of front of figure 22. (Art Institute of Chicago, Wirt D. Walker Fund.)

q

r

s

t

Fig. 30 (continued). Houghton: q–s, Left, center, and right panels of figure 11. (Photos, Robert B. St. George.) t, Right panel of figure 10. (Photo, Robert B. St. George.) u, Detail of figure 3. (Photo, Robert F. Trent.)

u

v

w

Related examples: v, Detail of top front rail of figure 6. (Photo, Robert B. St. George.) *w,* Detail of front of figure 29. (Photo, Robert B. St. George.)

Fig. 31. Carved lozenge panels. *a,* Detail of figure 1. (Photo, Robert F. Trent.) *b,* Back of figure 12. (Photo, Robert B. St. George.) *c,* Back of figure 26. (Photo, Robert B. St. George.) *d,* Right panel of figure 28. (Photo,

e

f

Robert B. St. George.) *e,* Left panel of figure 6. (Photo, Robert B. St. George.) *f,* Left panel of figure 7. (Metropolitan Museum of Art, gift of Mrs. Russell Sage, 1909.)

Appendix

Biographies of Craftsmen Working in Dedham or Medfield

This Appendix contains biographical sketches of the twenty-five furniture craftsmen who worked in Dedham or Medfield between 1635 and 1685. The list is arranged chronologically by the earliest date that each craftsman could have begun working in the region. An asterisk beside a name within an entry indicates a craftsman whose biographical sketch is included in the Appendix.

1635   JONATHAN FAIRBANKS arrived in Boston with his wife and six children from Sowerby, North Riding, Yorkshire, in 1633. Three years later they moved to Dedham, where, on March 23, 1636/37, "Jonathan Fearebanke being presented by John Dwite was accepted & subscribed" to the town covenant. The next year he and Dwight were "chosen to be head workemen for the Caunsey at ye litle River." On August 14, 1646, after making a much quoted statement about his "scruples about publicke prfession of faith & ye Covenant," he was received into the Dedham congregation. Fairbanks's occupation as a wheelwright and turner is well documented by his inventory of December 16, 1668:

4 spinning wheeles   1:2:00
In the Roome called the new house:
   rimms for spinning wheeles & some
      lumber 5:00:00
   one betle foure wedges one draft chain &
      other irons 002:04:00
   2: Cross cutt sawes
In the working Celler:
   2: vises & one turning lath & other small
      things in that roome 001:00:00
In the Hall Chamber:
   many small tooles for turning & other like
      worke 003:00:00
Swamp in the great Cedar swamp, neere
   the saw mills 004:00:00

Fairbanks's son, John,* inherited his estate and continued in his trade.[56]

1637   GEORGE BARBER came to Dedham from Fressingfield, Suffolk, with no immediate family, although he may have been related to the Edward Barber who was also among the first settlers at Dedham. George Barber married Elizabeth Clarke on November 24, 1642. He was a member of the artillery company in 1646 and was made a freeman of the colony the following year. One of the original eleven signers of the Medfield Covenant in 1649, he was rated there in 1652. That same year he styled himself a "carpenter" in a deed to Henry Adams of Braintree. In Medfield Barber was continually active in woodworking trades. On January 16, 1654, he was paid by the town for procuring "slepers & plankes for the metting House," and on November 8, he received 9s. for additional work at the meetinghouse. In January 1659, there was "An Agrement made with John Thurston [*] Henry Smith [*] and Ser Barbur to make a galiry with two seates on the side of the meetinghouse from on[e] end gallery to the other." In 1668, Barber worked on the town's schoolhouse and repaired a bridge, and on December 8–9, 1675, he was paid for two days' work in shingling the meetinghouse. On February 10, 1676, the town "Agreed that ther shall be new frame orderd to hang the bell in and George Barbur and Sargt [Thomas] Thurston [*] are Desired to take som care about it." In addition to his work as a carpenter, Barber served as selectman and town clerk of Medfield for twenty-two years and a deputy to the general court for eight. His son John operated the Medfield sawmill until his death. The April 23, 1685, inventory of George Barber's estate included "carpenters and husbandry tools"

and a pine swamp valued at £12. One of the appraisers of his estate was Thomas Thurston.[57]

1637   EDWARD CULVER was in Dedham by November 28, 1637, when the town "ordered that Edward Colver wheelwright shall haue twoe acres layd out for ye present for imploymt in his trade & after to haue an addicon els wher as shalbe fownd needfull. In the meane tyme to haue free liberty of taking Timber for his trade every mans ppriety Reserved." As a wheelwright, Culver would not only have made wheels but probably would also have used a lathe to make turned furniture. As one of the six documented craftsmen who would have owned turning tools in Dedham and Medfield prior to 1685, Culver may also have done work for joiners who did not own lathes. By his wife Anne, he had three sons between 1640 and 1645. His death passed unnoticed.[58]

1637   THOMAS FISHER reportedly received a house lot in Dedham on July 28, 1637. He died on August 10, 1638, while building the first meetinghouse. The town meeting of November 23, 1638, noted him as he "whoe vndrtooke ye Meetinghouse [but] dieth before it was finished." On March 25, 1639, it was "Agreed yt Forty shillings shalbe allowed unto ye wedowe of Tho: Fisher toward yt bargayne yt he tooke in building ye meetinghouse, wch or towne is to make good unto her." Slightly more than a year later, his widow Elizabeth was given "liberty to take administration of the goods of her husband. & hath liberty to sell halfe her lot, for the bringing up of her children." When she died in 1651, her inventory included "two great wimbles"

---

[56] Lorenzo Sales Fairbanks, *Genealogy of the Fairbanks Family in America, 1633–1897* (Boston: Privately published, 1897), pp. 31–33. Don Gleason Hill, ed., *Early Records of the Town of Dedham*, 6 vols. (Dedham, Mass.: Transcript Press, 1886–1936), vol. 2, *Church and Cemetery, 1638–1845* (hereafter *Dedham Church and Cemetery*) (1888), p. 29; vol. 3, *Town and Selectmen, 1636–1659* (hereafter *Dedham Town and Selectmen, 1636–59*) (1892), pp. 28, 49, 116, 118, 124. Suffolk County Probate Records, Suffolk County Court of Probate, Boston, 5:112–14.

[57] Fred Carlisle, *Genealogy of George H. Barbour, 1635–1897* (Detroit: Winn & Hammond, [1901?]), p. 6; Forman, "Mill Sawing," p. 128 (see n. 27 above); Savage, 1:113; Medfield Town Records, Town Office, Medfield, Mass., passim; Don Gleason Hill, ed., *Early Records of the Town of Dedham*, vol. 4, *Town and Selectmen, 1659–1673* (hereafter *Dedham Town and Selectmen, 1659–73*) (1894), p. 247; J. Gardner Bartlett, "Edmund Dane Barbour," *New England Historical and Genealogical Register* 79, no. 316 (October 1925): 339; Suffolk Co. Probate Records, 1:13, 9:118, 13:697.

[58] Frank Smith, *A History of Dedham, Massachusetts* (Dedham, Mass., 1936), p. 45; *Dedham Town and Selectmen, 1636–59*, pp. 37, 57, 96–97, 1101; Savage, *Genealogical Dictionary*, 1:438.

valued at 3s. which may have been her husband's. Thomas Fisher may have been related to the Fisher family in Dedham which came from Syleham, Suffolk, or to the Thomas Fisher of Cambridge, an emigrant from Winston, Suffolk.[59]

1637 JOHN ROPER was born in England in 1611. On April 13, 1637, "John Ropear of New Bucknam [New Buckenham, Norfolk,] Carpentar ageed 26 yeares and Alles [Alice] his wife ageed 23 years with 2 children Alles and Elizabeth" announced they were "desirous to goe for New England there to remaine." Accompanied by Henry Smith,* Roper settled in Dedham, was granted a house lot on August 11, 1637, and began attending town meetings the following November. It is likely that Roper helped Thomas Fisher* build the first meetinghouse, for he was one of the committee chosen to "estimate what was left vndone of ye agremt made wth him [Fisher]: as also other worke done by others interniscuously wthin ye sayd house to be soe distinguished yt ye Towne may beare ye one & ye wedowe beare ye other accordingly." On February 28, 1641, it was noted that "John Roper, being destitute of Corne, craveth licence to make sale of some board wch he hath ready sawne," some of which was bought by John Fairbanks. His wife Alles bore him four more children. After 1645 there is no mention of him in the records.[60]

1637 HENRY SMITH came to New England in the company of John Roper* in 1637 from New Buckenham, Norfolk. Like Roper, he testified that "Henry Smith of Newbucknam husbandman ageed 30 years and Elizabeth his wife ageed 34 yeares with 2 children John and Sethe ar desirous to passe into New England to in-

habitt." Smith arrived in Boston on June 20, 1637, and by the following November owned land in Dedham and had signed the town covenant. Smith signed the original Medfield Covenant in 1649 and had moved there by 1652. Although he had called himself a husbandman when he left England, the Medfield records reveal that he was a woodworker. In January 1659, he, George Barber,* and John Thurston* built a gallery in the Medfield meetinghouse. Smith's work was itemized in an account of December 13, 1661:

Rickned with Brother Smith this 13 of 10 moth. 1661
and found Due to hi[m] for worke at the new gallery [£]0-15-0
and for the ballesters 0-11-0
and for sawing 0-08-0
and for boord 0-02-6
and for a days work 0-02-0
paid to Henry smith by the constables 0-9-2

In 1667 Smith was paid for laying the meetinghouse floor, and in December 1675, he did a day's work in shingling the meetinghouse and received 2s. Smith was capable of carpentry and turning, and he probably taught these skills to his son Seth, who continued in the trade. Smith's will was written on August 2, 1683; no inventory was made of his estate.[61]

1638 JOSEPH MOYCE, joiner, probably came from Dennington, Suffolk. On September 21, 1638, the town of Dedham granted "Joseph Moyce Joyner" four acres of land in "ye wigwam playne." However, he may never have settled in Dedham, because he never was rated in the town nor did he attend any town meetings. Instead, he probably left soon for Salisbury, where his name appears twelve times in local town and court records beginning in the 1650s. The last time he appears in the public record is on March 19, 1668/69, when "Joseph Moys of Salisbury, joyner" con-

[59]Donnelly, *New England Meeting Houses*, pp. 18–19 (see n. 15 above); Winifred Lovering Holman, "Anthony Fisher Genealogy," typescript (Boston: New England Historic Genealogical Society, 1935), pp. 93–94; *Dedham Town and Selectmen, 1636–59*, pp. 49–51; Suffolk Co. Probate Records, 2:56.

[60]James Savage, "More Gleanings for New England History," *Collections of the Massachusetts Historical Society*, 4th ser. 1 (1852): 99; Savage, *Genealogical Dictionary*, 3:574–75; *Dedham Town and Selectmen, 1636–59*, pp. 33, 35, 45, 49–50, 83, 109, 168.

[61]Savage, "More Gleanings," p. 99; Savage, *Genealogical Dictionary*, 4:116; "Register of Births in Dedham," *New England Historical and Genealogical Register* 1, no. 1 (January 1847): 99; Medfield Town Records; *Dedham Town and Selectmen, 1636–59*, pp. 34–38, 83; Suffolk Co. Probate Records, 11:56.

veyed all of his land holdings to his grand-children. Moyce has been confused re-peatedly with Joseph Morse of Dorchester and Medfield, beginning with a misread-ing of the records by Frank Smith which were published in *A History of Dedham* in 1936. Fortunately, a land account bearing the names of both men simultaneously confirms their separate identities. Moyce, active in Salisbury during the 1650s, may have been responsible for the Salisbury communion table now in the Wadsworth Atheneum.[62]

1639   THOMAS EAMES, born in England in 1618, was twenty-two years of age when he first appeared in the Dedham town records. On December 2, 1640, the select-men ordered Joseph Kingsbury, John Hayward, and John Bacheler "to search for Bricke earth & pvide a place nec-essary to burn bricke vpon & also to appoynt wood sufficient for ye same & all this in ye greate Iland wher conueniently they maye be had to the satisfaction of the Brickemaker Thomas Eames." By 1652, he had moved to Medford. On May 1, 1660, while still living in Medford, Eames submitted a deposition concerning the behavior of his apprentice, Joseph Mirri-ble. Two years later, on June 17, 1662, he married Mary, widow of John Paddlefoot, joiner of Cambridge. Eames and his wife lived in Sudbury when their son Samuel was born, January 15, 1664, but Eames's carpentry work was first recorded in 1674, when he was the master builder of the meetinghouse in Sherborn. On February 1, 1676, an Indian attack resulted in the death or capture of his wife and children and the burning of his house in Sherborn. He petitioned the General Court for monetary compensation and counted among his material losses £5 worth of car-penter's and joiner's tools. Eames lived in

Sherborn until his death on January 25, 1680. Because he worked during the latter part of his career as a carpenter and joiner, he may have been a woodworker as well as a brickmaker while in Dedham in the 1640s.[63]

1639   JOHN THURSTON may have been born in Suffolk, for when he embarked for New England in 1637, listed himself "of Wrenton in Suff., carpentar." He settled in Salem but moved in 1639 to Dedham, where he and his wife Marg[a]ret were re-ceived into the church in 1641 and 1640, respectively. He first obtained land in Dedham on July 10, 1642, and began at-tending town meetings on January 2 of the same year. While in Dedham, Thurston built the seats in the meeting-house in 1646 and built the town's first schoolhouse in 1648 (see pp. 12–13 above). In 1649, Thurston and his son Thomas* signed the Medfield Covenant, and he was rated on the Medfield tax list in 1652. John Thurston must have been involved with the building of Medfield's first meetinghouse; on May 26, 1655, he was paid for planks and for work done on that building a total of £3.14.10. In 1657 and 1658, he was paid £13.5.1 for seat-ing the meetinghouse and the gallery and 30s. for making the "seate about the tabell"—the same table made for the con-gregation by John Houghton* of Dedham (see p. 13 above). In January 1659, Thurston assisted carpenters Henry Smith* and George Barber* in building the new gallery in the meetinghouse (see p. 38 above). Thurston was probably the master builder of the addition made to the meetinghouse in 1664, for on November 20 of the following year he received £8 in payment for his work. When he died on November 1, 1685, he was one of the most prominent members of the Medfield community. In his will, proved on October 21, 1686, he gave two-ninths of his estate to his son Thomas and one-ninth to his son Joseph,* both of whom had followed in his trade. Thurston's inventory, taken

[62]Mary Lovering Holman, *Ancestry of Charles Stinson Pillsbury and John Sargent Pillsbury*, 2 vols. (Concord, N.H.: Rumford Press, 1938), 1:493–94; Smith, *History of Dedham*, p. 46; Johnston, p. 33 (see n. 17 above); *Dedham Town and Selectmen, 1636–59*, p. 48; "Old Norfolk County Records," *Essex Institute Historical Collections*, n.s. 56, no. 4 (October 1920): 299–300; 57, no. 4 (October 1921): 318; 60, no. 2 (April 1924): 152; 60, no. 3 (July 1924): 232; 62, no. 2 (April 1926): 127–28; 67, no. 2 (April 1931): 176.

[63]Trent, pp. 56–57 (see n. 17 above); *Dedham Town and Selectmen, 1639–59*, pp. 74, 80–81, 95–96, 109–11; Suffolk Co. Probate Records, 9:16, 13:191.

by Benjamin Clarke* and Samuel Bullen on March 1, 1685/86, included "Carpenters tooles" in an estate valued at £169.3.10.[64]

1640 JOHN FAIRBANKS emigrated from Sowerby, Yorkshire, with his father Jonathan* in 1633. In 1640, John received six acres of land at the east end of his father's house lot in Dedham. John was a wheelwright and turner and must have learned the trade from his father. In 1641, he bought a quantity of sawn boards from carpenter John Roper.* In 1661, he was on a committee which evaluated a bridge built by Lt. Joshua Fisher,* and on December 31, 1663, he and John Houghton* were paid £1.2.0 for mending a cart bridge. Fairbanks and John Aldis* served as a committee in 1672 to find carpenters to build the second meetinghouse, finally settling on Daniel Pond* and John Baker.* The only record of Fairbanks's work as a wheelwright is that of November 29, 1675, when the town promised him 10s. "for a payre of wheels to lay the great gune vpon." John Fairbanks died on November 13, 1684, and the inventory of his estate taken on December 10 valued his worldly possessions at £491.0.6. Included in that sum were "Turning tooles & wheelwright tooles" apprized at £8.7.0, a high valuation that could only have corresponded to a large quantity of tools. No doubt some of them belonged to his father and came to John when he inherited his father's estate in 1678.[65]

1642 Lt. JOSHUA FISHER was baptized on April 2, 1621, at Syleham, Suffolk. He probably started his apprenticeship while still in Syleham and may have followed his master to the New World, for when he joined the Dedham church in 1639 he was listed as servant. He married Mary Aldis, daughter of elder Nathan Aldis and sister of carpenter John Aldis,* in 1643. His first recorded work as a carpenter dates from January 17, 1651, when he agreed to "shingle the meeting house and doe all the worke & beare all the charge thereof that is the takeing of the old couering & make the spares feite & set them on. lay on the board shingle & flewe boards at one end & one pyrāmedy at ye south end and shingle the penthouse ouer the Bell." On January 4, 1657, Fisher was one of three people appointed to establish the first sawmill in Dedham. It was operating by 1660, and Fisher retained a share of ownership. The next year, he built a bridge for the town. The 1661 rating listed Fisher's house as the best in town (worth £31). In February 1664, the town asked Fisher to see about "repairing and make[ing] a new gate for the pound" and "allso desired [him] to cutt oake planke fitt to make a new payer of stocks." If Fisher did this at his sawmill, as the words "oake planke" suggest, it would be the second earliest known reference to mill-sawn oak, the first being at Salisbury prior to 1658. By August 27, 1672, Fisher was dead. No probate papers for him survive.[66]

1645 JOHN HOUGHTON, born in England in 1624, came to New England aboard the *Abigail* in 1635 at age eleven. He was probably from Eaton Bray, Bedford, where his father was warden of the parish church of St. Mary in 1629 and 1630. John must have received his training in

[64]Tilden, pp. 63–65, 70 (see n. 2 above); Frank Thurston to author, December 15, 1977; the parish records of all Suffolk churches were searched by Richard B. Allnutt of Ipswich, Suffolk; Brown Thurston, comp., *Thurston Genealogies*, 2d ed. (Portland, Me.: Brown Thurston, 1892), p. 357; John Camden Hotten, *The Original Lists of Persons of Quality, 1600–1700* (1880; reprint ed., Baltimore: Genealogical Publishing Co., 1962), p. 294; *Dedham Town and Selectmen, 1636–59*, pp. 24–25, 131–32, 156–57, 160; Medfield Town Records, passim; Suffolk Co. Probate Records, 9:171, 11:32.

[65]Fairbanks, *Genealogy of the Fairbanks Family*, pp. 34–37; Smith, *History of Dedham*, p. 52; *Dedham Church and Cemetery*, p. 52; *Dedham Town and Selectmen, 1636–59*, pp. 36, 68, 85; *Dedham Town and Selectmen, 1659–73*, pp. 31, 42; Hill, ed., *Early Records of Dedham*, vol. 5, *Town and Selectmen, 1672–1706* (hereafter *Dedham Town and Selectmen, 1672–1706*) (1899), p. 4; Suffolk Co. Probate Records, 9:114.

[66]Holman, "Fisher Genealogy," p. 1; Smith, *History of Dedham*, p. 45; B. Katherine Brown, "Puritan Democracy in Dedham, Massachusetts: Another Case Study," *William and Mary Quarterly*, 3d ser. 24, no. 3 (July 1967): 392; Forman, "Mill Sawing," p. 122; note of publication (Philip Anthony Fisher, *Record of the Descendants of Joshua, Anthony and Cornelius Fisher of Dedham, Massachusetts, 1636–1840* [Everett, Mass., 1898]) in *New England Historical and Genealogical Register* 53, no. 212 (October 1899): 462; *Dedham Church and Cemetery*, p. 21; *Dedham Town and Selectmen, 1636–59*, pp. 148, 186–87, 195–97; *Dedham Town and Selectmen, 1659–73*, pp. 42, 101, 223–24.

the woodworking trades after arriving in Dedham and probably served his apprenticeship between 1637 and 1645. References to his being a carpenter-joiner and turner appear in 1655, when he was paid for making the pulpit, communion table, and balusters for the Medfield meetinghouse (see pp. 5–7 above), and in 1664, when he built a bridge with John Fairbanks.* By 1658 he had married Beatrix Buckminster, and their first child, Robert, was born the following year. Two more children, John and Mary, were born at Dedham in the next six years. Houghton signed the petition to settle Lancaster in 1653 and moved there in 1665. The uncontrolled use of wood in that town must have threatened his livelihood, for on February 3, 1667, "it was ordered by a voate of the towne that John Houghton should have Libertie to fall Timber in the Comons for his trade use, And If he take the barke of it And sett his marke vpon it, Then it is not Lawfull for any to take or make vse of any such Timber." Anticipating the destruction of Lancaster in King Philip's War, Houghton moved his family to the safety of Charlestown, where by April 15, 1676, he had a grant of commonage. Houghton died in Charlestown in 1684 at age sixty. After he was laid to rest in the Granary burial ground, his family resettled in Lancaster, where his widow married Benjamin Bosworth. In 1706 his eldest son, Robert, who may have trained with his father, received thirty-seven acres of land in payment of "work done by him at the meeting house" and "for making the pulpit" in the third Lancaster church. Some of the "Tools for Joinery work" that were valued at £2.12.04 in Robert's inventory taken in 1723 may have belonged to his father.[67]

[67]John W. Houghton, *The Houghton Family Genealogy* (New York: Frederick H. Hitchcock, 1912), pp. 299–304; Henry S. Nourse, ed., *Early Records of Lancaster, Massachusetts, 1643–1725* (Lancaster, Mass., 1881), pp. 81, 248, 293–94; Annie Lane Burr and Thomas Hovey Gage, "John Houghton of Lancaster, Massachusetts, and Some of His Descendants," *New England Historical and Genealogical Register* 79, no. 316 (October 1925): 392–400; Medfield Town Records; *Dedham Town and Selectmen, 1636–59,* pp. 139, 145; *Dedham Town and Selectmen, 1659–73,* pp. 99, 123.

1646 JOHN ALDIS, born in Fressingfield, Suffolk, around 1625, came to New England with his father, Nathan Aldis, and was in Dedham by 1640. Aldis may have trained in Dedham with George Barber,* a carpenter from Fressingfield who must have known his father. John married Sarah Eliot of Roxbury on September 27, 1650, and they had five children between 1652 and 1666. Aldis first appears as a carpenter on February 24, 1664, when the town asked him to see about "repayering the meeting house in the clapboarding the wales. and the seats in the east gallery and what else may be at prsent to be needfull." In 1672, Aldis and John Fairbanks* chose the builders of the second meetinghouse. On April 15, 1674, Aldis was "deputed to set up a post neer the meeting House for to nayle publications vpon also to set up a conuenient Horse bloock neere" and on March 13, 1675/76, he repaired the town pound. He died on December 21, 1700, in Dedham. His inventory, taken four days after his death, indicates that he may have been a carver as well as a joiner:

axes 8s
Spades, hoes & Saws 14s, 6d
An adze, augurs a Square & plains 13s 6d
4 chizels 4s a burs 1d
3 gouges & 3 Sickles 2s
2 joynters & a plow 4s
A hammer 1s
a knife and needle case 1s
beetle rings & 3 wedges 3d
Two Lots in the great Cedar Swamp 1:0:00[68]

1647 CORNELIUS FISHER came from Syleham, Suffolk, to Dedham by 1647, the year he joined the church. His brothers Anthony Fisher and Joshua Fisher and his nephews Daniel Fisher and Lt. Joshua Fisher* had preceded him to Dedham. On January 3, 1652, he was admitted a townsman of Dedham. In two separate deeds of July 18 and February 2, 1665, he called himself a carpenter. On December 4, 1672, the town "ordered that a bill shall be giuen to Cornell Fisher to receaue of

[68]Banks, *Topographical Dictionary,* p. 153; Savage, *Genealogical Dictionary,* 1:24; *Dedham Church and Cemetery,* p. 32; *Dedham Town and Selectmen, 1636–59,* p. 132; *Dedham Town and Selectmen, 1659–73,* p. 101; *Dedham Town and Selectmen, 1672–1706,* pp. 16, 40; Suffolk Co. Probate Records, 14:358.

the Constable 20s out of the town rate. for Fence by him set about the buriall place." Sometime afterward he removed to Wrentham, where he died early in 1699. His inventory taken on June 20 of that year includes unspecified "Carpenters Tools" in a total estate valued at £242.19.8.[69]

1649 SETH SMITH was the second son of Henry Smith* and came with his parents and brother John from New Buckenham, Norfolk, in 1637. His father probably trained him in carpentry and joinery. By 1652 they had moved to Medfield. In the 1661 Medfield town rate, he was taxed on an estate valued at £92.10.0. On January 23, 1676, he was paid 2*s.* for doing work with his father at the meetinghouse. His inventory, taken on August 12, 1682, valued his possessions at £234.3.0 and included "Carperters tooles, hoaes & sythes" worth £2.3.6, "Board and Timber" worth £1.4.0, and several shares of swamp.[70]

1651 DANIEL POND first appears in the Dedham town records in 1651, when he was retained by Lt. Joshua Fisher* and Eleazer Lusher to make alterations to the first meetinghouse. The work required that he "vndertake to frame & set vp 2 windowes vpon the back side of ye meeting house," "set vp a sufficient frame vpon the north end of ye meeting house for ye hanging of ye Bell," and "make & set vp one conueanient & sufficient payer of flewe boards at the said end of ye meeting house." Shortly thereafter, Pond married Abigail Shepard, the daughter of Edward Shepard of Cambridge, which suggests that Pond may have lived there prior to his arrival in Dedham. Their seven children were born before Abigail's death on July 5, 1661. In September 1661, Pond married Ann Shepard (no relation of his

first wife) and had seven more children by 1680. Pond's long career in carpentry proves him to have been one of the most active Dedham craftsmen. The town repeatedly called on him to do work on its meetinghouses. In 1662, he was "freed of his highway worke for 7 years for building the gallarie in the meeting house," and in 1669 he was paid for "altering the 2 seats in the meeting house." In February 1672, he and John Baker,* who may have been one of his apprentices, were chosen by John Aldis* and John Fairbanks* to build the second meetinghouse. The building was probably completed by 1674, when Pond received £47.5.0 for his share of the work. In 1675 he built two more seats in the church, and in 1677, the town "Agreed wth Ser Ponde to build a seat at the table in the meeting House." In 1681, he was again paid for making "the two Last seates run the north side of the meeting house into thre forthwith for Boyes to Sit in," for which he received additional compensation in 1683 and 1685. Pond served as a selectman beginning in 1660, was made a freeman of the colony in 1690, and attained the rank of lieutenant in the militia before his death on February 4, 1697. His inventory included "Carpenter Tools [£]3:0:0" in a total estate prized at £185.19.0. Pond's son Robert was one of two carpenters responsible for saving the two carved panels from Houghton's Medfield pulpit in 1706 (see p. 1 above).[71]

1655 THOMAS MASON came to New England with his father Robert from Waldon, Essex, and was living in Dedham by 1642. Arriving as a child, he must have trained in the shop of one of the Suffolk craftsmen working in Dedham between 1642 and 1649. By 1652 he lived in Medfield, and on April 23, 1653, he married Margery Partridge. Their six chil-

[69] Holman, "Fisher Genealogy," p. 26; *Dedham Church and Cemetery*, p. 30; *Dedham Town and Selectmen, 1636–59*, p. 138; *Dedham Town and Selectmen, 1659–73*, pp. 9, 209, 223; *Suffolk County Deeds*, 14 vols. (Boston: Rockwell & Churchill, 1880–1906), 5:38, 7:326; Suffolk Co. Probate Records, 14:53–55.

[70] Savage, "More Gleanings," p. 99; *Dedham Town and Selectmen, 1672–1706*, pp. 44, 101; Medfield Town Records; Suffolk Co. Probate Records, 9:47.

[71] Edward Doubleday Harris, *A Genealogical Record of Daniel Pond and His Descendants* (Boston: William Parsons Lunt, 1873), pp. 9–13; *Dedham Town and Selectmen, 1636–59*, pp. 186–87, 207; *Dedham Town and Selectmen, 1659–73*, pp. 53, 55, 92–93, 108, 142, 145, 186; *Dedham Town and Selectmen, 1672–1706*, pp. 4–5, 10, 14, 29, 35, 40, 63–64, 119, 147, 177; Suffolk Co. Probate Records, 17:429–30. The inventory of Daniel Pond is not dated.

dren were born between 1655 and 1669. Mason worked as a joiner, as the Medfield town records of May 26, 1655, indicate:

Thomas mason the town indebted
    to him for planks 0-12-6
paid to thomas mason by the town
    Rate for the seating of the meeting Hous
        0-5-7

Because John Thurston* installed most of the seating in the first meetinghouse of Medfield, perhaps Mason worked under his aegis and possibly he was one of Thurston's former apprentices. Mason was killed by the Indians on February 21, 1675, leaving an estate valued at £226.[72]

1658   THOMAS THURSTON, eldest son of John* and Marg[a]ret Thurston, probably was born in Wrentham, Suffolk. He immigrated to Salem and then Dedham with his parents in late 1639. He probably learned woodworking skills from his father. By July 2, 1662, he was described as a carpenter of Medfield in a deed with Daniel Morse. He married Sarah Thaxter of Hingham on December 13, 1655, and they had ten children before she died on September 1, 1678. On April 16, 1669, the town of Medfield paid "Thomas Thurstun for worke at the Schoole house £00:02:08." This reference, probably only for a day's work, is the only recorded instance of his practicing his trade. He moved to Wrentham after that town incorporated in 1673 and died there May 20, 1704. Prized in his inventory of February 9, 1704, were "Carpenters Tooles 4:16:8." His total estate was valued at £563.17.11.[73]

1660   JOSEPH THURSTON was the third son of John* and Marg[a]ret Thurston and the brother of Thomas Thurston.* He was born on September 13, 1640, soon after his parents arrived in Dedham from Salem, and was baptized two days later. Like his brother, he too must have learned

the skills of carpentry and joinery from his father. He was probably working by 1660, when he first appeared in the Medfield town rate with an estate valued at £33. Later that year, however, he moved to Jamaica, Long Island, where in 1663, or shortly thereafter, he married Anne Foster, widow of Thomas Foster of Lauralea. Thurston must have had a large family, for in the rate returns for Jamaica for the seven years prior to 1683, he reported one marriage, eight christenings, and one death. He died at age forty-eight in 1688, and his inventory listed three augurs, seven axes of various sizes, a handsaw, two broad chisels, a narrow chisel, a gouge, a drawknife, a crosscut saw, beetles, wedges, pincers, two great gimlets, and "two pieces of chair" among an estate valued at £220. Because Thurston was trained in the Suffolk dialect, he probably carried that with him to his new location near New York City, thus adding yet another variant to an area already settled by the Dutch, French, English, Irish, and Germans.[74]

1662   THOMAS BOYDEN arrived in New England in 1634. He was listed as a "joiner, ae. 21" when he embarked from Ipswich, Suffolk, on April 30, 1634, on board the ship *Francis.* The place of his birth is unrecorded, but he seems to have come from the ancestral village of Boyton, about ten miles from Ipswich. He may have been trained as a joiner in either place. After landing in New England, he settled first at Scituate, where the Reverend John Lothrop noted: "Thomas Boiden, Brother Gilsons Servaunt joyned [the congregation] May 17, 1635." His master was William Gilson, the town's first miller. Boyden was probably responsible for the construction of the first windmill at Scituate, which was owned and operated by Gilson. Because Boyden was the first known joiner to have been working at Scituate, he may also have made some, if not all, of the furni-

[72]Tilden, *History of Medfield,* p. 249; Savage, *Genealogical Dictionary,* 1:170; Medfield Town Records; Suffolk Co. Probate Records, 5:337.
    [73]Frank Thurston to St. George, December 15, 1977; Thurston, *Thurston Genealogies,* pp. 357–58; Medfield Town Records; Suffolk Co. Probate Records, 15:508–9.

[74]Thurston, *Thurston Genealogies,* pp. 357, 361; Charles Myrick Thurston, *Genealogy of Charles Myrick Thurston* (New York: John F. Trow & Co., 1865), p. 5; *New York Genealogical and Biographical Record,* 4:109; Failey, p. 288; *Dedham Church and Cemetery,* p. 24.

ture so carefully itemized in his master's inventory in 1639:

one framed bedsteed	[£]00:15:00
one framed Table	00:08:00
two great chests	00:10:00
two smale chests	00:01:00
1 joyned chaire	00:01:00
three smale chaires	00:01:00
1 smale table	00:00:04
1 stoole	00:00:02
1 smale form	00:00:02
1 joyned cupboard	00:02:00

By 1639 Boyden had married his first wife, Frances, and had moved to Watertown, where his first son, Thomas, was born September 26, 1639. In the ensuing eleven years, three more children were born in Watertown. On May 23, 1647, Boyden was made a freeman of the Bay Colony. By March 27, 1650, he had moved his family to Muddy River (Brookline), where two more children were born before his wife died on March 17, 1658. The following November he married Hannah Morse, the widow of Joseph Morse of Dorchester and Medfield. In a deed of August 22, 1660, Boyden conveyed his lands in Muddy River to Joshua Scottow, a Boston joiner with whom he may have been well acquainted, and moved to a house in Sudbury Lane, Boston. If Boyden had a shop, it was probably included in the property transferred to Scottow. The 1660 settlement of Joseph Morse's Medfield estate stipulated that Boyden should care for the Morse children until they had married or reached their majorities. In return for the Morse property, the Suffolk County Probate Court directed him to give each child £26.13.4 and to see that they were taught to read and write. Boyden was thus bound by the court for the sum of £180 in a deposition of June 27, 1665, in which he styled himself "late of Boston, now of Medfield." The youngest Morse child under Boyden's guardianship was Jeremiah,* who may have trained with his stepfather while learning the wheelwright's trade. John Ferniside, another Boston joiner with whom Boyden might have worked while living in the Plymouth

Colony prior to 1639, witnessed the agreement. Boyden had sold his property in Sudbury Lane on September 12, 1662, and moved to Medfield shortly thereafter, where he remained for at least twenty years. On February 24, 1667, the selectmen of Medfield paid "Thomas Boydon for a days work with his team at [the] schooll house 0:5:0." In 1678 as a resident of Medfield, he subscribed "one bushel of wheat to the new brick college" at Harvard, and in 1682 he was chosen a tithingman of the town. His unrecorded death must have occurred sometime thereafter. Boyden's son Thomas was a joiner in Groton.[75]

1665 BENJAMIN CLARK, born in Dedham in 1644, was the son of Joseph Clark who moved to Medfield in 1651. In 1665 Benjamin married Dorcas Morse, and in 1668 he was granted a house lot "near the way as you go out at Nantasket," either in Hingham or Hull. However, according to Tilden, he remained in Medfield and followed the trade of a wheelwright. The Indians burned his house in 1676, but he returned to rebuild on the very same house lot. Clark became a freeman in 1682. On November 30, 1685, he agreed with the selectmen to "take care for ye falling, drawing, & squiring of timber" for the rebuilding of the Great Bridge. On February 25, 1696, there was "due to Benjamin Clarke for work at ye meetinghouse—0-3-0." His inventory of January 20, 1724, valued his estate at £569.12.10.[76]

1665 NATHANIEL FRENCH was active in Dedham for about three years, appearing in the Country Rates for 1665, 1666, and 1667. On January 1, 1665, the town "Granted to Nathaneell French Libertie to take so much timber in the Townes comõn as may make 6 payer of wheeles to be sold & vsed in this Towne." He was still active

[75]Trent, "The Joiners and Joinery of Middlesex County, Massachusetts," pp. 78–79; Wallace C. Boyden et al., comps., *Thomas Boyden and His Descendants* (Boston: Privately printed, 1901), p. 57; *Mayflower Descendant* 3, no. 3 (July 1901): 160–62; Benno M. Forman, "Boston Furniture Craftsmen, 1630–1730," typescript (1969), nos. 6, 12.

[76]Tilden, *History of Medfield*, pp. 348–49; Medfield Town Records; Savage, *Genealogical Dictionary*, 1:392.

on October 2, 1667, when "Vpon the request of Nathaneell French Liberty is granted to him to fell such Timber for the vse of his Trade as he shall emproue for any [of] the Inhabitants of this Towne pvided he fell it within the Comon lands of the Towne, and be carefull that he waste no timber." After 1667 he disappears from the Dedham town records. He may have been the Nathaniel French who married Mary Tisdale in Taunton on January 9, 1677, and who died on June 14, 1711. If so, French had stopped working in his trade by the time of his death.[77]

1665 JOHN PRATT of Medfield was probably the son of the John Pratt who joined the Dorchester congregation on January 27, 1642. He may have been among the Dorchester contingent that migrated to Medfield when John Wilson, Jr., coadjutor of the Dorchester church under Richard Mather, was called to take charge of the Medfield congregation in 1653. According to Tilden, Pratt was a carpenter, having shingled "the new end of the meeting house, and the side of the old house next to the new end at 16s. a thousant, to be done before the 15 of June 1665." Pratt's inventory, taken at Medfield August 29, 1707, listed "Carpentry Tools" in a total estate valued at £158.7.4.[78]

1666 JOHN BAKER, born in Lynn, Massachusetts, in 1645, was living in Dedham by December 17, 1668, the date of his marriage to Abigail Fisher, daughter of Daniel Fisher. His first major undertaking in the carpentry trade came in 1672, when he and Daniel Pond* built the second Dedham meetinghouse. On January 6, 1678, he was "Granted . . . liberty to take a Chestnut tree: for a table leafe of his own use." The use of chestnut in seventeenth-century American furniture has appeared previously only in the drawer and chest bottom boards in objects from the East

Narragansett region of coastal Connecticut near Guilford and a chest of drawers with doors made in Boston. Baker used chestnut on more than one occasion. Earlier an entry in the Dedham town records for January 7, 1677, when liberty was granted him "to fell . . . a tune of Chesnut: timber" for which the town "Reseaiued: of: John Baker in mony 1s for on Tune of Chesnut timber," a partial payment made on January 6, 1678. Like most carpenters, Baker also served as a procurer of timber. On May 14, 1677, he was appointed to satisfy Eleazer Lusher's "request to have a tree or two for a grou[nd]sel for his Barne." Baker's will of October 2, 1713, mentions a son Samuel to whom he had "given . . . a trade," but no inventory survives.[79]

1672 JEREMIAH MORSE was born at Dedham on June 10, 1651, the seventh child of Joseph and Hannah Morse. He was brought up and perhaps trained in Medfield by his stepfather, Thomas Boyden.* Morse is said to have followed the wheelwright's trade, although he probably made most of his living as owner and operator of the sawmill at Wrentham. He married Elizabeth Hamant sometime between 1672 and 1678 and had ten children by her between 1678 and 1704. He died on February 19, 1715. His will mentioned his house and shop, and his inventory of March 13, 1715/16, included

To Several Sorts of Tool
To Ten acres of Land and four in Wrentham all lying near the Saw Mill in two parcells 7:00:00
To a Saw Mill one Acre at the Daming and 3 acres of Meadow it flowes in Wrentham 40:00:00
To Five Acres of pine Swamp in Wrentham 2:10:00

The total value of his estate was £372.7.6.[80]

[77]Smith, *History of Dedham*, p. 45; *Dedham Town and Selectmen, 1659–73*, pp. 110, 138; Savage, *Genealogical Dictionary*, 3:207.

[78]Tilden, *History of Medfield*, p. 70; *Records of the First Church of Dorchester in New England, 1636–1734* (Boston: George H. Ellis, 1891), pp. 6–7.

[79]Nelson M. Baker, *A Genealogy of the Descendants of Edward Baker of Lynn, Massachusetts* (Syracuse, N.Y.: Journal Office, 1867), pp. 83–84; *Dedham Town and Selectmen, 1672–1706*, pp. 4–5, 14, 28, 53, 63, 77.

[80]Tilden, *History of Medfield*, pp. 440–41; Savage, *Genealogical Dictionary*, 3:238; *Vital Records of Medfield, Massachusetts, to the Year 1850* (Boston: New England Historic Genealogical Society, 1903), p. 224; Suffolk Co. Probate Records, 19:113, 115.

Wallace Nutting

Collector and Entrepreneur

William L. Dulaney

ON OCTOBER 4, 1941, Parke-Bernet sold at auction antiques from the estate of Wallace Nutting. Nutting had died four months earlier, leaving his wife Mariet in debt. Among over 200 items put on the block were Queen Anne, Chippendale, Hepplewhite, and Sheraton furniture and "an important Rhode Island block-front desk . . . attributed to John Goddard." The desk, which had come from Israel Sack, sold for $3,000; the rest of his collection of antiques, including a number of items illustrated in Nutting's *Furniture Treasury,* brought only $20,942.50.[1] Ironically, a comparable collection of Nutting reproduction furniture would sell today for six to seven times this amount, not because the reproductions are likely to be mistaken for antiques by knowledgeable collectors (although this may happen occasionally), but because of their association with Nutting, a major figure who stimulated interest in early American decorative arts.

Wallace Nutting (fig. 1) was something of a New England institution during his lifetime and today is best known to the general public through his handtinted photographs of landscapes and colonial interiors and to students of antique furniture through his writings. Yet Nutting's role in the world of American antiques was more colorful than his photographs and larger than his three-volume *Furniture Treasury.*

I am grateful for the encouragement and assistance of William F. Deuser during the preparation of this article. Deuser, of Shawnee Mission, Kansas, was an early collector of Nutting furniture reproductions and accumulated one of the most extensive collections in existence.

[1]The Parke-Bernet auction also included "a group of six superbly hooked carpets made under the personal supervision of Mrs. Wallace Nutting." "Early American Furniture," Parke-Bernet Galleries sale catalogue, no. 299, October 4, 1941, Winterthur Museum Library.

Nutting was a Congregationalist minister who, at age forty-four, began a study of early decorative arts that led to his total immersion in the subject. A man of tremendous energy and monumental ego, he pronounced upon, photographed, collected, reproduced, bought and sold, and lectured and wrote about American antiques with a sweep unmatched before or since.

There were more affluent collectors (Nutting never enjoyed great wealth); there were better art historians (Nutting was more concerned with line than authenticity); there is also evidence that Nutting at times preferred commerce to craftsmanship (promotion of his furniture and iron reproductions at times bordered on the shameful). But the variety of Nutting's antiquarian activities and the single-mindedness with which he pursued them merit the attention of those interested in early American decorative arts and a seemingly endless colonial revival.

In the world of antiques between the world wars, Nutting sought and enjoyed the reputation of a prolific and authoritative writer, a connoisseur and collector, an overseer of a workshop whose reproductions were sought by both collector and curator (fig. 2). Nowhere is this better illustrated than in his relationship with Colonial Williamsburg, a relationship which also illustrates the contradictions that give pause to judgments of his work and his principles.

In 1932, representatives of Colonial Williamsburg, seeking furnishings for restored and reconstructed buildings and unable to secure sufficient period pieces of furniture, turned to Nutting. Using volumes one and two of Nutting's *Furniture Treasury,* they located needed antiques and reproduced them with the owners' permission. They also visited the Wadsworth Atheneum

Fig. 1. Wallace Nutting in a photograph used for promotional materials. (Private collection.)

Fig. 2. A tag attached to some Nutting reproduction furniture. The wording reflects his philosophy of "copy and avoid bad taste." (Private collection.)

in Hartford to view the collection of seventeenth-century furniture purchased from Nutting and given to the museum by J. P. Morgan. They then placed an order with Nutting for twelve reproduction Flemish armchairs to be used in the council chambers of Colonial Williamsburg's capitol.[2]

Had the chairs been reproduced and accepted without incident, the transaction would have added luster to Nutting's image. Such was not the case. The prototype chair, reproduced under Nutting's direction (Nutting himself could not plane a board), was rejected. Colonial Williamsburg's representative reported that the arms were clumsy, that the posts were not properly tapered, and that the carving was not faithful to the original (fig. 3). Unfortunately, he added, Nutting had proceeded with work on the remaining eleven chairs before having the first one approved. Nutting resisted efforts to rework the chairs or start over but finally agreed to produce another model after viewing the prototype alongside the original in the Wadsworth Atheneum. The second chair was also carried to Hartford for comparison with the original and was found to need additional work on the stretchers.[3]

Nutting eventually produced twelve chairs acceptable to Colonial Williamsburg and was paid $112.50 each. There is confusion over whether he was stuck with the unacceptable chairs on which he had begun work before receiving approval for the model. It is, however, a matter of record that before the transaction Nutting advertised reproductions of the chair as "Flemish, Maple." After Colonial Williamsburg placed the order, he advertised the same reproductions as "Williamsburg Restoration" chairs. Nutting acted to assuage his vanity by offering a negative critique of the chair in volume three of *Furniture Treasury.* After disposing of the chair's merits in two sentences, Nutting used the remainder of a page to pick the piece apart and question its structural soundness. "This chair," he concluded, "affords a rich opportunity for the study of the old

[2]The chair is illustrated in Wallace Nutting, *Furniture Treasury,* 2 vols. (Framingham, Mass.: Old America Co., 1928), 2:1985. See also, Bland Blackford, assistant archivist, Colonial Williamsburg, to A. R. Carter, June 3, 1971, Colonial Williamsburg Archives, Virginia (hereafter cited as CWA).

[3]Robert C. Dean, designer in charge for Perry, Shaw and Hepburn, architects for Williamsburg restoration, to William G. Perry, April 20, May 1, 1933, CWA.

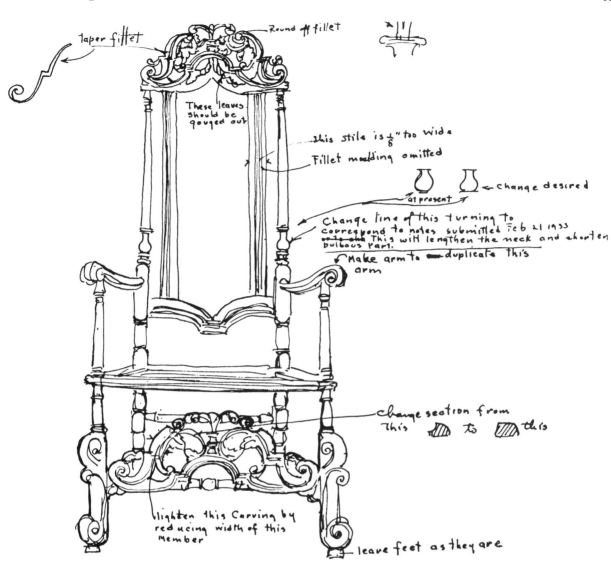

taper fillet

Round off fillet

These leaves should be gouged out

this stile is $\frac{1}{8}$" too wide

Fillet molding omitted

at present

change desired

Change line of this turning to correspond to notes submitted Feb 21 1933 onto one This will lengthen the neck and shorten bulbous part.

Make arm to duplicate this arm

change section from this to this

lighten this Carving by reducing width of this member

leave feet as they are

Note: these changes were noted in pencil on the work itself and all such notations should be preserved until such changes are made notations on the work itself should be followed for detail This drawing should be used only as a memorandum.

Memorandum of Changes To be made in Reproduction of Chair No 1985 in the Hartford Morgan Memorial Museum.
Perry Shaw + Hepburn Architects
141 Milk St Boston Mass
Apr 20 1933

Fig. 3. Sketch of the Flemish armchair designed by Wallace Nutting for Colonial Williamsburg. The prototype produced from this design was rejected by Colonial Williamsburg. (Colonial Williamsburg.)

methods, and one is bound to say that in this example everything was sacrificed to appearances."[4]

A harsh judge of Nutting's behavior in the Colonial Williamsburg transaction might regard him as an opportunist more concerned with profit than perfection. A more humane and probably more correct judgment is that Nutting behaved as he often did—as a man of contradictions whose inconsistencies were accentuated by a lifelong struggle to reconcile idealism with earthly realities. Nutting sought perfection and often came close to achieving it (Colonial Williamsburg ordered yet another dozen Flemish armchairs from Nutting plus an oak table and ten Cromwellian chairs). But when Nutting found his carver standing idle and his costs mounting, he

behaved as a businessman making his way in a capitalist society.

By the mid-1930s, Nutting estimated that he had superintended the reproduction of some 1,000 different pieces of furniture, most of which were produced for a mass market. In recent years an increasing number of Nutting reproductions have reappeared. Many are from the estates of those who sought to furnish their homes tastefully forty or fifty years ago. These reproductions are now being purchased both by private collectors and by museums for study collections. With prices paid for the reproductions rising, there is concern over establishing the authenticity of pieces attributed to Nutting. For example, a Connecticut sunflower chest advertised for $275 in 1928 recently brought $1,285 at auction (fig. 4). There is also speculation that Nutting might have produced two grades of furniture: one for the general public, clearly marked and clearly reproductions; the second, for collectors and others interested in superior products, unmarked, and on the surface indistinguishable from the original except, perhaps, for the finish. There is no solid evidence of such a practice by Nutting. There are, however, to the eyes of both amateur collector and connoisseur clear differences in quality of comparable items produced in Nutting's shop.

[4]Robert C. Dean recalled recently that Nutting was stuck with twelve chairs rejected by Colonial Williamsburg; Dean to Dulaney, August 18, 1975. However, other correspondence indicates that Perry accepted for Colonial Williamsburg all of the chairs ordered from Nutting; Dean to Perry, May 1, 1933, and Dean to Nutting, May 5, 1933, CWA. The correspondence does not indicate a happy relationship between Nutting and Colonial Williamsburg. For example, Nutting refused to permit the chair finisher chosen by Williamsburg to enter his shop; Dean to Perry, June 12, 1933, CWA. See also Nutting, *Furniture Treasury*, vol. 3 (New York: Old America Co., 1933), p. 158.

Fig. 4. Nutting reproduction of a Connecticut sunflower chest. From *Wallace Nutting Products Catalog*, 7th ed. (Framingham, Mass., 1927, 1928), p. 55, no. 931. (Winterthur Museum Library.)

Fig. 5. Nutting reproduction of a bow-back Windsor chair. From *Wallace Nutting Windsors: Correct Windsor Furniture* (Framingham, Mass., 1918), p. 28. (Winterthur Museum Library.)

Added support for the two standards of production theory is that early students and important collectors of American antiques such as Luke Vincent Lockwood and Francis P. Garvan are known to have bought Nutting reproductions.[5] Also, Nutting himself made reference to some of his products being bought and sold as antiques.

Three different markings were used on Nutting reproductions: paper label, Wallace Nutting's signature carved in script, and WALLACE NUTTING burned into the wood (chair bottom or drawer side). The paper labels appear to have been used on the first reproductions in 1917 and until at least 1927. However, Nutting noted in a 1920s catalogue that henceforth he would acknowledge as furniture reproduced under his supervision only those items with his name burned into them in block letters. He added: "I will not be responsible for a script letter formerly used as a mark." Possibly the script letter was used during the 1922–23 period when Nutting sold his businesses and retired. Unhappy with the new owner's conduct, Nutting repurchased the businesses. To further confuse identification of Nutting reproductions, there are pieces of furniture with a Nutting catalogue number burned into them but not the Nutting name. And, finally, some items left Nutting's shop without mark or label.[6] A piece of furniture suspected to be of this nature was recently removed by a museum from an eighteenth-century exhibition room. Privately, Nutting would have been pleased and doubly so had he known the chair was earlier put on exhibition abroad as an outstanding example of American workmanship and design. Although he railed against fakery by telling the story of a reproduction windsor high chair made and sold by his

shop for $19 that was resold for $1,000 after being artificially aged, he predicted that his reproduction furniture would be the antiques of the future.[7]

In his Saugus, Massachusetts, shop (later moved to Ashland and then to Framingham), Nutting sought to reproduce "the best form, put together in the finest manner." He had posted above each worker's bench his Ten Construction Commandments:

1. All work to be of the best quality.
2. If the old method is best, use it.
3. If the work can be done better by hand, do it that way.
4. Use long and large mortises, and large square white oak pins.
5. Make all joined work to fit perfectly, using draw bore where it is better.
6. Match the color where two pieces come together.
7. Follow the sample strictly. Take no liberties.
8. The hand and mouth do not work effectively at the same time.
9. Keep busy, do your best, and no fault will be found.
10. Let nothing leave your hands until you are proud of the work.[8]

Initially Nutting found little merit in furniture styles and woods used after the early eighteenth century and noted in an early catalogue that "a stop is made just short of the cabriole leg style." He cited as one specialty "the finest type of Windsor Chair." Nutting's catalogue description for the example shown in figure 5 claimed it to be "the supreme Windsor side chair. Very popular for dining. . . . A heavy man may tilt the chair and swing over the back without hearing a creak or feeling anything give a particle. . . . It has the perfect vase pattern, with a cusp below the bowl which is in a manner my trade mark, as its sharp edge is only possible in hand turning." Other specialties were the substantial cabinet pieces in maple, oak, pine, and walnut which, to Nutting, characterized the Pilgrim life and the American development up to 1720 (see, for example, the chest-on-frame in fig. 6). Persons "looking for 'mahoganized' imitations" need not stop at his shop. However, Nutting had to adapt his taste to changing market demands, and he began to see the virtue of a

[5]Wallace Nutting, *Wallace Nutting's Biography* (Framingham, Mass.: Old America Co., 1936), p. 130; Steve Koltuniak, Steve's Auction Barn, Norfolk, Conn., to Benno M. Forman, research fellow and teaching associate, Winterthur Museum, Winterthur, Del., July 15, 1976. Ernest Donnelly, Nutting's aide for many years, wrote that Garvan "bought almost one each of all the samples of Wallace Nutting's finest reproductions" (Donnelly to Arthur Whallon, June 12, 1962, Dulaney collection).

[6]A curly maple trencher with a Nutting label dated 1927 on the back is in the Dulaney collection; *Wallace Nutting Period Furniture* (Framingham, Mass., n.d.), p. [15]; Nutting, *Biography,* p. 286. An unmarked piece is owned by William F. Deuser, whose house was at one time furnished with Nutting reproductions in several rooms. He recalls that the carefully crated reproductions always arrived in perfect condition. Nutting's promotional material stated that his name would not be stamped on furniture sold without finish "because of danger of swelling and unsatisfactory finish" (promotional material, undated, Dulaney collection).

[7]*Wallace Nutting Supreme Edition General Catalog* (Framingham, Mass., 1930), p. 4.

[8]Nutting's Ten Construction Commandments, photocopy, Dulaney collection.

Fig. 6. Nutting reproduction of a chest-on-frame. From *Wallace Nutting Products Catalog*, 7th ed. (Framingham, Mass., 1927, 1928), p. 63, no. 920. (Winterthur Museum Library.)

Fig. 7. Nutting reproduction of a "Savery School" lowboy. From *Wallace Nutting Products Catalog*, 7th ed. (Framingham, Mass., 1927, 1928), p. 39, no. 692. (Winterthur Museum Library.)

Fig. 8. Nutting reproduction of a "Goddard School" blockfront secretary. From *Wallace Nutting Products Catalog,* 7th ed. (Framingham, Mass., 1927, 1928), p. 43, no. 733. (Winterthur Museum Library.)

cabriole leg and the beauty of mahogany (fig. 7). There is evidence, too, that Nutting began to appreciate Queen Anne and Chippendale furniture if the latter was not too highly carved.[9] He recalls in his autobiography: "My first attempt at mahogany was to copy the most beautiful and elaborate piece of American furniture—a secretary in Providence which had been bought from Goddard. I took six of my craftsmen to study it by the hour and to make all measurements and sketches. . . . I knew if I made that piece as well as the old, that I could make anything."[10] Nutting was apparently satisfied with his craftsmen's efforts, for he regarded the blockfront secretary with its nine shell carvings as the gem of his reproductions (fig. 8). One of Nutting's catalogues describes the secretary as a "supreme type." It was his most expensive reproduction and wholesaled for $1,450. A cabinetmaker who worked for Nutting recalls only six being produced.

While Nutting the romantic could wax rhapsodic over blockfronts, court cupboards, and windsor chairs ("no new style has been evolved that can bear comparison side by side, for a moment, with the old styles"), Nutting the businessman was, by 1930, producing seventeenth-century versions of an oak radiator cover, a stenographer's swivel chair, an oak chest adapted for typewriters, and a check writing desk intended for bank use. Such practical products appear to have been but a nod by Nutting toward commercial realities, for, while the country was heading deeper into economic depression, Nutting continued reproducing furniture "of all good periods including mahogany." As economic conditions continued to deteriorate, Nutting cut his work force, which had numbered as many as twenty-five craftsmen, and asked remaining employees to accept furniture reproductions in lieu of pay. Nutting estimated in 1936 that he had lost $100,000 in the furniture business. He also observed: "I do not look to see the general public estimate good work properly. It never did, even in the ages of better taste."[11]

It is doubtful Nutting would have rendered a similar harsh judgment with respect to his picture

[9]*Wallace Nutting Period Furniture,* pp. [12, 14]. Nutting used many Queen Anne, Chippendale, and Federal period styles as backgrounds for his tinted photographs. He also furnished his home with several mid- and late eighteenth-century pieces of furniture.

[10]Nutting, *Biography,* p. 132.

[11]Nutting, ibid., p. 126; *Supreme Edition General Catalog,* p. 5; Nutting, *Biography,* p. 128.

business, for it was the public's purchase of his handtinted photographs that kept his furniture reproduction business afloat. Nutting took up photography in 1897 and shortly after leaving the ministry in 1904 began marketing his photographs. Assisted and encouraged by his wife, Mariet Griswold Caswell Nutting, he employed up to 100 colorists, referred to as "Nutting girls," to tint his photographs of apple blossoms and birch trees, winding streams, early doorways, and meticulously arranged interiors (fig. 9). Photographs numbering in the tens of thousands were sold in twenty-six states and thirteen foreign countries.[12] In 1933, Nutting estimated that his signed (generally by an employee who could copy Nutting's signature) prints hung in 10 million American homes.[13] Consigned to attics by a World War II generation, Nutting's prints are today being collected enthusiastically by the public whose taste Nutting derided. Ironically, this same public today pays as much as $50 for a 1930 edition of a Nutting furniture reproduction catalogue that initially sold for $2.[14]

Nutting's writings were another source of income that financed his furniture business and his expanding collection of antiques. He wrote eighteen books (more if revised editions are counted) and numerous magazine articles.[15] Promoting volumes one and two of *Furniture Treasury*—his most lasting work—Nutting predicted that it would be "a monumental work, to contain many times more careful information and illustrations than any other work." He was right in two out of three of his assertions. *Furniture Treasury*, with its 5,000 pictures, is monumental and does contain more illustrations than any other work of its kind. The same cannot be said for its "careful information."[16] As critics have noted, Nutting misidentified provenance and maker in more than one instance. But such errors were few, and some were corrected in volume three of *Furniture Treasury*. A greater fault for the researcher into American decorative arts is the paucity of historical information accompanying the photographs. Style and line were Nutting's interests. He cared little for the social history of furniture. Despite this shortcoming and others—southern furniture is ignored, some pictures are small, several are under- or overexposed—*Furniture Treasury*, in its twelfth printing, remains an indispensable reference work for those interested in American antique furniture.

Nutting incorporated in *Furniture Treasury* much of the content of his *Furniture of the Pilgrim Century,* published in 1921 and revised in 1924. In the revised edition Nutting explained he had taken the opportunity "to omit a few pieces which, owing to their similarity to others, or for other competent reasons, could be spared." He added somewhat gratuitously that the omission of an item pictured earlier should not be taken as "a reflection on its authenticity."[17] This cryptic caution was no doubt a response to an allegation by Edward Guy that Nutting, in his 1921 edition of *Furniture of the Pilgrim Century,* had represented as old, iron made only three years earlier.

---

[12]Mariet Griswold married her sister's widower, Albert Caswell. After Caswell's death, she married Nutting, eight years her junior. There is some evidence that Mrs. Nutting, her stepchildren, and other relatives played a larger role in Nutting's achievements—particularly in the early stages of his picture and furniture reproduction businesses—than Nutting publicly acknowledged. A great-niece remembers Mrs. Nutting as a stabilizing influence in her husband's life, keeping him "one step ahead of bankruptcy because he never counted the costs." She also recalls that Mrs. Nutting's old-fashioned flower garden was kept "entirely for W. N.'s pictures" (Eleanore B. Monahon to Dulaney, January 6, 1976).

[13]Nutting advertised his products widely but not always accurately. His promotional material urged customers to look for the Wallace Nutting signature, and an advertisement in *Good Housekeeping* stated: "His own signature guarantees the artistic value of each picture." However, interviews with Nutting colorists reveal that Nutting rarely signed his photographs—generally only upon special request.

[14]A Wallace Nutting Collectors Club, "Dedicated to the Preservation of Wallace Nutting's Achievement," was formed in 1973. Some 200 members pay annual dues and receive a newsletter. Three national conventions have been held. While club members primarily collect Nutting photographs, they also buy, sell, and trade his books, and a few have acquired Nutting reproduction furniture pieces.

[15]Nutting's books include *Old New England Pictures* (1913), *A Windsor Handbook* (1917), *Furniture of the Pilgrim Century* (1921, expanded in 1924), *The Clock Book* (1924), *Photographic*

Art Secrets (1927), *Furniture Treasury* (vols. 1 and 2, 1928; vol. 3, 1933), and *Wallace Nutting's Biography* (1936). The States Beautiful series was published between 1921 and 1935 and focused on Connecticut, Maine, Massachusetts, New Hampshire, New York, Pennsylvania, Vermont, and Virginia. Although heralded in promotional literature, books on California, Florida, New Jersey, and Ohio were never published. There is, however, among Nutting's papers in the Framingham (Mass.) Public Library a twenty-two-page portion of a manuscript for "Florida Beautiful." Perhaps Nutting decided the manuscript would never qualify for his States Beautiful series, for, in one passage, he wrote: "The present trend of Florida life, so far as it is rich, is toward total depravity. The hard-earned money of fathers is wasted in riotous living, and the cost of one feast would support many a Northern family for a year. Ideas are at a discount amongst many of the rich and vicious crowd that rush to Florida. . . . The third generation of the Northerner who settles in Florida will be a cracker." Nutting also published books on England and Ireland.

[16]Promotional literature, undated, Dulaney collection.

[17]Nutting, *Furniture of the Pilgrim Century*, p. 7.

Fig. 9. A sampling of the handtinted photographs marketed by Nutting. From *Wallace Nutting Pictures* (Framingham, Mass., 1912), p. 27. (Winterthur Museum Library.)

Ironwork of the Pilgrim Century Made in 1918

A STATEMENT BY EDWARD GUY, MAKER OF HAND WROUGHT IRON

To Whom it May Concern:—

A copy of the book written by Wallace Nutting showing furniture and ironwork of the Pilgrim century was sent to me, and I thought it was strange business when I saw pictures of ironwork made by me a few years ago, now known as antique ironwork, for students and collectors to study.

I thought it was strange again when the last lines of the author are: "Finally the author begs a kindly judgment on his work, trusting it will be understood all has been guided by fidelity in dealing with the work of the faithful artificers of the Pilgrim century."

For five years I made wrought iron for Wallace Nutting, Inc. Mr. Nutting wrote about my work and praised it. In a booklet given to the public in November, 1917, he wrote: "In Mr. Edward Guy, the mastersmith, he (Mr. Nutting) has secured a man who is a descendant of a line of forgemen of five generations. His ancestors were trained in the Lancashire region of England, famous for its cunning and beautiful wrought ironwork. The workmanship challenges comparison with anything of the sort produced in modern times. The daintiness of the work, together with its feeling of taste, will certainly commend itself to all discriminating persons."

On page 559 of the Nutting book are two iron candleholders. Both were made by me in 1918. I have the original sketch used by me to make them, which was copied from a book called "Village Homes of England," page 137. They are from Sussex. We changed the candle sockets.

On page 553 of the Nutting book there is shown a pair of pipe tongs or brand tongs. They came out of the same book of English work. They are four years old. They are numbered 184. I also made 181 and 183, but they are copies of the old American tongs. I still have the shop drawings used to make the pair captured at some fort according to Nutting.

On page 573 there are nine door-knockers shown. I made every one of them, and seven out of the nine are my original designs. I have witnesses who saw me make them, and they will say so any time, anywhere.

All the illustrations in the Nutting book, with numbers on the pictures of ironwork, were taken from the catalogue of ironwork sold by Wallace Nutting, Inc. Why show catalogue numbers in a $15 book?

I have counted over 150 pieces shown in both the catalogue and the book. Old and new are mixed together. I make this statement in self defense, because I made much of this ironwork to be sold as modern work in old style, and I still make it.

Honest ironwork is my living. I want to keep the record straight.

Very truly yours,

(Signed)   EDWARD GUY.

Saugus Center, Mass., April 1, 1922.

Fig. 10. "Ironwork of the Pilgrim Century Made in 1918." Statement of Edward Guy, Saugus Center, Mass., April 1, 1922. (Private collection.)

Guy was an ironmaster, who, with his family, worked for Nutting at the Saugus Iron Works from about 1916 until 1921. Nutting bought the ironworks property and located his picture, furniture, and iron reproduction business there. In 1917 he praised Guy as "a master smith of rare skill . . . a descendant of a line of forgemen of five generations." In 1922 Guy circulated to booksellers and librarians a one-page signed statement (fig. 10) accusing Nutting of picturing, in *Furniture of the Pilgrim Century*, candleholders, pipe tongs, and door knockers made by Guy in 1918 and shown in Nutting's 1919 catalogue of reproduction ironwork (figs. 11, 12).[18]

Whether the record favors Nutting or Guy (there is not much to go on), the 1924 revised edition of *Furniture of the Pilgrim Century* contained not a single door knocker. If Guy's assertions were correct, what might have been Nutting's motive in depicting new iron as old? The

reason could hardly have been commercial. More likely, Nutting simply thought there *should have been* seventeenth-century American door knockers of the style designed and produced under his supervision. The Guys' work is highly prized by collectors today, but it is difficult to identify since they did not mark their reproductions.

Ecclesiastical in pronouncement and Olympian in judgment, Nutting frequently sought to improve upon the originals by making reproductions with bolder turnings and deeper carvings. For others to alter the work of master craftsmen was akin to barbarism; for Nutting to do so was conferring perfection. A craftsman who worked for Nutting in the mid-1920s and who had been directed by Nutting to modify reproductions from the originals later wrote a book on colonial furniture design. He dedicated it "To Wallace Nutting whose kindly teaching and early guidance inspired this book." Nutting, displeased with some design modifications in the book, failed to acknowledge the dedication.[19]

[18]Nutting promotional literature, 1917, Dulaney collection. Guy asked librarians to paste the sheet to the front matter of Nutting's book, and many did so. Guy's son owns a copy of the original statement.

[19]Interview with Franklin Gottshall. Gottshall dedicated *Simple Colonial Furniture* (New York: Bruce Publishing Co., 1931–35) to Nutting.

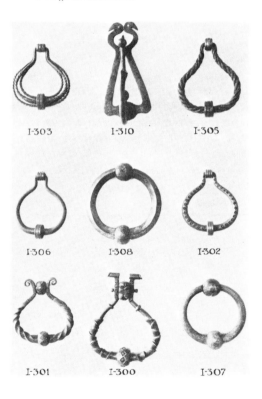

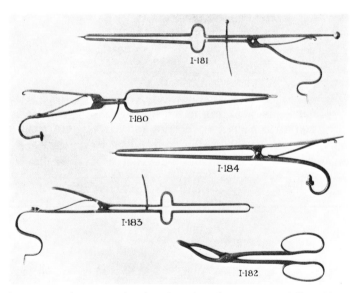

Fig. 11. Nutting reproduction door knockers. From Wallace Nutting, *Early American Ironwork* (Saugus, Mass., 1919), p. 13. (Winterthur Museum Library.) The illustration is identical to one in Wallace Nutting, *Furniture of the Pilgrim Century, 1620–1720* (Boston: Marshall Jones Co., 1921), p. 573.

Fig. 12. Nutting reproduction pipe tongs. From Wallace Nutting, *Early American Ironwork* (Saugus, Mass., 1919), p. 4. (Winterthur Museum Library.) The illustration is identical to one in Wallace Nutting, *Furniture of the Pilgrim Century, 1620–1720* (Boston: Marshall Jones Co., 1921), p. 553.

Nutting wrote for the masses as well as for the connoisseur. He wrote about windsor chairs, spoon racks, and court cupboards for *Antiques*. He championed early American furniture and warned against fakes in such mass circulation magazines as *Woman's World* and the *Saturday Evening Post*. He also wrote for a furniture salesmen's trade magazine. These writings, along with slide-show lectures before such gatherings as a Springfield, Ohio, women's club and a New York antiques exposition, no doubt fueled the colonial revival and stimulated interest in antique collecting among the general public.

Nutting came late to antique collecting, but he came with a vengeance.[20] Despite Nutting's admonition to collectors to behave civilly and his assertion that "only selfish boors become angry because an owner will not sell," Nutting was a buccaneer of a collector. Lacking a fortune with which to buy antiques, he wheedled, conspired, sermonized, and all but promised salvation to get the antique he wanted. He argued that the owner of a fine antique without the means to properly protect or display it had a moral obligation to turn it over to someone who could—namely Wallace Nutting.

This argument, according to court testimony given by Abby Howes, a Danvers, Massachusetts, high school teacher, was used by Nutting to obtain from her the Prence-Howes court cupboard, ca. 1665, an ancestral piece (fig. 13). Upon learning that Nutting, who paid her $3,000 for the cupboard, was planning to sell it to J. P. Morgan for $20,000 as part of a collection to be presented to the Wadsworth Atheneum, Miss Howes sued to recover the cupboard. She alleged that she had contacted Nutting in 1921 to appraise the cupboard for insurance purposes and that he had persuaded her that it was her civic duty to let him

Fig. 13. Prence-Howes cupboard. From Wallace Nutting, *Furniture Treasury* 2 vols. (Framingham, Mass.: Old America Co., 1928), 1:455. (Winterthur Museum Library.)

buy the cupboard and put it on display at his Framingham studio. She also asserted that Nutting had indicated he wished to hire her as his secretary so she might continue to be close to the cupboard. Nutting told the court the cupboard was worth no more than the purchase price when he bought it, but that his possession of the cupboard and his writings on antiques had increased its value. This claim was supported by testimony from antiques dealers and Nutting won the case; the Prence-Howes cupboard is today on display in the Nutting collection in the Atheneum.[21]

Speaking from the witness stand, Nutting told the court that "Morgan didn't know any more about the value of an antique cupboard than a hole-in-the-wall."[22] There is no record of Morgan's reaction to this judgment. There is, however, evidence that Nutting could count few of the major collectors or antiques dealers among

---

[20]Conflicting accounts of how and when Nutting began collecting antiques are in Nutting, *Biography*. He states on p. 129 that he had been collecting antiques for thirty-five years, or since 1901 when he was forty years old and serving Old Union Church in Providence, R.I. He notes on pp. 94 and 284 that his desire to photograph colonial interiors spurred his interest in antiques but that his first colonial interiors were not photographed until 1904. Another version is on pp. 95 and 96. While waiting for a train, his wife suggested that he might pass the time by visiting a nearby antiques shop. "It will educate you," she supposedly told him. Nutting returned to report to his wife that he had bought the entire contents of the shop, half of which he auctioned off and half of which he kept, thus beginning his interest in antiques. This last incident most likely occurred about 1918, a year after Nutting had published his book on windsor chairs and a year after he had begun making reproductions.

[21]*Boston Globe* (May 17, 1928). See also *Boston Globe* clipping, undated, Nutting Papers, Framingham Public Library. The Nutting collection in the Wadsworth Atheneum is regarded as the most complete of its kind and secured Nutting's reputation as a premier collector of American furniture and accessories of the seventeenth century.

[22]Clipping stamped "Express," May 17, 1928, Nutting Papers, Framingham Public Library.

his friends. Some sought his judgment and many used his *Furniture Treasury* as a guide to acquisitions, but, except for Henry Wood Erving (1851–1941), none offered lasting friendship.[23]

Erving began collecting at an early age in the area around his Hartford, Connecticut, home and later discovered and named the so-called Hadley chest, which he found in Hadley, Massachusetts. Nutting's elder by ten years, Erving tutored Nutting and welcomed his visits. Nutting illustrated more than 100 items from Erving's collection in *Furniture Treasury* and acknowledged his debt by dedicating to Erving both *Furniture of the Pilgrim Century* and *Furniture Treasury*.

Less cordial was Nutting's relationship with Israel Sack. Although Nutting used a number of Sack's photographs in *Furniture Treasury*, Harold Sack, Israel's son, recalls that Nutting "very rarely returned them." Harsher recollections of Nutting may be found in Israel Sack's "Reminiscences." Sack recalled Nutting as a major collector of early American decorative arts but also remembered him as a meddler and a man who could not keep his word. In the 1920s Henry Ford had been looking for furniture to furnish the Wayside Inn near Sudbury, Massachusetts. Sack suggested he purchase the Nutting collection of seventeenth- and early eighteenth-century furniture. Ford had seen the collection, liked it, and authorized Sack to negotiate a price with Nutting. Sack met with Nutting and, after establishing his commission at 10 percent, agreed to recommend that Ford purchase the collection on one condition—that Nutting stay away from the Wayside Inn for thirty days and let Sack handle the sale. Nutting, according to Sack, agreed to the terms, shook hands, and parted. The deal fell through when two days later Sack unexpectedly visited the Wayside Inn, found Nutting there, and learned that Nutting had been visiting the inn regularly to give unsolicited advice on its restoration.[24]

Undoubtedly Nutting would have preferred to deal directly with Ford, not so much to save paying a commission but because he sought social acceptance by the great collectors of his day. This was the case with Henry Francis du Pont who invited Nutting to visit his home at Henry Wood Erving's suggestion. While du Pont described Nutting as "really quite agreeable and very interesting," correspondence between the two indicates that Nutting desired a closer relationship than did du Pont. In one letter to du Pont, Nutting noted: "You have never done us the honor of a call."[25]

That Nutting failed to secure the favor and social acceptance of the "gentlemen collectors" of his age may in part be explained by the fact that he was as much a dealer as he was a collector. Often overextending himself financially in buying antiques and reproducing them, Nutting occasionally had to retrench. This he did when he sold the major portion of his windsor chair collection, numbering some 140 different styles, and a large number of eighteenth-century mahogany pieces to John Wanamaker's department store in New York City. The items came from three of the five houses described in Nutting promotional material as "The Wallace Nutting Chain of Colonial Houses." Furnished with antiques, the houses were open to public tour for a 25¢ admission price. The interiors, many of which appear in the pages of *Furniture Treasury*, were also used for Nutting's tinted photographs.[26] Needing money, during World War I Nutting had offered all five of the houses and their contents to the Society for

[23]In his waning years, Nutting kept lists of "First Line Friends" and "Second Line Friends." Of the forty names on both lists, only Erving could be associated with antiques in a major way. The other names are those of employees, boyhood friends, relatives, and parishioners of churches served by Nutting. Two names on the list of "First Line Friends" were of particular importance in Nutting's business ventures. Esther Svenson and Ernest John Donnelly worked for Nutting for many years—Svenson as head colorist and office manager and Donnelly as bookkeeper, artist, and general aide to Nutting Donnelly created both a series of silhouettes which Nutting marketed and the sketches for volume three of *Furniture Treasury*. When Mariet Nutting died in 1944, she left the picture business to Donnelly and Svenson. The latter bought Donnelly's share of the business in 1946 and continued to take orders for pictures until 1952. When Svenson entered a nursing home in 1971, she directed that all of the glass negatives of Nutting's photographs be destroyed. She feared that picture quality might not be maintained, and the plates were taken to the city dump and smashed. Donnelly worked for dealer David Stockwell but later went into the antiques business for himself before returning to his native Ireland. Copies of the lists are in the Dulaney collection; Mary Donnelly to Dulaney, November 12, 1975; Kathleen Donnelly to Dulaney, October 6, November 12, 1975; interview with Hilda Svenson Cushing, November 18, 1975.

[24]Harold Sack to Dulaney, May 21, 1975; Israel Sack, "Reminiscences," Ford Archives, Henry Ford Museum and Greenfield Village, Dearborn, Mich.

[25]Registrar's files, Winterthur Museum, Winterthur, Del.

[26]*New York Evening Sun* (August 27, 1918); "The Wallace Nutting Collection of American Antiques," John Wanamaker exhibition and sale catalogue, 1918, Dulaney collection. The five houses are Wentworth-Gardner House, Portsmouth, N.H.; Saugus Iron Works House, Saugus, Mass.; Webb House, Wethersfield, Conn.; Hazen Garrison House, Haverhill, Mass.; and Cutler-Bartlett House, Newburyport, Mass.

the Preservation of New England Antiquities for $125,000—an offer the society was unable to finance.[27] Wanamaker's retailed the items bought from Nutting at a 1918 exhibition and sale. Included were 9 high chests, 10 dressing tables, 22 candlestands, 27 beds, 20 sets of chairs, 40 looking glasses, and 120 hooked rugs.

While Nutting continued to buy and sell antiques and "sneak in a find now and then," in his waning years he displayed little heart for collecting. Instead of slipping gracefully into old age, content with the knowledge of his contributions to American decorative arts, Nutting (as revealed by his correspondence) was an unhappy man.

Beset by financial problems, trying to make a few dollars on antiques with which he would rather not be publicly associated (bucket benches and strap hinges), lashing out in shrill prose at the New Deal, and doubting the value of his life's work to more than a few people, in 1938 Nutting wrote a series of letters to a friend and former employee.

Business is worse and worse here. We cannot sell anything because so few people are earning and when the people have to leave us then we are taxed to support them and then we have nothing to pay the terrible taxes with. . . . I wonder whether there is a little old iron in your vicinity that can be had right to sell again. . . . Do you know of a water bench that I can buy so as to make a profit? . . . It is one of the temptations that we have to overcome to buy more than we are able. I have been through that myself and must constantly fight it. We shall have to allow our taste in design to rest upon the possessions of others rather than in our own. . . . Business is very hard with us and I have not paid my taxes.

In April 1941, three months before he died of cancer, Nutting wrote:

I have aged a good deal in the last six months. We intend to close out the furniture business this summer.

Don't know how, but we shall. Am not buying any antiques, except to exchange the third volume for them. Have been pretty sick and am now. Stay in the office only three hours a day. Cannot eat and am weak. . . . It is age that really compels me to quit. But the fad for different styles would also be enough. We make some very fine pieces, several each, and the public is stuck in another tack. Another thing, they want a different color mostly.[28]

Few, if any, art historians regard Nutting as a scholar. Henry P. Maynard, former curator of American decorative arts at the Wadsworth Atheneum, once said of Nutting: "He rarely practiced the scholar's detached evaluation of a subject or an object. He was not a dweller in an ivory tower but rather a rugged hunter and every discovery was his personal trophy. There were some collectors who rivaled him, but there were no other collectors like him."[29]

Nutting was more a perfectionist than a purist, altering this or that reproduction from the original to fit his idea of how it should look (fortunately, he was often right). His manners when collecting were sometimes akin to those of a polished picker (he once took the old door knocker from his wife's homestead and replaced it with a reproduction). And he was for nearly half of his life as much entrepreneur as he was connoisseur. Nutting did, however, with his prodigious energy, mastery of photography and the English language, and eye for line and style, manage to leave in print and picture and his collection of furniture of the pilgrim century a legacy that continues to interest, inform, and occasionally awe students of American decorative arts.

[27]William Sumner Appleton to Mrs. Wallace Nutting, February 8, 1944, Nutting Papers, Framingham Public Library.

[28]Nutting to William Bowers, January 6, June 8, September 30, and December 7, 1938; April 29, 1941; photocopies, Dulaney collection.

[29]Henry P. Maynard, "The Wadsworth Atheneum and Wallace Nutting," copy of undated article, Nutting Papers, Framingham Public Library.

Furniture in Philadelphia

The First Fifty Years

Cathryn J. McElroy

DURING THE MIDDLE YEARS of the eighteenth century, Philadelphia furniture craftsmen produced some of the finest American furniture in the Queen Anne and Chippendale styles. It survives in quantity and it has been studied extensively. The preceding period, from the founding of the city in 1682 until about 1730, is another matter. Very few examples of furniture that can be attributed to Philadelphia craftsmen during the city's first fifty years survive today. (Only three pieces bearing inscriptions are known at this time: two chests of drawers signed by William Beake and the desk bearing the stamp of Edward Evans.) Since furniture historians tend to concentrate their work in periods that produced furniture in quantity (which still survives) and where there is a body of documented pieces, Philadelphia's first fifty years have been neglected. As a consequence, we lack adequate studies on which to base attributions.

There is, nevertheless, a great deal of information available about the furniture owned by the first two generations. It is largely contained in the probate records, especially wills and inventories, where personal property is enumerated, given values, and sometimes described. This paper is based on a survey of a large number of Philadelphia inventories in an attempt to derive as much information as possible concerning the furniture actually used in Philadelphia during this period. The survey is not confined to the

original boundaries of the city because residents of nearby areas sometimes filed their probate records in Philadelphia. It is presumed, however, that furnishings owned by residents of outlying areas reflect the same regional preferences and characteristics as those owned by city residents. William Macpherson Hornor, Jr., provided most of the information previously known about furniture of this era in the first chapter of his classic *Blue Book* of Philadelphia furniture, published in 1935. For the most part, this paper confirms the outline drawn by Hornor.

In 1685, William Penn, proprietor of Pennsylvania, could report with pride that Philadelphia had "advanced to Three-hundred and fifty-seven Houses; diverse of them large, well built, with good Cellars, three stories, and some with balconies." Penn further reported the houses to be inhabited by "most sorts of useful Tradesmen as Carpenters, Joyners . . . Turners, etc."[1] In 1691 merchant James Claypoole described "very pretty houses" of two stories being built of stone and brick, "Except by the very meanest sort of People," who built frame houses.[2]

The furniture made for these houses was necessarily influenced by the technical ability of the immigrant craftsmen, the economic status of their customers, and the restraining influence of Quaker discipline. Although the Charter of Privileges, granted in 1701, broke the political control the Quakers had previously exercised, the

Research for this article was largely undertaken while I was a fellow in the Winterthur Program in Early American Culture under the direction of the late Charles F. Montgomery, whose contribution in constructive criticism and enthusiasm is difficult to acknowledge adequately. Benno M. Forman has given continued support with new information and provocative objections and was kind enough to critique this paper.

[1]William Penn, "A Further Account of the Province of Pennsylvania and Its Improvements . . ." (1685), in *Narratives of Early Pennsylvania, West New Jersey and Delaware, 1630–1707,* ed. Albert Cook Meyers (New York: Charles Scribner's Sons, 1912), p. 251.

[2]"Extracts from the Letter-Book of James Claypoole," *Pennsylvania Magazine of History and Biography* 10, no. 2 (1886): 197 (hereafter cited as *PMHB*).

sect continued to influence standards of dress and domestic appointments. However, not all Quakers were willing to restrict themselves to "the best sort but plain." The 1698 Yearly Meeting of Women Friends entreated "that no superfluous furniture be in your houses, as great fringes about your valances, and double valances, and double curtains, and many such needless things."[3] Evidence from the survey of inventories substantiates the need for such a plea.

One of the earliest surviving Philadelphia inventories is that of Christopher Taylor, a substantial merchant who had served in the lucrative office of register general of the province. In 1685 appraisers noted the contents of his two houses. A dwelling on High Street was sparsely furnished with a table, a chest, two wooden chairs, and Taylor's small library. His "Logg House" was furnished more lavishly. It was, apparently, a two-and-one-half story building with two rooms and the "Roome where they Dress Victuals" on the ground level, chambers above each of these, and garret rooms over all. Among the thirty chairs listed were six turkey work, six cane, eight wood, two serge, one wicker, and one "elboe." Cedar was used for a table and chest of drawers, oak for another chest of drawers, and deal (pine or fir) for three chests. Other furniture included two tables with carpets, a close stool case, a stand for a basin, a looking glass, a spice box, a chest of drawers "marked M.T.," a clock, and numerous smaller household furnishings.[4]

Although Pennsbury Manor, the home of William Penn, was some distance upriver from Philadelphia, the influence exerted by Penn in light of his role as proprietor makes his household furnishings of special interest. When called back to England in 1684, Penn appointed James Harrison "the Steward of my Household & what relates to the Place where I live." Penn's letters to Harrison, written while he was in England, are revealing. On October 6, 1685, Penn wrote "Here comes a Dutchman, A Joyner and a Carpenter. . . . Let him wainscot and make tables and stands for some of the rooms, but chiefly help with the Out-

houses, because we shall bring much furniture." In November he asked for "two or three Eating Tables to flap down—one less than another as for 12-8-5—some wooden chairs of Walnut with long backs, 4 Inches lower than the old ones because of Cusheons."[5] Penn's specifications show that he followed .English post-Restoration taste in his preference for walnut and the fashion of dining in small groups. Then—and later—many colonists chose to import at least some of their furniture, undoubtedly to keep up with fashions in the homeland and possibly because resident craftsmen could not produce furniture in sufficient quantity or quality to meet the demand. However, Pennsylvania walnut, cedar, and other woods were being sent to Europe, and it is not impossible, or even improbable, that some of the wood exported was then imported as furniture.

Walnut was the fashionable wood of the period and it is the predominant wood mentioned in Philadelphia area inventories until 1730. An abundant supply of walnut and other fine furniture woods discouraged the practice of veneering, and, indeed, no veneered Philadelphia furniture from this period is known. Nevertheless, some Philadelphia craftsmen had in their shops olivewood veneers, veneering screws, and plentiful supplies of glue. The extravagant use of fine local woods caused two Swedish pastors traveling through Philadelphia between 1700 and 1702 to remark on one church with "pews made of cedar and a pulpit of walnut" and another where the "entire chancel and the pulpit are of black walnut, intricately turned."[6] Such massive pieces would have been made by local craftsmen.

Beds were the principal and most highly valued article of house furnishings. They were uniformly the first item listed on an inventory and practically the only furniture mentioned in wills. The seventeenth-century custom of having a bed in nearly every room was followed in Philadelphia, but the practice declined in the eighteenth century. When a room-by-room account was made in 1687 of the contents of Pennsbury Manor, all rooms except the "Govr's Paller" and the "Passaige" room contained beds.[7]

[3] Frederick B. Tolles, *Meeting House and Counting House: The Quaker Merchants of Colonial Philadelphia, 1682–1763* (Chapel Hill: University of North Carolina Press, 1948), p. 128.

[4] The location of the log house is given in neither will nor inventory. MS 26-1685, Office of Wills and Administration Papers, City of Philadelphia (hereafter information from wills, inventories, and administrations will be cited only by the manuscript number and year filed).

[5] J. Francis Fisher Copies, Penn Papers, p. 14, Historical Society of Pennsylvania (hereafter cited as HSP).

[6] "Two Early Letters from Germantown," *PMHB* 84, no. 2 (April 1960): 201–2 (hereafter cited as "Two Early Letters").

[7] Hubertis M. Cummings, "An Account of the Goods at Pennsbury Manor," *PMHB* 86, no. 4 (October 1962): 397–

Differences between modern and period terminology can prove misleading. In the parlance of the period, the term "bed" referred to the mattress. The wood frame for holding the mattress, if there was one, was identified separately as the bedstead. A frequent verbal formula was "bed and furniture," with the latter term encompassing curtains, valance, blankets, coverings, and whatever else made it complete and usable. Appraisers usually neglected to mention the bedstead, although such descriptive notes as "sacking bottomed" and "Cords" among the bed furnishings confirm that a bedstead was employed. Others specified the items involved. An inventory of 1706 listed a "Pine bedstead, ordinary Quilt, &c." at £3.10. Another, in 1719, valued "Feather bed bolster pillow Sheets 3 Blankets 2 Coverlids Curtains rods & Mahogany bedstead" at £6.5.[8]

There were alternatives to bedsteads. Hammocks were listed on a number of inventories, and they were not necessarily makeshift affairs. In 1708, an extraordinary group was left by Quaker merchant John Jones, who had immigrated from Barbados in 1683:

1 Old Hammack	£1: 0:0
1 Ditto with fringe	1:10:0
1 Ditto old	1: 5:0
1 Ditto Double ffringe	2: 0:0
1 old Do no strings	0:12:0[9]

Cots, cot bedsteads, pallets, pallet bedsteads, and couches were also in use. Merchant James Logan paid joiner Thomas Stapleford 25s. for a pallet bedstead in 1717. In 1725, Logan paid only 6s. for a couch and 34s. for "plush for a Couch bed." Couches, now called daybeds, were in use in the colony by 1689 when joiner Edward Stanton died, leaving couch chains as well as drops and locks among his shop goods.[10]

Of the eleven beds listed at Pennsbury Manor in 1687, six were accompanied by bedsteads, two were described as bed and "tester," and three had no mention of a bedstead. The form of a feather bed in the parlor with "cordes and stetell" is an enigma, but it provokes the imagination.

Elizabeth Tibby, a joiner's widow, and Sarah Quary, a rich widow, left "canopied bedsteads" in 1688 and 1717, respectively. Bedsteads in 1704 were described with "standing" and "turned" posts. Widow Margaret Beardsley in 1701 left a "Large Walnut Bedstead wth ffurniture" in her great chamber and an old bedstead at the home of Thomas England, who was probably an upholsterer.[11] Other walnut bedsteads, when independently valued, were worth from 20s. to 30s.

Another widow, Sarah Eckley, left a particularly interesting group of beds in 1692:

1 Black wallnut bedsted & Sacking bottom to it with wooden Screws	£2: 0:0
1 Ditto with Sacking bottom & Iron Screws	1:12:0
1 Oak bedsteed Short post & cord	0: 4:0
1 pallat bedsteed	0: 8:0
1 Oak bedsteed with long post & Cord	0:10:0[12]

The specific itemization of bed screws, both wood and iron, suggests that the appraisers considered them a distinctive feature. At his death in 1694 John Fellows, joiner, had bed screws among his shop goods, along with logs of walnut, cedar, and pine, and "one pallet bedstead partlie made."[13] Bed screws were probably used to hold the frame together, but in the absence of any recognized bedsteads from the period, their function remains uncertain. Indeed, without such artifactual evidence, our knowledge of beds in this early period is dependent on the limited information provided by appraisers in inventories.

The shop inventory of Charles Plumley, a joiner who died in 1708, contains an interesting list of unfinished work:

1 Walnutt Table framd	£1: 0:0
1 Pine Table	0: 5:0
7 Sett Gum bedstead pillows [pillars] at 2s4d	0:16:4
15 Sett Sydes and Ends at 2s4d	1:15:0
8 parcele of Walnutt & Pine Ends	1: 5:0
2 black Carved Chair frames	0:18:0
1 Walnut Case Drawers not finished	1:16:0

For the four beds listed in Plumley's house, appraisers recorded only two bedsteads: "1 small Sacking beddstead" and "1 Beddstead Bottom Iron Rods and Cornishes &c.," dressed with "1 pr Green Curtens and Vallens" or "1 pr

416. This is a transcription of the inventory taken in 1687, now deposited at the Pennsylvania Bureau of Land Records (MS no. PP 8-3), Department of Internal Affairs, Harrisburg, Pa.

[8]MSS 34-1706, 159-1719.
[9]MS 83-1708.
[10]James Logan Account Book, 1712–20, p. 245, HSP; James Logan Ledger, 1705–25, p. 46, HSP; MS 97-1689.

[11]MSS 53-1688, 113-1717, 42-1701, 143-1704.
[12]MS 84-1692. Oak furniture, popular elsewhere in the seventeenth century, is rarely mentioned in Philadelphia inventories and generally given low valuations.
[13]MS 104-1694.

blew Printed Curtins fringed."[14] Gum bedsteads were later specified in inventories of 1702 and 1722.

Bedsteads were also imported. John Christopher Sauer suggested that immigrants from Holland bring as much merchandise with them as possible because goods would cost twice as much in Pennsylvania. He warned that such items would be confiscated if discovered by English customs "because the merchants of England do not tolerate it. They are not supposed to check in bedsteads, however."[15]

Feather and flock beds were the most common types listed. Other adjectives used to describe beds include "small," "large," "old," "old fashioned," "low," and "trundle." Perhaps the most intriguing example found was the "good Sacking bottom bedstead wth large wrought head," in the lodging room of the "Great and Stately Palace" of merchant John Tatham in Burlington, New Jersey. Tatham died in 1700 and his wife Elizabeth died in childbirth in 1701; although residents of New Jersey, their wills and inventories were filed in Philadelphia. One wishes to suppose their bed had a carved wood headboard, but it was probably a plain wood headboard covered with a worked textile as found elsewhere in the same inventory: "1 feather Bed, bolster & Pillow, a Sett of Camlet Curtains lin'd wth Sarsnett Vallens above and below, Sacking bottoms, bedstead. 3 Iron rods wth a high head lin'd & quilted, 1 Silk Quilt lin'd wth bags all at £30:0:0."[16]

While beds and their furnishings were undoubtedly the most important item on the majority of inventories, chairs were the most numerous. In inventories of the 1680s, cane, turkey-work, walnut, wood, serge, wicker, "calfe leather," canvas, "wanded," oak, and Bermuda chairs were listed. The earliest reference to Bermuda chairs was found in the inventory of William Frampton, a merchant who died in 1686. It is unclear whether the term "Bermuda chair" refers to any cedar chair or to a specific form also in cedar, imported from Bermuda. Nathaniel Allen may have provided a description of a Bermuda chair in his request to a Bermuda correspondent in 1720: "I would desire thee to send 3 red Sedar

Chairs with White Straw Bottoms and of the newest fashion   16 inches   high in the seate with Low Backs."[17]

Despite the large number and great variety of descriptive adjectives applied to chairs in Philadelphia inventories, Old World associations of certain forms with social rank continued. The ceremonial connection between the "great" or armed chair and a person of authority is pointed out in William Markham's account of the appearance in court of Patrick Robinson in 1686:

As soon as he Came in he squatts himselfe downe opposite to me, at the table I writt which was before the Judges; Arthur Cook spoak to him thus, wee sent for you not to sit There. He replyed he Came not in obedience to their warrant but voluntaryly to Know what they had to say to him, and said he, if you are offended at my sitting here I will sit there. He then Removed into an Elbow Chaire with a Cushing in it that had been sett for President Lloyd. His posture when there was very Indecent, much like a mad Man. I was astonished to see it in a Man of his understanding.[18]

A "Great Chair" was only valued at 6*s.* in a 1719 inventory, but another "Great Arme Chaire wood" in 1727 was valued at 20*s.*[19]

The widow Anna Salter had two large wooden chairs, valued at 6*s.*, and four smaller wooden chairs with four turkey-work cushions.[20] The most expensive chairs found in any of the Philadelphia inventories surveyed were six turkey-work chairs valued at 20*s.* each in 1697, which emphasizes the value and importance of textiles to the furnishings of this period. Turkey-work chairs of various values were listed on a number of inventories, but no examples of this fabric from the Philadelphia area are known to have survived.[21]

James Claypoole, a Philadelphia merchant, was one of the few people who referred in his will to furniture other than beds. After distributing the beds, he gave his wife "household goods for the Common and necessary Furniture of One Room." Each daughter was assured of receiving her wearing apparel and her own chest of drawers; the eldest daughter was also given eighteen

---

[14]MS 113-1708.
[15]"Two Early Letters," p. 231.
[16]Inventories of John and Elizabeth Tatham, 1700/1, Society Miscellaneous Collection (photostats), HSP (hereafter cited as Tatham Inventories).

[17]MS 31-1686; September 7, 1720, Letterbook of Nathaniel and Hannah Allen, 1716–35, Joseph Downs Manuscript and Microfilm Collection, Winterthur Museum, Winterthur, Del. (hereafter cited as DMMC).
[18]"The First Decade in Pennsylvania: Letters of William Markham and Thomas Holme to William Penn," *PMHB* 90, no. 3 (July 1966): 345.
[19]MSS 159-1719, 73-1727.
[20]MS 47-1688.
[21]MS 160-1697.

"High chairs" and six "low ones." The inventory taken in 1688 does not list the chairs (perhaps because the eldest daughter had already married and removed them), but a single high leather chair was valued at 6s. and two low ones at 5s. apiece. Other seating furniture in Claypoole's house included a leather stool (4s.), eight cane chairs (80s.), ten canvas-bottom chairs (20s.), a cane couch (20s.), and a "Cloath Elboed Chair" (8s.). The last item may have been an easy chair, but it could also have been a turned armchair with upholstered seat and back. Claypoole's appraisers also noted that some of the chairs were "old," but whether this means the chairs were worn or simply out of fashion is open to question.[22]

Rush, flag, matted, turned, cedar, green, child's, "fiare," and "groaning" chairs were listed in inventories of the 1690s. "Ordinary," shalloone, and bass chairs were noted before 1715. Four dozen leather chairs valued at 8s. each were found in a 1723 merchant's home. The large quantity suggests they were intended for resale, but that would not have been the case for the fourteen other chairs in his parlor or the sixteen chairs in a back chamber. In only one instance before 1730 were all the chairs inventoried in one house of the same type; Abel Cottey, clockmaker, left seventeen bass-bottom chairs in 1711.[23]

Sets consisting of one or two armchairs with six to twelve side chairs are found in seventeenth-century Philadelphia inventories, but they are more frequent after 1700. In 1718 James Logan asked a London friend to obtain for him "8 handsome but plain new fashioned Cane Chairs of about 11 or 12 S & 2 Arm Chairs of ye same for a chamber." These were probably the "8 Walnut Cane Chairs at 11s & 2 Elbow at 15s" recorded in his accounts for 1719.[24] Logan purchased other furniture from the cargo of the ship *Richmond* in 1718, including:

2 fine Walnut Chairs & 1 Elbow ditto		
cost £1:11:6	£3:	3:0
9 black Chairs at 6s 2 Elbow dito at 9s		
£3:12:0	7:	4:0
1 black couch £1:2:0	2:10:0	
6 Cane Chairs at 5s6d Do at 4s & 1 Elbow		
8s £3:2:0	6:	4:0[25]

It is interesting to compare the prices of the chairs Logan imported with those in Philadelphia inventories. Those without descriptive notations in inventories were generally valued at 1s. Rush, wooden, and other undescribed chairs constituted most of those priced at one to four shillings. Cane, leather, and walnut chairs were generally appraised at between 4s. and 12s.

Cane chairs were the most frequently listed type in the period. They were usually found in sets of six with an armchair, but sets of twelve were not rare. In 1719, mariner Isaac Leader had a set of six cane side chairs and one armchair in both his parlor and back chamber and six "stickback" cane chairs and an armchair to match in his front chamber.[26] The latter were possibly what we call banister backs, although a banister back and a cane seat is an unusual combination. Jonathan Dickinson owned forty-four side chairs and twenty-six armchairs in 1722, as well as a cane couch and two cane stools. To make them more comfortable, the chairs had cushions and the couch had a squab and pillows, "all flowered satin."[27]

Suites of seating furniture, including sets of chairs with couches and/or stools, were fairly common in inventories after 1715. Cane stools were listed frequently. Couches, first listed in 1693 at 12s., had a standard value of 20s. and were usually fitted with squabs. A blacksmith's "best lower room" contained a black bass couch and squab and six bass chairs in 1717. James Logan credited his London agent with 45s. for a cane couch in his 1727 accounts; on the same day he purchased "Plush for a couch bed &c. 4½ yds at 8s."[28]

The cane chair in figure 1 is thought to have been the property of Gov. Thomas Lloyd. The turnings used for the arm supports and legs are not common among chairs attributed to Pennsylvania, but they are similar to a stool with a tradition of ownership in the Logan family.[29] Elongated vase turnings, such as those on the leather chair in figure 2, are more common, as are the

[22]MSS 34-1687 (will and inventory filed under same number).

[23]MSS 244-1712, 302-1723.

[24]James Logan, Logan Letter Book, 1717-31, p. 49, HSP; Logan Account Book, p. 347.

[25]Logan Account Book, p. 35. The two sets of prices in-

dicate a two-to-one ratio of colonial currency to British sterling.

[26]MS 169-1719.

[27]"The Estate of Jonathan Dickinson (1663–1722)," *PMHB* 59, no. 4 (October 1935): 420–29 (hereafter cited as Dickinson Inventory).

[28]MSS 20-1693, 106-1717; Logan Ledger, 1720–27, p. 89, HSP.

[29]The stool is owned by the Historical Society of Pennsylvania.

Fig. 1. Armchair, possibly Philadelphia, 1700–1720. Black walnut (*Juglans nigra*) and cane; H. 43⅝″, W. 25⅜″, D. 22¾″. (Winterthur Museum, gift of David Stockwell.)

Fig. 2. Armchair, possibly Philadelphia, 1700–1720. Black walnut (*Juglans nigra*), leather upholstery; H. 49⅞″, W. 24¾″, D. 23¾″. (Winterthur Museum.)

blocks, rather than flattened balls, into which the stretchers are mortised. The arched crest rail of the maple chair in figure 3 might be what an appraiser described as a "high back arch" chair. Maple was not often noted in inventories. Joiner Charles Plumley left carved maple chairs among his goods in 1708, but maple chairs are not listed on another inventory until 1724.[30] Since the seat of this chair is rush, it was probably listed as a rush, flag, or "wanded" chair.

Leather chairs were second only to cane in popularity. Russia leather chairs were specified in 1697, and twelve "rusia" chairs were listed again in 1708. A 1714 inventory included a leather couch (30*s.*) and six "High Rush Leather chairs" (15*s.*) "In the Lower roome," as well as "five old Chairs of Leather and Rush bottoms" (2*s.*5*d.*

each). In 1725, James Logan, always particular and specific in his wants, ordered "6 handsome Leather Chairs" from London, for which he was willing to pay about 7*s.* each. In 1729, an appraiser valued a set of six leather chairs left by wealthy physician Edward Owen at 10*s.* each.[31]

Few new descriptive terms were used for chairs between 1715 and 1730. In 1717, "stuff" and "course" chairs, both fabric-covered types, were listed, as well as a widow's two "easie" chairs, valued together at £8.[32] Easy chairs, such as the maple framed example in figure 4, represented a new concept in seating comfort, previously a matter of removable cushions or solid padded seats and straight backs. The ball and bobbin turnings of the rather overwhelming underbracing detract

[30]MSS 113-1708, 309-1724.

[31]MSS 157-1697, 83-1708, 1-1714, 139-1729; James Logan to J. Askew, Logan Letter Book, p. 399.
[32]MS 113-1717.

Fig. 3. Side chair, possibly Philadelphia, 1740–80. Maple (*Acer pennsylvanicum*) and rush; H. 43⅜″, W. 19¼″, D. 15⅞″. (Winterthur Museum.)

Fig. 4. Easy chair, possibly Philadelphia, 1720–40. Maple; H. 49¾″, W. 32¼″, D. 31¼″. (Winterthur Museum.)

somewhat from the graceful lines of the arms and wings and mark it as an early version, as do the still upright back and Spanish feet.

The values placed on tables ranged upward from 6*d*. Size, wood, form, condition, and decoration were all factors. Several table "boards" were listed before 1700, possibly tops which were, as in the medieval fashion, set on some type of separate frame. Dining rooms, as such, were a new concept in Restoration England. Philadelphia inventories first record such a room in 1693, furnished by merchant Thomas Hooton, Jr., with a table, six chairs, a warming pan, and eight glasses. Another, in 1711, contained a chest of drawers, six cane chairs, two leather chairs, an oval table and carpet, a looking glass, and a spice box. Rooms such as baker James Fox's "New Roome" (1701), furnished with twelve chairs and a walnut table, obviously served as dining rooms.[33]

Oak, pine, walnut, and cedar tables—as well as a small table with an olivewood leaf—were listed before 1700. Slate tables, good for use with food or beverages, were recorded in 1693, 1699, and in several inventories after the turn of the century. A black walnut "Sideboard Table" was listed in one 1724 inventory. "Spanish" tables were reported in 1687 and 1698 and "Dutch" tables in 1717 and 1723. Whether such listings refer to country of origin or style is problematic. The most frequent descriptive term was "oval," but "long," "round," and "square" tables in large and small sizes were also mentioned. A "large folding

[33]MSS 91-1693, 202-1711, 41-1701.

table" was appraised at the remarkable sum of 90*s*. in 1699.[34] The extraordinary turnings of the heavy legs on the table in figure 5 suggest that it is one of the earliest tables made in Pennsylvania, although this type of turning persisted well into the eighteenth century.

"Large walnut oval" tables, such as the one in figure 6, were specified in inventories of 1705 (50*s*.), 1711 (35*s*.), and 1716 (40*s*.).[35] The vaselike turnings on this table as well as the single drawer are characteristic features. Tables with drawers were often specifically noted on Philadelphia inventories. The turnings on tables attributed to the middle colonies are bolder than those made in New England.

A small walnut table appraised at 24*s*. in 1697 was described as "inlaid." This style of decoration was mentioned again in the inventories of John and Elizabeth Tatham, whose "One rich Ollave inlaid Table & 2 Stands" were valued at 90*s*. and a "Dressing box being inlaid Olive, wth 2 square & 3 Essence bottles wth silver screws and a good large looking glass" at 50*s*. It is probable that the Tathams's inlaid furniture was imported, although the veneering tools owned by Philadelphia craftsmen could have been used for inlay work.[36]

As indicated earlier, the account books of James Logan, influential merchant and secretary of the colony, provide the best single record of furniture imported prior to 1730. In 1712, Logan debited his account for a chest of drawers (£8), a walnut chamber table (£2.16), three looking glasses (£9), a quilt, blankets, six side chairs, a small chair, and an armchair, all in walnut (£9). In 1718, Logan received part of a cargo including "1 Case Chairs &c.," which seems to indicate they were sent in pieces, ready for assembly. For his quarter of the cargo in the ship *Adventure*, received in March 1718, Logan accounted "each Guilder to advance to 4s of our money." Seven tables of various sizes with two separate leaves, three oval tables, four "Hangore" tables, a side table, a black stand, three close stools, a "Sempters box," and five bottle cases were among the merchandise. Logan's accounts show that he sold some of this furniture. Thomas Lindsley

Fig. 5. Gateleg folding table, possibly Philadelphia, 1675–1710. Black walnut (*Juglans nigra*); H. 31 5/16″, W. 60½″, D. (open) 47⅜″. (Winterthur Museum.)

Fig. 6. Gateleg table, possibly Philadelphia, 1685–1710. Walnut; H. 28¾″, W. (closed) 23⅛″, (open) 73⅛″, D. 60¾″. (Philadelphia Museum of Art, gift of Letitia Humphreys.)

bought one of the cases "wth 12 Bottles in" for 20*s*. Charles Brockton purchased a stand and one table. In May 1718, Thomas Sharp sold Logan a bed bottom and bought from him three tables: a large "Hangore" (20*s*.), a small "Hangore" (15*s*.), and an oval (18*s*.).[37]

Among his other purchases of furniture in 1718, Logan acquired a "scallop'd falling table" for 12*s*. and one "Japan'd Oval Table" for 15*s*. In the Tatham's inventories of 1700 and 1701, japanned ornamentation is mentioned on a dressing box, looking glass, and other small items. Similar japanned pieces are not uncommon in

[34]MSS 20-1693, 214-1699, 309-1724, 34-1687, 179-1698, 113-1717, 302-1723; William Macpherson Hornor, Jr., *Blue Book: Philadelphia Furniture, William Penn to George Washington* (Philadelphia: n.p., 1935), p. 3.
[35]MSS 6-1705, 220-1711, 81-1716.
[36]MS 160-1697; Tatham Inventories.

[37]Logan Account Book, pp. 25, 259, 262, 267, 279, 349, 375. For further information on furniture imports, see R. W. Symonds, "English Export Trade in Furniture to Colonial America, Part II," *Antiques* 28, no. 4 (October 1935): 156–59.

Philadelphia inventories after 1715. Edward Shippen is known to have owned a japanned cabinet in 1711, and Ralph Assheton is said to have had a japanned cabinet, two card tables, and a tea table in 1727. Values are not known for any of those pieces, but japanned cupboards owned by a mariner in 1719 and a merchant in 1723 were valued at 30s. and 80s., respectively. The merchant also owned a japanned mirror valued at 120s. Japanned stands were listed in 1722 and 1724. Unfortunately, such decoration is very susceptible to damage and little survives from any area except Boston.[38]

It is sometimes difficult to recognize the form, even when the inventory provides a description. An interesting example is the walnut combination sliding stool and table in a 1713 inventory. The most difficult problem of interpretation occurs with tables, particularly those described "wth drawers," listed in conjunction with case pieces. Were they simple tables, what we term "dressing tables," or perhaps the stands or frames for the associated case pieces? Group listings could merely have been an expedient method of taking an inventory, instead of implying that the pieces were en suite. Furthermore, usage and meaning may have varied according to the practice of each appraiser. "A Chest of drawers, c[um] another chest and table," all valued at 40s., may just have been a group listing. However, the single line grouping of "1 Chest of Drawers . . . £5 and Table 30s," when other items are put on separate lines, suggests a high chest and matching dressing table.[39]

Dressing tables were specifically listed on several inventories. Pipemaker John Warder's black walnut chest and dressing table were valued at 40s. in 1711. The term "chamber table," such as that imported by Logan in 1712, was also used. Valuations for such tables vary greatly. Logan's walnut chamber table, valued at 56s., was listed just after an expensive (160s.) chest of drawers. In 1727, another black walnut chamber table was valued at only 18s. and an accompanying chest of drawers at 30s. Samuel Carpenter, a merchant in Bucks County and treasurer of the province, left one "Square Chamber table wth Ceddar upper-

part & Carpt" valued at 12s., and a small walnut chamber table valued with a cedar chest at 30s.[40]

Features usually attributed to Philadelphia area case furniture are found on the uniquely documented dressing table in figure 7. The date 1724 inlaid in the top is probably the year it was made (fig. 8). The concave molding under the top, forming the upper edge of the drawer openings, seems to be a Pennsylvania characteristic. Cup-and-trumpet–turned legs are also common to furniture from the area; they are not usually interrupted by a vase turning before the flange fitting the leg to the stretcher.

Three dressing tables with arcades similar to those on the dressing table in figure 9 are known. The legs do not have differentiated cup turnings, but the upper slope of the trumpet turning is articulated in such a way that it resembles a cup compressed onto the trumpet. In other examples, the lines of the trumpet are simplified and the vase turnings above are less bulbous, just as the ball feet are generally rounded and smooth instead of having a ribbed contour.

The dressing table is matched by a high chest (fig. 10), both of which descended in the Morris family of Philadelphia. The lower case of the high chest is wider than the dressing table; hence the separation of the lower drawers is proportionally greater, a feature almost exclusive to Pennsylvania case furniture in the William and Mary style. The moldings at the juncture of upper and lower cases are often flat and relatively broad. The cornice moldings are quite simple, pleasantly flared, and of moderate height.

There are several other features of construction and style which seem common, although not exclusive, to Pennsylvania case furniture of this period. The wood grain of drawer bottoms generally runs from back to front. Most drawer bottoms are not rabbeted into but extend over and are nailed onto the sides. Bottom runners (extra applied strips) were not generally used. The upper edges of drawer sides are usually flat, and the sides are more often dovetailed to the drawer back as well as to the front than they are nailed.

Drawers in bureau forms are often separated from each other by whole or partial dividers. In dressing tables and high chest bases, the drawers rest on slides mortised into the case but not piercing the backboard. Drawer fronts commonly fit

[38]Logan Account Book, pp. 299, 399; Tatham Inventories; Hornor, p. 12; MSS 169-1719, 302-1723, 317-1724; Dickinson Inventory.

[39]MSS 277-1713, 131-1709, 202-1711.

[40]Logan Account Book, p. 25; MSS 217-1711, 73-1727, 1-1714.

Fig. 7. Dressing table, possibly Philadelphia, dated 1724. Walnut with maple and elm inlay; H. 30″, W. 40¼″, D. 23⅜″. (Philadelphia Museum of Art, bequest of R. Wistar Harvey.)

Fig. 8. Inlaid top on dressing table shown in figure 7. (Philadelphia Museum of Art, bequest of R. Wistar Harvey.)

Fig. 9. Dressing table, possibly Philadelphia, 1690–1720. Black walnut (*Juglans nigra*); H. 29″, W. 33⅝″, D. 21½″. (Philadelphia Museum of Art, bequest of Lydia Thompson Morris.)

Fig. 10. High chest, possibly Philadelphia, 1690–1720. Black walnut (*Juglans nigra*); H. 66⅞″, W. 42⅛″, D. 23 3/16″. (Philadelphia Museum of Art, bequest of Lydia Thompson Morris.)

flush within an opening edged with double half-round moldings. Even small drawers in dressing tables and high chests are often fitted with a pair of brasses.

Cedar chests and tables were listed frequently, and they were often more highly valued than the fashionable but common walnut. Cedar chest and table groups in 1717 and 1718 were valued at 100*s.* and 150*s.* In contrast, a "Walnut Chest wth drawers & Table" was valued at 50*s.* in 1722. A cedar chest and table, appraised at 190*s.* in 1720, was listed with "3 pr of sheets & Table linen in the drawers," as well as "Glasses & Earthenware over ye drawers & Chimney pc." When the widow Martha Waite made her will in 1720, the property left to her daughter Johanna Biles included: "my best Bed with its Furniture and the Wallnut Chest of Drawers and Table which are called hers together with my Spice Box. And I Give and Bequeath unto my Daughter Phoebe my next best Bed and Furniture with my Cedar Chest of Drawers." The subsequent inventory appraised the "Cedar Chest Drawers   table & Cloth Something more" at 150*s.* and the walnut chest of drawers and table with a looking glass for the same amount.[41]

In 1717, widow Sarah Quary grouped a looking glass with each of her two dressing tables. She was also equipped to deal with the increasingly popular and fashionable pastime of tea drinking. Since tea was expensive, the habit was at first limited to the wealthy or to those who wished to project an image of social status regardless of cost. Ownership of a tea table and stand was thus a statement of the widow's wealth and social standing. Two walnut tea tables were listed in Philadelphia in 1686. James Logan charged 5*s.* for "1 hand Tea Table" in 1718, and merchant-silversmith Francis Richardson (d. 1729) sold a "Tea Board" for 4*s.* in 1719. These were probably trays, because Richardson sold a tea table for 12*s.* 6*d.* the same year.[42]

Jonathan Dickinson kept all the necessary furnishings as well as the "Tea Table and fframe" (45*s.*) in his best parlor in 1722:

Sett large Tea Cups & Saucers	£2: 0:0
Sett Small do	1:18:0
Do Bason	0: 9:0
Sugar Cup 9 milk pot 12s &	
3 large saucers 6s	1: 7:0

[41]MSS 271-1722, 96-1717, 132-1718, 195-1720, 210-1720.

[42]MSS 113-1717, 31-1686; Logan Account Book, p. 270; Francis Richardson, "His Book," pp. 27, 32, 40, DMMC (n. 17 above).

4 Dishes 12 plates edged and		
2 Basons		5: 0:0
China Bowl Stand		1: 0:0
2 doz. Courser China plates at		
36/p. Doz.		3:12:0
3 China Chocolate Cups	0:6	0: 6:0
8 fine earthen plates & 12 Saucers		
sorted		0:12:0

Dickinson also had a "Tea Tray and 16 ps China ware" (21*s*.) in his best chamber. Other inventories provide further evidence that the tea service was left on display. In 1719, "2 Tea Tables & furniture" were valued at 35*s*., and a "Tea Table c[um] China Ware" at 30*s*. A physician's "Tea Table   40 ps China Ware & Stand" were valued at 80*s*. in 1720.[43]

Dickinson's estate, appraised in 1722, included the first mahogany tables found; nine were listed from four to six feet in size. Five of these were inventoried as "Mahogany Chest Drawers and Table," three valued at 150*s*., one at 110*s*., and one at 90*s*. The four other tables, including one in the "Upper Kitchen," were valued between 40*s*. and 200*s*.; two mahogany clothespresses, in the front parlor and on the stairhead, were valued at 100*s*. apiece. The only other wood noted in Dickinson's household inventory was walnut for two small chests of drawers, one with a swinging glass, each valued at 40*s*. Mahogany had been noted in use for a screen in 1708 and a bedstead in 1719, but Dickinson obviously favored mahogany over any other wood, perhaps because he immigrated to Philadelphia from Jamaica, where he would have been acquainted with the wood.[44]

Dickinson also had an oval mahogany table and mahogany planks in his shop. This is significant in light of the order Dickinson placed with his brother Caleb in 1698: "A Few fine woods for ye Joyners & Some Mohogany & [?] in board or Plank for Chest of Drawers & Tables & quarters for Frames, [also] . . . Lignum Vita for Turners Bastard Lignum Vita & Bully Tree—for Loggs & Round for Millwrights."[45] It is probable that some if not all of Dickinson's mahogany furniture was made in Philadelphia. Joiner Abraham Hooper paid Dickinson £18.5.10 for mahogany planks in 1701 and bequeathed his wife a mahogany chest of drawers and spice box in

1707. Another joiner, William Till, who died in 1711, had a substantial stock of mahogany boards as well as cedar, walnut, cherry, pear, and oak. Surprisingly, Till's own furniture was extremely undistinguished. A mahogany chest of drawers left by a shipwright in 1711 was valued at 80*s*., and a carpenter's "Old Fashioned" mahogany chest of drawers at 60*s*. in 1722.[46]

Chests, chests of drawers, desks, cupboards, and presses were increasingly important in the eighteenth-century Philadelphia home, although they had been present in a great range of woods and prices from the earliest years. Chests of drawers were often fitted with scarves, such as the "One pr Cedar Chest drawers & Cloth" valued at 110*s*. in 1707, and a "Chest of drawers c[um] Wrought cloth" in 1700.[47]

An old-fashioned chest of drawers listed as early as 1697 was probably in the seventeenth-century mode, but the style of an "old-fashioned" piece in later years is harder to determine.[48] A walnut chest of drawers with geometrically paneled drawer fronts and extended stiles forming the feet (fig. 11) is one of the few seventeenth-century style case pieces thought to have been made in Pennsylvania. The drawers are not

[46]MSS 46-1707, 216-1711, 228-1711, 271-1722; Jonathan Dickinson, Ledger, 1699–1701, p. 15, HSP.
[47]MS 64-1707; Tatham Inventories.
[48]MS 157-1697.

Fig. 11. Chest of drawers, possibly Philadelphia, 1685–1700. Walnut; H. 44″, W. 45½″, D. 23¼″. (Philadelphia Museum of Art.)

[43]Dickinson Inventory; MSS 169-1719, 173-1719, 201-1720.
[44]Dickinson Inventory; MSS 159-1719, 83-1708.
[45]February 25, 1698, Jonathan Dickinson, Letterbook, 1698–1701, HSP.

grooved for slide rails; instead, the drawer bottoms rest directly on simple side supports. The drawers are of different heights, but they are not ranged in the graduated order common in later chests of drawers. Although the present brasses are replacements, evidence suggests that single drops and escutcheons (rather than wooden pulls) were installed when the chest was made.

Although the frequent inventory notation "broken" suggests why relatively little furniture of this period remains, case furniture was expected to have a long life. A Bristol County yeoman decreed in 1719: ". . . and my will is that After my wifes Decease afforsd the Chest of Drawers that She now hath Be Delivered to my Daughter Esther to her use during her life and After her Decease to her Eldest Daughter to be by her freely enjoyed."[49] Even an old-fashioned oak chest of drawers was valued at 60*s.* in 1714 and an old-fashioned English chest of drawers at 70*s.* in 1716. In comparison, a "new" chest of drawers and table were valued at 80*s.* in 1722.[50]

Among the various woods used for chests of drawers, a "black Cherry tree Chest Draws" valued at 50*s.* in 1708 was unique. It was left by joiner Charles Plumley, whose shop goods included an unfinished walnut case of drawers appraised for 36*s.* A "Case of black walnut drayers" valued at 35*s.* in 1688 was the first of many of that wood listed in Philadelphia. Soft woods were also used but were not as popular. A pine chest was listed in 1712 (30*s.*) and an "old painted fir chest of drawers" (20*s.*) in 1697.[51]

Walnut chests of drawers were usually valued around 40*s.* The most expensive one listed was appraised at 120*s.* and none was valued at less than 20*s.* Five of seven cedar chests listed were appraised for more than 80*s.* A majority of the chests of drawers were valued between 35*s.* and 50*s.*; a smaller number were valued from 90*s.* to 200*s.*, which may indicate that they were high chests. The first listing of the more expensive group was in 1702 at 120*s.* Some case pieces were given remarkable valuations: an "Olivewood Chest of Drawers & cloth" was appraised at 150*s.* in 1697 and a "pr of Olivewood Drawers & Stand" at 200*s.* in 1698. Merchant Philip Richards owned the latter as well as a standard "Chest of Drawers Black Walnut" (£3) and "1 pr ffine inlaid Drawers

& Glass" (£18). A "flowered Chist of Drawers" in 1708 may have been either painted or inlaid; no value is known. In 1713, two "Inlaid" chests of drawers were appraised with two dressing boxes at 200*s.*[52]

Inventory references to stylistic features of chests of drawers are rare. A walnut chest of drawers "on balls" is mentioned in a 1722 inventory.[53] A number of surviving chests of drawers in the William and Mary style have ball feet, but the most important Philadelphia example is one inscribed "William/Beake 1711" (fig. 12). William Beake, Jr., was an apprentice to joiner William Till in 1709; Till died in 1711. Cedar drawer bottoms and pine secondary woods were used in the walnut case and the drawers are separated by dust dividers.

Chests were listed more frequently than chests of drawers. Only chests valued at more than 10*s.*, or with specific descriptive notes, were considered

[52]MSS 160-1697, 182-1698, 84-1702, 277-1713; Hornor, p. 30.
[53]MS 271-1722.

Fig. 12. Chest of drawers, probably Philadelphia, dated 1711. Walnut, cedar, pine; H. 36¾", W. 40⅛", D. 22⅛". Inscribed on inside of right side panel "William/Beake 1711." (Collection of Mr. & Mrs. Joseph A. McFalls, Jr.: Photo, Winterthur Museum.)

[49]MS 155-1719.
[50]MSS 1-1714, 82-1716, 253-1722.
[51]MSS 113-1708, 157-1697, 239-1712; Inventory of John Moon, 1688, DMMC.

in this survey; others, of lesser value, were probably simple storage boxes. Prior to 1700, pine, fir, cedar, "Danzick" (oak), and "framed" (joined) chests were listed. A pine chest "with draws" was valued at 8s. in 1711.[54] Other chests listed in this way or as "two drawer" (and with low valuations) were probably not chests of drawers.

John Moll owned a "Learge painted" chest valued at 12s. in 1701. Chests of "wainscot," oak, pine, cedar, and walnut ranged from 10s. to 50s. in value. In 1728, two chests of drawers and two chests were specifically "Irish" oak.[55] Since chests of drawers were often listed in the same inventory with expensive chests, it seems clear that chests are not to be confused with chests of drawers.

The value of an inventory to a researcher always rests on the amount of descriptive detail provided. While an appraiser might be exact enough to detail the "Little beas Wax, oringe peel, & some odd things" found in an old pine chest in 1714, he did not feel the need to describe what to him was ordinary. Different interpretations are possible for listings such as "Part of a Chest of drawers & frame" (6s.), "1 low frame for a chist" (4d.), and "1 Chest of drawers & frame & prcll of trumpery in ye upper drawer" (10s.) in 1688, although all seem to refer to chests on frames or high chests; this could also explain the "part of an old Chest of Draurs" (5s.) mentioned in 1708.[56]

The widow Margaret Beardsley's great chamber was furnished in 1701 with

1 Stand Chest Drawers Delivered BW	£3: 0:0
1 Ditto wth feet	2:15:0
1 Walnutt Table wth 2 Drawers	2: 5:0
1 Small Dressing box	1:10:0[57]

The second item may have been a high chest or a chest with ball feet. The widow also stocked her shop with "Drops for Drawers" and "Bell Drops" for customers such as joiner James Chick. "Wrought drops" and "drawer rings" are listed on another 1701 inventory and "ring brass drops" on a 1734 inventory.[58] Either description would fit the brasses on the chest-on-frame in figure 13 which seem to be original. The stretchers on this piece relate more to other high chests than do the vase-and-bobbin–turned legs and the use of a single long drawer in the frame.

[54]MS 210-1711.
[55]MSS 52-1701, 73-1727.
[56]MSS 1-1714, 47-1688, 83-1708.
[57]MS 42-1701.
[58]MSS 41-1701, 42-1701, 387-1734.

The dressing box, as indicated by the valuation above, was sometimes an elaborate form. Dressing boxes were in use by 1687 when both a merchant and a "gentleman" left boxes valued at 8s. each. Walnut, japanned, and inlaid boxes were noted, as well as "old" boxes in 1699 and 1722.[59]

Looking glasses were listed frequently, often in conjunction with tables, chests of drawers, or dressing boxes. Merchant Nathaniel Puckle, for instance, had among the furnishings of his best chamber in 1706 "1 Wallnutt Table & Dressing Box & 2 Pewdor boxes and a Large Looking glass . . . £10:0:0." Most looking glasses were probably imported. Among those purchased from a ship's cargo by James Logan were an "arch'd black" looking glass and a "Swinging glass with a draw." Puckle also had two maps hanging in his best chamber, and others hung elsewhere in the house. Frequent inventory references to maps, as well as later newspaper advertisements, show that

[59]MSS 34-1687, 37-1687, 214-1699, 253-1722, 239-1712, 272-1713; Tatham Inventories.

Fig. 13. Chest-on-frame, possibly Philadelphia, 1680–1720. Walnut and pine. (Collection of Mr. and Mrs. Miodrag B. Blagojevich: Photo, Winterthur Museum.)

maps were a popular wall decoration in Philadelphia homes.[60]

There are many specific inventory references to spice boxes in Philadelphia; the first itemized was valued at 5s. in 1685. A "cabinet of Drawers" valued at 12s. in 1701 may also have been what is popularly called a spice box. Since most of the twelve cabinets listed between 1687 and 1730 were given low valuations (1s.6d.–5s.), they were probably small, simple cupboards with shelves. One cabinet was described as oak; no woods were mentioned in the other inventory references. Hornor refers to a japanned cabinet along with a black table in the widow's chamber of the Edward Shippen house.[61]

Merchant James Claypoole bequeathed to his son George "my writing cabinett and all written books." His inventory of 1688 listed two cabinets valued at 8s. and 10s. and a "Scrutore" valued at 20s.[62] It is probable that the latter is what is referred to in Claypoole's will. The wide range of values attached to desks and escritoires (the latter spelled in a number of imaginative ways), however, does not preclude its being one of the cabinets.

Desks in many forms were common in the Philadelphia area. The first desks listed were in the home of Zechiah Whitpaine, who died in 1693. He left both a "Desk box Cover'd with paper" and "One Table & drawers with a desk covered with Green Linsey." The first was only valued at 9d. and probably denoted a simple slant-top box form. The latter was valued at 9s. and it may have been what is now termed a "desk-on-frame." An "old desk box without drawers" left by merchant Charles Pickering in 1694 was valued at 3s. and merchant John Day's "old" desk in 1696 at 2s.6d. Other probable desk-on-frame forms include an "Escrutore & Table" valued at 100s. in 1719, an "escrutore" at 65s., and, several entries later, an "escrutore frame" at 8s. in 1716. The maple desk-on-frame in figure 14 is an unsophisticated version of this form. The desk has nicely shaped dividers and arched pigeonholes, but it is set rather awkwardly into the simple one-drawer frame.[63]

A "Black Walnut desk & feet" listed at 24s. in 1699 may have been a desk-on-frame or a desk with ball feet such as the one shown in figure 15.[64]

Fig. 14. Desk-on-frame, possibly Philadelphia, 1715–40. Soft maple, hard pine, white pine, tulip; H. 38⅛″, W. 28″, D. 17⅛″. (Winterthur Museum.)

Fig. 15. Desk, possibly Philadelphia, 1700–1725. Walnut, hard pine, tulip, white cedar, white oak; H. 42⅜″, W. 40¾″, D. 22″. (Winterthur Museum.)

[60]MS 34-1706; Logan Account Book, p. 247.
[61]MSS 26-1685, 52-1701, 34-1687; Hornor, p. 12.
[62]MS 34-1687.
[63]MSS 20-1693, 103-1694, 139-1696, 173-1719, 81-1716.
[64]MS 214-1699.

This desk, with its distinctive five ball feet and scalloped skirt, has a tradition of ownership in the Richardson family of Philadelphia.

In 1705 a walnut desk was valued at 30*s.*, and in 1706 an "Inlaid" walnut desk was appraised at 100*s.* "Writing" desks were specified in 1700, 1724, and 1729, and a "reading" desk in 1719. Oak desks were listed in 1699, 1711, and 1716. Desks were occasionally imported. Logan received one in 1718 and Samuel Powell honored a London invoice of £1.11.16 for a desk in 1717.[65]

Escritoires were listed twenty-five times on inventories before 1730. They ranged in value from 8*s.*6*d.* to 240*s.* Listings such as a 1714 "Large Oval Table & Scrutore and Carpet" (170*s.*) indicate that the term was also used for desks in the form of slant-top boxes. Most desks and escritoires were owned by merchants, but a butcher, a baker, and two widows also left them in their homes. Surprisingly, wealthy merchant Jonathan Dickinson had only an "Old Broken Escrutore wch Joseph Claims," but it was valued at 40*s.* The wide range of forms that must have been listed under this name is demonstrated by the two "scrutores" left by a sadler in 1724. An undescribed version was valued at 80*s.* and an inlaid one at 25*s.* Physician Edward Owen's was the most highly valued example at 240*s.* in 1729.[66]

The fall-front desk stamped "Edward Evans 1707" (figs. 16, 17) undoubtedly represents the form called an "escritoire"; it is comparable to English desks of the period. The drawer masquerading as a torus molding is not a common feature of Pennsylvania case furniture. The arrangement of two drawers side by side over two full-width drawers is common practice—but not standard. The well-crafted interior arrangement of drawers and pigeonholes relates to English rather than American case furniture.

Edward Evans may have been the son of William Evans who settled in New Jersey in 1683. In that case he would have been trained in this country and, indeed, an Edward Evans received his

Fig. 16. Fall-front desk, probably Philadelphia, dated 1707. Walnut, white cedar, red pine; H. 66½″, W. 44½″, D. 20″. Stamped on base of a small drawer in upper section "Edward Evans 1707." (Colonial Williamsburg.)

[65]MSS 2-1705, 34-1706, 309-1724, 127-1729, 173-1719, 214-1699, 200-1711, 68-1716; Tatham Inventories; Logan Account Book, p. 25; Invoice Book, Commercial Correspondence, 1683–1747, Powell Collection, p. 22, HSP.
[66]MSS 8-1714, 314-1724, 139-1729; Dickinson Inventory.

Fig. 17. Stamp on desk shown in figure 16.

freedom in Philadelphia in October 1704. On the other hand, Edward Evans, the joiner, was making and selling furniture as early as 1701. Records of the London Joiners Company show that one Edward Evans gained his freedom in 1674 and another in 1685. The similarity of the Evans desk to English prototypes plus his early appearance on the Philadelphia scene suggest that Edward Evans was a first-generation immigrant craftsman.

Evans's first documented work in Philadelphia was for William Penn's daughter Letitia, who paid him £7 for a chest of drawers in 1701. He did some "Joyners Work" for Lt. Gov. Andrew Hamilton in 1702, and he had accounts with merchants Isaac Norris and James Logan. In short, Evans worked for important and style-conscious customers. He made a stand (9s.) and an expensive oval table (£2.12.6) for Logan in 1712. That same year Evans included sixteen dozen "drops" among his purchases from Logan. Evans's frequent work for William Trent, who launched the ship *Diligence* in 1707, indicates he may have been a ship's joiner. Since the earliest known provenance for the desk is the estate of the Reverend Thomas Grant, who died in New Jersey in 1802, such reasoning remains speculation. A fall-front desk is not described in a Philadelphia inventory before 1730, but joiner Thomas Stapleford purchased sets of "writing desk locks" and locks "for the fall" in 1719. Evans lived until 1754, but he seems to have given up cabinetwork some years earlier.[67]

Two references in the inventory of merchant Joseph Redman give especially interesting and descriptive information. In 1722 his "Looking Glass Scrutore 1 glass broke" was appraised for £8, and earthenware and glass worth 18s. were stored in "ye Bowfett & Escretore head."[68] With this helpful information, we can surmise that Redman owned something similar to the desk and bookcase with mirrored, arch-topped doors now in the Philadelphia Museum of Art (fig. 18). The interior is composed of drawers, spaces

Fig. 18. Desk-and-bookcase with mirrored doors, probable Philadelphia, ca. 1720. Walnut and tulip; H. 90″, W. 40″, D. 22¾″. Inscribed on bottom of top section "D. John 2/20." (Philadelphia Museum of Art, gift of Mrs. John Wintersteen.)

[67]*Philadelphia: Three Centuries of American Art* (Philadelphia: Philadelphia Museum of Art, 1976), pp. 13–15 (hereafter cited as *Philadelphia*); "Registers of Freedom Admissions," vol. 1, December 1674, and May 1, 1685, Joiners's Company, London, microfilm no. 928, DMMC; Philadelphia Account Book, 1694–98, p. 2, HSP; Ledger, 1709–40, Norris Papers, pp. 93, 168, HSP; Logan Account Book, pp. 7, 9, 98; Logan Receipt Book, pp. 2–3, HSP; and J. Thomas Scharf and Thompson Westcott, *History of Philadelphia, 1609–1884*, 2 vols. (Philadelphia: L. H. Everts & Co., 1884), 1:183.

[68]MS 257-1722; *Philadelphia*, pp. 22–23.

for ledgers, and a central shelf with an arched head surrounded by twenty-four pigeonholes. The refined exterior styling of the walnut desk is not matched by the heavy, tulip-drawer sides and crude dovetailing. The chalk inscription "D. John 2/20" on the bottom of the bookcase section may relate the desk to the family of Philip John, a joiner who died in 1741, but no firm connection has yet been established. Such a desk and bookcase was not unique; when merchant Thomas Master made his will in December 1723, he left "unto him my Sd Son Thomas . . . one of my Clocks and the Scrutore with Glass Doors to it. . . . unto my Sd Son William . . . the other of Clocks & Scrutores vizt that which hath the Book Case Together with the Books to it."[69]

Nineteen clocks valued from 6s. to 200s. and thirty-four clocks and cases valued from 40s. to 450s. were listed in the Philadelphia area before 1730. All the clocks mentioned in seventeenth-century inventories were owned by merchants; after 1700 clocks were also owned by a variety of craftsmen and some farmers as well. Widow Barbara Pritchard gave clocks to two of her daughters and an "ould" clock to her son in her 1699 will.[70] The wide range of economic and social status of the people who owned clocks is further evidence of the cosmopolitan character of the early city. Two-thirds of those owning clocks left estates valued at more than £400, but the wealthiest men did not always own the most expensive clocks.

Clocks were made in Philadelphia prior to 1730. Abel Cottey, who died in 1711, was probably the first clockmaker to work in the city. Cottey's inventory included "Three Clocks unfinished & watch Clook & 2 watches . . . £30:0:0," as well as "A wheele Ingin with Sundry tooles &c. . . . £15:0:0." Other early clockmakers included Peter Stretch, John Copson, Joseph Wills, and Francis Richardson, Jr. (fig. 19). Richardson was primarily a goldsmith, but he advertised that he made, sold, cleaned, and repaired clocks and watches in 1736 and 1737.[71]

The only reference to a cupboard before 1700 was the "Old stand and Cupboard of drawers in ye Kitchin" of a Sussex County gentleman in

Fig. 19. Tall-case clock, probably Philadelphia, ca. 1725. Walnut; H. 73″, W. 18″. Clock face engraved "Francis Richardson." (Philadelphia Museum of Art, museum purchase from Fanny Magee Fund, gift of Henry V. Weil.)

[69] MS 302-1723.

[70] MS 216-1699.

[71] MS 244-1712; Martha Gandy Fales, *Joseph Richardson and Family, Philadelphia Silversmiths* (Middletown, Conn.: Wesleyan University Press, 1974), p. 28; Carolyn Wood Stretch, "Early Colonial Clockmakers in Philadelphia," *PMHB* 56, no. 3 (1932): 233.

1687, but they were not uncommon in the early eighteenth century. Walnut cupboards were listed in 1701 and 1702 and an oak cupboard in 1722. Of eight corner cupboards inventoried, two were japanned; one was valued at 30s. in 1719, the other at 80s. in 1723. The mariner who owned the first japanned corner cupboard put "earthen & Glass Furniture on ye mantle ps & Cuppard head." He also left a "Painted Press" which appraisers valued at 35s. A press of "walnut wood" was first listed in a baker's home in 1701 (30s.); walnut presses were listed again in 1716 and 1724. Clothespresses were inventoried in 1719 (12s.) and 1722 (25s.). Appraisers priced Jonathan Dickinson's two mahogany clothespresses at 200s. each. Since joiner John Crosswhitt left a "Press pt made" (15s.) on his death in 1715, the form was being made in Philadelphia. A single dresser of black walnut was listed in 1714.[72]

Some type of stand was found on most inventories. Most of them were not described and many lacked individual valuation. Again, the most common descriptive term was walnut, first noted in 1686. The only other wood cited was "Black't" pine in 1711, a descriptive term further applied to a small square table, a chest of drawers, and a "hatt Case" in the same room. A large number of stands must have been what we call candlestands. One of two japanned stands listed was accompanied by a cup. Such listings as "stand for a Bason" in 1685 and "China bowl stand" in 1722 indicate the function of other stands.[73]

Another useful and common article of furniture in early Philadelphia was the screen. Three were recorded before 1700; one of the three was made of walnut. A "broaken Mahogany Skreen" was valued at only 2s. in 1708. A screen with four leaves was left in 1709; screens of six leaves were cited in 1693, 1698, and 1706. Other descriptive terms included "small," "old," "leather," "oilcloth," "landskip," and "wheat." Valuations ranged from 2s. to 40s.[74]

The documentation of first use by inventory listings is necessarily equivocal. The rare notation "new" is, therefore, especially interesting. Two new chests of drawers were noted at Pennsbury

Manor in 1687. A "new chest draws and table" in brewer Joshua Cart's home was valued at 80s. in 1722. The old styles inevitably lingered on; people did not throw out furniture in good condition merely because it was old fashioned. In some cases there was active continuance of an old style. In 1735 Thomas Mullan made six cane chairs at 12s. apiece for Thomas Penn; the same year he mended two mahogany chairs. Thomas Stapleford, a chair-frame maker in Philadelphia in 1695, did not make his will until 1739, at which time he bequeathed to his daughter Elizabeth "a Maple Chest of Drawers & Chamber Table & Tea Table Varnished and half a dozen of Cane Chairs All to be finished at the Charge of my Estate."[75] It is probable that the former were in the Queen Anne style and the latter in the William and Mary style.

At least eighty joiners, turners, carvers, and cabinetmakers can be documented in Philadelphia and its environs prior to 1730. Joiner John Fellows, for instance, left the following work in progress at his death in 1694:

To stuff partlie wrought for an ovall table	£1: 0:0
To stuff for 3 side tables partlie done	
To one case of drawers partlie done	0:15:0
To 2 chests partlie made & one box	0: 6:4
To one pallet bedsted partlie made	0: 6:0
To one dozen chair frames	4: 4:0

In 1709 Edward Mayo, a merchant in Bristol, Bucks County, specified that the chest of drawers to be given his daughter Mary was to be "bought of John Crosswhite ye Joyner," and joiner Thomas Carus left his "scrittore" to his friend Richard Heath. The same year a Philadelphia widow left "unto Wm Beakes Junr who is now an Apprentice wth Wm Till of Phil. Aforesd Joyner the sum of £5." These and other references suggest that the furniture trade was not only active but that the craft was being perpetuated.[76]

The transition to a new, more indigenous American tradition in Philadelphia is demonstrated by some members of the large Claypoole family. Joseph Claypoole (b. 1677) immigrated with his family in 1683. Hornor thinks that he was trained by joiner Charles Plumley in this country. Various records after 1710 indicate that

[72]MSS 37-1687, 52-1701, 112-1702, 271-1722, 169-1719, 302-1723, 41-1701, 81-1716, 313-1724, 173-1719, 251-1722, 50-1715; Dickinson Inventory; MS Inventory PH-712, Mary Harrison, December 8, 1714, no. 4535/3, DMMC.

[73]MSS 26-1685, 31-1686, 216-1711, 317-1724; Dickinson Inventory.

[74]MSS 215-1711, 83-1708, 152-1709, 20-1693, 142-1698, 34-1706.

[75]MSS 253-1722, 30-1739; Pennsbury Account; MSS A-27, May 9, June 7, 1735, documents, 1261-1874, Henry Armitt Brown Collection, HSP.

[76]MSS 104-1694, 124-1709, 172-1709, 128-1709.

Claypoole made furniture, coffins, and did other joinery work. In January 1738, Claypoole drew his will leaving his son Josiah all the tools of his trade and all his stock down to "Locks, drops and Scutchins." Although some of these brasses are firmly associated with the William and Mary style, he left a maple cabinet and black walnut writing desk to his son James and the largest cedar chest and the "Black walnut Drawers case upon case" to his daughter. If surviving pieces are the criterion, the last was almost certainly made in what we would call the Queen Anne style, a further indication that the two fashions existed side by side.

In May 1738, Joseph Claypoole announced that he had left active work in his trade and recommended patrons to his son who was prepared to supply "all Sorts of Furniture of the best Fashion: as Desks of all Sorts, Chest of Drawers of all Sorts, Dining Tables, Chamber Tables, and all Sorts of Tea Tables and Sideboards." To fashion this furniture, Josiah inherited "the largest and oldest Stock of Timber, of the Produce of this country and the West-Indies of any in this Province, some of which having been in Piles near 25 Years; he has likewise a Parcel of choice curl'd Maple." Joseph did not die until 1744. Josiah, the son he wished to carry on his trade, was indicted for theft in 1739 and fled to Charleston, South Carolina, where he advertised himself as a joiner in 1740.[77]

Inventory and account-book evidence can thus support a statement that Philadelphia homes were often copiously fitted with a wide variety of furniture in the first fifty years after the founding of the city. While substantial quantities of furniture were imported, there is no doubt that local furniture craftsmen were actively pursuing their trade and training apprentices from the earliest years.

[77]MSS 81-1744; *Pennsylvania Gazette* (May 18, 1738); November 10 and 21, 1739, Indictments, 1717–90, Philadelphia County Court Papers, HSP; *South Carolina Gazette* (March 22, 1740).

Cabinetmaking in Philadelphia 1820–1840

Transition from Craft to Industry

Kathleen M. Catalano

COMMENTING ON PHILADELPHIA'S cabinetmaking industry in the post-Revolutionary years, William Macpherson Hornor, Jr., author of the standard work on eighteenth-century Philadelphia furniture, observes:

Although the prevailing style of the day may be said to have deteriorated, the occupation of cabinetmaker became more popular and unquestionably more lucrative. The one hundred and nineteen of this calling in 1799 . . . increased to two hundred and eleven by 1824. The seventeen Windsor and twenty-two fancy chairmakers of 1799 were supplanted by sixty-seven twenty-five years later. Where eleven carvers and gilders were sufficient in 1799 thirty-two were required by the trade a quarter of a century later. Are not these statistics, which are as accurate as can be obtained, convincing enough proof that the antique furniture world has paid too little attention to the development and progress of Philadelphia's artificers during her post-Revolutionary days?[1]

While Hornor's remarks are intended to draw attention to the early nineteenth century, they are especially appropriate for the third and fourth decades as well. During the 1820s and 1830s Philadelphia possessed a well-organized furniture-making community, with over 1,290 cabinetmakers, 300 chairmakers, 250 turners, 80 pianoforte makers, 55 framemakers, and 40 chair and ornamental painters (see Checklist).[2] Despite these figures, furniture historians have tended to

neglect these decades. The lack of interest is even more surprising considering the fact that this was perhaps the most critical time in the city's furniture-making history. During this twenty-year period the expansion of the market, the growth of wholesale merchandising, the weakening of the apprenticeship system, and the increased antagonism between employers and their journeymen interacted to alter the nature of the business, transforming cabinetmaking from an eighteenth-century craft into a modern industry.

Philadelphia's cabinetmakers in the 1820s and 1830s were in the enviable position of having an ever-widening market for their products. Improvements in transportation and the rapid growth of the West encouraged unprecedented commerce with the hinterland as well as with coastal and foreign ports. This expansion in sales was aided by the city's reputation as a fashion and financial center and by her ideal geographical location which made delivery of goods convenient and cheap.[3]

During the period under discussion the city exported more than 128,529 items of furniture to over fifty American cities and twenty foreign ports.[4] In the domestic coastal trade most items

The author thanks Nancy Richards of the Winterthur Museum for her assistance and encouragement in the research of this article.

[1] W. M. Hornor, Jr., "Henry Connelly, Cabinet and Chairmaker," *International Studio* 93, no. 384 (May 1929): 43.

[2] A list of furniture craftsmen working in Philadelphia between 1820 and 1840 is contained in the appendix to this article.

[3] Except as noted, the following information on Philadelphia's foreign and coastal trade is based on a systematic study of the city's exports from 1820 to 1840, as recorded in the Bureau of Customs shipping manifests: U.S. Bureau of Customs, Outward Coastwise Manifests, District of Philadelphia, 1820–40, Record Group 1059, National Archives, Washington, D.C.; and U.S. Bureau of Customs, Outward Foreign Manifests, District of Philadelphia, 1820–40, Record Group 1059, National Archives, Washington, D.C.

[4] The breakdown of this exported furniture, as listed in the outward manifests, is as follows: in the coastal trade, 19,063 articles, 2,355 boxes, 5,176 bundles, 342 shipments, and 4 sets of cabinet wares; in the foreign commerce, 109,466 articles, 3,093 boxes, 3,849 bundles, and 37 shipments, all valued at $441,361.35.

went southward, two-thirds of the importing cities being located below Washington, D.C., with Charleston as the major depot (table 1).[5] In the foreign trade, the islands of the West Indies— Cuba, Puerto Rico, Haiti—together with Mexico, Argentina, Venezuela, Uruguay, and Brazil were the favorite recipients (table 2). That Philadelphia should have found so ready a market in Latin America and the southern part of the United States is not surprising, considering the fact that while the northern states had built up numerous cabinetmaking centers plantation economies of these regions had discouraged extensive craft development.

Of the more than 500 people shipping furniture, approximately one-third can be identified according to occupation. Most of these were either craftsmen or merchants, the latter group playing a much larger part in the export trade than in local sales. The merchant-exporters were of two types. The first consisted of persons from other cities who traveled to Philadelphia on buying trips. Jenkins and Milton of Suffolk, Virginia, sent back 8½ dozen chairs in November 1830, and Hatch and Kinsey of New Bern, North Carolina, consigned 15½ dozen windsors to themselves for shipment September 27, 1826.[6] The other, a much more numerous group, included merchant-exporters living and operating in Philadelphia. Between 1820 and 1840 over twenty of the city's commercial houses shipped cabinet wares to domestic and foreign ports; the most important were the firms of John Ohl, Peter Logan, John Latour, John Vaughan, Peter Bousquet, Eyre and Massy, and Samuel and William Welsh. Since Latour, Vaughan, and the others traded with foreign nations, as well as with other American ports, it is difficult to determine what percentage of the furniture they shipped was Philadelphia made. It is possible that a portion originated in another city; however, that some shipments came from Philadelphia's cabinetmaking shops can be inferred from their frequent contacts with craftsmen and from advertisements

like that of Loud and Brothers, a piano manufacturing firm: "Merchants shipping to the West Indies or South America, can be supplied with first rate Piano Fortes, to stand the climate and on favourable terms."[7]

In addition to merchants, ninety-five cabinet- and chairmakers participated in the domestic and foreign trade. Of these, only fourteen can be considered major exporters: Michel Bouvier, Joseph H. Campion, the firm of Cook and Parkins, Bennet Fling, William B. Fling, Philip Halzel, William Haydon, John Huneker, Loud and Brothers, Thomas H. Moore, John Patterson, Crawford Riddle, Charles H. White, and John F. White. In the foreign commerce, Philip Halzel was the most active, shipping his wares to eight different countries throughout Latin America. In the coastal trade, Michel Bouvier had the widest range of activity, dealing with ten cities ranging from New York to New Orleans.

Among the articles exported was a variety of case pieces, tables, and seating furniture (tables 3 and 4). Chairs were by far the most common form shipped, for over 126,331 left Philadelphia in the 1820s and 1830s. Other types of furniture frequently exported included desks, bureaus, bedposts, tables, and pianos. Nine "billard tables" were also shipped during this period, eight to the West Indies and one to Calcutta.[8] Although most descriptions are not specific enough to determine the style of the items exported, the few references which listed wood indicate that mahogany was the preferred material.[9]

In addition to the more commonly exported finished articles, shippers also found a ready market for some of the raw materials needed in furniture making.[10] Cabinetmaker John F. Johnson sent fifty-six cherry boards to New Orleans in 1839, while Michel Bouvier forwarded "1 lot veneers" to Baltimore in 1828. Bouvier also exported 2 table planes, 1 tooth plane, 1 iron

---

[5]Philadelphia had figured prominently in the southern furniture trade since the early 1790s. Between 1789 and 1815, for instance, she had led all foreign and American ports— except New York—in the quantity of cabinet wares shipped to Savannah (see Katherine Wood Gross, "The Sources of Furniture Sold in Savannah, 1789–1815" [M.A. thesis, University of Delaware, 1967], pp. 9, 62, 93).

[6]Outward Coastwise Manifests, November 1, 1830; September 27, 1826.

[7]Loud and Brothers advertisement, *Desilver's Philadelphia Directory and Stranger's Guide for 1828* (Philadelphia: Robert Desilver, 1828), n.p.

[8]Business papers, February 28, 1838, William C. Coles, Correspondence and Business Papers, 1813–61, Historical Society of Pennsylvania, Philadelphia (hereafter HSP).

[9]Outward Coastwise Manifests, March 14, 1820; December 7, 1833.

[10]Outward Coastwise Manifests, May 9, July 3, July 29, 1820; September 8, 1838; February 1, 1839; November 7, 1834; December 20, 1820. Outward Foreign Manifests, September 10, 1826.

Table 1. Furniture Exported from Philadelphia in Coastwise Trade, 1820–40

Destination	Individual pieces	Boxes	Bundles	Shipments	Sets
Albany	...	21	8	1	...
Alexandria	81	33	89	9	...
Apalachicola, Fla.	...	10	...	...	...
Attakapas, La.	25	19	9	...	...
Baltimore	333	290	341	140	...
Beauford, N.C.	6	...	...	...	...
Boston	230	33	214	1	...
Brooklyn	...	...	2	...	...
Charleston	5,877	299	517	4	...
City Point, Va.	...	40	...	...	...
Currituck, N.C.	8	...	...	...	...
Darien, Ga.	...	...	...	1	...
Delaware (no city specified)	24	...	...	...	...
Edenton, N.C.	...	3	...	...	...
Elizabeth City, N.C.	16	...	...	...	...
Exeter	26	...	16	...	...
Folly Landing, Va.	132	...	1	...	...
Fort Brooke (Tampa), Fla.	60	...	...	...	...
Franklin, La.	34	4	...	...	...
Fredericksburg, Va.	406	...	...	...	...
Georgetown, D.C.	134	24	198	12	...
Grand Gulf, Miss.	...	18	...	...	...
Hartford	...	...	12	...	...
Mobile	589	315	134	2	...
Nantucket, Mass.	24	...	...	...	...
Natchez	1	...	21	...	...
New Bern, N.C.	1,669	26	33	...	...
New Castle, Del.	...	...	2	1	...
New Iberia, La.	94	...	...	...	...
New Orleans	903	396	501	4	4
Newport, R.I.	...	...	...	1	...
New York City	815	167	1,097	105	...
Norfolk	321	41	296	6	...
Pensacola, Fla.	240	9	18	...	...
Petersburg, Va.	580	79	139	1	...
Pitch Landing, N.C.	11	...	...	...	...
Portland, Me.	26	...	42	1	...
Portsmouth, Va.	6	...	...	...	...
Providence	22	18	55	12	...
Richmond	359	96	287	3	...
St. Augustine, E. Fla.	...	17	61	1	...
St. Joseph, E. Fla.	...	45	1	...	...
St. Mary's	...	...	...	2	...
Savannah	955	142	485	3	...
Snow Hill, Md.	82	...	25	2	...
Suffolk, Va.	4,062	...	...	1	...
Vicksburg, Miss.	...	22	12	...	...
Washington, D.C.	313	180	463	25	...
Wilmington, Del.	150	...	16	...	...
Wilmington, N.C.	449	8	81	4	...

SOURCE.—U.S., Bureau of Customs, Outward Coastwise Manifests, District of Philadelphia, 1820–40, Record Group 1059, National Archives.

Table 2. Furniture Exported from Philadelphia in Foreign Trade, 1820–40

Destination	Individual pieces	Boxes	Bundles	Shipments	Value
Argentina	8,853	77	14	. . .	$ 12,564.00
Brazil	13,980	92	82	3	19,880.21
Chile	1,354	302	294	. . .	9,008.46
Ecuador	156	. . .	28	. . .	156.00
England	5	3	32	. . .	1,650.00
France	. . .	10	. . .	. . .	500.00
Germany	96	31	7	. . .	6,424.00
Gibraltar	354	11	33	. . .	4,656.50
Holland	. . .	. . .	15	. . .	460.00
India	905	. . .	13	. . .	2,646.50
Java	204	. . .	. . .	. . .	170.00
Liberia	23	. . .	. . .	. . .	164.00
Mexico	5,575	219	325	2	37,536.14
Nova Scotia	1	. . .	. . .	. . .	35.00
Peru	588	10	. . .	. . .	654.00
South America (no country specified)	6,269	63	12	. . .	8,059.00
Spanish Main	132	2	. . .	. . .	340.00
Texas	303	78	25	1	2,898.94
Uruguay	9,388	2	374	4	12,418.13
Venezuela	8,969	622	180	3	62,344.94
West Indies	52,311	1,571	2,415	24	258,795.53

SOURCE.—U.S., Bureau of Customs, Outward Foreign Manifests, District of Philadelphia, 1820–40, Record Group 1059, National Archives.

cramp, over 64 mahogany veneers, a quantity of hair seating, and glass knobs to Havana.[11]

The cabinet wares were shipped in a variety of ways to a variety of people.[12] Wholesale selling and shipping in bulk occurred frequently in the coastal and foreign trade, and export records and newspaper advertisements document cabinetmakers' willingness to sell to merchants "who want to purchase in large quantities."[13] (This type of marketing will be discussed later in greater detail.) A second category, custom order or "bespoke work," also appears on the manifests. Although by 1820 this was no longer the most popular form of merchandising, it was still used for the specialized, superior kinds of orders. Anthony Quervelle, for instance, shipped two boxes of custom-made furniture to Secretary of Navy Samuel L. Southard who lived in Washington, D.C., while chairmaker Isaac H. Laycock sent fourteen custom chairs and one lounge to W. A. Hayne, the bookkeeper of the Bank of the State of South Carolina.[14] Craftsmen preferred this type of marketing because they retained the greatest control over the prices of their wares.

When shippers were unable to dispose of their furniture by custom order, they frequently consigned their goods to factors and commission merchants in other cities for wareroom or auction sales. Between 1820 and 1840 Philadelphians forwarded their exports to no less than thirty-five such agents. Thus, Messrs. Taylor, Licard, and Company, merchants, were placed in charge of the three settees and five dozen chairs which J. H.

[11] Outward Coastwise Manifests, November 30, 1839; Shipment of October 21, 1828, Shipments between Philadelphia and Baltimore, 1827–28, Western Transportation Line, HSP; Outward Coastwise Manifests, April 3, December 8, 1828; March 30, 1829.

[12] Unlike coastwise shipping records, foreign manifests ordinarily do not specify the consignee. Consequently, it is difficult to determine from this source alone the types of persons to whom the furniture was exported. Fortunately, a number of outside references are more specific; from these we discover that, as in the coastal trade, factors and commission merchants were the chief recipients of the shipments.

[13] Outward Coastwise Manifests, December 9, 1820; March 1, July 14, December 7, 1821; November 20, 1822; June 12, 1824; September 9, 1826; October 3, October 16, 1827; September 20, 1828; October 21, 1830; November 19, 1831; November 11, 1837. Outward Foreign Manifests, March 9, June 6, July 7, 1820; April 26, 1821; May 30, December 12, 1822; October 9, October 17, November 15, 1823; April 26, August 11, 1824; May 11, August 7, 1826; August 27, 1828; April 12, April 14, 1831; May 9, 1839; *Poulson's American Daily Advertiser* (Philadelphia) (September 22, 1820).

[14] Outward Coastwise Manifests, October 16, 1827; November 15, 1823.

Table 3. Furniture Forms Exported from Philadelphia in Coastwise Trade, 1820–40

Form	Individual pieces	Boxes	Bundles	Shipments	Sets
Tables and case pieces:					
Tables	39	. . .	. . .	. . .	. . .
Desks	8	. . .	. . .	. . .	. . .
Chests	7	. . .	. . .	. . .	. . .
Bureaus	20	. . .	. . .	. . .	. . .
Pianos	88	. . .	. . .	. . .	. . .
Sideboards	6	. . .	. . .	. . .	. . .
Organs	1	. . .	. . .	. . .	. . .
Seating furniture:					
Fancy chairs	686	. . .	30	. . .	. . .
Windsors	922	. . .	. . .	. . .	. . .
Rocking chairs	14	. . .	6	. . .	. . .
Table chairs	2	. . .	. . .	. . .	. . .
Armchairs	25	. . .	. . .	. . .	. . .
Unspecified types of chairs	16,197	56	1,376	1	. . .
Sofas	25	2	. . .	. . .	. . .
Settees	51	. . .	. . .	. . .	. . .
Lounges	13	. . .	. . .	. . .	. . .
Couches	2	. . .	. . .	. . .	. . .
Small furniture and miscellaneous forms:					
Looking glasses	. . .	40	12	. . .	. . .
Foot and piano stools	3	. . .	. . .	. . .	. . .
Frames	. . .	1	75	. . .	. . .
Clocks	5	12	4	. . .	. . .
Clock cases	1	. . .	. . .	. . .	. . .
Cradles	1	. . .	. . .	. . .	. . .
Bedposts and bedsteads	130	1	31	. . .	4
Wash- and candlestands	30	. . .	. . .	. . .	. . .
Unspecified furniture	787	2,243	3,642	341	. . .

SOURCE.—U.S., Bureau of Customs, Outward Coastwise Manifests, District of Philadelphia, 1820–40, Record Group 1059, National Archives. Form names are listed here as they appear on the manifests.

Stevenson shipped to Alvarado, Mexico, in 1825. Similarly, when merchant John W. Rulon exported three imitation mahogany chairs and seven children's chairs to Calcutta in 1838, he consigned them, at commission and charges of 8 percent, to the Exchange Commission Sales Room for disposal by public auction.[15]

Although J. Simmons Bee, the operator of the Charleston Depository Furniture Warehouse and Auction Mart, does not appear to have done any business with Philadelphia, the workings of his firm may typify the operations of other warerooms. In 1825 Bee advertised in a Boston newspaper that he would receive cabinet wares of every description from northern ports to be disposed of at "Private Sale and at Auction." Such sales, he explained, would be subject to the following rules:

1. Every article received for sale shall be charged a sum proportioned to its size and value, and remain one month free of storage; after which time it shall be charged as above.

2. Sales at Auction will be held on the 1st Monday in every month . . . and all articles bid in shall be charged one fourth of the usual commission, if bid in a second time, one half, and a third time a full commission.[16]

[15]Invoice of Goods of J. H. Stevenson, September 14, 1825, Joseph Downs Manuscript and Microfilm Collection, Winterthur Museum, Winterthur, Del. (hereafter DMMC); business paper, April 18, 1838, Coles Collection.

[16]*Repertory* (Boston) (December 8, 1825).

Table 4. Furniture Forms Exported from Philadelphia in Foreign Trade, 1820–40

Form	Individual pieces	Boxes	Bundles	Shipments	Value
Tables and case pieces:					
Tables	87	6	1	. . .	$ 2,828.50
Desks	31	1	13	. . .	1,216.50
Bureaus	59	22	1	. . .	2,418.00
Pianos	63	4	. . .	. . .	14,832.50
Sideboards	14	. . .	. . .	. . .	819.00
Wardrobes	3	. . .	. . .	. . .	134.00
Secretaries	12	. . .	. . .	. . .	642.00
Billiard tables	8	. . .	. . .	. . .	2,128.00
Seating furniture:					
Fancy chairs	1,326	25	81	. . .	4,923.68
Windsors	4,463	3	3	. . .	4,971.85
Rocking chairs	256	3	12	. . .	2,728.59
Armchairs	3	. . .	. . .	. . .	35.00
Unspecified types of chairs	102,437	615	1,705	22	181,292.88
Sofas	259	53	14	. . .	12,571.12
Settees	219	1	6	. . .	2,268.50
Lounges	22	5	. . .	. . .	860.00
Couches	20	. . .	. . .	. . .	94.00
Small furniture and miscellaneous forms:					
Foot and piano stools	70	3	. . .	. . .	485.25
Frames	1	6	. . .	. . .	852.00
Clocks	4	19	5	. . .	1,359.00
Cradles	3	. . .	. . .	. . .	50.00
Portable desks	2	. . .	. . .	. . .	35.00
Bedposts and bedsteads	88	. . .	17	. . .	1,213.00
Wash- and candlestands	14	. . .	3	. . .	654.87
Unspecified furniture	2	2,327	1,988	15	201,948.11

SOURCE.—U.S., Bureau of Customs, Outward Foreign Manifests, District of Philadelphia, 1820–40, Record Group 1059, National Archives. Form names are listed here as they appear on the manifests.

If sales through agents were unfeasible, exporters occasionally reverted to the older and less popular practice of consigning their wares to a ship's captain. In 1827 merchant Richard Ashurst "gave over" nine bundles of chairs and three boxes of furniture to Capt. George W. White for sale in New Orleans.[17] Since the shipmaster had the final say regarding the price and disposal of the goods in his charge, this method of selling was a financial risk and, hence, became less and less common.

Sometimes, craftsmen and merchants accompanied their own shipments. Pianoforte maker John Loud did so on a couple of occasions, as did cabinetmaker John F. Johnson.[18] And, as previously indicated, southern merchants frequently journeyed to Philadelphia on business trips and consigned furniture purchases to themselves for shipment back home.

While such coastwise and foreign trade comprised the bulk of the furniture exported, cabinetmakers and merchants also sold goods to residents of western and northern Pennsylvania. Encouraged by an expanding transportation network, craftsmen frequently advertised their willingness to ship to the interior part of the state.[19] Charles W. James, for example, assured

[17]Outward Coastwise Manifests, May 17, 1827.

[18]Outward Coastwise Manifests, April 5, 1821; December 18, 1822; November 30, 1839. With two exceptions all exports by the various members of the Loud family were made under the firm name, initially Thomas and John Loud and later Loud and Brothers.

[19]In the early 1820s businessmen had revived the Union Canal and the Chesapeake and Delaware Canal projects in the hope of diverting the trade of the Susquehanna Valley from Baltimore. Similarly, the city had sponsored a canal along the Schuylkill to provide a link northward to Pottsville. In 1826 Pennsylvania had inaugurated a system of railroads designed to cross the Susquehanna and capture the commerce of the West, specifically Pittsburgh and the Ohio River Valley. Although these improvements never brought the business boon expected, they did boost the city's export rate and provided the method by which many Philadelphia-made goods found their way to the hinterland.

the public that the quality and low prices of his chairs had "obtained him customers from the remotest parts of this and neighboring cities, as well as all the populous and fashionable towns in this state."[20] James Kite, owner of a cabinet warehouse on Walnut Street, similarly notified his clientele: "The Subscriber continues to carry on the cabinet business in all its branches at the above mentioned stand. He has on hand a general assortment of furniture which he will dispose of at the lowest prices. . . . He particularly invites the attention of southern and western merchants to his establishment, as he will endeavor to execute all orders he may be favored with, with punctuality and dispatch. Goods will be carefully packed and a liberal discount will be made on large purchases."[21]

Unfortunately, documentation about the actual shipment of furniture to the hinterland is sketchy, which makes a systematic study of exports impossible. There are, however, in addition to the newspaper advertisements, some indications that the city's cabinet wares found their way west and north. In Pottsville, Pennsylvania, for instance, the managers of the Schuylkill Navigation Company estimated that thirty-two tons of household furniture had passed up that canal system from Philadelphia in 1826. Three years later, again in Pottsville, a James Burge deposited three dozen windsor chairs, "lately brought from Philadelphia," in a local store. In 1837 Henry Sterling of Pittsburgh received five shipments of furniture from the eastern metropolis, via the Pittsburgh Transportation Line. The railroad company's consignment included 2 sideboards, 1 chest, 2 cot-bedsteads, and over 25 boxes of unspecified furniture.[22] Although such references make it difficult to determine whether the recipients were moving older household goods or purchasing new furniture, they do reveal a definite trade pattern and, at the very least, indicate ways newly made cabinet wares might have reached the hinterland.

An increased reliance on new merchandising methods was connected with the growth of the domestic and foreign trade. In preceding periods, cabinetmakers had contented themselves with two major forms of selling: custom order or bespoke work and, by the late 1700s, retail sales or "shop work."[23] But, as facilities for transporting goods expanded, furniture craftsmen adopted a third sales technique, wholesale or "order work."

In this new form of marketing, craftsmen were not able to set their own prices or deal directly with their customers, as they could in custom order or retail selling. Instead, they conducted their business through middlemen who, aided by improvements in transportation, sold to the ever-widening market. Since price soon became the key factor in the competition for sales, these intermediaries pressed their cabinetmaking suppliers to keep costs at a minimum. Thus, those master craftsmen who succeeded managed to reduce the number and wages of their skilled journeymen, while simultaneously increasing the number of apprentices and cheap unskilled laborers. The cabinetmaker became less and less a craftsman and merchant and more and more an employer, directing the work of an enlarged, relatively inexperienced staff. By 1835 it was estimated that the products of a good many master cabinetmakers were primarily the result of apprentice labor. Upset with inadequate wages and the lack of job security, journeymen defended themselves: "We do not say that this work is imperfectly or unsubstantially made, we merely wish to appraise the public of the fact, that they may be enabled to judge whether, in the nature of things, it can be as well manufactured by an inexperienced boy, as by an experienced man, who had spent his youth in acquiring a knowledge of the rudiments and the vigor of his man hood in perfecting himself in all the minutae of this difficult art."[24] On this point a bitter conflict arose in Philadelphia between the master cabinetmakers and their skilled journeymen.

Conflicts between employers and their journeymen were, of course, nothing new; they had existed in Philadelphia since the second half of the eighteenth century.[25] But, with few excep-

---

[20]*Poulson's American Daily Advertiser* (Philadelphia) (December 22, 1822).

[21]*United States Gazette* (Philadelphia) (March 30, 1833).

[22]*Report of the President and Managers of the Schuylkill Navigation Company to the Stockholders* (Philadelphia: Lydia R. Bailey, 1827), p. 11; *Pottsville Journal* (October 10, 1829); Henry Sterling Papers, September 27, October 28, November 8, October 2, 1837, University of Pittsburgh Libraries, Pittsburgh.

[23]Custom-made work involved small-scale selling with the cabinetmaker remaining essentially a craftsman. Shop work was the retail wareroom marketing of ready-made furniture. Here, the cabinetmaker became a merchant as well as a craftsman, selling his goods either in his own wareroom or in those of commission merchants or auctioneers.

[24]*United States Gazette* (March 30, 1835).

[25]For details of the 1796 strike by Philadelphia's journeymen cabinetmakers, see Charles F. Montgomery, *American Furniture: The Federal Period* (New York: Viking Press, 1966), pp. 19–26. In 1825 another strike was called by the journeymen to enforce higher wages. Although this seems to have

tions, these early clashes were not especially militant. Perhaps this was because the first journeymen's organizations functioned more as benevolent societies than as trade unions. Beginning in the 1820s, however, a change occurred. Journeymen became more aggressive; as a result, their association took on more of the qualities of a labor union. Conflicts now became more sustained and severe. A good illustration of this is provided by the history of the Society of Journeymen Cabinetmakers.

Instituted in 1806, the Society of Journeymen Cabinetmakers began as a benevolent association. Each member paid a $2.00 admission fee and then 12½¢ per month, "for the benefit of the Society," and 6¼¢ at each session "for the benefit of the house in which they were meeting." Provisions were also made for a kind of fire insurance whereby, in case a member suffered any damage by fire, the society contributed "to repair the loss sustained." Funeral benefits amounting to $40 were paid to relatives of deceased members; after the burial, deficiencies in the fund were replenished by a 25¢ contribution levied on surviving members.[26]

By the early 1820s journeymen sensed their position as skilled workmen was endangered. Under the old system of custom-made and retail-order work, employer-employee antagonism had been kept at a minimum. Masters still had controlled the prices charged for their own products and had granted their journeymen's wage increase requests simply by raising the prices of their furniture. With the new wholesale method of selling, however, this was no longer possible. Faced with competition from other centers of manufacture, masters could not continue passing along the cost of wage increases to their customers and remain in business. Accordingly, they solved the problem by taking the only course of action they saw open to them—reducing both the number and wage rate of their journeymen and increasing the quantity of cheap laborers, that is, apprentices and unskilled workmen.

Journeymen protested that their standard of life was threatened. When the Society of Jour-

neymen Cabinetmakers revised its constitution in 1829, a noticeable change in the organization's original objective had occurred. While benefits still were provided, primary emphasis now was laid upon protection of the trade. The society's immediate concern was over the competition from inferior workmen. To alleviate this problem, it suggested a minimum wage based ultimately on the 1828 book of prices. This volume, a revision of the Philadelphia price books of the 1790s, contained lists of suggested wages to be paid to journeymen cabinet- and chairmakers on a piecework basis. It fixed day salaries at $1.33⅓, a one-third increase over that established in 1795, and set the length of the working day at eleven hours, "employers to find candles."[27] The society also gave standing committees the duty of drawing up bills for members unacquainted with the book of prices and made special provision for the arbitration of labor disputes. Apparently, the Philadelphia association communicated with similar groups in other cities, for one section permitted the free admission of "any person presenting a certificate from any Society in the United States with whom the Society shall hold correspondence."[28]

The revised constitution was an effort on the part of the journeymen cabinetmakers to face the challenge of unskilled labor and to relieve the growing tension between themselves and their masters. Unfortunately, this attempt failed. The masters did not feel they could grant concessions and still make a profit. Therefore, after five years of continued frustration, the Society of Journeymen Cabinetmakers took a more aggressive stand.

In the spring of 1834 the society—totaling more than 200 members—established its own wareroom at 48 South Fifth Street under the supervision of Crawford Riddle. The association contended that this was done not to accumulate property but to defend the members against "a system of tyranny, exaction, and injustice—to submit to which would be to lose sight altogether of the dignity of men." According to the journeymen, masters had given them the alternative of quitting their jobs or working for an inadequate wage. Some of the society's members

been settled quickly, it was a prelude to the more sustained and acrimonious conflict of 1834 (see *Freeman's Journal* [Philadelphia] [June 27, 1825]; and John R. Commons et al., *History of Labour in the United States*, 4 vols. [New York: Macmillan Co., 1918–35], 1:157).

[26] *The Constitution of the Pennsylvania Society of Journeymen Cabinet-Makers of the City of Philadelphia* (Philadelphia: Garden & Thompson, 1829), pp. 16, 7, 19–20.

[27] *The Philadelphia Cabinet and Chair Makers' Union Book of Prices for Manufacturing Cabinet Ware* (Philadelphia: Printed for a Committee of Employers and Journeymen by William Stavely, 1828), p. 7.

[28] *Constitution of the Pennsylvania Society of Journeymen Cabinet-Makers*, pp. 14, 17.

already had left their employers before the establishment of the cooperative; the rest were fired when the wareroom opened.[29]

In May the society published a full vindication of its actions:

JOURNEYMEN
Cabinet-Makers' Warerooms,
No. 48 South Fifth Street.
Read and Reflect

. . . The history of the principle employing Cabinet-Makers of this city, for the last five years, has been unhandsome in the extreme. They have endeavored to reduce us to a state of vassalege and poverty, below the meanest of our race—it has been their custom, in the most inclement season of the year, when employment could not be obtained, to force upon us the alternative of quiting their shops or working for a price entirely inadequate to the amount of labor performed, and entirely insufficient for the maintenance of our families. They have involved us in law suits, harassing and ruinous in their effects, and they have deprived us of the just recompense of our labor. In the land of our nativity, the very birth place of Liberty, they have thrown every obstacle in our way, and they have prosecuted their object with a zeal and perserverance that would have done them credit, if bestowed in an honorable cause.

In consequence of this ungenerous treatment we were compelled to institute an establishment, for the purpose of disposing of such articles of furniture, as should be manufactured by and of our men, who might be compelled to avail themselves of the little assistance it was then able to afford. By this act of self-defence we incurred their determined opposition, and it was followed by an immediate discharge of the balance of our men, to the amount of nearly two hundred, thrown suddenly upon the slender resources of our infant Institution, for the purpose of crushing us the more effectually. It ought to be known and remembered, that this was done in the dead of winter, and the little pittance that was due them, was and is still witheld from many of them.[30]

The society further explained that apprentices were not permitted to work at the cooperative and, as a consequence, the cabinet wares were of a superior quality.[31]

The new wareroom proved quite successful. In fact, it soon became one of the largest furniture retail stores in the city. By June it occupied six rooms; and two years later, in 1836, the society made further enlargements in response to "the great and rapidly increasing demand" for its furniture.[32] The association drew its clientele mainly from the middle and upper middle classes. Included among its patrons were several lawyers, merchants, and grocers, as well as a number of craftsmen. The society's cabinetmaking customers included William V. Griffith, Daniel Binder, Elias Reed, John Connelly, William Riley, and Charles M. Gilbert.[33]

The wareroom itself was stocked with a large quantity of furniture in a variety of forms and prices (table 5). But as a result of the unsettling effects of the depression of 1837, the society on one occasion found itself in serious financial difficulty. Unable to discharge its debts, it assigned all its property, on September 12, 1837, to cabinetmaker and society member Robert T. Coane, in trust for the payment of its creditors. This action apparently proved effective, for less than a year later the cooperative was again in operation and continued selling furniture at least until the end of the period under discussion. By 1838 the journeymen had total assets amounting to $20,741.91.[34]

The establishment and operation of the society's wareroom brought to a head more than a decade of antagonism between workmen and their employers. Never before in Philadelphia had there existed such sustained labor unrest. As historian John R. Commons has remarked, the modern struggle between capital and labor began between 1820 and 1840.[35]

The expansion of the market and the rise of wholesale merchandising had no less a disturbing effect on the apprenticeship system. Although apprenticeship was still the major institution for the transmittal of technical skills in the 1820s and 1830s, evidences of the system's continued decline were apparent.[36] With the growing demands for increased output at lower cost, masters

---

[29]*Pennsylvanian* (Philadelphia) (March 6, May 31, 1834).

[30]*Pennsylvanian* (May 31, 1834).

[31]*Pennsylvanian* (May 31, 1834). The society maintained strict quality control throughout its existence. In 1835 it expelled some members whose work it felt did not meet certain standards. At that time it also raised the initiation fee, presumably for the purpose of barring "undesirables" from the organization (*United States Gazette* [July 15, 1835]).

[32]*Pennsylvanian* (July 3, 1834); *United States Gazette* (June 16, 1834; March 10, 1836).

[33]Miscellaneous Book, A. M., 2, 10, pp. 663–65, Municipal Archives, Philadelphia.

[34]Miscellaneous Book, pp. 658–60; *United States Gazette* (September 19, 1837); *Pennsylvania Inquirer and Daily Courier* (Philadelphia) (January 2, April 26, 1838); *United States Gazette* (April 5, 1838); *Public Ledger* (Philadelphia) (March 22, 1838); Miscellaneous Book, p. 665.

[35]Commons et al., 1:63–65.

[36]The apprenticeship system had shown signs of breakdown as early as the eighteenth century (see Ian M. G. Quimby, "Apprenticeship in Colonial Philadelphia" [M.A. thesis, University of Delaware, 1963], pp. 149–56).

Table 5. Furniture for Sale at the Journeymen Cabinetmakers'
Wareroom, 1836

Form	Quantity	Price range
Consul table	1	$60.00
Center table	9	43.00–60.00
Card table	4	22.50
Pier table	7	37.50–70.00
Work table	6	10.00–18.00
Dining table	8	25.00–27.50
Dressing table	3	35.00
Lounge, upholstered	3	49.00–60.00
Lounge, unupholstered	2	20.00
Sofa, upholstered	4	45.00–48.00
Sofa, unupholstered	7	27.00
Sideboard	7	37.00–90.00
Bedstead	6	18.00–55.00
Bedpost	5 sets	7.16/set–22.50/set
Bureau	2	32.50–44.00
Chair	28	7.00–11.66
Music stool	2	8.50
Marble slabs	5	7.75–12.00
Glass plate	2 pieces	6.00
Crib mattress	1	8.00
Hardware	1 lot	88.82

SOURCE.—Miscellaneous Book, A.M., 2, 10, pp. 662–63, Municipal Archives, Philadelphia.

came to regard their apprentices not as craft trainees but as sources of cheap labor. It was, after all, less expensive to use bound laborers than full-fledged journeymen. The *Mechanics' Free Press* explained:

The practice of many master mechanics in this city in employing none but apprentices in their manufacturing establishments, is an evil severely felt by the journeymen of all denominations; for whenever there is a greater number of mechanics than the demand of labour requires, it is evident the surplus must be thrown out of employ. There are men in this city who have from 15 to 20 apprentices, who never or very seldom have a journeyman in their shops, but to supply the place of journeymen, and to monopolize to themselves trade and wealth, as one apprentice becomes free, another is taken to fill up the ranks.[37]

The master had become more and more of a manager and delegated traditional responsibilities to others. The transfer of moral and liberal arts instruction to external agencies, practiced as early as the American Revolution, increased during the 1820s and 1830s. Religious guidance, hitherto supervised by the master, was

[37]*Mechanics' Free Press* (November 29, 1828).

given over to the Sunday school; and education in nonvocational matters became increasingly relegated to formal sessions at day or evening schools. The evening school was, after all, originally established "to instruct apprentices whose indentures stipulated a certain amount of reading, writing, & ciphering."[38] By the 1820s and 1830s, most of the indentures specifically stipulated that the master permit his apprentices to attend school for a certain amount of time each year.[39] Thus, Abraham McDonough permitted

[38]John Farron to John Jamison, March 24, 1828; Lawrence Shaw to Enoch Tomlin, April 21, 1828; Charles Mason to Joseph White, November 29, 1830; George Davenport to Sidney Hiscox, March 14, 1831; William Donnell to Joseph Walraven, August 22, 1831; John Coyle to Samuel Meyers, November 4, 1833; Dared Mintzer to Thomas P. Sager, September 13, 1830, Guardians of the Poor Indenture Papers, 1827–29, 1830–33, Municipal Archives; Carl Bridenbaugh as quoted in Bernard Bailyn, *Education in the Forming of American Society* (Chapel Hill: University of North Carolina Press, 1960), p. 32.

[39]John Barr to George Ball, July 8, 1822; Eleazer Toram to Jacob Wayne, June 21, 1824; Richard Thomas to Thomas P. Sherborne, June 6, 1825; Collin W. Puttinger to Isaac H. Laycock, October 2, 1826, Alms House Indenture Book, Municipal Archives; see also Indenture of Silas Wilson to Jacob F. Wilkins, July 19, 1829, and Indenture of Henry Manderson to Benjamin Thompson, Indentures of Apprenticeship, 1677–1849, Society Miscellaneous Collection, HSP.

John Brooks to receive seven quarters of half-day schooling per year, and Noah Gee allowed John Rutland sixteen quarters of half days.[40] The master's influence over his workers was further limited by the increase in the number of apprentices boarding at home. In cases where the apprentice continued living with his master, the latter sometimes provided his worker's family a sum of money in lieu of furnishing clothing, washing, and mending.[41]

[40]John Brooks to Abraham McDonough, April 4, 1831; John Rutland to Noah Gee, February 10, 1834, Guardians of the Poor Indenture Papers, 1830–33, 1834–35.

[41]*Public Ledger* (June 27, 1839); see also Indenture of Silas Wilson to Jacob F. Wilkins, July 19, 1829, DMMC, and Indenture of Henry Manderson to Benjamin Thompson, Indentures of Apprenticeship, 1677–1849, Society Miscellaneous Collection, HSP.

The apprenticeship system with its traditional network of corresponding duties and obligations had been considerably weakened. Regarded increasingly as a source of cheap manpower, the indentured child of the 1820s and 1830s was not far from becoming the child laborer of later industrial periods.

On the whole, cabinetmaking in 1840 was a different business from what it had been twenty years earlier. The availability of new markets, the increased reliance on wholesale distribution, the growing tension between masters and journeymen, and the continued decline of the apprenticeship system, all had combined to transform the furniture trade from the eighteenth-century craft to the nineteenth-century industry.

Checklist of Cabinetmakers and Related Craftsmen in Philadelphia, 1820–40

The checklist contains the names of over 2,100 furniture craftsmen who worked in Philadelphia between 1820 and 1840. Included are cabinetmakers, chairmakers, sofamakers, turners, pianoforte makers, organ makers, rush bottomers, portable-desk manufacturers, framemakers, ornamental chair painters, and curled-hair and sacking-bottom manufacturers. All names are arranged alphabetically. Beside each name is the craftsman's occupation as listed in the records. Only primary craft occupations are given, despite the fact that furniture makers in the 1820s and 1830s often engaged in additional business as sidelines. Craftsmen were an exceptionally versatile group and frequently acted as general repairmen, replacing knobs, making cornices and venetian blinds, hanging doors, repairing steps, and doing other carpentry work. Many branched out into the lumber, undertaking and coachmaking trades, and a few even took on added duties as innkeepers, grocers, distillers, stonecutters, booksellers, and real estate speculators. Such diversification enabled craftsmen to adjust to changing conditions in the economy and con-

tributed to the general prosperity of the cabinetmaking community in the 1820s and 1830s.

An asterisk (*) to the left of the name indicates a member of the Society of Journeymen Cabinetmakers; a dagger (†) indicates an exporter of furniture to either domestic or foreign ports.

Beneath each name various short titles indicate the major sources of information for that individual. Because of the large number of craftsmen, shop addresses have been omitted, although generally the greatest concentration of workrooms lay in the area of Front, Second, Third, and Walnut Streets. The short titles used are given below.

Directories

D 1820   Whitley, Edward, *The Philadelphia Directory and Register, for 1820.* Philadelphia: Printed for M'Carty & Davis, 1820.

D 1821   *The Philadelphia Directory and Register, for 1821.* Philadelphia: M'Carty & Davis, 1821.

D 1822   *The Philadelphia Directory and Register, for 1822.* Philadelphia: M'Carty & Davis, 1822.

D 1823   Desilver, Robert. *The Philadelphia Index, or Directory, for 1823.* Philadelphia: Robert Desilver, 1823.

D 1824   Desilver, Robert. *The Philadelphia Directory, for 1824.* Philadelphia: Robert Desilver, 1824.

D 1825   Wilson, Thomas, ed. *The Philadelphia Directory and Stranger's Guide, for 1825.* Philadelphia: Thomas Wilson, 1825.

D 1828   *Desilver's Philadelphia Directory and Stranger's Guide, for 1828.* Philadelphia: Robert Desilver, 1828.

D 1829   *Desilver's Philadelphia Directory and Stranger's Guide, 1829.* Philadelphia: Robert Desilver, 1829.

D 1830   *Desilver's Philadelphia Directory and Stranger's Guide, 1830.* Philadelphia: Robert Desilver, 1830.

D 1831   *Desilver's Philadelphia Directory and Stranger's Guide, 1831.* Philadelphia: Robert Desilver, 1831.

D 1833   *Desilver's Philadelphia Directory, and Stranger's Guide, for 1833.* Philadelphia: Robert Desilver, 1833.

D 1835/36   *Desilver's Philadelphia Directory and Stranger's Guide, for 1835 & 1836.* Philadelphia: Robert Desilver, 1835–36.

D 1837   *Desilver's Philadelphia Directory and Stranger's Guide, for 1837.* Philadelphia: Robert Desilver, 1837.

D 1839   *A. M'Elroy's Philadelphia Directory, for 1839.* 2d ed. Philadelphia: A. M'Elroy, 1839.

D 1840   *A. M'Elroy's Philadelphia Directory, for 1840.* 3d ed. Philadelphia: A. M'Elroy, 1840.

Newspapers

Aurora	*Aurora* (Philadelphia)
Franklin Gaz.	*Franklin Gazette* (Philadelphia)
Freeman's Jnl.	*The Freeman's Journal* (Philadelphia)
Mechanics' Free Press	*Mechanics' Free Press* (Philadelphia)
Nat. Gaz.	*National Gazette and Literary Register* (Philadelphia)
Pennsylvanian	*Pennsylvanian* (Philadelphia)
Poulson's Advertiser	*Poulson's American Daily Advertiser* (Philadelphia)
Pa. Inquirer	*Pennsylvania Inquirer and Daily Courier* (Philadelphia)
Public Ledger	*Public Ledger* (Philadelphia)
Public Record	*Public Record* (Philadelphia)
Sun. Dispatch	*Sunday Dispatch* (Philadelphia)
Sat. Eve. Post	*Saturday Evening Post* (Philadelphia)
U.S. Gaz.	*United States Gazette* (Philadelphia)
Vill. Record	*Village Record* (West Chester, Pennsylvania)

Records in the Archives of the City and County of Philadelphia, City Hall, Philadelphia

Men's Register	Men's Register, Alms House Hospital, 1828–44.
Misc. bk. 1	Miscellaneous Book, G. W. R., 1, 7.
Misc. bk. 2	Miscellaneous Book, G. W. R., 2.
Misc. bk. 3	Miscellaneous Book, A. M., 2, 10.
Convict Docket	Convict Description Docket, Prison and Financial Records, 1826–31.
Mayor's Court	Mayor's Court Docket, 1820–37.
Quarter Sessions	Court of Quarter Sessions Dockets, and Bonds, 1820–40.
Indenture Papers	Indenture Papers and Bonds, 1820–40, Guardians of the Poor.
Children's Register	Register, Children's Asylum, 1819–35.
Indenture Book	Almshouse Indenture Book, 1819–49, Guardians of the Poor.

Other

1820 Census	U.S. Bureau of the Census. "Records of the 1820 Census of Manufacturers, Schedule for Pennsylvania," National Archives Microfilm Publications, microcopy no. 279, roll 14.
1829 Const.	*The Constitution of the Pennsylvania Society of Journeymen Cabinet-Makers, of the City of Philadelphia.* Philadelphia: Garden & Thompson, 1829.
Fire Surveys	Franklin Fire Insurance Company Surveys, Historical Society of Pennsylvania, Philadelphia.
Girard Papers	Stephen Girard Papers, ser. 2 (microfilm), American Philosophical Society, Philadelphia.
HSP Indentures	Indentures of Apprenticeship, 1677–1849, Society Miscellaneous Collection. Historical Society of Pennsylvania, Philadelphia.
Unger Coll.	Bills, 1772–1860, Claude W. Unger Collection, Historical Society of Pennsylvania, Philadelphia.
Wills	Wills and Inventories, Department of Records, City Hall, Philadelphia.

Craftsmen

Achilles, George, *cabinetmaker*
  D 1820, 1823
Ackhuff, James, *turner*
  D 1839–40
Adams, Charles, *cabinetmaker*
  D 1840
Adams, John, *chairmaker*
  D 1825
Adams, Jonathan, *turner*
  D 1823
*Adams, Samuel, *cabinetmaker*
  D 1839
  1829 Const., p. 11
Aken & Co., *cabinetmakers*
  D 1836
†Aken, Joseph, *cabinetmaker*

  D 1828–31, 1833, 1835/36, 1837, 1839–40
  U.S. Gaz., September 29, 1826; December 6, 1828; August 9, 1830; September 3, 1831
*Akins, James, *cabinetmaker*
  Misc. bk. 3, pp. 658–65
†Albrecht, C. F. L., *pianoforte maker*
  D 1820, 1823, 1825, 1828–31, 1833, 1835/36, 1837, 1839–40
  Freeman's Jnl., July 21, 1825
  U.S. Gaz., January 11, 1832
  Wills, no. 54 (1843)
*Alexander, John, *cabinetmaker*
  1829 Const., p. 12
Alexander, Richard, *cabinetmaker*
  D 1820, 1823
Alforce, William, *cabinetmaker*
  D 1835/36
Alfred, William, *cabinetmaker*
  D 1831, 1833
Alice, Christian, *cabinetmaker*
  D 1840
Allen, William, *cabinetmaker*
  D 1831, 1833
Alsop, Samuel, *cabinetmaker*
  D 1839
Altemus, William, *ornamental painter, gilder*
  D 1830–31, 1833, 1837, 1839–40
Altmeyer, A., *cabinetmaker*
  D 1839
Ambler, Henry, *cabinetmaker*
  D 1840
Ames, Henry, *pianoforte maker*
  D 1835/36
Anderson, George, *turner*
  D 1823
Anderson, George R., *cabinetmaker*
  D 1839–40
Anderson, James, *cabinetmaker*
  D 1840
*Anderson, James A., *cabinetmaker*
  D 1835/36
  Pennsylvanian, November 1, 1834
  1829 Const., p. 12
Anderson, R., *cabinetmaker*
  U.S. Gaz., July 15, 1835
Andrews, John, *turner*
  D 1820
Andrews, John, *cabinetmaker*
  D 1840
Antone, Joseph, *cabinetmaker*
  D 1839
Apenhouse, Frederick, *pianoforte maker*
  D 1835/36

App, Jacob, *cabinetmaker*
    D 1840
†Apple, George, *carver and gilder, looking glass and
        fancy chairmaker*
    D 1823, 1828–31, 1833
    Misc. bk. 2, pp. 53–55
Applebaugh, Henry, *cabinetmaker*
    D 1820
Applegate, Daniel, *cabinetmaker*
    D 1835/36, 1837
Apt, Jacob, *cabinetmaker*
    D 1840
Armistead, James, *cabinetmaker*
    D 1823
*Armstrong, James, *cabinetmaker*
    Misc. bk. 3, pp. 658–65
*Armstrong, William, *cabinetmaker*
    D 1837
    Misc. bk. 3, pp. 658–65
†Ashmead, John B., *cabinetmaker*
    D 1828–31, 1833, 1835/36, 1837, 1839–40
    Girard Papers, reel 201, June 13, 1821
Ashton, Samuel, *cabinet- and chairmaker*
    D 1820, 1822, 1823, 1825, 1828–31, 1833,
        1835/36, 1837
    Samuel Ashton Accounts, DMMC
†Ashton, Thomas, *chairmaker*
    D 1820, 1823, 1825, 1828–31, 1833, 1835/36,
        1839
    Poulson's Advertiser, July 20, 1830
Atkinson, John, *cabinetmaker*
    D 1820
Atkinson, Samuel S., *cabinetmaker*
    D 1828–31, 1833
*Auchinleek, Thomas, *cabinetmaker*
    Misc. bk. 3, pp. 658–65
    1829 Const., p. 12
Avis, Joseph, *cabinetmaker*
    D 1837
Axe, Horatio J., *cabinetmaker*
    D 1830–31, 1833
Axton, Samuel, *turner*
    D 1829–31, 1833

Babcock, Alpheus, *pianoforte maker*
    D 1835/36
    U.S. Gaz., December 31, 1832
Babcock, H., *pianoforte maker*
    D 1831, 1833
Babe, J., *cabinetmaker*
    D 1825
Babe, Luke, *cabinetmaker*
    D 1823, 1828–30, 1833, 1835/36, 1837,

    1839–40
    Freeman's Jnl., April 5, 1825
Bacon, Benjamin R., *cabinetmaker*
    D 1835/36, 1837, 1839–40
Bacon, Isaac, *cabinetmaker*
    D 1820, 1823, 1825, 1828–31, 1833
Bacon, Richard, *cabinetmaker*
    D 1825, 1828–31, 1833, 1835/36
Bacon, Thomas, *cabinetmaker*
    D 1820, 1829–31, 1833, 1836–37, 1839–40
Bacon, Uriah, *cabinetmaker*
    D 1839–40
Bailey, John, *turner*
    D 1835/36
Bailey, Samuel, *sofamaker*
    D 1835/36
†Bailey, Samuel B., *chairmaker*
    D 1837, 1839–40
Baken, Richard, *cabinetmaker*
    D 1837
Baker, Adam, *cabinetmaker*
    D 1820
Baker, Bartholomew, *chairmaker*
    D 1820, 1823, 1839–40
Baker, Bassett, *cabinetmaker*
    D 1837
Baker, Charles, *cabinetmaker*
    D 1820, 1823–24, 1839–40
    Nat. Gaz., April 8, 1822
Baker, Christian, *cabinetmaker*
    Men's Register, February 26, 1836
Baker, Henry, *ornamental painter*
    D 1823
Baker, John J., *cabinetmaker*
    D 1840
Baker, John L., *cabinetmaker*
    D 1839
*Baker, Joseph, *framemaker*
    D 1830, 1833, 1835/36
    1829 Const., p. 11
Baker, Joshua, *cabinetmaker*
    D 1837
Baker, Thomas, *cabinetmaker*
    D 1835/36
Baldwin, Joseph, *chair painter*
    D 1840
Ball, George, *cabinetmaker*
    D 1823, 1825, 1830, 1833, 1835/36, 1840
    Indenture Papers, June 17, July 8, 1822
    Indenture Bk., July 8, 1822
Ball, Jesse, *cabinetmaker*
    D 1840
Bannister, Edward, *cabinet warerooms* [*proprietor*]

D 1835/36, 1837, 1839
Baptist, Eugene, *cabinetmaker*
    D 1840
*Barbazet, Jacob, *cabinetmaker*
    D 1820, 1824–25, 1828–31, 1833
    1829 Const., p. 11
Barnes, Henry, *cabinetmaker*
    D 1839
Barnet [Barnitt], Thomas, *turner*
    D 1823, 1825, 1828–31, 1833
*Barnett, Francis, *cabinetmaker*
    D 1829–31, 1833, 1835/36, 1837
    1829 Const., p. 11
Barr, John, *cabinetmaker*
    D 1840
Barrett, G. B., *cabinetmaker*
    D 1833, 1835/36, 1839–40
Barrett, William, *ornamental painter*
    D 1829–31, 1833, 1835/36
Barry, J. B., *cabinetmaker*
    D 1820, 1823, 1825, 1828–31, 1833
    Aurora, January 5, 1822
Barry, Joseph, Jr., *cabinetmaker*
    D 1820, 1823, 1829–31, 1836, 1839–40
†Barry, Joseph, & Co., *cabinetmakers*
    D 1831–33, 1835/36
Bartle, George, *turner*
    D 1820
Bartlett [Bartling], Henry, *cabinetmaker*
    D 1825, 1828–31, 1833
Bartlett & Kehr, *cabinetmakers*
    D 1825, 1828–29, 1831, 1833
Barton, J. R., *cabinetmaker*
    D 1835/36
*Barton, William, *cabinetmaker*
    D 1839–40
    1829 Const., p. 11
Bates, James A., *cabinetmaker*
    D 1840
†Bauer & Frick, *cabinetmakers*
    D 1839–40
Bauer, William, *cabinetmaker*
    D 1839–40
Baugh, Harman, *turner*
    D 1823, 1829–31, 1833, 1835/36, 1837, 1840
Bavies, Samuel, *chair painter and ornamenter*
    D 1825
Bavis, Samuel C., *chairmaker*
    D 1831, 1833, 1835/36
Bayne, N., *turner*
    D 1839
Bayne, Nathaniel, *turner*
    D 1820, 1823, 1833, 1837, 1839

Beale, Joseph, *cabinetmaker*
    D 1820, 1835/36
    Wills, no. 233 (1844)
Beale & Jamison, *cabinetmakers*
    D 1820
Beasinger, Adam, *cabinetmaker*
    Men's Register, August 4, 1833
Beasley, Edward, *turner*
    D 1837
Beasley, Rawle, *cabinetmaker*
    D 1837
*Beaumont, John, *cabinetmaker*
    D 1835/36
    1829 Const., p. 12
Beaurette, Charles, *cabinetmaker*
    D 1833, 1835/36
Beck, Anthony, *cabinetmaker*
    D 1837
Beck, Edward, *chairmaker*
    D 1829–31, 1833, 1835/36, 1837
Beck, Edward C., *chairmaker*
    D 1839
Beck, Jacob, *turner*
    D 1840
*Beck, Peter, *cabinetmaker*
    D 1829–31, 1833, 1835/36, 1837, 1839–40
    Misc. bk. 3, pp. 658–65
    1829 Const., p. 11
*Beck, William, *cabinetmaker*
    D 1835/36
    Misc. bk. 3, pp. 658–65
    1829 Const., p. 12
Becker, Christian, *pianoforte maker*
    D 1820
Beebe, Alexander, *chair painter*
    D 1829–31, 1833, 1835/36, 1837, 1839
Beers, John, *turner*
    D 1828–29, 1831, 1833
Beisley, Jacob, *cabinetmaker*
    D 1839
*Bell, David, *cabinetmaker*
    D 1824
    1829 Const., p. 11
Bell, David H., *cabinetmaker*
    D 1839–40
Bell, Elijah, *cabinetmaker*
    D 1837
Bell, Richard, *turner*
    D 1824
Bellerjeau, Samuel, *cabinetmaker*
    D 1837, 1839–40
*Bellingham, Thomas, *cabinetmaker*
    1829 Const., p. 11

Benkoff, George, *cabinetmaker*
D 1839
Benner, Sebastian, *cabinetmaker*
D 1823, 1828–31, 1833
Freeman's Jnl., April 5, 1825
Benson, John, *cabinetmaker*
D 1833
Benstead, John M., *cabinetmaker*
D 1837, 1840
Benstead & Tatem, *cabinetmakers*
D 1840
Berguin, Frederick, *cabinetmaker*
D 1837
Berks, John, *cabinetmaker*
D 1829–31, 1833
Berrett, William, *ornamental painter*
D 1823, 1825, 1830, 1833
Berry, William B., *chairmaker*
D 1835/36, 1837, 1839–40
Berryman, Matthew W., *cabinetmaker*
D 1835/36, 1837
*Besson, George, *cabinetmaker*
Misc. bk. 3, pp. 658–65
*Bessun [Bessan], Jacob, *cabinetmaker*
D 1837, 1839–40
Misc. bk. 3, pp. 658–65
Betts, Edward, *pianoforte maker*
D 1837
Betzold, C. F., *cabinetmaker*
D 1839–40
Beyer, Joseph, *chairmaker*
D 1835/36
Bickel, Conrad, *cabinetmaker*
D 1830–31, 1833, 1839
Bickerton, Joseph, *pianoforte maker*
D 1828–31, 1833, 1835/36, 1839
Bignell, T. George, *chairmaker*
D 1835/36
Bilson, John, *cabinetmaker*
D 1820
Binder, Daniel, *cabinetmaker*
D 1825, 1828–31, 1833, 1835/36, 1837,
1839–40
Bingham, Robert, *cabinetmaker*
D 1837
Binns, Thomas, *cabinetmaker*
Men's Register, October 3, October 25, 1830;
January 13, 1831; February 17, October
4, 1832; December 14, 1833
Bioret, Charles, *cabinetmaker*
D 1820, 1825, 1830–31, 1833, 1836, 1839–40
Biral, Charles, *cabinet warehouse [proprietor]*
D 1829–31

Birnbaum, George, *turner*
D 1829–31, 1833, 1835/36, 1837, 1839–40
Bishop, Benjamin, *cabinetmaker*
D 1820, 1822–23, 1825, 1828–31, 1833,
1835/36
Bishop, Uriah, *furniture store [proprietor]*
D 1837
Bitting, George, *joiner, cabinetmaker*
D 1820, 1825, 1828–31, 1833
Black, George, *cabinetmaker*
D 1840
Black, Jesse, *turner*
D 1839
Blackwell, Sydney, *cabinetmaker*
D 1835/36
*Blakey [Blakie], John, *cabinetmaker*
D 1825, 1828–31, 1833
1829 Const., p. 11
Bleyler, Henry, *cabinetmaker*
D 1829–31, 1833
*Blondon, Joseph, *cabinetmaker*
1829 Const., p. 11
Bloom, Charles, *turner*
D 1839
Bloomer, Arnold, *framemaker*
D 1839
Boardman, R., *cabinetmaker*
D 1839–40
Bockius, Caspar, *cabinetmaker*
D 1840
Bode, Rudolph, *chairmaker*
D 1829–31, 1833
Boden, Joseph, *cabinetmaker*
D 1837, 1839–40
Bodey, Rudolph, *chairmaker*
D 1820
Boes, Jacob, *chairmaker*
D 1839
Bogg, John, *pianoforte maker*
D 1837
Boggs, Daniel, *cabinetmaker*
D 1828–31, 1833
Boggs, David, *cabinetmaker*
D 1820
Boggs, David, *pianoforte maker*
D 1829–31, 1833, 1835/36, 1837, 1840
Boggs, George, *chairmaker*
D 1837, 1839–40
Indenture Bk., January 8, 1838
Boikman, William, *cabinetmaker*
D 1840
Bond, Charles P., *cabinetmaker*
D 1837

Bond, James, *cabinetmaker*
  D 1831, 1833
Bond, James F., *cabinetmaker*
  D 1837, 1840
Bond, Thomas, *cabinetmaker*
  D 1820, 1825, 1828, 1830–31, 1833, 1835/36,
    1837
Bond, Thomas, *looking glass framemaker*
  D 1839–40
Bond, William, *cabinetmaker*
  D 1837
Bonnell, J., *chairmaker*
  D 1837
Bonsall, C. S., *turner*
  D 1840
†Booth, Benjamin, *chairmaker*
  D 1828–31, 1833, 1835/36, 1840
†Booth, Isaac, *cabinetmaker, stone cutter*
  D 1828–29, 1833, 1835/36, 1839–40
Booth, J. K., *furniture store [proprietor]*
  D 1837
Booth, John, *turner*
  D 1839–40
Bossert, Adam, *turner*
  D 1831, 1833
*Bossert, Charles, *cabinetmaker*
  D 1823
  Misc. bk. 3, pp. 658–65
  1829 Const., p. 11
Bossert, Charles, *pianoforte maker*
  D 1829–31, 1833, 1835/36, 1837, 1839–40
Bossert, Charles, *framemaker*
  D 1839
Bossert & Schomacher, *pianoforte maker*
  D 1840
Bosskirk, Benjamin, *chairmaker*
  D 1829–31, 1833, 1835/36, 1839–40
Bosthwick, Robert, *cabinetmaker*
  D 1837, 1840
Boswell, Clement S., *turner*
  D 1835/36
Botham, James, *turner*
  D 1837
Boulden, David P., *chairmaker*
  D 1830–31, 1833
*Boulten, John G., *cabinetmaker*
  1829 Const., p. 11
Bourgains, Fred, *cabinetmaker*
  D 1830–31, 1833, 1835/36, 1839
†Bouvier, Michel, *cabinetmaker, mahogany and marble dealer*
  D 1821–25, 1828–31, 1833, 1835/36, 1837,
    1839, 1840

  Unger Coll., October 24, 1828
  Public Record, June 11, 1874
  Sun. Dispatch, June 14, 1875
  Girard Papers, reel 210, July 28, 1829; August 26, 1829; September 1, 1829
  U.S. Gaz., November 22, 1824; July 21, 1825;
    August 4, 1828; May 21, 1829; February
    27, July 14, 1830; July 3, October 11,
    1832; January 4, February 19, August 13,
    1833; August 15, 1834; June 18, 1835;
    May 24, 1836; April 15, 1837; July 18,
    1838; November 9, 1838
  Wills, no. 463 (1874)
Bowen, A., *cabinetmaker*
  D 1823
Bowen, A. I., *cabinetmaker*
  D 1821
Bowen, Ananias, *cabinetmaker*
  D 1825, 1828–31, 1833, 1840
Bowen, David H., *cabinetmaker*
  D 1835/36, 1837, 1839–40
*Bowen, Philip, *cabinetmaker*
  Misc. bk. 3, pp. 658–65
Bowen, William, *cabinetmaker*
  D 1839–40
Bower, John, *turner*
  D 1837
Bower, John A., *cabinetmaker*
  D 1839–40
*Bower(s), Samuel, *cabinetmaker*
  D 1829–31, 1833, 1835/36
  Men's Register, August 27, 1838
  Misc. bk. 3, pp. 658–65
  1829 Const., p. 11
Bower, William, *cabinetmaker*
  D 1839
Bowers, Jacob, *turner*
  D 1829–31, 1833
Bowers, Peter, *chairmaker*
  D 1833, 1835/36, 1837, 1839–40
*Bowers, William V., *cabinetmaker*
  1829 Const., p. 12
Bows, Jacob, *chairmaker*
  D 1840
*Boyd, Matthew, *cabinetmaker*
  1829 Const., p. 12
Boyer, Abraham, *cabinetmaker*
  D 1840
Boyer, Joseph, *chairmaker*
  D 1829–31, 1833
Boyer, Nathan, *cabinetmaker*
  D 1839
*Bozear, John, *cabinetmaker*

D 1831, 1833
1829 Const., p. 12
Bracken, Henry, *cabinetmaker*
D 1839–40
Braklin, Samuel, *cabinetmaker*
D 1823
Bramaker, Andrew, *cabinetmaker*
D 1837
*Branson, John G., *cabinetmaker*
1829 Const., p. 12
Breinig, J., *cabinetmaker*
D 1840
Brelsford, John, *cabinetmaker*
D 1829–31, 1833, 1836, 1839–40
Brenholts, Lewis, *framemaker*
D 1830, 1833
Brenizer, Amos, *turner*
D 1837
Brewer, Robert, *chairmaker*
D 1840
Brewer, Samuel, *ornamental painter*
D 1833, 1835/36, 1837, 1839
*Briceland, Benjamin, *cabinetmaker*
Misc. bk. 3, pp. 658–65
Brindley, Jacob, *pianoforte maker*
D 1840
Bringhurst, Robert R., *cabinetmaker*
D 1820, 1823, 1825, 1828–31, 1833, 1835/36,
1837, 1839–40
Britzell, Joseph, *turner*
D 1820
Brock, Frederick, *cabinetmaker*
D 1835/36
Brock, William, *cabinetmaker*
D 1825, 1829–31, 1833, 1836, 1839–40
*Brooks, Samuel, *cabinetmaker*
1829 Const., p. 11
Brooks, William, *cabinetmaker*
D 1839
Brooks, William H., *turner*
D 1835/36
*Brown, George, *cabinetmaker*
D 1829–31, 1833
1829 Const., p. 11
Brown, Henry L., *cabinet- and sofamaker*
D 1823
Brown, Thomas, *turner*
D 1833
Brown, Thomas W., *cabinetmaker*
D 1839–40
Brown, William, *cabinetmaker*
D 1820, 1823, 1829–31, 1836, 1840
Brown, William, *cabinetmaker*

D 1825
Brown, William, *cabinetmaker*
D 1825
Indenture Papers, December 1, 1823
Brown, William, *cabinetmaker*
D 1829–31, 1833
Brown, William, *cabinetmaker*
D 1837, 1839
Brown, William, *cabinetmaker*
D 1839
Browne, Louis Henri, *pianoforte maker*
D 1839–40
Brownholtz, Lewis, *framemaker*
D 1837
Brownlee, H., *cabinetmaker*
D 1839
Brumaker, A., *cabinetmaker*
D 1839
Brusstar, Samuel B., *cabinetmaker*
D 1820, 1823
Bryan, John, *cabinetmaker*
D 1820, 1823, 1825, 1828–31, 1833, 1835/36,
1839–40
Bryant, William, *cabinetmaker*
D 1820–24
Bryant, William, *cabinetmaker*
D 1825
Bryant, William, *cabinetmaker*
D 1825, 1828
Bryant, William, *chairmaker*
D 1829–31, 1833
Bryne, William, *chairmaker*
D 1835/36, 1840
Buck, Benjamin, *cabinetmaker*
D 1833
Buck, John, *framemaker*
D 1835/36
Buckmaster, Charles, *cabinetmaker*
D 1837
Budd, Thomas W., *cabinetmaker*
D 1820, 1823, 1829–31
Buffington, Isaac, *cabinetmaker*
D 1820, 1823, 1828–31, 1833, 1835/36,
1839–40
Buffington, Joseph, *chairmaker*
D 1829–31, 1833, 1835/36, 1837
Buffington, William, *chairmaker*
D 1837
Burden, Alexander, *fancy and windsor chairmaker*
D 1822–23, 1825, 1828–31
†Burden, Joseph, *fancy chairmaker*
D 1820, 1823–25, 1828–31, 1833, 1837
Girard Papers, reel 210, November 4, 1820

Burdge, Ira, *cabinetmaker*
  D 1835/36
  Pennsylvanian, June 26, 1835
Buret, Charles, *cabinetmaker*
  D 1822–23
Burkett, Charles, *cabinetmaker*
  D 1837
Burkart, Adam L., *turner*
  D 1820, 1823, 1825, 1829–31, 1833, 1836,
    1840
Burkart, F. R., *pianoforte maker*
  D 1825, 1828–31, 1833
  U.S. Gaz., October 10, 1823
Burkhard & Smith, *chairmakers*
  D 1839
  Public Ledger, January 14, 1839
Burkhart, A., *turner*
  D 1839
Burkhart, Jacob, *cabinetmaker*
  D 1820
Burkhart, L. A., *turner*
  D 1837
Burkhart, Melchoir, *chairmaker*
  D 1839
Burkhart, R. F., *pianoforte maker*
  D 1823
Burn, Lawrence, *cabinetmaker*
  D 1829–31, 1833
Burn, Peter, *cabinetmaker*
  D 1828, 1830–31, 1833
Burnbum, George, *turner*
  D 1839
Burns, Pellellassy, *cabinetmaker*
  D 1840
Burry, Matthew, *cabinetmaker*
  D 1830–31, 1833
Burt, Joseph, *pianoforte maker*
  D 1833
Burton, John, *turner*
  D 1835/36, 1839
Bush & Ollis, *turners*
  D 1840
Butler, William W., *cabinetmaker*
  D 1820
Buzer, Henry, *framemaker*
  D 1839
Byers, Andrew, *chairmaker*
  D 1833, 1835/36, 1839–40
Byrne, William, *chairmaker*
  D 1837, 1839

Cady, Horace, *cabinetmaker*
  D 1831

Cady, Patrick, *cabinetmaker*
  Men's Register, April 20, 1832
Cahill, George, *cabinetmaker*
  D 1835/36
Calvert, John W., *chairmaker*
  D 1829–30
Campbell, David, *cabinetmaker*
  D 1820, 1823, 1825, 1828–31, 1833
Campbell, James, *cabinetmaker*
  Men's Register, May 6, 1835; September 3,
    1836
Campbell, Joseph, *turner*
  D 1831, 1833
Campbell, William, *cabinetmaker*
  D 1820, 1823
†*Campion, Joseph H., *cabinetmaker*
  D 1835/36, 1837, 1839, 1840
  1829 Const., p. 12
†Caner, John, *cabinet- and chairmaker*
  D 1820, 1823, 1825
Canter, Jacob, *cabinetmaker*
  D 1820, 1823, 1825
Caracourt, Henry, *turner*
  D 1840
Carlley, Nathan, *cabinetmaker*
  D 1829–31, 1833
Carlyle, John, *cabinetmaker*
  Wills, no. 19 (1828)
Carman, Charles, *cabinetmaker*
  D 1839–40
Carpenter, John, *cabinetmaker*
  D 1823
*Carr, John, *cabinetmaker*
  D 1840
  Public Ledger, May 14, 1839
  Misc. bk. 3, pp. 658–65
Carr, Thomas, *cabinetmaker*
  D 1829–31, 1833
*Carrey, Thomas, *cabinetmaker*
  D 1823
  1829 Const., p. 12
Carson, Thomas, *cabinetmaker*
  D 1820, 1823, 1828–31, 1833
Carter, Daniel, *chairmaker*
  D 1825
Carter, William M., *turner*
  D 1828–31
Carteret, Daniel, *chairmaker*
  D 1820, 1824, 1828–29
  Wills, no. 46 (1830)
Carteret, J. W., Jr., *cabinetmaker*
  D 1839
Carteret, Joseph W., *cabinetmaker*

D 1820, 1825, 1828–31, 1833, 1835/36
Carteret, Joshua, *cabinet- and chairmaker*
   D 1823
Cartner, Joseph, *cabinetmaker*
   D 1840
Cartwright, Joseph, *cabinetmaker*
   D 1840
Caruthers, Samuel, *chairmaker*
   D 1829–31, 1833, 1840
Carver, Isaac, *turner*
   D 1839–40
Cascady, George, *cabinetmaker*
   D 1825
Casledine, Richard, *chairmaker*
   D 1840
Caswell, W. R., *cabinetmaker*
   D 1831, 1833
Cavenaugh, Michael, *cabinetmaker*
   D 1835/36
Cavil, L. S., *cabinetmaker*
   D 1840
*Cays, Robert, *cabinetmaker*
   1829 Const., p. 12
Chanceaulme, Martin, *cabinetmaker*
   D 1823, 1825, 1828–31, 1833
Chapman, J., *cabinetmaker*
   D 1835/36
Chapman, John, *turner*
   D 1825
Chapman, John, *cabinetmaker*
   D 1825, 1828–31, 1833
Chapman, John, *cabinet warerooms* [*proprietor*]
   D 1837
Chapman, Lewis, *turner*
   D 1829–31, 1833
Chapman, Lucas, *turner*
   D 1820, 1823
Chapman, Luke, *turner*
   D 1833
Chapman, S. B., *turner*
   D 1839
Charnock, Thomas, *cabinetmaker*
   D 1839–40
Chattam, Abraham, *chairmaker*
   D 1837, 1839
Chatting, Abraham, *chairmaker*
   D 1835/36
Cheavens, Frederick, *cabinetmaker*
   D 1823, 1829–31, 1833
*Chesnut, Benjamin, *cabinetmaker*
   D 1829–31, 1833
   1829 Const., p. 11
*Chesnut, William, *cabinetmaker*

1829 Const., p. 11
*Chevers, George, *cabinetmaker*
   Misc. bk. 3, pp. 658–65
   1829 Const., p. 11
Chew, James, *chairmaker*
   D 1823, 1825
Chew, James, *chair painter*
   D 1835/36, 1837, 1839
*Chipman, Isaac, *cabinetmaker*
   1829 Const., p. 12
Christian, Anthony, *cabinetmaker*
   D 1835/36
Christine, John, *turner*
   D 1820–21, 1823
*Christopher, William H., *cabinetmaker*
   1829 Const., p. 12
Chur, John, *turner*
   D 1828–31, 1833
Ciirn, Loudn, *cabinetmaker*
   D 1839
Clair, Charles, *cabinetmaker*
   D 1837, 1839–40
Clair, William, *furniture store* [*proprietor*]
   D 1837, 1839
Clancey, Thomas F., *cabinetmaker*
   D 1839–40
Clapp, Henry, *turner*
   D 1839
Clark, Charles, *looking glass framemaker*
   D 1824
Clark, Hawkins, *cabinetmaker*
   D 1837, 1839–40
Clark, James, *cabinetmaker*
   D 1829–31, 1833
Clark, John, *chairmaker*
   D 1820, 1831, 1833
Clark, John, *turner*
   D 1820, 1823, 1825, 1828–31
Clark, Moses, *pianoforte maker*
   D 1833, 1837
*Clark, Moses H., *cabinetmaker*
   D 1837, 1839–40
   Misc. bk. 3, pp. 658–65
Clark, Thomas, *cabinetmaker*
   D 1840
Clark, William, *looking glass framemaker*
   D 1820, 1823, 1825, 1828–31
Clark, William, *chairmaker*
   D 1840
Clauson, Moses L., *cabinetmaker*
   Men's Register, May 21, 1836
Clavaux, M., & Liomin, E., *turners*
   D 1835/36

Clemens, Benjamin, *turner*
 D 1823, 1833, 1837, 1839
Clement, Henry A., *pianoforte maker*
 D 1839–40
Clemo, James, *cabinetmaker*
 D 1829–31, 1833
Clopp, Henry, *cabinetmaker*
 D 1823
Cloud, William, *chairmaker*
 D 1829–31, 1833
Cluley, Henrietta, *chair wareroom [proprietor]*
 D 1840
Clump, John, *cabinetmaker*
 D 1839
Coad, John, *cabinetmaker*
 D 1839
*Coane, Robert, T., *cabinetmaker*
 D 1830, 1831, 1833, 1835/36
 Misc. bk. 3, pp. 658–65
 U.S. Gaz., September 19, 1837
 1829 Const., p. 11
Cobb, W., *cabinetmaker*
 D 1825, 1828–31, 1833
Cocherell, James, *furniture store [proprietor]*
 D 1837, 1839
Cohen, Barnett, *cabinetmaker*
 D 1823, 1828–31, 1833, 1835/36, 1837,
  1839–40
 Public Ledger, January 14, 1839
Cohen, Robert, *cabinetmaker*
 D 1831, 1833, 1835/36
Cohill, George, *cabinetmaker*
 D 1833, 1840
Cole, George, *cabinetmaker*
 D 1839
Cole, Nelson, *turner*
 D 1839
Coleman & Briggs, *turners*
 D 1829–31, 1833
*Colgan, James, *cabinetmaker*
 Misc. bk. 3, pp. 658–65
Colson, Samuel, *turner*
 D 1840
Colvin, D., & Corbin, H. W., *turners*
 Pennsylvanian, April 20, 1833
Combes, Stephen, & Co., *cabinetmakers*
 D 1829
Combes, Thomas, *cabinetmaker*
 D 1820, 1823, 1828–31
Comfort, Cyrus, *framemaker*
 D 1839
Comley, Martin, *turner*
 D 1839

Compier, Lavier, *cabinetmaker*
 D 1820
Condie, J., *pianoforte maker*
 D 1840
Coner, John, *cabinetmaker*
 D 1823
Conger, John, *chairmaker*
 D 1829–31, 1833
Conie & Hubic, *organ builders*
 D 1837
Connelly, Davis, *cabinetmaker*
 D 1824
*Connelly, Dennis, *cabinetmaker*
 D 1828–31, 1833, 1839
 1829 Const., p. 11
Connelly, Henry, *cabinetmaker*
 D 1820, 1823
 Wills, no. 36 (1827)
*Connelly, John, *cabinetmaker*
 D 1828–31, 1833, 1835/36
 1829 Const., p. 12
Connor, George, *cabinetmaker*
 D 1837
Connor, M., *looking glass framemaker*
 D 1825, 1828–30, 1833, 1839
Conover, Michael F., *ornamental, fancy and*
  windsor chair and lounge maker
 Public Ledger, January 24, 1840
Conover, William, *cabinetmaker*
 D 1839–40
*Conwell, John, *cabinetmaker*
 1829 Const., p. 11
Cook, Edward, *cabinetmaker*
 D 1840
Cook, Edward W., *turner*
 D 1820, 1823, 1825
Cook, Elisha, *pianoforte maker*
 D 1835/36
Cook, Elisha, W., *turner*
 D 1824, 1828–31, 1833, 1835/36, 1837, 1839
 Children's Register, July 3, 1825
 U.S. Gaz., July 4, 1832
Cook, Henry D., *cabinetmaker*
 D 1835/36, 1837
Cook, Philip, *cabinetmaker*
 D 1823
†Cook, Thomas, *cabinetmaker*
 D 1824–25, 1828–31, 1833, 1835/36, 1837
 Unger Coll., May 13, 1834
†Cook & Parkins, *cabinetmakers*
 D 1820, 1823, 1825, 1828–31, 1833
 Unger Coll., January 1, 1828
Cooper, Alpheus, *cabinetmaker*

D 1833
Cooper, Hugh D., *turner*
    D 1831, 1833, 1835/36
Cooper, Samuel M., *cabinetmaker*
    D 1833
Cope, Thomas, *cabinetmaker*
    D 1840
Corbin, Horace W., *turner*
    D 1835/36, 1840
Corbin & Williams, *turners*
    D 1837
Corbitt, Christopher, *cabinetmaker*
    D 1825, 1828–29
Corndius, William, *chairmaker*
    D 1824
Cortham, –, *turner*
    D 1829–31, 1833
Cortz, William, *cabinetmaker*
    D 1829–31, 1833
Cost, George, *turner*
    D 1820, 1823
Costello, Cornelius, *cabinetmaker*
    D 1840
Costen, Levi, *cabinetmaker*
    D 1825, 1828
Coston, Benton, *cabinetmaker*
    D 1823, 1825, 1828–31, 1833
*Cotter, William R., *cabinetmaker*
    Misc. bk. 3, pp. 658–65
Cottman, William B., *turner*
    D 1823
Coulston, Israel, *cabinetmaker*
    D 1820, 1823
Coulston, Samuel, *turner*
    D 1837
Countryman, C., *ornamental painter*
    D 1823
*Coursalt, L., *cabinetmaker*
    D 1839
    Misc. bk. 3, pp. 658–65
Cowen, Jacob, *windsor chairmaker*
    D 1820
Cowley, John, *cabinetmaker*
    D 1833
Cox, Anthony, *chair painter*
    D 1825, 1828–30, 1833
Cragg, J., *cabinetmaker*
    D 1828–31, 1833
Cragg, William, *cabinetmaker*
    D 1820, 1829–31, 1833, 1839
†Craig, William, *cabinetmaker*
    D 1825
*Crane, David, *cabinetmaker*

1829 Const., p. 11
Crawford, W., *cabinetmaker*
    D 1823
Creamer, Francis, *turner*
    D 1837, 1839
Cross, Robert, *cabinetmaker*
    D 1840
Crouding, Charles, *ornamental painter*
    D 1822, 1825
Crout, Anthony, *cabinetmaker*
    D 1837
Crout, J., & Crout, A., *cabinetmakers*
    D 1839–40
    Unger Coll., January 6, 1836
    Pa. Inquirer, April 26, 1838
Crout, J., & Crout, C., *cabinetmakers*
    D 1837
Crout, Joseph, *cabinetmaker*
    D 1835/36, 1837, 1839–40
Crowther, George, *turner*
    D 1829–31, 1833
Crowther(s), John, *turner*
    D 1829–31, 1833, 1835/36, 1837
Cruthers, Samuel, *cabinetmaker*
    D 1840
Culley, Elias, *turner*
    D 1831, 1833
Cumming, Charles, *glue and curled-hair
        manufacturer*
    D 1830–31, 1833, 1840
*Cummings, Samuel, *cabinetmaker*
    D 1835/36
    1829 Const., p. 12
†Currin [Curvin], Thomas, *cabinetmaker*
    D 1825, 1828–29
Curry, Enoch, *turner*
    D 1823, 1837
Cursault, Leopold, *cabinetmaker*
    D 1837
*Cuskaden, George, *cabinetmaker*
    D 1829–31, 1835/36, 1837, 1840
    Misc. bk. 3, pp. 658–65
    1829 Const., p. 11

Dach, Stephen, *turner*
    D 1829–31, 1833
Daily, Nicholas, *cabinetmaker*
    D 1820, 1823
*Dalhoff, Nicholas C., *cabinetmaker*
    1829 Const., p. 11
Daniel, John, *turner*
    D 1825
Davie, John, *cabinetmaker*

D 1820

Davies, A. H., *cabinetmaker*
D 1840

Davis, Abram, *cabinetmaker*
D 1829–31, 1833

Davis, Alfred H., *cabinetmaker*
D 1835/36

Davis, Charles S., *cabinetmaker*
D 1839

Davis, David, *cabinetmaker*
D 1837

Davis, David, *cabinetmaker*
D 1837

Davis, Jeremiah S., *chairmaker*
D 1835/36, 1837, 1839–40

Davis, John, *cabinetmaker*
D 1820

Davis, John, *pianoforte maker*
D 1839

Davis, Samuel, *chairmaker*
Men's Register, October 30, 1833

†Davis, Thomas, *cabinetmaker*
D 1820, 1823, 1825, 1829–31, 1833, 1835/36, 1837, 1839–40

Davis, Thomas, *cabinetmaker*
D 1839–40

Davis, Thomas H. J., *cabinetmaker*
D 1839

Davis, William, *framemaker*
D 1837, 1839

Davis, William, *turner*
D 1839–40

Davy, John, *cabinetmaker*
D 1835/36
Men's Register, June 8, 1833; December 6, 1833; March 18, 1834

Dawson, P., *cabinetmaker*
D 1829–31, 1833

Day, Augustus, *carver and gilder, looking glass maker, painter*
1820–23, 1833

Dayton, Charles, *chairmaker*
D 1840

Deacon, James, *cabinetmaker*
D 1835/36, 1839–40

Deak, John, *cabinetmaker*
D 1837

Deal, Michael, *cabinetmaker*
D 1837, 1839

Dean, Bradley, *turner*
D 1824

Deates, William, *pianoforte maker*
D 1835/36

Deaves, James, *ornamental painter*
D 1825, 1829–31, 1833

Deaves & Mitchell, *chairmakers*
D 1831, 1833

Deaves, William, *chairmaker*
D 1840

DeBeust, Charles, *chairmaker*
D 1840

Debree, William, *cabinetmaker*
D 1824–25

DeForrest, George, *chairmaker*
D 1825, 1828–31, 1833

Deighton, Thomas, *pianoforte maker*
D 1837, 1839

Deitz, George, *turner*
D 1840

*Deitz, William, *cabinetmaker*
1829 Const., p. 12

Delavau, William, *ornamental painter, fancy chairmaker*
D 1820, 1823, 1828–31, 1833
Wills, no. 89 (1832)

Delavau & Jones, *japanned furniture wareroom [proprietors]*
D 1820

Denning, John, *cabinetmaker*
D 1835/36

Dennis, John W., *cabinetmaker*
D 1820

*Dennis, Robert, *cabinetmaker*
D 1824, 1829–31, 1833, 1835/36, 1837
1829 Const., p. 11

Denny, James, *chair painter*
D 1840

Deperven, Henry, *cabinetmaker*
D 1839–40

Derkheim, David, *cabinetmaker*
D 1821

Devamy, George W., *chairmaker*
D 1835/36

Devine, George, *chairmaker*
D 1837

Devine, George, *cabinetmaker*
D 1839–40

Deviney, George, *chairmaker*
D 1839–40

Dews, Thomas, *cabinetmaker*
D 1820

Dick, Abel, *turner*
D 1840

*Dick, James, *cabinetmaker*
D 1829–31, 1833, 1835/36, 1837, 1839–40
1829 Const., p. 12

Dietz, William, *cabinetmaker*
  D 1825
Dilge, George, *cabinetmaker*
  D 1840
Dillworth, J., *turner*
  D 1828–31, 1833, 1835/36, 1837, 1839–40
*Disbrow, Benjamin, *cabinetmaker*
  D 1829–31, 1833
  1829 Const., p. 12
*Ditmars, J. V. H., *cabinetmaker*
  D 1839–40
  1829 Const., p. 11
Ditmars, John, *cabinetmaker*
  D 1829–31, 1835/36
Ditmars, John, *cabinetmaker*
  D 1833
Ditmars & Beoraft, *cabinetmakers*
  D 1840
Ditz, William, *framemaker*
  D 1839
Doak, John, *cabinetmaker*
  D 1839
Doake, –, *cabinetmaker*
  D 1825
Dobelbower [Doublebower], John H., *chair
    painter*
  D 1839–40
Dockman, David, *cabinetmaker*
  D 1828–31
Dodd, Stephen, *cabinetmaker*
  D 1840
Doig, Thomas, *chairmaker*
  D 1835/36
*Domniguim [Dominique], Charles, *cabinetmaker*
  D 1829–31, 1833
  Misc. bk. 3, pp. 658–65
  1829 Const., p. 11
Don(n)avan, James, *framemaker*
  Men's Register, September 28, 1830;
    December 13, 1831
Donnelly, James, Jr., *cabinetmaker*
  D 1839
Dorey, Thomas, *cabinetmaker*
  D 1823
Dorey, Thomas, *cabinetmaker*
  D 1823
Dorey, Thomas, *cabinetmaker*
  D 1824–25
Dougherty, John, *turner*
  D 1837
Douglass, R., *ornamental painter*
  D 1835/36, 1837
Downing, Hugh, *cabinet- and chairmaker*

D 1823
Downing & Hook, *cabinetmakers*
  D 1825
Doyer, George, *cabinetmaker*
  D 1840
Dreer, Frederick, *cabinetmaker*
  D 1820–23, 1825, 1828–31, 1833, 1835/36
  Unger Coll., April 2, 1826
Dubois, Cornelius, *cabinetmaker*
  D 1823
Dubois, James, *cabinetmaker*
  D 1833
Duke, John, *chairmaker*
  D 1825, 1829–31, 1833
*Duke, Tristrim, *cabinetmaker*
  1829 Const., p. 11
Dumac, Frederick, *cabinetmaker*
  D 1839
Dumac, John, *cabinetmaker*
  D 1840
Dungan, David, *cabinetmaker*
  D 1829–31, 1833
Dunn, George, *turner*
  D 1823
Durburrow, Edward, *cabinetmaker*
  Men's Register, August 29, 1820
Dyer, Samuel, *cabinetmaker*
  Men's Register, April 9, 1836

Earheart, John P., *turner*
  D 1820–21
Earle, James, *carver and gilder*
  D 1820, 1823, 1828–29, 1831, 1840
Earle, John H., *cabinetmaker*
  D 1835/36
*Earley, John, *cabinetmaker*
  D 1824, 1830–31, 1833
  1829 Const., p. 11
Earley, John H., *pianoforte maker*
  D 1840
Eckard, Leopold, *cabinetmaker*
  D 1839
Eckel, William, *cabinetmaker*
  D 1837, 1839
Eckhardt, Frederick, *turner*
  D 1822
Edwards, Henry, *cabinetmaker*
  D 1839–40
  U.S. Gaz., June 6, 1837
†Eglee, Jacob, *cabinetmaker*
  D 1820–21, 1823
  Mayor's Court, December 23, 1820
  Unger Coll., January 8, 1821

Eldridge, Eli, *cabinetmaker*
  D 1822, 1825, 1828–31, 1833, 1835/36, 1837,
    1840
Elfrey, Jeremiah, *cabinetmaker*
  Men's Register, December 13, 1831; March
    16, April 17, 1832; March 4, 1835
Elias, Christian, *cabinetmaker*
  D 1837
Elk, Frederick, *turner*
  D 1833
Elkinton, Charles, *cabinetmaker*
  D 1837
Ellis, Enos, *cabinetmaker*
  D 1820, 1823
Ellis, John, *cabinetmaker*
  D 1825
Ellis, Joseph, *chairmaker*
  D 1837
Ellis, William, *cabinetmaker*
  D 1824
Ellwine, Emmanuel, *cabinetmaker*
  Men's Register, August 1, 1840
Elmes, Thomas, *cabinetmaker*
  D 1837
Elmore, Robert, *cabinetmaker*
  D 1839
Elvin, J., *cabinetmaker*
  Public Ledger, July 23, 1839
Elwell, Joseph M., *cabinetmaker*
  D 1820, 1825, 1828–31, 1833
Elwine, Michael, *turner*
  D 1830–31
Ely, Christian, *cabinetmaker*
  D 1839
*Emery, Charles, *cabinetmaker*
  D 1825, 1829–30, 1833
  1829 Const., p. 12
Emery, George, *cabinetmaker*
  D 1828–31
Emery, T. B., *chair- and cabinetmaker*
  D 1823–25
  U.S. Gaz., September 24, November 21, 1822
Engard, Caspar, *turner*
  D 1829–31, 1833, 1835/36
English, S., *cabinetmaker*
  D 1820
Enos, Thomas T., *cabinetmaker*
  D 1839
†Enston, Daniel, *chairmaker*
  D 1829–31, 1833
Eppsgood, Lewis, *cabinetmaker*
  D 1840
Esher, Charles, *pianoforte maker*

  D 1839–40
Esler, Benjamin, *turner*
  D 1824–25, 1833, 1835/36
*Esler, James, *cabinetmaker*
  1829 Const., p. 12
Essex, Christian, *turner*
  D 1835/36
Estell, Benjamin, *turner*
  D 1828–29, 1831
Estlow, Charles, *framemaker*
  D 1839
Etinger, John, *cabinetmaker*
  Men's Register, May 1834
Etris, David, *cabinetmaker*
  D 1820
Etriss, Samuel, *cabinetmaker*
  D 1825, 1828–31, 1833, 1835/36, 1837,
    1839–40
Etriss, Samuel, Jr., *cabinetmaker*
  D 1839–40
Evans, John, *cabinetmaker*
  D 1831, 1833
Evans, Joseph, *turner*
  D 1837, 1840
Ewell, M., *furniture store* [*proprietor*]
  D 1837
Ewing, Samuel, *cabinetmaker*
  D 1824
Ewins, John, *cabinetmaker*
  Convict Docket, October 2, 1829

Facker, John, *cabinetmaker*
  D 1829, 1831, 1833
Faron, Samuel, *cabinetmaker*
  D 1825
Faxis, John, *cabinetmaker*
  D 1823
Fayette, Lewis, *cabinetmaker*
  D 1833, 1837, 1839–40
  U.S. Gaz., December 10, 1838
Fees, Christopher, *cabinetmaker*
  D 1831, 1833, 1839
Feet, Christian, *turner*
  D 1839
*Fell, Penrose, *cabinetmaker*
  1829 Const., p. 12
Felmey, Frederick, *chairmaker*
  D 1839
Felten, Henry, *framemaker*
  D 1839–40
Felton, Jacob, *cabinetmaker*
  D 1835/36, 1837
Ferguson, James, *chairmaker*

D 1839
Ferguson, John, *cabinetmaker*
    D 1839
†*Ferguson, William, *cabinetmaker*
    D 1831, 1833, 1835/36
    1829 Const., p. 11
Ferman, Elijah, *chairmaker*
    D 1835/36
Ferre, Soloman, *cabinetmaker*
    D 1837, 1840
Fesler, Stephen, *framemaker*
    D 1837
*Fesmore [Fesmire], Christian, *cabinetmaker*
    D 1820
    1829 Const., p. 11
Fess, John L., *cabinetmaker*
    D 1825, 1828–31, 1833
Feurring, William, *pianoforte maker*
    D 1839–40
    Pennsylvanian, November 8, 1834
    U.S. Gaz., March 6, 1839
Field, Oliver W., *turner*
    D 1840
Fiet, Clemens, *looking glass framemaker*
    D 1830–31, 1833
Fink, John, *cabinetmaker*
    D 1837
Finn, Morris, *cabinetmaker*
    D 1823
Fisher, John, *cabinetmaker*
    D 1837, 1839–40
Fisher, John, & Fisher, Philip, *cabinetmakers*
    D 1829–31, 1833, 1835/36, 1837, 1839–40
Fisher, Philip, Jr., *cabinetmaker*
    D 1829–31, 1833, 1835/36, 1837, 1839–40
*Fiss, Samuel, *cabinetmaker*
    D 1820, 1822, 1825, 1829–31, 1833, 1837,
    1839
    Misc. bk. 3, pp. 658–65
Fite, Clemens, *picture framemaker*
    D 1825
Fitten, Isaac, *cabinetmaker*
    D 1824
*Fitten, John, *cabinetmaker*
    D 1825
    1829 Const., p. 12
Flager, Henry, *cabinetmaker*
    D 1825
Flake, Edwin R., *turner*
    D 1839
Fleetwood, David, *cabinetmaker*
    D 1833, 1835/36, 1837
    Mayor's Court, April 2, April 16, 1836

Fleming, Aaron, *cabinetmaker*
    D 1837, 1840
Fling, Bennet, *cabinetmaker*
    D 1824–25, 1833, 1835/36, 1837, 1839
†Fling, Bennet, & Fling, William B., *cabinetmakers*
    D 1820–21
†Fling, William B., *cabinetmaker*
    D 1823, 1825, 1828–31, 1833
    Fire Surveys, no. 316, March 20, 1832;
        no. 849, July 3, 1834
    Poulson's Advertiser, March 3, 1826
Flint, Achilles, *cabinetmaker*
    D 1820, 1825, 1828–31, 1833
Flint, Archelaus, *cabinetmaker*
    D 1823, 1833, 1835/36
Flint, Erastus, *cabinetmaker*
    D 1820, 1823, 1825, 1828–31, 1833, 1835/36,
    1837
Flood, William, *chairmaker*
    D 1837, 1839–40
Flowers, Thomas, *chairmaker*
    D 1839
Folwell, Joseph, *turner*
    D 1829–31, 1833
Fontanell, Rose, *cabinetmaker*
    D 1825, 1828–31, 1833
Fontmein, Frederick, *pianoforte maker*
    D 1835/36
Fopless, Adam, *chairmaker*
    D 1837, 1839
Fordyce, Abraham, *chairmaker*
    D 1820
Fouser, David, *cabinetmaker*
    D 1820
Fox, Frances, *cabinet wareroom [proprietor]*
    D 1825, 1828–31, 1833
Fox, John, *cabinetmaker*
    D 1820, 1823, 1824, 1828–31, 1833
Fox, Samuel, *cabinetmaker*
    D 1837, 1840
Fradonfol, Charles, *cabinetmaker*
    D 1840
Frankland, William, *pianoforte maker*
    D 1840
*Franklin, Walter, *cabinetmaker*
    D 1823, 1825, 1828–30
    1829 Const., p. 11
Frederick, J. G., *cabinetmaker*
    D 1828
Freed, A., *mahogany framemaker*
    D 1820
Freed, George, *mahogany framemaker*
    D 1820

Frick, Christian, *cabinetmaker*
    D 1839–40
Frick, William, *cabinetmaker*
    D 1839
Fricke, Frederick, *cabinetmaker*
    D 1823, 1825, 1828–31, 1833
Fricke, Henry, *cabinetmaker*
    D 1820
Fricker, John, *cabinetmaker*
    D 1820, 1823, 1825, 1828–31, 1833
    Wills, no. 179 (1836)
Frisby, Charles, *cabinetmaker*
    D 1837, 1839–40
Fritz, Christian, *turner*
    D 1835/36
Fritz, Jacob, *cabinetmaker*
    D 1820, 1825, 1828–31, 1833, 1835/36, 1837,
        1839–40
Fritz, John, *cabinetmaker*
    D 1823, 1831, 1833
Fritz, John, *chairmaker*
    D 1835/36
Fritz, John S., *cabinetmaker*
    D 1837, 1839–40
Fritz, William, *cabinetmaker*
    D 1839–40
Fry, George, *windsor and fancy chairmaker*
    D 1820
Fryer, William A., *pianoforte maker*
    D 1823, 1825
Fryer, William M., *pianoforte maker*
    D 1833, 1839–40
Fullerton, Ely, *turner*
    D 1840
Fullerton, Josiah [Isaiah], *turner*
    D 1835/36, 1837
Fulton, John, *turner*
    D 1829–31, 1833, 1835/36, 1837, 1839–40
    Mechanics' Free Press, June 5, 1830
    Sat. Eve. Post, July 31, 1830
Fulwiler, John, *cabinetmaker*
    D 1835/36
Funk, Charles F., *cabinetmaker*
    D 1839–40
Fysmier, Christian, *cabinetmaker*
    D 1825, 1828–31, 1833

Gambling, William, *cabinetmaker*
    D 1839
Gammit, John, *cabinetmaker*
    Men's Register, May 4, 1837
Gardiner, Peter, *chairmaker*
    D 1820

*Gard(i)ner, James H., *cabinetmaker*
    D 1839
    1829 Const., p. 11
Gardner, Richard, *furniture store* [*proprietor*]
    D 1837
*Garman, Charles, *cabinetmaker*
    D 1820
    1829 Const., p. 11
*Garret(t), Samuel, *cabinetmaker*
    Misc. bk. 3, pp. 658–65
    1829 Const., p. 12
Garrett, John, *turner*
    D 1823
Garrison, Jacob, *cabinetmaker*
    Men's Register, July 28, 1834; July 25, 1835;
        April 1, 1839
Gartland, Michael, *cabinetmaker*
    D 1833
Gar(e)y, Thomas, *cabinetmaker*
    Men's Register, January 13, 1832
Gates, Peter, *turner*
    D 1837
Gates, Washington, *cabinetmaker*
    D 1837
Gaw, Gilbert, *cabinetmaker*
    D 1820, 1823
    Wills, no. 54 (1824)
†Gaw, Robert, *fancy and windsor chairmaker*
    D 1820, 1823, 1825, 1828–30, 1833
    Indenture Bk., April 9, 1827
Gaw, Robert, Jr., *chairmaker*
    D 1828–31, 1833
Gee, Noah, *cabinetmaker*
    D 1835/36
    Indenture Papers, February 10, 1834
Gell, Noah, *cabinetmaker*
    D 1829–31, 1833
Genn, James, *turner*
    D 1829–31, 1833
Gerker, H., *curled-hair manufacturer*
    D 1839
Gerrin, Stephen, *cabinetmaker*
    D 1823, 1825, 1828–31, 1833
    Mayor's Court, March 29, 1834
Gideon, George, *chairmaker*
    D 1820, 1823, 1825, 1828–31, 1833
Giffin, Furman, *cabinetmaker*
    D 1825, 1828–31, 1833
Gifford, Bethuel, *cabinetmaker*
    D 1839
*Gilbert, Charles M., *cabinetmaker*
    D 1839
    1829 Const., p. 12

Gilbert, Theophilus, *chairmaker*
  D 1828–31, 1833
Gilbert, William, *cabinetmaker*
  Men's Register, July 30, 1828
*Gildea, H. A., *cabinetmaker*
  Misc. bk. 3, pp. 658–65
Gilder, John, *cabinetmaker*
  D 1839
Gilder, John, *cabinetmaker*
  D 1839
Gilkey, James E., *cabinetmaker*
  D 1824
Gilkey, John, *cabinetmaker*
  D 1823
Gilkey, Joseph, *cabinetmaker*
  D 1820
Gill, Elisha, *chairmaker*
  D 1837, 1839
Gill, Thomas, *cabinetmaker*
  D 1820
Gill, Thomas, *cabinetmaker*
  D 1820
*Gill, William, *cabinetmaker*
  1829 Const., p. 11
*Gilloire, Charles, *cabinetmaker*
  D 1830, 1831, 1833
  Men's Register, February 17, 1836
  1829 Const., p. 11
Gilmore, Thomas, *cabinetmaker*
  D 1837
*Gilpin, William, *cabinetmaker*
  Misc. bk. 3, pp. 658–65
*Gilson, Robert, *cabinetmaker*
  1829 Const., p. 12
Glace, Isaac, *cabinetmaker*
  D 1824
Glanden, James, *chairmaker*
  1835/36
Glass, Francis, *chairmaker*
  D 1837
Glenn, James, *turner*
  D 1835/36, 1837
*Glenn, William, *cabinetmaker*
  D 1828–31, 1833
  Misc. bk. 3, pp. 658–65
  1829 Const., p. 11
Good, John, *cabinetmaker*
  D 1837
  U.S. Gaz., September 13, October 4, 1837
Gorman, John, *cabinetmaker*
  D 1837
Gorman, Jonn, *cabinetmaker*
  D 1837

Gosnell, Brise, *looking glass framemaker*
  D 1837
Gossman, John, *cabinetmaker*
  D 1831, 1833
Gouilart, John, *cabinetmaker*
  D 1835/36, 1837
Goujon, Lewis, *turner*
  D 1828–31, 1833, 1835/36
Gould, Walter, *chairmaker*
  D 1820
Grace, George, *cabinetmaker*
  D 1839
Gragg, Thomas, *cabinetmaker*
  Men's Register, October 14, 1835
*Graham, Elisha P., *cabinetmaker*
  1829 Const., p. 12
†Graham, John, *cabinetmaker*
  D 1823, 1825, 1828–31, 1833, 1835/36, 1839
Graham, William, *cabinetmaker*
  D 1839
Graham, William, *cabinetmaker*
  D 1839
Gravenstine, George, *turner*
  D 1825, 1828–29, 1831, 1833
Gray, James M., *turner*
  D 1837
Gray, John, *turner*
  D 1829, 1831, 1833
Gray, William, *chairmaker*
  D 1835/36, 1837
Green, Francis, *cabinetmaker*
  D 1823
Green, Jacob, *windsor chairmaker*
  D 1823
Green, Job, *chairmaker*
  D 1820, 1824–25, 1828–31, 1833
Greenleaf, John, *cabinetmaker*
  D 1829–31, 1833
Greer, William, *turner*
  D 1825, 1835/36
Gregory, John, *cabinetmaker*
  D 1820, 1823, 1825, 1828–30, 1833, 1835/36
  Wills, no. 153 (1836)
Gregory, Nathaniel, *turner*
  D 1837
Griffith, William V., *cabinetmaker*
  D 1823, 1825, 1828–31, 1833, 1835/36
Griswell, Gilbert, *cabinetmaker*
  D 1820
Groff, Thomas, *cabinetmaker*
  D 1829–31, 1833
Grose, Thomas, *cabinetmaker*
  D 1839

*Grove, Daniel, *pianoforte maker*
    D 1830–31, 1833, 1835/36, 1837, 1839
    Fire Survey, no. 804, July 6, 1833
    1829 Const., p. 11
  Grove & Wohlien, *pianoforte makers*
    D 1835/36, 1837
    U.S. Gaz., June 21, 1834; November 27, 1837
  Groven, William, *chairmaker*
    D 1839
  Grubb, William, *chairmaker*
    D 1828–29, 1831, 1833
*Guilkey, Joseph, *cabinetmaker*
    D 1825, 1829–31, 1833
    1829 Const., p. 11
  Gwinn, William, *ornamental painter*
    D 1837, 1839
  Gwyn, William, *chairmaker*
    D 1828–31, 1833

  Haas, William, *cabinetmaker*
    D 1825
*Haines, John, *turner*
    D 1828–31
    1829 Const., p. 11
*Halberstabt, James, *cabinetmaker*
    Misc. bk. 3, pp. 658–65
    1829 Const., p. 12
  Hall, E. C., *chair ornamenter*
    D 1839–40
  Hall, James, *organ builder*
    D 1833
  Hallman, George, *cabinetmaker*
    D 1837
  Hallman & Brothers, *cabinetmakers*
    D 1833
†Halzel, Philip, *fancy chairmaker*
    D 1823, 1825, 1828–31, 1833, 1835/36, 1837,
      1839–40
    Fire Survey, no. 148, May 27, 1830
    Quarter Sessions, October 10, 1825
    Poulson's Advertiser, December 28, 1825
  Hamarsley, George, *turner*
    D 1839
  Hamilton, Isaac, *cabinetmaker*
    D 1835/36
  Hamilton, William, *cabinetmaker*
    D 1820
  Hamilton, William, *turner*
    D 1828–31, 1833
  Hamilton, William, *cabinetmaker*
    D 1835/36, 1837, 1839
  Hammar, Andrew, *turner*
    Mechanics' Free Press, February 28, 1829

  Hank, David C., *cabinetmaker*
    D 1840
  Hanley, William, *cabinetmaker*
    D 1837
  Hansell, James S., *turner*
    D 1837, 1840
  Hansell, Thomas, *turner*
    D 1820, 1823, 1828–29, 1831, 1833, 1835/36,
      1837, 1840
  Harding, James, *cabinetmaker*
    D 1829–31, 1833, 1835/36, 1837, 1839
  Hardman, Frederick, *cabinetmaker*
    D 1840
  Hargesheimer, William, *cabinetmaker*
    D 1837, 1839
  Harker, Joseph, *chairmaker*
    D 1828–31, 1833
  Harman, John, *chairmaker*
    D 1839–40
  Harmich, Julius, *cabinetmaker*
    D 1840
  Harmstead, James, *cabinetmaker*
    D 1828–29
  Harper, John, *cabinetmaker*
    D 1831, 1833
  Harris, David, *cabinetmaker*
    D 1839
  Harris, Gebhard, *cabinetmaker*
    D 1825, 1828–31, 1833, 1835/36, 1839
  Harris, William, *chairmaker*
    D 1823, 1825, 1828–29, 1831, 1833
  Harris & Van Aken, *cabinetmakers*
    D 1823
  Harrison, Obit, *cabinetmaker*
    D 1823
  Hart, John, *chairmaker*
    D 1829–31, 1833
  Hart, John, *pianoforte maker*
    D 1833
  Hart, Peter, *cabinetmaker*
    Men's Register, August 8, 1834
  Haug, Casper, *pianoforte maker*
    D 1830, 1833
  Hauser, Matthias, *turner*
    D 1840
  Havenstrite, Jacob, *cabinetmaker*
    D 1839
*Havenstrite, Samuel, *cabinetmaker*
    D 1820, 1829–31, 1833, 1835/36, 1839
    1829 Const., p. 12
  Haworth, Stephen, *chairmaker*
    D 1837, 1839–40
†Haydon, William, *fancy chair painter, fancy*

chairmaker
D 1820–23, 1825, 1830, 1833
Nat'l Gaz., April 17, 1823
Hayes, Robert, *cabinetmaker*
D 1823
Hayle, Robert B., *chairmaker*
D 1835/36
Hays, James, *cabinetmaker*
D 1820, 1825, 1828–31, 1833
Hays, John, *chairmaker*
D 1820, 1822, 1828–31, 1833
Hays, William, *cabinetmaker*
D 1822–23, 1825, 1828–31, 1833
Hayward, James, *chairmaker*
D 1839
Hayward, Richard, *chairmaker*
D 1835/36, 1837, 1839–40
Hayward, Robert B., *chairmaker*
D 1822, 1829–31, 1833, 1835/36, 1837, 1839
Hazard, John, *cabinetmaker*
D 1837, 1839
Hazelet, William, *cabinetmaker*
D 1837
Hazzard, Joseph, *cabinetmaker*
D 1839–40
Hedges, E., & Co., *cabinetmaker*
D 1840
Heideann, Edward, *cabinetmaker*
D 1840
Helffenstine, Jacob, *cabinetmaker*
D 1823
Helverson, Jonathan, *cabinetmaker*
D 1820, 1823, 1829–31, 1833
Helverson, Nicholas, *cabinetmaker*
D 1828–31, 1833, 1835/36, 1837
Henderson, William, *cabinetmaker*
D 1833
Henry, –, *cabinetmaker*
D 1825, 1828–31, 1833
*Henry, Abraham, *cabinetmaker*
D 1829, 1831, 1833
1829 Const., p. 11
Wills, no. 27 (1836)
Herman, Sebastian, *cabinetmaker*
D 1839
Hesson, John, *chairmaker*
D 1830–31, 1833
*Heyl, Peter, *cabinetmaker*
1829 Const., p. 12
High, Samuel, *cabinetmaker*
D 1839–40
Hiles, Peter, *pianoforte maker*
D 1828–31, 1833

Hill, David, *cabinetmaker*
D 1839
Hill, Henry, *cabinetmaker*
D 1829–31, 1833
Hill, Robert, *cabinetmaker*
D 1820, 1837
Hillen, Jacob, *chairmaker*
Men's Register, November 18, 1832
Hilt, Ernest, *chairmaker*
D 1840
Hines, Samuel, *turner*
D 1824
Hipple, M. H., *cabinetmaker*
D 1835/36
Hiscox, John S., *cabinetmaker*
D 1829–31, 1833, 1835
Hoare, Robert, *ornamental painter*
D 1825, 1830, 1835/36, 1837
Hodge, William, *chairmaker*
D 1840
Hodges, Benjamin O., *cabinetmaker and
upholster*
D 1820, 1822, 1828–31, 1833, 1835/36
Hodges, John, *cabinetmaker*
D 1835/36
Hoffman, Charles, *cabinetmaker*
D 1829–31, 1833
Hoffman, John, *cabinetmaker*
D 1839–40
Hoffman, Jonathan, *cabinetmaker*
D 1820
Hoguet, Francis, *cabinetmaker*
D 1840
Holloday, Thompson, *cabinetmaker*
Men's Register, May 17, 1828
Hollowbush, Joseph, *turner*
D 1830–31, 1833
Hollowell, John, *cabinetmaker*
D 1837
Hollven, George, *cabinetmaker*
D 1837
Hollwarth, John M., *cabinetmaker*
D 1840
Holmes, Thomas, *cabinetmaker*
D 1833, 1835/36, 1839
†*Holst, Charles, *cabinetmaker*
D 1829–31, 1833, 1839
1829 Const., p. 12
Holt, Jacob, *cabinetmaker*
D 1825, 1828–31, 1833
Holt, Jacob, *cabinetmaker*
D 1828
Homan, Abraham, *cabinetmaker*

D 1823, 1825, 1828–31, 1833
*Hooding, Charles, *cabinetmaker*
 1829 Const., p. 12
*Hook, Francis, *cabinet wareroom* [*proprietor*]
 D 1825, 1829–31, 1839–40
 1829 Const., p. 11
Hookey, Anthony, *cabinetmaker*
 D 1820, 1825, 1828–31, 1833, 1835/36, 1837,
  1840
Hooton, Andrew, *cabinetmaker*
 D 1820, 1822
Hopel [Hoppel], William, *framemaker*
 D 1835/36, 1839–40
*Hopkins, Thomas, *cabinetmaker*
 D 1831, 1833, 1839–40
 Misc. bk. 3, pp. 658–65
*Hopper, Daniel G., *cabinetmaker*
 D 1833, 1835/36
 1829 Const., p. 11
*Hosea, Thomas I., *cabinetmaker*
 1829 Const., p. 12
*Hottenhauser, L., *cabinetmaker*
 Misc. bk. 3, pp. 658–65
Houck, Gilbert, *cabinetmaker*
 D 1823
Houck, Joseph, *chairmaker*
 D 1839
*Hough, John T., *cabinetmaker*
 D 1835/36
 1829 Const., p. 12
Houptman, John, *turner*
 D 1829–31, 1833
House, Peter, *cabinetmaker*
 D 1820
Householder, Adam, *cabinetmaker, looking glass
  and picture framemaker*
 D 1823, 1825, 1828–31, 1833, 1835/36, 1837,
  1839
 Fire Survey, no. 1391, October 18, 1834
 Indenture Papers, June 27, 1831
Houston, Jeremiah, *chairmaker*
 Men's Register, March 17, 1829
Hovel, Richard, *cabinetmaker*
 D 1820
Howarth, G. N., *furniture store* [*proprietor*]
 D 1837
Howell, John C., *chairmaker*
 D 1837, 1839–40
Hoxhemer, William, *cabinetmaker*
 D 1840
Hubbert, Christian, *cabinetmaker*
 D 1820, 1823, 1825, 1828–31, 1833, 1835/36,
  1837

Hubic, John, *organ builder*
 D 1833
Huckel, Francis, *chairmaker*
 D 1820, 1823, 1825, 1829–31, 1833, 1837,
  1839–40
 Indenture Bk., July 9, 1821; January 23,
  1832
Huff, John, *cabinetmaker*
 D 1831, 1833
Hugh, John F., *cabinetmaker*
 D 1835/36
Hughes, George, *chairmaker*
 D 1825, 1828–31, 1833
Hughes, George, *pianoforte maker*
 D 1835/36, 1839–40
*Hughes, Thomas M., *cabinetmaker*
 1829 Const., p. 12
Hughes, William, *cabinetmaker, coffin maker*
 D 1820, 1825, 1828–29, 1833
Humphreville, Joshua, *cabinetmaker*
 D 1820
Hundredmark, Matthias, *cabinetmaker*
 D 1840
†Huneker, John, *chairmaker*
 D 1820, 1828, 1830–31, 1833, 1835/36, 1837,
  1839–40
Huneker, Joseph, *chairmaker*
 D 1823, 1829–31, 1833, 1835/36, 1837,
  1839–40
Hunt, Humphrey, *cabinetmaker*
 D 1820, 1825, 1828–31, 1833, 1835/36, 1837,
  1839–40
Hunt, Robert, *pianoforte maker*
 D 1840
Hurdman, Peter, *chairmaker*
 D 1820
Hurst, John, *framemaker*
 D 1839–40
Hutchinson, John, *cabinetmaker*
 D 1835/36
*Hutchinson, William, *cabinetmaker*
 D 1829–31, 1833, 1835/36
 1829 Const., p. 11
Hutchinson & Powell, *cabinet warehouse*
  [*proprietors*]
 D 1837
Hyde, Isaac, *chairmaker*
 D 1828–31, 1833

Ilig, Frederick, *turner*
 D 1835/36
Ingham, John, *cabinetmaker*
 D 1820

Jackson, David D., *cabinetmaker*
  D 1839–40
Jackson, John, *cabinetmaker*
  Men's Register, April 6, 1838
Jacobs, Joseph, *chairmaker*
  D 1829–31, 1833
Jacoby, Charles, *cabinetmaker*
  D 1839–40
†James, Charles W., *fancy chairmaker*
  D 1824–25, 1828–30
  Poulson's Advertiser, December 22, 1822; December 12, December 22, 1825
James, Israel E., *cabinetmaker*
  D 1820, 1835/36
James, John, Jr., *cabinetmaker*
  D 1820, 1822–23, 1825
†James, Otto, *cabinetmaker*
  D 1820, 1821, 1823, 1825, 1828–31, 1833
  U.S. Gaz., October 11, 1820; July 11, October 2, 1823; March 4, 1824; May 1, 1826; April 17, 1827; April 2, 1829
†Jamison, John, *cabinet- and chairmaker*
  D 1820, 1823, 1825, 1828–31, 1833, 1839–40
  Unger Coll., January 9, 1821; February 25, 1822; January 14, October 4, 1823; November 12, 1824; January 2, 1826; April 20, 1827; January 19, 1828; March 4, April 11, May 4, November 24, 1829; September 30, October 5, 1831; August 11, September 5, 1832
  Mayor's Court, January 16, 1832
  Indenture Papers, September 25, 1820; March 24, 1828; April 28, 1834
  Children's Register, October 29, 1826
  1820 Census, no. 560
Jarman, Charles, *cabinetmaker*
  D 1820, 1829–31
Jarman, Daniel, *chairmaker*
  D 1820
†Jarrett, Jacob, *cabinet warehouse [proprietor]*
  D 1829, 1839
  Mayor's Court, no. 5, January 16, 1830
*Jenkins, Benjamin, *cabinetmaker*
  D 1833, 1835/36
  1829 Const., p. 12
Jennings, John D., *turner*
  D 1839
Jewell, Daniel, *cabinetmaker*
  D 1829–31, 1833, 1839
Jile, George, *cabinetmaker*
  D 1840
Johnson, Edward, *turner*
  D 1835/36

*Johnson, Francis, *cabinetmaker*
  D 1828–31, 1833, 1840
  1829 Const., p. 12
Johnson, Francis S., *cabinetmaker*
  D 1831, 1833, 1835/36, 1840
Johnson, Henry, *turner*
  D 1825, 1828–31
Johnson, James, *cabinetmaker*
  D 1835/36, 1839
*Johnson, Jesse, *cabinetmaker*
  D 1839
  Pennsylvanian, November 1, 1834; July 6, 1840
  Misc. bk. 3, pp. 658–65
Johnson, John, *chairmaker*
  D 1833
Johnson, John D., *chairmaker*
  D 1839–40
†Johnson, John F., *cabinetmaker*
  D 1835/36, 1839
Johnson, John P., *cabinetmaker*
  D 1835/36
Johnson, John R., *cabinetmaker*
  D 1823
Johnson, Richard B., *turner*
  D 1820, 1822–23, 1825, 1828, 1830–31, 1840
Johnson, Robert C., *turner*
  D 1840
*Johnson, Thomas S., *cabinetmaker*
  D 1839–40
  Misc. bk. 3, pp. 658–65
Johnson, William, *cabinetmaker*
  D 1830–31, 1833
Johnson & Corsault, *cabinetmakers*
  D 1840
Johnston, James, *cabinetmaker*
  D 1835/36
Jones, Abraham, *turner*
  D 1820, 1823, 1825, 1828–31, 1833, 1835/36, 1839–40
Jones, Benjamin, *cabinetmaker*
  D 1820, 1823, 1839–40
  Men's Register, February 22, 1830
Jones, Ephraim, *chairmaker*
  D 1829–31, 1833, 1840
  U.S. Gaz., March 28, 1837
Jones, George D., *cabinetmaker*
  D 1820–23, 1825, 1828–31, 1839–40
Jones, George W., *ornamental painter*
  D 1825, 1833, 1835/36
Jones, George W., *cabinetmaker*
  D 1835/36
†*Jones, Isaac, *cabinetmaker*

D 1820, 1823, 1825, 1828–31, 1833, 1835/36,
1839–40
Girard Papers, reel 202, July 6, 1824
1829 Const., p. 12
Jones, J., *cabinetmaker*
D 1835/36
Jones, Jacob, *chairmaker*
D 1829–31, 1833
Jones, John K., Jr., *cabinetmaker*
D 1823
Jones, Joseph, *turner*
D 1828–29, 1831, 1833, 1839
Jones, Joseph, *cabinetmaker*
D 1833
Jones, Joseph, *turner*
D 1835/36
Jones, Joseph, *looking glass framemaker*
D 1839–40
Jones, Joshua B., *pianoforte maker*
D 1839–40
Jones, Samuel, *cabinetmaker*
D 1820, 1823, 1825, 1828–31, 1833
Jones, Samuel P., *cabinetmaker*
D 1828–31, 1833
Jones, Thomas J., *cabinetmaker*
D 1829, 1831, 1833
Jones, Thomas P., *pianoforte maker*
D 1830–31, 1833
†*Jones, William, *cabinetmaker*
D 1823, 1828–29, 1839–40
Misc. bk. 3, pp. 658–65
1829 Const., p. 12
Jordan, Conrad, *framemaker*
D 1835/36
Jordon, Levi, *cabinetmaker*
D 1839
Jouber, Frederick William, *chairmaker*
D 1824
*Julian, Edmond, *cabinetmaker*
D 1823
1829 Const., p. 11
Julien, Edward, *cabinetmaker*
D 1831, 1833, 1835/36, 1840
Juper, Michael, *cabinetmaker*
D 1835/36

Kane, Andrew, *cabinetmaker*
D 1831, 1833
Kane & Burge, *cabinetmakers*
D 1833
Kates, Samuel, *chairmaker*
D 1837, 1839–40
Katom, Peter, *chairmaker*

D 1837
Keare, Henry, *cabinetmaker*
D 1840
Keefer, Andrew, *pianoforte maker*
D 1840
Keel, Jacob, *cabinetmaker*
D 1828–29, 1831, 1833
Kehr, Samuel, *cabinetmaker*
D 1825, 1828–29
Kehrer, George, *cabinetmaker*
D 1839
Keim, George, *turner*
D 1829–31, 1833, 1837, 1839
Keim, John, *turner*
D 1820, 1823, 1825, 1829–31, 1833, 1835/36,
1837, 1839, 1840
Keim, Joseph, *turner*
D 1839–40
*Keim, Peter, *cabinetmaker*
D 1833
1829 Const., p. 12
Keim, William, *turner*
D 1820, 1823, 1825, 1829, 1831, 1833,
1835/36, 1837
Wills, no. 180 (1821)
Keith, Nathaniel, *cabinetmaker*
D 1839
Keller, Adam, Jr., *cabinetmaker*
D 1829–31, 1833, 1835/36
Keller, Conrad, *turner*
D 1839–40
Kelly, Alexander, *cabinetmaker*
D 1839–40
Kelly, Charles F., *turner*
D 1823
*Kemp, Elias K., *cabinetmaker*
D 1829–31, 1833, 1835/36, 1837
1829 Const., p. 11
Kemp, K., *cabinetmaker*
D 1837
Kemp, Thomas, *cabinetmaker*
Men's Register, January 21, 1831
Kennedy, James, *cabinetmaker*
D 1823
†Kennedy, William, *chairmaker*
D 1835/36
Kennedy & Riat, *cabinetmakers and upholsterers*
D 1840
Kenner, Ludwick, *cabinetmaker*
D 1823
Kenny, William, *cabinetmaker*
D 1840
Kerby, Nathan, *cabinetmaker*

D 1825
Kerk, Charles H., *turner*
    D 1830
*Kerr, Thomas, *cabinetmaker*
    D 1835/36, 1837, 1839, 1840
    1829 Const., p. 12
Kerr & Kitmars, *cabinetmakers*
    D 1835/36
    Public Ledger, March 25, 1836
    U.S. Gaz., October 11, 1834
Kesler, Charles, *cabinetmaker*
    D 1839
Keyser, John, *cabinetmaker*
    D 1837
Keyser, John, *chairmaker*
    D 1839–40
Keyser, Joseph, *fancy chairmaker*
    D 1820
Kiefer, A., *pianoforte maker*
    D 1839
Kiersted, Joseph, *cabinetmaker*
    D 1825
Kimble, Joseph, *cabinetmaker*
    D 1820, 1823
King, John, *chairmaker*
    D 1829–31, 1833
King, John, *chairmaker*
    D 1829–31, 1833
King, Joseph R., *cabinet-, chair-, and sofamaker*
    D 1825
King, Thomas, *cabinetmaker*
    D 1829–31, 1833, 1840
*Kingston, John, *cabinetmaker*
    D 1829–31, 1833, 1835/36, 1837, 1839–40
    1829 Const., p. 12
Kinnan, John C., *turner*
    D 1820, 1822, 1823, 1828–30
    U.S. Gaz., December 15, 1828
Kirchoff, Henry, *turner*
    D 1839
Kirk, Robert, *cabinetmaker*
    D 1820
Kirkpatrick, Ferguson, *cabinetmaker*
    D 1820, 1833
Kirkwood, Alexander, *pianoforte maker*
    D 1839
Kisser, John, *chairmaker*
    D 1829–31, 1833
Kite, Isaac S., *looking glass framemaker*
    D 1828–30
†Kite, James, *cabinetmaker*
    D 1828–31, 1833, 1835/36, 1837, 1839–40
    U.S. Gaz., December 10, December 31, 1831;

December 11, 1832; January 3, March
    30, 1833
Kitler, John L., *windsor chairmaker*
    D 1820
†Klemm, J. G., *pianoforte warehouse [proprietor]*
    D 1825, 1828–31, 1833, 1835/36, 1840
Kline, Frederick, *turner*
    D 1840
Klinesmith, Lewis, *cabinetmaker*
    D 1820
Kloss, William, *cabinetmaker*
    D 1840
Knight, Edward, *cabinetmaker*
    D 1833, 1835/36
Knight, John, *cabinetmaker*
    D 1828–31, 1833
Knight, Stephen, *cabinetmaker*
    D 1831, 1833, 1835/36, 1837, 1840
    Fire Survey, no. 315, February 11, 1832
Knipe, John R., *furniture store [proprietor]*
    D 1837
Koch, Edward, & Co., *cabinetmakers*
    D 1837, 1839–40
Kollock, David H., *cabinetmaker*
    D 1825, 1828–31, 1833, 1835/36, 1839–40
Kraffues, Jacob, *framemaker*
    D 1839
Kraft, George, *cabinetmaker*
    D 1820, 1823, 1825, 1828–31, 1833, 1835/36,
        1839–40
    Unger Coll., August 22, 1833
    Indenture Papers, December 2, 1822
    Wills, no. 475 (1863)
Kraft, George W., *cabinetmaker*
    D 1839
Kramer, Francis, *turner*
    D 1835/36, 1840
Krerner, Francis, *turner*
    D 1840
Krickbaum, J., *cabinetmaker*
    D 1839–40
Krips, Jacob, *chairmaker*
    D 1820, 1823, 1825, 1828–31, 1833
Kurtz, William, *cabinetmaker*
    D 1823, 1833
Kuser, Thomas F., *cabinetmaker*
    D 1833
Kutz, William, *framemaker*
    D 1839

Labbree, John H., *cabinetmaker*
    D 1837, 1839–40
Lackman, Ferdinand, *cabinetmaker*

D 1840

Lafayette, Lewis, *cabinetmaker*
    D 1835/36

Lafferty, William, *cabinetmaker*
    D 1837

Lafourn, John, *chairmaker*
    D 1824

Lake, David, *fancy chairmaker*
    D 1825
    Children's Register, November 6, 1826

Lake, Joseph E., *cabinetmaker*
    D 1825, 1828–31, 1833

Laland, John, *cabinetmaker*
    D 1820

Lalanne, Dominick, *cabinetmaker*
    D 1821, 1825, 1830, 1833, 1835/36

*Lame, Joseph, *cabinetmaker*
    D 1837, 1839–40
    1829 Const., p. 11

Landers, Joseph, *turner*
    D 1840

Lane, Joseph, *cabinetmaker*
    D 1829–31, 1833

*Lang, Urban, *cabinetmaker*
    D 1830–31
    1829 Const., p. 12

Lange, U., *cabinetmaker*
    D 1829–31, 1833

Lansinger, Nicholas, *framemaker*
    D 1835/36

Lapier, John, *chairmaker*
    D 1829–31, 1833

Large, David, *cabinetmaker*
    D 1837, 1839–40

Large, Stephen, *cabinetmaker*
    D 1820

Law, Robert, *cabinetmaker*
    D 1837, 1839–40

Lawrence, Joseph, *cabinetmaker*
    D 1829, 1831

*Lawrence, William, *cabinetmaker*
    D 1829–31, 1833, 1839–40
    1829 Const., p. 11

†Laycock, Isaac H., *chairmaker*
    D 1822, 1824–25, 1829–31, 1833
    Misc. bk. 1, March 30, 1827
    Mayor's Court, April 18, 1826
    Indenture Bk., October 2, 1826

†Laycock, J. H., *fancy chairmaker*
    D 1820–21, 1823
    Poulson's Advertiser, September 22, 1820
    U.S. Gaz., August 23, September 15, 1825

Lee, Caroline, *chairmaker*

D 1839–40
    Public Ledger, June 25, 1839

Lee, James, *cabinetmaker*
    D 1839

Lee, John, *chairmaker*
    D 1824–25, 1829–31, 1833, 1835/36, 1837

Lee, Nathan, *cabinetmaker*
    D 1829–31, 1833

†Lee, William, *chairmaker*
    D 1820, 1823

Lee, William, *cabinetmaker*
    D 1822–23, 1825, 1828–31, 1833, 1835/36,
        1837, 1840
    Men's Register, December 19, 1829; April
        30, 1833

Lee, William, *furniture polisher*
    D 1837

Leeds, Gordon, *cabinetmaker, mahogany dealer*
    D 1830–31, 1833, 1835/36, 1839–40

*Leeds, Thomas, *cabinetmaker*
    Misc. bk. 3, pp. 658–65

Lees, John, *chairmaker*
    D 1823

Legrange, Paul, *cabinetmaker*
    Men's Register, May 22, 1833

Lehman, Charles, *cabinetmaker*
    D 1820

Lehr, William, *cabinetmaker*
    D 1829

Leiderer, Charles, *cabinetmaker*
    D 1840

Leidy, Emanuel, *chairmaker*
    D 1829–31, 1833

*Leland, John, *cabinetmaker*
    D 1825, 1828–31, 1833
    1829 Const., p. 11

Lemonier, Joseph, *cabinetmaker*
    D 1828–31, 1833

Lenhart, John H., *cabinetmaker*
    D 1840

Lentner, George C., *fancy chairmaker*
    D 1820

†Lentner & Patterson, *fancy chairmakers*
    D 1822

†Lentz, John, *cabinetmaker*
    D 1820, 1825, 1829–31, 1833, 1835/36, 1837

Le Roye, A., *cabinetmaker*
    D 1828–31, 1833
    Men's Register, September 2, 1839

Lesley, Peter, *cabinetmaker*
    D 1820, 1823, 1825, 1828–31, 1833, 1835/36,
        1837

Letchworth, John, *windsor chairmaker*

Vill. Record, April 16, 1823; February 25,
    1824
Levan, Jacob, *cabinetmaker*
    D 1839–40
Levering, Nathan, *cabinetmaker*
    D 1839–40
Levy, James, *cabinetmaker*
    Men's Register, January 12, 1831
Lewan, William, *framemaker*
    D 1839–40
Lewis, Adam, *cabinetmaker*
    D 1837, 1839
Lewis, David, *cabinetmaker*
    D 1839
Lewis, George W., *cabinetmaker*
    D 1839
Lewis, Henry, *cabinetmaker*
    D 1829–31, 1833, 1840
Lewis, John, *cabinetmaker*
    D 1840
Lewis, Joseph, *cabinetmaker*
    D 1835/36
*Lewis, Reynear, *cabinetmaker*
    1829 Const., p. 11
Lewis, Samuel, *cabinetmaker*
    D 1837
Lewis, Samuel M., *turner*
    D 1830–31, 1833
Linbarger, W., *chairmaker*
    D 1839–40
Lincoln, Abel, *cabinetmaker*
    D 1829–31, 1833
Lindall, Daniel, *chairmaker*
    D 1825, 1828–31, 1833
Lindsay, Robert, *cabinetmaker*
    D 1820
Linvill, Aaron, *turner*
    D 1837
Linvill, Arthur, *turner*
    D 1825, 1829–31, 1833
Lippincott, George, *turner*
    D 1835/36, 1837, 1839
Lippincott, Samuel E., *cabinetmaker*
    D 1829–31, 1833
Lippincott, Tyler, *turner*
    D 1837
Lithgow, David, *cabinetmaker*
    D 1828–31, 1833
Littleton, Thomas, *cabinetmaker*
    D 1828–31, 1833
Lockwood, George, *cabinetmaker*
    D 1835/36
Lockwood, Richard, *cabinetmaker*

D 1820
*Lodge, S. G., *cabinetmaker*
    D 1839, 1840
    Public Ledger, June 10, 1839
    1829 Const., p. 12
Lodge, Samuel B., *cabinet warehouse [proprietor]*
    D 1833, 1835/36, 1837
Lodor, Benjamin, *turner*
    D 1820, 1823–25, 1828–31, 1833, 1835/36,
        1839–40
Loffan, Jonathan, *cabinetmaker*
    Men's Register, May 9, 1834
Logue, John J., *fancy chairmaker*
    D 1828, 1830, 1833
Long, Abraham, *cabinetmaker*
    D 1837
Long, James, *turner*
    D 1835/36
Long, Mathias, *cabinetmaker*
    D 1833
Longmire, Emanuel, *cabinetmaker*
    D 1839–40
Longstreth, John, *curled-hair manufacturer*
    D 1840
Lorrilliere, Julius, *cabinetmaker*
    D 1840
Loud, John, *pianoforte maker*
    D 1820, 1825, 1828–31, 1833, 1835/36, 1839
    U.S. Gaz., September 24, 1834
Loud, Joseph, *pianoforte maker*
    D 1828–31, 1833, 1835/36, 1837, 1839
Loud, Philologus, *pianoforte maker*
    D 1825, 1828–31, 1833, 1835/36, 1837, 1839
Loud, Thomas, *pianoforte maker*
    D 1820, 1825, 1828–31, 1833, 1835/36, 1837,
        1839
Loud, Thomas C., *pianoforte maker*
    D 1835/36, 1837, 1840
    Pennsylvanian, September 26, 1838
†Loud & Brothers, *pianoforte makers*
    D 1825, 1828–31, 1833, 1835/36, 1837, 1839
    Fire Surveys, nos. 245–47, January 26, 1831
    1820 Census, no. 553
    U.S. Gaz., February 24, 1825; November 16,
        1826; October 2, 1829; October 4, 1833;
        June 26, September 24, 1834
†Loud, Thomas, & Loud, John, *pianoforte makers*
    U.S. Gaz., September 25, 1821
Loudenslager, Christian F., *cabinetmaker*
    D 1839
Loughead, Robert, *turner*
    D 1831, 1833, 1835/36
Loughead, W. H., *turner*

D 1825, 1829, 1831, 1833

Loughlin, David, *turner*
  D 1839–40

Lovenberg, Lewis, *cabinetmaker*
  D 1839–40

Lowber, Bowers, *cabinetmaker*
  D 1823

Lower, Abraham, *cabinetmaker*
  D 1820, 1823–24, 1828–31, 1833, 1835/36,
    1839–40

*Lowry [Lowary], John, *cabinetmaker*
  D 1820, 1829–31, 1833, 1837
  1829 Const., p. 11

*Lukens, Chilion, *cabinetmaker*
  D 1829, 1831, 1833, 1835/36, 1837, 1839–40
  Misc. bk. 3, pp. 658–65
  1829 Const., p. 11

Lukens, Edward, *cabinetmaker*
  D 1824

*Lukens, Lewis A., *cabinetmaker*
  1829 Const., p. 12

*Lukens, William, *cabinetmaker*
  Misc. bk. 3, pp. 658–65
  1829 Const., p. 12

Lumick, Joseph, *cabinetmaker*
  D 1835/36

Lutes, J., *chairmaker*
  D 1828–31

Lutz, Henry, *cabinetmaker*
  D 1835/36, 1837

Lutz, John G., *chairmaker*
  D 1830–31

Lye & Hoare, *ornamental painters*
  D 1825

*Lynch, Urban, *cabinetmaker*
  D 1835/36
  1829 Const., p. 11

†Lyndall, David, *chairmaker*
  D 1820, 1823–25, 1828–31, 1833, 1835/36,
    1837, 1839

Lyndall, James, *chairmaker*
  D 1839–40

Lyndall, Joseph W., *cabinetmaker*
  D 1820, 1822–23
  Wills, no. 80 (1824)

Lyndall, Robert, *cabinetmaker*
  D 1825, 1829–31, 1833, 1835/36, 1837, 1839

Lyndall, Samuel, *cabinetmaker*
  D 1820

Lyndall & Dietz, *cabinetmakers*
  D 1825

Lyndall, Joseph W., & Lyndall, Samuel,
    cabinetmakers

D 1820

McAdan, Thomas F., *windsor chairmaker*
  D 1820

McAfee, Robert, *turner*
  D 1825, 1828–31, 1833, 1835/36

McCarter, William, *turner*
  D 1820, 1825, 1829–31, 1833

*McCartney, Samuel, *cabinetmaker*
  1829 Const., p. 12

McCarty, John, *chairmaker*
  D 1833

McCauley, Rebecca, *furniture store [proprietor]*
  D 1840

McClary, John, *chairmaker*
  D 1840

McClaskey, William, *cabinetmaker*
  D 1831, 1833

McClean, Archibald, *cabinetmaker*
  D 1825, 1828–31

McClean, Archibald, *cabinetmaker*
  D 1828–31, 1833

McClintock, Robert H., *cabinetmaker*
  D 1833

McCluskey, William, *cabinetmaker*
  D 1829–31, 1833, 1835/36, 1840

McConnell, John, *turner*
  D 1835/36

*McCormick, Thomas B., *cabinetmaker*
  D 1839–40
  Misc. bk. 3, pp. 658–65

*McCutcheon, John, *cabinetmaker*
  Misc. bk. 3, pp. 658–65

McDaniels, Joseph, *framemaker*
  D 1837

McDermond, George, *cabinetmaker*
  D 1840

McDermond, Isaac, *cabinetmaker*
  D 1822, 1825

McDevitt, Bernard, *chairmaker*
  D 1829–31, 1833

McDevitt, Burnet, *chairmaker*
  D 1839–40

*McDonald, David, *cabinetmaker*
  1829 Const., p. 12

McDonald, J., *furniture store [proprietor]*
  D 1837

McDonald, John, *cabinetmaker*
  D 1835/36

McDonald, Patrick, *cabinetmaker*
  D 1837

McDonald, Samuel, *turner*
  D 1828–31, 1833

†McDonough, Abraham, *ornamental chair painter and gilder, chairmaker*
    D 1830–31, 1833, 1835/36, 1837, 1839–40
    Indenture Papers, April 4, 1831; May 13, 1833
    Pennsylvanian, January 5, 1833
    Public Ledger, March 25, 1836; January 30, December 12, 1837
    U.S. Gaz., December 6, 1832; December 28, 1835; September 28, 1839
    Wills, no. 341 (1852)
McEffee, Robert, *turner*
    D 1829–31, 1833
McElwee, Matthew, *cabinetmaker*
    D 1825
*McEwen, James, *cabinetmaker*
    D 1824–25, 1828–31, 1833
    1829 Const., p. 11
McFadden, William, *turner*
    D 1839
McGee, George, *turner*
    D 1835/36
*McGill, William, *cabinetmaker*
    1829 Const., p. 12
McGinnis, John, *turner*
    D 1837
McGlen, Francis, *cabinetmaker*
    D 1839
McGonigal, Thomas, *cabinetmaker*
    D 1840
*McGonigle, John, *cabinetmaker*
    D 1835/36
    1829 Const., p. 12
McGowen, William, *cabinet- and chairmaker*
    D 1837
McGrays, John, *turner*
    D 1837
*McGuier, Thomas, *cabinetmaker*
    Misc. bk. 3, pp. 658–65
Machan, Thomas, *chairmaker*
    D 1820
McHeron, Edward, *chairmaker*
    D 1831, 1833
*McIlvaine, A., *cabinetmaker*
    Misc. bk. 3, pp. 658–65
McIntire, Samuel, *cabinetmaker*
    D 1823
Mackey, Jacob, *cabinetmaker*
    D 1839
McKinley, Samuel, *chairmaker*
    D 1835/36, 1837
McKintz, Cornelius, *framemaker*
    D 1839

McKnight, William, *cabinetmaker*
    Men's Register, June 14, 1838
McMackin, Samuel, *chairmaker*
    D 1820–23, 1825, 1828–31
McManus, J., *cabinetmaker*
    D 1837
McManus, John, *cabinetmaker*
    D 1840
    Public Ledger, July 12, 1838
McMay, John, *cabinetmaker*
    D 1837
McMurray, Samuel, *cabinetmaker*
    D 1831, 1833
Magee, George, *turner*
    D 1839
*Maguire, John, *cabinetmaker*
    Misc. bk. 3, pp. 658–65
Manderfield, John, *cabinetmaker*
    D 1824–25, 1828–31, 1833
Manley, R., *cabinetmaker*
    D 1835/36, 1837, 1839
    Public Ledger, March 25, 1836
    U.S. Gaz., January 11, 1836
Manning, Charles, *cabinetmaker*
    D 1837, 1839
Mansure, Robert, *cabinetmaker*
    D 1829–31, 1833, 1835/36
*Mare, Hypolite, *cabinetmaker*
    1829 Const., p. 11
Marks, John, *chairmaker*
    D 1837
Marks, Tobias, *chairmaker*
    D 1823
Marot, Samuel, *cabinetmaker*
    D 1821, 1828–31, 1833
Marott, Davenport, *chairmaker, turner*
    D 1825, 1828–29, 1831
Marple, Jacob, *cabinetmaker*
    D 1837, 1839
Marshall, Edward, *cabinetmaker*
    D 1839
Marshall, James, *cabinetmaker*
    D 1823
Marshall, James, *framemaker*
    D 1830, 1833, 1835/36, 1837
†Marshall, Thomas, *cabinetmaker*
    D 1828–31, 1833
Martel, George, *cabinetmaker*
    D 1831, 1833
Martin, Jacob, *chairmaker*
    D 1837
†Martin, John, *cabinetmaker*
    D 1835/36

Martin, Joseph, *cabinetmaker*
    D 1835/36
Martin, Lewis, *cabinetmaker*
    D 1823
Martin, Peter, *chairmaker*
    D 1830–31, 1833, 1839
    Wills, no. 12 (1867)
Martin, William, *cabinetmaker*
    D 1820, 1823, 1825, 1828–31, 1833
Martin & Parham, *cabinetmakers*
    D 1820, 1822, 1825, 1829–31, 1833
Marson, Francis, *cabinetmaker*
    D 1835/36
Mason, George, *rush bottomer*
    D 1840
Mason, Thomas, *cabinetmaker*
    D 1837
Mason, William, *cabinetmaker*
    D 1820–21, 1823, 1828–31, 1833, 1835/36,
        1837
Mason, William, *cabinetmaker*
    D 1829–31, 1833, 1835/36
*Matlack, William, *cabinetmaker*
    D 1831, 1833, 1837, 1839
    1829 Const., p. 12
Matthews, Henry W., *turner*
    D 1839
Matthews, John, *pianoforte maker*
    D 1831, 1833, 1835/36, 1837, 1839
Matthews, Thomas, *cabinetmaker*
    D 1825
May, John, *cabinetmaker*
    D 1829–31, 1833, 1835/36, 1839
May, John, *pianoforte maker*
    D 1839
Mayer, Andrew, *ornamental painter*
    D 1837
Mayer, Charles, *cabinetmaker*
    D 1837
Maynard, Henry, *turner*
    D 1839
Mears, John, *chairmaker*
    D 1824
Mecke, George, *cabinetmaker*
    D 1835/36, 1837, 1839
    Fire Surveys, no. 1630, July 7, 1836
    Public Ledger, December 4, 1840
Mecke, Henry, *cabinetmaker*
    D 1835/36, 1837, 1839
Mecke, H., & Mecke, G., *cabinetmakers*
    D 1829, 1831, 1833
Mecke, John, *cabinetmaker and upholsterer*
    D 1820–21, 1823, 1828

Wills, no. 33 (1829)
Mellon, Michael, *cabinetmaker*
    D 1825
Mench, George C., *cabinetmaker*
    D 1837, 1839
Mench, John O., *cabinetmaker*
    D 1839
    Public Ledger, May 10, 1839
Mentzer, Stephen, *cabinetmaker*
    D 1835/36
Merkle, Jacob, *chairmaker*
    Men's Register, December 26, 1829; January
        1, 1835; June 8, 1840
*Merrihew, Kelley E., *cabinetmaker*
    D 1839
    Misc. bk. 3, pp. 658–65
    1829 Const., p. 12
Merrihew & Thompson, *cabinetmakers and
    upholsterers*
    U.S. Gaz., March 2, 1838; January 12, 1839
Mershon, Daniel, *fancy chair ornamenter*
    D 1831, 1833, 1835/36, 1837
Mershon & Meyers, *fancy chair ornamenters*
    D 1831, 1833, 1835/36
*Metcalf, Thomas, *cabinetmaker*
    D 1823, 1825
    1829 Const., p. 11
Metler, David, *cabinetmaker*
    D 1837
Meyer, Conrad, *pianoforte maker*
    D 1830–31, 1833, 1835/36, 1837, 1839
Meyer, Ernst, *cabinetmaker*
    Men's Register, October 29, 1834
Meyers, Charles, *cabinetmaker*
    D 1835/36
Meyers, Daniel, *cabinetmaker*
    D 1823, 1825
Meyers, John, *fancy chairmaker, fancy chair
    ornamenter*
    D 1825, 1831
Mickley, Joseph J., *pianoforte maker*
    D 1825, 1828–31, 1833, 1837, 1839
Middleton, Jacob R., *cabinetmaker*
    D 1830–31, 1833
Middleton, Lewis, *cabinetmaker*
    D 1820, 1823, 1825, 1828–31, 1833
    Quarter Session, October 27, 1827
Miley, William, *cabinetmaker*
    D 1820
Mill, George, *looking glass frame and
    toilet box maker*
    Indenture Papers, January 26, May 17,
        May 31, December 20, 1824

Indenture Bk., May 2, 1825
Millard, William, *cabinetmaker*
D 1837
Miller, Alexander, *cabinetmaker*
D 1839
Miller, Charles, *cabinetmaker*
D 1825, 1828–31, 1833
Miller, Charles, *pianoforte maker*
D 1839
Miller, F. W., *piano warehouse* [*proprietor*]
D 1835/36
*Miller, Henry, *cabinetmaker*
D 1829–31, 1833
1829 Const., p. 11
Miller, Jacob, *cabinetmaker*
D 1837
Miller, Joel, *cabinetmaker*
D 1825
†Miller, John, *cabinetmaker*
D 1820, 1829–31, 1833
Miller, John, *turner*
D 1820
Miller, John, *cabinetmaker*
D 1829–31, 1833
Miller, John Charles, *cabinetmaker*
Men's Register, May 14, 1837
Miller, John G., *turner*
D 1829, 1831, 1833
*Miller, Mark, *cabinetmaker*
D 1837
Misc. bk. 3, pp. 658–65
Miller, Matthew, *cabinetmaker*
D 1835/36
Miller, Nehemiah, *cabinetmaker*
D 1833, 1835/36
Miller, Samuel, *turner*
D 1830, 1833
Miller, Simon, *turner*
D 1829–31, 1833, 1835/36
Miller, William, *chairmaker*
D 1839
Miller & Osbourin, *piano warehouse* [*proprietors*]
D 1833
Milligan, Samuel, *turner*
D 1825, 1828–29, 1833
Millikan, Samuel, *furniture store* [*proprietor*]
D 1837
Millis, Nehemiah, *cabinetmaker*
D 1820, 1823, 1825, 1828–30, 1833, 1837, 1839
Mills, George, *looking glass framemaker*
D 1820, 1823, 1831, 1833, 1835/36
Mills, George, Jr., *cabinetmaker, looking glass*

framemaker
D 1820, 1823, 1825, 1828–31, 1833
Mills, Henry, *cabinet- and looking glass framemaker*
D 1825, 1828–31, 1833
Milne, Michael, *cabinetmaker*
Franklin Gaz., March 21, 1821
Minahan, Michael F., *cabinetmaker*
D 1839
Mitchell, George H., *chairmaker*
D 1835/36, 1837, 1839
†Mitchell, James, *chair and furniture store* [*proprietor*]
D 1820, 1822–23, 1825, 1828–31, 1833, 1835/36, 1837, 1839
Unger Coll., May 29, 1822
U.S. Gaz., October 3, 1833
Mitchell, John, *fancy chairmaker*
D 1820–21, 1829–31, 1833, 1835/36, 1839
Unger Coll., February 24, 1821
Mitchell, Thomas L., *fancy chairmaker*
D 1820
Men's Register, December 24, 1828
†Mitchell, William, *chairmaker*
D 1828
Moffitt, Thomas, *turner*
D 1835/36
Monnison, Daniel, *turner*
D 1837
*Montgomery, Henry, *cabinetmaker*
1829 Const., p. 11
Montgomery, James, *chairmaker*
D 1824
Montgomery, James R., *chair ornamenter, chairmaker*
D 1835/36, 1837
Montgomery, Robert, *cabinetmaker*
D 1831, 1833
Montier, Robert L., *turner*
D 1829–31, 1833
*Moore, David, *cabinetmaker*
D 1820, 1828–31, 1833
Misc. bk. 3, pp. 658–65
1829 Const., p. 11
Moore, James S., *furniture store* [*proprietor*]
D 1837
†*Moore, Thomas H., *cabinet warerooms* [*proprietor*]
D 1835/36
1829 Const., p. 12
†*Moore, William, *cabinetmaker*
D 1828–31, 1833, 1835/36
Misc. bk 3, pp. 658–65
1829 Const., p. 11

Moore, William H., *cabinetmaker*
  D 1829–31, 1833
  Mayor's Court, January 11, 1834
Moore & Campion, *cabinetmakers*
  D 1837, 1839
  Unger Coll., January 12, 1838
Moren, William, *turner*
  D 1820
*Morford, E. F. R., *cabinetmaker*
  Misc. bk. 3, pp. 658–65
Morgan, Gilbert, *cabinetmaker*
  D 1823
Morgan, James, *picture framemaker*
  D 1828, 1830, 1833
Morow, Peter, *windsor chairmaker*
  D 1820
Morris, Pearson, *chairmaker*
  D 1820
Morris, Thomas, *cabinetmaker*
  D 1837
Morris, William, *turner*
  D 1820, 1823, 1825, 1837, 1839
*Morris, William, *cabinetmaker*
  D 1823–25, 1829–31, 1833, 1835/36, 1837,
    1839
  1829 Const., p. 11
Morris, William, *cabinetmaker*
  D 1837, 1839
*Morrison, Abraham, *cabinetmaker*
  D 1820, 1824, 1829, 1833, 1835/36, 1839
  1829 Const., p. 11
Morse, Henry, *pianoforte maker*
  D 1825
*Morton, Mark, *cabinetmaker*
  D 1837, 1839
  Public Ledger, July 27, 1839
  Misc. bk. 3, pp. 658–65
Mosley, George, *cabinetmaker*
  D 1839
Mosley, Samuel, *cabinetmaker*
  D 1823, 1825, 1829–31, 1833, 1835/36, 1839
Mosley, William, *cabinetmaker*
  D 1837
Mount, Eli, *cabinetmaker*
  D 1837, 1839
*Mullen, Samuel, *cabinetmaker*
  1829 Const., p. 12
Murphy, James, *cabinetmaker*
  D 1820, 1824–25, 1828–31, 1833, 1835/36,
    1837, 1839
Murphy, James, *chairmaker*
  D 1835/36
Murphy, John, *turner*

  D 1835/36, 1837
Murphy, William N., *sacking bottom maker*
  D 1831, 1833, 1835/36, 1839
Murrow, Peter, *chairmaker*
  D 1821, 1823
Murrow, Peter, *chairmaker*
  D 1823
Murry, James, *cabinet warehouse [proprietor]*
  D 1829, 1831
Musgrove, James, *looking glass and chair manufac-
    turer*
  D 1837
  Unger Coll., September 16, 1835; December
    14, 1837; March 9, 1838
  U.S. Gaz., December 3, 1833
*Musser, Henry M., *cabinetmaker*
  1829 Const., p. 12
Myer, C., *pianoforte maker*
  D 1825, 1829, 1831, 1833
Myer, Charles, *cabinetmaker*
  D 1839
Myer, Lewis, *cabinetmaker*
  D 1839
Myers, Daniel, *cabinetmaker*
  D 1820
Myers, George, *cabinetmaker, framemaker*
  D 1829–31, 1833, 1837, 1839
Myers, John, *fancy painter*
  D 1835/36
Myers, Samuel, *cabinetmaker*
  Quarter Sessions, November 4, 1833
Myers, Thomas, *chair painter*
  D 1839

Napier, Alexander, *turner*
  D 1837
Napier, John, *chairmaker*
  D 1833, 1835/36, 1839
Naylor, David, *turner*
  D 1839
*Neal, Henry, *cabinetmaker*
  1829 Const., p. 12
Neal, Thomas, *cabinetmaker*
  D 1837
Neb, Stephen, *turner*
  D 1839
Neff, Jacob, *turner*
  D 1820, 1828–31, 1833
*Nehns, Richard, *cabinetmaker*
  Misc. bk. 3, pp. 658–65
*Neilds, Joseph, *cabinetmaker*
  1829 Const., p. 11
*Neill, Thomas J., *cabinetmaker*

D 1839
    Misc. bk. 3, pp. 658–65
*Neinhause, Arnold, *cabinetmaker*
    1829 Const., p. 12
Nelms, Thomas, *cabinetmaker*
    D 1839
*Newkirk, J., *cabinetmaker*
    Misc. bk. 3, pp. 658–65
Newlyn, Daniel, *cabinetmaker*
    D 1820
Newman, Melchior, *turner*
    D 1830–31, 1833
Newton, Thomas W., *turner*
    U.S. Gaz., July 25, 1830
Nice, John, *cabinetmaker*
    D 1820, 1823
Nice, John, *chairmaker*
    D 1835/36, 1839
Nice, Levi, *turner*
    D 1820, 1823, 1825, 1828–31, 1833
*Nice, Samuel, *cabinetmaker*
    1829 Const., p. 12
Nichols, Daniel, *cabinetmaker*
    D 1839
Nicholson, Daniel, *cabinetmaker*
    D 1837
Nicholson, Thomas, *turner*
    D 1828–31, 1833, 1835/36
Noblet, Stephen, *cabinetmaker*
    D 1831, 1833, 1839
†Nolen, Charles, *furniture warehouse* [*proprietor*]
    D 1820, 1822, 1823, 1825
    Poulson's Advertiser, January 27, 1823
    U.S. Gaz., March 28, 1820; March 13,
        December 1, 1821; July 1, 1822;
        February 3, 1827; October 2, 1828
Nolen, Spencer, *looking glass manufacturer*
    D 1828–29, 1831
Norris & Tatem, *cabinetmakers*
    D 1835/36
North, John, *cabinetmaker*
    D 1835/36
North, Joseph, *cabinetmaker*
    D 1839
Nossitter, Thomas, *cabinetmaker*
    D 1825
Nunnelly, Nathaniel, *turner*
    D 1830–31, 1833, 1835/36
Nunns, J. P. *pianoforte warehouse* [*proprietor*]
    D 1837
    U.S. Gaz., February 14, 1837

O'Conner, Kelley, *cabinetmaker*

D 1820
Ogburn, Aaron, *framemaker*
    D 1837
Ogden, John, *cabinetmaker*
    D 1837, 1839
Olway, A. T., *cabinetmaker*
    D 1839
O'Neill, James, *furniture store* [*proprietor*]
    D 1839
Ortlip, John, *turner*
    D 1829–31, 1833
Osborne, Richard, *cabinet warerooms* [*proprietor*]
    D 1837
    U.S. Gaz., January 10, 1839
Ossback, John, *chairmaker*
    D 1820
Ott, Jacob C., *turner*
    D 1825, 1828–31, 1833, 1835/36
Ottinger, Robert, *chairmaker*
    D 1837, 1839
*Ottinger, William, *cabinetmaker*
    1829 Const., p. 11
Ottinger & Lee, *chairmakers*
    D 1822
Otto, John, *cabinetmaker*
    D 1820, 1823
Owens, Thomas, *cabinetmaker*
    D 1830–31, 1833
    Mechanics' Free Press, September 18, 1830

Pacey, Lewis, *looking glass framemaker*
    D 1823
Painter, John, *turner*
    D 1820
Palmer, Amos, *cabinetmaker*
    D 1829–31, 1833, 1835/36, 1839
*Palmer, George, *cabinetmaker*
    D 1840
    1829 Const., p. 11
Palmer, Richard, *furniture store* [*proprietor*]
    D 1820
Parham, Robert, *cabinetmaker*
    D 1823, 1825, 1828–31, 1833, 1835/36,
        1839–40
Paris, Benjamin, *turner*
    D 1824
Park, Pascal, *cabinetmaker*
    D 1825
Parker, Benjamin, *cabinetmaker*
    D 1820, 1823, 1825, 1828–31, 1833, 1835/36,
        1839
Parker, Benjamin, *cabinetmaker*
    D 1825

Parker, George H., *cabinetmaker*
D 1839–40
*Parker, John, *cabinetmaker*
1829 Const., p. 12
Parker, Joshua B., *cabinetmaker*
D 1840
†Parkin, Richard, *cabinetmaker*
D 1825, 1828–31, 1833, 1835/36, 1837, 1839–40
Unger Coll., May 9, May 28, 1834
*Parks, P. T., *cabinetmaker*
1829 Const., p. 11
Parris, Benjamin, *chairmaker*
D 1823
Parris, Benjamin, *turner*
D 1825, 1828–31, 1833, 1835/36
Parselles, William, *chairmaker*
D 1840
Passmore, Samuel, *cabinetmaker*
D 1840
Pastor, John, *cabinetmaker*
D 1839
*Patten, Nathaniel, *cabinetmaker*
Misc. bk. 3, pp. 658–65
†Patterson, John, *fancy chairmaker*
D 1820, 1823, 1825, 1828–31, 1833
Quarter Sessions, June 23, 1823, p. 272
*Patterson, Joseph, *chairmaker*
D 1824, 1825, 1839
U.S. Gaz., July 15, 1835
1829 Const., p. 12
Patton, John, *turner*
D 1823, 1828–31, 1833, 1835/36
*Paul, John, *cabinetmaker*
D 1823, 1825, 1837, 1839
Misc. bk. 3, pp. 658–65
Paul, John B., *cabinetmaker*
D 1837
Paul, John T., *cabinetmaker*
D 1839–40
*Paynter, Samuel, *cabinetmaker*
1829 Const., p. 12
Pearce, Peter, *turner*
D 1835/36
Pearl, A. F., *cabinetmaker*
D 1835/36
Pearl, Alexander, *cabinetmaker*
D 1831, 1833
Pearson, Cyrus, *turner*
D 1823
Pearson, John, *turner*
D 1823
Peart, Abraham, *cabinetmaker*

D 1824, 1839–40
Peart & Gilky, *cabinetmakers*
D 1824
Peck, Joseph, *chairmaker*
D 1829–31, 1833
Peckworth, Charles, *turner*
D 1831, 1833, 1835/36
Peckworth & Waters, *turners*
D 1835/36
Peco, Zenah, *cabinetmaker*
D 1837
Pendergast, Joseph L., *cabinetmaker*
D 1823, 1825, 1828
Pepperd, Standish, *chair painter*
D 1820
Perkins, William, *chairmaker*
D 1829–31, 1833
Perry, Felix, *cabinetmaker*
D 1837
*Peters, Charles B., *cabinetmaker*
1829 Const., p. 12
Peterson, James, *cabinetmaker*
D 1831, 1833
Peterson, Samuel, *cabinetmaker*
D 1820
Pettit, Robert, *chairmaker*
D 1835/36
Peze, Lewis, *framemaker*
D 1839
Pezey, Louis, *cabinetmaker*
D 1830–31, 1833
Pfeil, John, *cabinetmaker*
D 1820, 1825, 1829–31, 1833
Phiesth, Phillip, *pianoforte maker*
D 1840
Phile, Daniel, *cabinetmaker*
D 1820
Piccot, Xaver, *cabinetmaker*
D 1840
Pickering, Joseph, *turner*
D 1835/36
Pierce, Peter, *turner*
D 1829–30
Pierce, William M., *pianoforte maker*
D 1835/36
*Pierpoint, Michael, *cabinetmaker*
1829 Const., p. 12
†Pippitt, Isaac, *cabinetmaker*
D 1820, 1823, 1825, 1828–31, 1833, 1835/36
Freeman's Jnl., April 26, 1826
Mayor's Court, December 31, 1824; January 8, 1825
U.S. Gaz., January 25, 1825

Pirtt, Abraham F., *cabinetmaker*
D 1837
Plowman, John, *pianoforte maker*
D 1840
*Poinset(t), Thomas, *pianoforte maker*
D 1839–40
Misc. bk. 3, pp. 658–65
Polis, George, *chairmaker*
D 1835/36, 1837, 1839
Public Ledger, August 3, 1837; May 3, 1838
Pomeroy, Benjamin F., *turner*
D 1825, 1828–29
Pommer, Charles, *pianoforte maker*
D 1820, 1823, 1825, 1828–31, 1833, 1835/36,
1837
Porter, Henry, *turner*
D 1820
Porter, Isaac, *turner*
D 1830, 1833
Porter, Stephen, *cabinetmaker*
D 1823
Potter, Edward, *chair painter*
D 1835/36
Powell, Eli, *chairmaker*
D 1825, 1829–31, 1833
Powell, John, *turner*
D 1828–31, 1833
Powell, Richard, *cabinetmaker*
D 1825, 1828–31, 1833 1835/36, 1837,
1839–40
Public Ledger, June 27, 1839
†Prall, Edward, *chairmaker*
D 1820, 1825, 1828–31, 1833, 1835/36, 1837,
1839–40
Prall & Fritz, *chairmakers*
D 1828–31, 1833, 1835/36
*Pratt, Daniel, *cabinetmaker*
1829 Const., p. 12
*Pratt, George, *cabinetmaker*
1829 Const., p. 11
Pratt, John, *cabinetmaker*
D 1820
Pratt, Richard, *cabinetmaker*
D 1829–31, 1833
Prendergrast, J. L., *cabinetmaker*
D 1829–31, 1833
Presser, Warrington, *turner*
D 1840
Price, Thomas, *chairmaker*
D 1837, 1839–40
Price, William, *cabinetmaker*
D 1835/36
Priest, Aaron, *framemaker*

D 1840
Priest, George, *cabinetmaker*
D 1835/36, 1837
Pritchett, Jacob, *cabinetmaker*
D 1840
*Probasco, Abraham, *cabinetmaker*
1829 Const., p. 12
Pryor, Joseph, *cabinetmaker*
D 1820
Pryor, Joseph, Jr., *cabinetmaker*
D 1823, 1830–31, 1833
Pugh, Hugh, *chairmaker*
D 1831, 1833, 1839–40
Pugh, Jesse, *cabinetmaker*
D 1820, 1823, 1825
Pummer, Charles, *pianoforte maker*
D 1820

Quas, John, *cabinetmaker*
D 1825, 1828–31, 1833, 1835/36, 1837,
1839–40
†Quervelle, Anthony G., *cabinetmaker*
D 1820, 1823, 1825, 1828–31, 1833,
1835/36, 1837, 1839–40
Unger Coll., October 26, 1829; March 20,
August 13, December 7, December 30,
1830; October 11, 1831; May 11, [1833];
August 15, 1833
Poulson's Advertiser, January 6, 1830
Pa. Inquirer, January 2, 1838
Public Record, June 11, 1874
U.S. Gaz., February 17, November 16, 1826;
July 4, 1832; July 9, 1833; September 13,
1838; April 6, 1839; May 14, 1840

Rabe, Justin, *cabinetmaker*
D 1837, 1839–40
Ragen, William, *cabinetmaker*
D 1839
Rahman, Addar, *pianoforte maker*
D 1839
Ramage, Adam, *joiner and cabinetmaker*
D 1824
Ramsay, Henry, *cabinetmaker*
D 1829–31, 1833, 1837, 1839–40
Ramsay, Jacob, *cabinetmaker*
D 1839
Ramsay, James, *cabinetmaker*
D 1829–31, 1833
Ramsay, James B., *cabinetmaker*
D 1829–31, 1833, 1835/36, 1839–40
Ramsay, Joseph, *cabinetmaker*
D 1837, 1839–40

Randall, R. G., *turner*
   D 1835/36
Randolph, John, *cabinetmaker*
   D 1829–31, 1833
Randolph, Robert, *cabinetmaker*
   D 1828–30, 1833
Randolph, William, *chairmaker*
   D 1839–40
Ranken, William, *cabinetmaker*
   D 1824–25, 1828–31, 1833, 1835/36, 1837,
      1839–40
   Unger Coll., October 2, 1832; August 6, Oc-
      tober 22, 1833
Rankin, George, & Son, *cabinetmakers*
   D 1820, 1823, 1825, 1828–31, 1833, 1837,
      1839–40
Raphum, John, *chairmaker*
   D 1837
Rappoon, John, *chairmaker*
   D 1833
Rasber, John, *chairmaker*
   D 1820–21
Rawings, George, *cabinetmaker*
   D 1829–31, 1833, 1835/36, 1837
Rawlins, Thomas, *chairmaker*
   D 1833, 1839–40
Ray, Robert, *turner*
   D 1829–31, 1833
Raybold, Thomas, *windsor chairmaker*
   D 1820, 1823
Read, Elias, *cabinetmaker*
   D 1839
Readles, Adam, *turner*
   D 1824
Reaiger, Joseph S., *cabinetmaker*
   D 1831, 1833
Reazler, Ferdinand, *cabinetmaker*
   Men's Register, May 9, 1836
Reber, Samuel, *cabinetmaker*
   D 1837, 1839–40
Rebman, John, *cabinetmaker*
   D 1839–40
Redles, Adam, *turner*
   D 1820, 1828–31, 1833, 1835/36, 1837,
      1839–40
Redmond, John, *cabinetmaker*
   D 1837
*Redner [Rednor], Lewis, *cabinetmaker*
   D 1828–31, 1833
   Misc. bk. 3, pp. 658–65
   1829 Const., p. 11
†Redstreke, J., *cabinetmaker*
   D 1820, 1823, 1825, 1828–31, 1833, 1840

*Reed, Elias, *cabinetmaker*
   D 1830, 1831, 1833, 1835/36
   1829 Const., p. 12
Reed, Elijah, *cabinetmaker*
   D 1840
Rees, James, *chairmaker*
   D 1825
Rees & Berkelbach, *looking glass and framemakers*
   D 1839
Reeves, William, *cabinetmaker*
   D 1830–31, 1833
Refund, John, *chairmaker*
   D 1825
Reger, Joseph, *cabinet warehouse [proprietor]*
   D 1829, 1831, 1833
Reger, William, *cabinetmaker*
   D 1831, 1833, 1835/36
Rehn, Thomas J., *chairmaker*
   D 1829–31, 1833
Reichenbach, Frederick, *pianoforte maker*
   D 1939–40
Reilly, William, *cabinetmaker*
   D 1823
Reily, Charles, *chairmaker*
   D 1837
Reiter, Samuel, *turner*
   D 1839
Repburn, John, *fancy chairmaker*
   D 1828–31, 1833
Repsher, Leonard, *turner*
   D 1831, 1833, 1835/36
*Rest, John, *cabinetmaker*
   D 1840
   1829 Const., p. 12
Rethford, Jesse, *cabinetmaker*
   D 1830–31, 1833
*Reynear, Aaron, *cabinetmaker*
   1829 Const., p. 12
Rhoades, Joseph, *cabinetmaker*
   D 1825
Richards, Adam, *cabinetmaker*
   D 1840
Richey, Henry M., *cabinetmaker*
   D 1820
*Richmond, John, *cabinetmaker*
   D 1825
   1829 Const., p. 11
Richmond, D. John, *pianoforte maker*
   Men's Register, June 17, 1829
Ricketts, Andrew, *furniture store [proprietor]*
   D 1828–31, 1833
*Riddell, Christopher, *cabinetmaker*
   Misc. bk. 3, pp. 658–65

Riddle, Adam, *turner*
     D 1823, 1828–31, 1833
†*Riddle, Crawford, *cabinetmaker*
     D 1835/36
          Unger Coll., May 6, 1834; March 2, 1838
          Misc. bk. 3, pp. 658–65
          Pennsylvanian, November 1, 1834; June 9,
               1836
          Pa. Inquirer, January 2, April 26, 1838
          Public Ledger, March 25, 1836; March 22,
               1838
          1820 Census, March 8, 1834; March 30,
               1835; March 10, 1836, April 5, 1838
Riddle, John, *cabinetmaker*
     D 1823, 1825, 1835/36, 1837, 1840
Riddle, Robert, *cabinetmaker*
     D 1837
Ridgway, Samuel, *fancy chairmaker*
     D 1837
Rigby, Henry, *cabinetmaker*
     D 1820, 1823
          Wills, no. 85 (1823)
Rihl & Straum, *cabinetmakers*
     D 1825, 1828–31, 1833
†Riley, Charles, *chairmaker*
     D 1820, 1823
Riley, Charles, *chairmaker*
     D 1820, 1823
*Riley, William, *cabinetmaker*
     D 1825, 1829–31, 1833, 1835/36, 1839–40
          1829 Const., p. 11
Ristine, Frederick, *cabinetmaker*
     D 1840
Ritchie, Henry, *cabinetmaker*
     D 1835/36
Riterson, Joseph, *cabinetmaker*
     D 1829–31, 1833
Ritter, Edward, *chairmaker*
     D 1820, 1822–23, 1825, 1828–31, 1833
Ritter, Edward, *chairmaker*
     D 1823
Ritter, George, *cabinetmaker*
     D 1820, 1823, 1825, 1828–31, 1833, 1835/36
          George Ritter Receipt Book, 1834–39, HSP
          Pennsylvanian, July 2, 1835
          1820 Census, no. 565
          Wills, no. 235 (1849)
Roan, Joseph, *cabinetmaker*
     D 1823
Robb, James, *cabinetmaker*
     D 1823
Robb, Justen, *cabinetmaker*
     D 1835/36

Robbins, –, *chairmaker*
     D 1820
Robbins, John, *chairmaker*
     D 1823, 1828–31, 1833
Roberjohn, Thomas, *cabinetmaker*
     D 1823
*Roberts, Isaac, *cabinetmaker*
     1829 Const., p. 12
Roberts, John, *cabinet- and chairmaker*
     D 1820, 1823, 1825, 1828–31, 1833
Roberts, John P., *chairmaker*
     D 1825, 1828–31, 1833, 1835/36
Roberts, Thomas, *cabinetmaker*
     D 1823–24, 1833
Robertson, James, *cabinetmaker*
     D 1829–31, 1833, 1837
Robertson, John, *cabinetmaker*
     D 1829–31, 1833
*Robertson, Thomas, *cabinetmaker*
     D 1829–31, 1833, 1835/36, 1837, 1839–40
          Public Ledger, July 14, 1838
          1829 Const., p. 12
Robertson, William, *chairmaker*
     D 1820
Robinson, Charles C., *chairmaker*
     D 1820
Robinson, D., *turner*
     D 1828–31, 1833
Robinson, D., *turner*
     D 1828–31, 1833
Robinson, James, *cabinetmaker*
     D 1835/36
Robinson, Joel, *furniture car*
     D 1839
Robinson, John, *cabinetmaker*
     D 1837, 1839–40
Robinson, John, Jr., *cabinetmaker*
     D 1820
Robinson, John B., *chairmaker*
     D 1840
*Robinson, John V., *cabinetmaker*
     1829 Const., p. 11
Robinson, Joseph D., *turner*
     D 1824–25, 1828–31, 1833, 1835/36
*Robinson, Thomas, *cabinetmaker*
     D 1825, 1835/36, 1839
          Misc. bk. 3, pp. 658–65
*Robson, John, Jr., *cabinetmaker*
     1829 Const., p. 11
Rodes, Joseph, *cabinetmaker*
     D 1830–31, 1833, 1835/36, 1837, 1839–40
Roehm, Adam, *pianoforte maker*
     D 1839

Rogers, Francis, *turner*
  D 1830–31, 1833
Roland, John, *cabinetmaker*
  D 1829–31, 1833, 1835/36
Rollins, George, *cabinetmaker*
  D 1820, 1825
Rollins, Thomas, *chairmaker*
  D 1840
Rolph, William, *fancy chairmaker*
  D 1825, 1828–31, 1833
Ronaldson, George, *cabinetmaker*
  D 1824
Ronaldson, George, *cabinetmaker*
  D 1824
Ronaldson, George, *chair- and sofamaker*
  D 1825
*Rorty, Alexander, *cabinetmaker*
  D 1840
  Misc. bk. 3, pp. 658–65
Rose, Conrad, *pianoforte maker*
  D 1835/36, 1839
Rosi, John E., *cabinetmaker*
  Documented sideboard, 1829, illus., *Antiques*,
    January 1930, p. 80
Ross, Conrad O., *cabinetmaker*
  D 1829, 1831, 1833
Rouer, Peter, *furniture polisher*
  D 1837
Rovoudt, Peter, *turner*
  D 1823
*Rowand, Charles, *cabinetmaker*
  1829 Const., p. 12
Rowand, Samuel, *cabinetmaker*
  D 1837
Rowland, John, *cabinetmaker*
  D 1820, 1823, 1825, 1839
Rowland, Thomas, *chairmaker*
  D 1835/36, 1837
Roy, Rob, *turner*
  D 1835/36
Ruby, Philip, *chair painter*
  D 1829–31, 1833, 1840
Rudolf, Conrad, *turner*
  D 1820
Rudolph, Christian, *turner*
  D 1820, 1825, 1829–31, 1833, 1835/36, 1837,
    1839–40
Rudy, David, *cabinetmaker*
  D 1840
Rudy, Henry, *turner*
  D 1839–40
*Rue, Elijah, *cabinetmaker*
  D 1825, 1829–31, 1833, 1835/36, 1837,

  1839–40
  Misc. bk. 3, pp. 658–65
  1829 Const., p. 11
Rue, Samuel, *cabinetmaker*
  D 1835/36, 1837, 1839–40
  Freeman's Jnl. April 5, 1825
Ruffington, Isaac, *cabinetmaker*
  D 1825
Ruhl, Samuel, *cabinetmaker*
  D 1823
*Rumbaugh, George D., *cabinet-, chair-,
    and sofamaker*
  D 1837
  1829 Const., p. 12
*Rupert, Benjamin, *cabinetmaker*
  1829 Const., p. 12
Rupert, Francis, *cabinetmaker*
  Men's Register, October 15, 1836
Rushton, Thomas, *chairmaker*
  D 1835/36
Rutty, William, *cabinetmaker*
  D 1837
Ryckman, John, *cabinetmaker*
  D 1820, 1823

*Sackriter, David, *cabinetmaker*
  D 1820, 1823, 1825, 1828–31, 1833, 1835/36,
    1837, 1839–40
  Misc. bk. 3, pp. 658–65
  1829 Const., p. 11
  Wills, no. 259 (1849)
Sacriter, William C., *framemaker*
  D 1837
*Sager, Amos, *cabinetmaker*
  D 1831, 1833, 1837
  1829 Const., p. 11
Sager, Thomas, *cabinetmaker*
  D 1825, 1828–31, 1833, 1835/36
Sager, Thomas P., *framemaker*
  Men's Register, September 13, 1830
Sager, William, *cabinetmaker*
  D 1839–40
Sailer, John, *cabinet- and chairmaker*
  D 1820, 1822–23, 1825, 1828–31, 1833
St. John, Edward, *cabinetmaker*
  Men's Register, September 23, 1829
Salter, F. A., *cabinetmaker*
  D 1839–40
Salter, Phoenix, *cabinetmaker*
  D 1837
Samson, Joseph, *sacking bottom maker*
  D 1825, 1828–30, 1833
  Wills, no. 26 (1827)

Sanclera, –, *cabinetmaker*
D 1829–31, 1833

†*Sa(u)nders, James, *cabinetmaker*
D 1825, 1829–30
1829 Const., p. 11

Sanders, John E., *cabinetmaker*
D 1829–31, 1833

Sanderson, William, *chairmaker*
D 1839

*Sands, Aaron, *cabinetmaker*
1829 Const., p. 12

Sargent, John, *chairmaker*
D 1840

Sattler, F. A., *cabinetmaker*
D 1839–40

Savery, George, *turner*
D 1820

Schaeffer, Christian, *cabinetmaker*
D 1840

Schafer, Christopher, *pianoforte maker*
D 1839–40

Scharbach, Joseph, *cabinetmaker*
D 1839–40

†Scheer, Emilius N., *pianoforte and organ builder*
D 1825, 1828–31, 1833, 1835/36, 1837, 1839–40
Pa. Inquirer, January 4, 1838

Schell, Michael, *cabinetmaker*
D 1823

Schlosser, Washington, *cabinetmaker*
D 1830

Schmeiding, Frederick, *turner*
D 1820, 1825, 1828–31, 1833, 1835/36

Schoff, H. J., *pianoforte maker*
D 1840

Schopffel, Lewis, *cabinetmaker*
D 1840

*Schow, Ole, *cabinetmaker*
1829 Const., p. 11

Schrader, John H., *turner*
D 1822, 1825, 1828–31, 1833, 1835/36, 1840

Schreiner, Nicholas, *turner*
D 1820, 1823, 1828–31, 1833

*Schultz, Frederick, *cabinetmaker*
1829 Const., p. 11

Schultze, John, *cabinetmaker*
D 1840

Schuyler, Aaron, *cabinetmaker*
D 1833

Schuyler, P. R., *cabinetmaker*
D 1833

*Schwrenderwell, H., *cabinetmaker*
Misc. bk. 3, pp. 658–65

Scofield & Law, *looking glass and picture framemakers*
D 1825, 1828, 1830, 1833

Scott, H. C., *chairmaker*
D 1835/36

Scott, Hamilton C., *chairmaker*
D 1840

Sectzinger, William, F., *cabinetmaker*
D 1839

*Seeds, Thomas, *cabinetmaker*
D 1835/36, 1837, 1839
1829 Const., p. 12

Seibert, Jacob, *turner*
D 1837

Seibrecht, J. A., *cabinetmaker*
D 1833

*Seiwers, Jacob F., *cabinetmaker*
1829 Const., p. 12

Sellers, Nathan Y., *turner*
D 1820

Senseman, S., *pianoforte maker*
D 1839–40

Server, John, *cabinetmaker*
D 1820

Sevening, Charles, *framemaker*
D 1839

Severn, Charles, *framemaker*
D 1840

Shaffer, Christian, *cabinetmaker*
D 1837

Shannon, Hugh, *cabinetmaker*
D 1830–31, 1833, 1835/36, 1839–40

Shannon, William, *turner*
D 1829–30, 1833

Sharff, Fred, *cabinetmaker*
D 1840

Sharp, Jonah, *fancy chairmaker*
D 1825, 1828–31, 1833

Sharp, Joseph, *chairmaker*
D 1823

Sharp, Josiah, *chairmaker*
D 1820, 1823

Sharper, Charles, *turner*
D 1837

Sharper, Joseph, *cabinetmaker*
D 1837

Shaw, Henry P., *fancy chairmaker*
D 1823, 1825, 1830–31, 1833, 1835/36

*Shaw, James, *cabinetmaker*
D 1833, 1835/36, 1837, 1839–40
1829 Const., p. 11

*Shaw, John, *cabinetmaker*
D 1824

1829 Const., p. 12
Shaw, Jno., *cabinetmaker*
    U.S. Gaz., July 15, 1835
Shaw, Joseph, *turner*
    D 1837
*Shaw, Nathan, *cabinetmaker*
    D 1839
    1829 Const., p. 12
Shaw, P., *chairmaker*
    D 1835/36
Shaw, S. B., *turner*
    D 1837
Sheble, Jacob, Jr., *cabinetmaker*
    D 1820, 1823, 1825, 1829–31, 1833
Sheed, William, *chairmaker*
    D 1823, 1825
    Men's Register, December 10, 1831
Sheetz, Peter, *chairmaker*
    D 1820
Shelmire, –, *cabinetmaker*
    D 1825, 1829–31, 1833
Sheppard, Charles, *chairmaker*
    D 1835/36
Sheppard, Francis, *chairmaker*
    D 1835/36, 1837
†Sheppard, John W., *cabinetmaker*
    D 1828–29, 1831, 1833
Sheppard, Matthew, *cabinetmaker*
    D 1835/36, 1837
Sheppard, Randall, *cabinetmaker*
    D 1825
Sherborne, Thomas, *cabinetmaker*
    D 1828–31, 1833, 1835/36, 1840
    Unger Coll., July 23, 1830
    Fire Survey, no. 1314, July 10, 1835
    Indenture Bk., June 6, 1825
Shermer, A. & J., *cabinetmakers*
    D 1820, 1823, 1825, 1828–31, 1833, 1835/36,
      1837, 1839
Shermer, Jacob, *cabinetmaker*
    D 1820, 1823, 1825, 1828–29, 1831, 1833,
      1835/36, 1837, 1839–40
Sherwin, George R., *organ builder*
    D 1833
Shettleworth, John, *turner*
    D 1839
*Shibe, George, *cabinetmaker*
    D 1831, 1833
    1829 Const., p. 11
Shields, Joseph, *turner*
    D 1829–31, 1833, 1835/36, 1839–40
*Shingle, Jacob, *cabinetmaker*
    D 1839–40

Misc. bk. 3, pp. 658–65
Shoemaker, Daniel, *cabinetmaker*
    D 1829–31, 1833, 1839
    Poulson's Advertiser, October 4, 1830
Shoemaker, John, *pianoforte maker*
    D 1839
Shourds, Benjamin, *cabinetmaker and framemaker*
    D 1820, 1825, 1828–31, 1833, 1835/36,
      1839–40
    Misc. bk. 1, pp. 307–8
    U.S. Gaz., April 15, June 16, 1834
Shourds & Worn, *cabinetmakers*
    D 1822
Shue, William, *turner*
    D 1829–31, 1833
*Shuff, William, *cabinetmaker*
    D 1828–30, 1833
    1829 Const., p. 11
Shultz, Frederick, *cabinetmaker*
    D 1828–31, 1833
Shuster, Aaron, *turner*
    D 1840
Shuster, Jacob, *cabinetmaker*
    D 1839–40
Shute, William, *turner*
    D 1825, 1828, 1830, 1833, 1835/36, 1839–40
Sibbs, Joseph, *framemaker*
    D 1839–40
Siddall, William, *cabinetmaker*
    D 1833
Siddons, William, *cabinetmaker*
    D 1829–31, 1833, 1835/36, 1839
Siemers, William, *cabinetmaker*
    D 1839–40
Simmons, Peter, *turner*
    D 1829–31, 1833, 1835/36, 1839–40
Simmons, Stephen H., *ornamental chair painter*
    D 1825, 1828–29, 1831, 1833, 1835/36,
      1839–40
†Simmons & Bavis, *chairmakers*
    D 1829–31
Simpkins, Ellis, *cabinetmaker*
    D 1823
Simpson, Isaac, *cabinetmaker*
    D 1820, 1823, 1825, 1828–31, 1833, 1837,
      1839
Simpson, Peter, *cabinetmaker*
    D 1829, 1839–40
Sinclair, Kennedy, *cabinetmaker*
    D 1829–31, 1833, 1835/36, 1840
    Public Ledger, November 13, 1838
*Sinclair, William, *cabinetmaker*
    D 1820, 1823

Men's Register, November 12, 1837
  1829 Const., p. 11
Sink, Lawrence, *cabinetmaker*
  D 1822–23
  Wills, no. 1 (1828)
Sippel, Michael, *cabinetmaker*
  D 1830–31, 1833, 1835/36, 1837
Sites, George F., *chairmaker*
  D 1833, 1837, 1839–40
*Skelington, James W., *cabinetmaker*
  1829 Const., p. 12
*Skinner, Thomas, *cabinetmaker*
  D 1829–31, 1833
  1829 Const., p. 11
Skinner, William, *chairmaker*
  D 1840
Slammer, M., *cabinetmaker*
  D 1829–31, 1833
Slater, William, *furniture store [proprietor]*
  D 1837
  Public Ledger, June 10, 1836
Slemmer, Matthias, *cabinetmaker*
  D 1820, 1837, 1840
Slutzer, William, *cabinetmaker*
  D 1829–31, 1833
Small, Thomas, *cabinetmaker*
  D 1820, 1829–30, 1833, 1835/36, 1837
Smith, Christian C., *pianoforte maker*
  D 1840
Smith, Clement, *cabinetmaker*
  D 1840
Smith, Francis, *cabinetmaker*
  D 1820
Smith, G. W., *furniture store [proprietor]*
  D 1835/36, 1837, 1839
Smith, Garretson, *cabinetmaker*
  D 1831, 1833, 1835/36
Smith, George D., *chairmaker*
  D 1839
Smith, J., *furniture store [proprietor]*
  D 1837
Smith, Jacob, *cabinetmaker*
  D 1839–40
Smith, James, *portable desk manufacturer*
  D 1830, 1833
Smith, James, *cabinetmaker*
  D 1837, 1839
Smith, Joseph, *cabinetmaker*
  D 1839–40
Smith, Lewis L., *furniture store [proprietor]*
  D 1829, 1831
Smith, Richard, *turner*
  D 1820

Smith, Robert, *portable desk manufacturer*
  D 1830
Smith, Rowan, *cabinetmaker*
  D 1840
Smith, Samuel, *chairmaker*
  D 1830–31, 1833
Smith, Samuel, *turner*
  D 1837
Smith, Samuel F., *turner*
  D 1839–40
Smith, Samuel S., *chairmaker*
  D 1837
Smith, Stephen, *chairmaker*
  D 1837, 1839–40
  Public Ledger, May 30, November 5, 1838
Smith, Thomas, *chairmaker*
  D 1831, 1833
Smith, Thomas M., *chairmaker*
  D 1835/36, 1837, 1839–40
Smith, Wesley, *cabinetmaker*
  D 1839
†Smith, William, *cabinetmaker*
  D 1823, 1829–31, 1833
Smith, William, *furniture store [proprietor]*
  D 1829–31, 1833
†Smith, William A., *cabinetmaker*
  D 1840
Smith, C., & Smith, R. A., *cabinetmakers*
  D 1839
*Smyth, William B., *cabinetmaker*
  1829 Const., p. 12
Snowden, Benjamin, *chairmaker*
  D 1829–31, 1833, 1835/36, 1837, 1839–40
Snyder, Adam, *chairmaker*
  D 1820, 1823, 1825, 1828–31, 1833, 1835/36,
    1839–40
  Men's Register, October 24, 1829; September 29, October 27, December 7, 1833
  Convict Docket, December 24, 1835
Snyder, Adam, *chairmaker*
  D 1823
Snyder, Christian, *cabinetmaker*
  D 1820
Snyder, John, *cabinetmaker*
  D 1820
Snyder, John, *cabinetmaker*
  D 1820
Snyder, John, *cabinetmaker*
  D 1823
Snyder, John, *cabinetmaker*
  D 1823, 1825, 1828–31, 1833, 1835/36
Snyder, John, *cabinetmaker*
  D 1825, 1828–31, 1833, 1835/36

Snyder, John, *pianoforte maker*
  D 1830–31, 1833
Snyder, John, *cabinetmaker*
  D 1837, 1839–40
†*Snyder, Joseph, *gilder, fancy chairmaker, and
    looking glass manufacturer*
  D 1820, 1825, 1828–31, 1833, 1835/36, 1837,
    1839–40
  1820 Census, no. 529
  1829 Const., p. 12
Snyder, Matthias, *organ maker*
  D 1837
*Snyder, Nicholas J., *cabinetmaker*
  D 1835/36, 1837
  1829 Const., p. 12
Snyder, Thomas, *cabinetmaker*
  D 1840
Snyder, William, *chairmaker*
  D 1829–31, 1833, 1835/36, 1837, 1839–40
Somerset, Jacob, *cabinetmaker*
  D 1825, 1829–31, 1833, 1835/36, 1837
Souders, Nathaniel, *cabinetmaker*
  D 1837
Spade, John, *cabinetmaker*
  D 1839
*Spauldings, David F., *cabinetmaker*
  1829 Const., p. 12
Spears, Isaac F., *cabinetmaker*
  D 1837
Spencer, Philip, *cabinetmaker*
  D 1823, 1825
Spicer, James, *turner*
  D 1840
Springer, Abraham, *chairmaker*
  D 1833, 1837, 1839–40
Springer, Lewis R., *turner*
  D 1829–31, 1833
Stam, John L., *chairmaker*
  D 1835/36, 1839
*Stantz, F., *cabinetmaker*
  Misc. bk. 3, pp. 658–65
Stark, F., *pianoforte maker*
  D 1835/36, 1837, 1839
Starkey, Charles, *cabinetmaker*
  D 1820
*Starkey, Nathan, *portable desk manufacturer*
  D 1833, 1835/36, 1837, 1839–40
  Unger Coll., April 18, 1833
  1829 Const., p. 12
Steel, Thomas, *chairmaker*
  D 1820
Steel, William, *cabinetmaker*
  D 1837

Steele, William S., *cabinetmaker*
  D 1839–40
Steiner, Jacob, *cabinetmaker*
  D 1820
Steiner & Fries, *cabinetmakers*
  D 1820
Steitz, Jacob, *cabinetmaker*
  D 1840
Steitzer, John, *pianoforte maker*
  D 1840
Stellezell, Jacob, *turner and chairmaker*
  D 1820
Stemple, John, *chairmaker*
  D 1831, 1833
Sterret, John, *ornamental painter*
  D 1839
†Stevenson, William, *cabinetmaker*
  D 1835/36
Steward, Joseph, *framemaker*
  D 1839
Stewart, Henry, *cabinetmaker*
  D 1829–31, 1833
Stewart, Henry D., *cabinetmaker*
  D 1835/36
  Children's Register, October 29, 1826
Stewart, James, *pianoforte maker*
  D 1820
†Stewart [Stuart], John, *cabinetmaker*
  D 1820–21, 1823, 1828–31, 1833, 1835
Stewart, John, *chairmaker*
  D 1839–40
†Stewart, John A., *cabinetmaker, chairmaker*
  D 1823, 1825, 1828–31, 1833, 1835/36, 1837,
    1839–40
Stewart, Thomas, *pianoforte maker*
  D 1820
Stewart, Thomas, *cabinetmaker*
  D 1830–31, 1833, 1840
Stewart, Thomas, *chair- and cabinetmaker*
  D 1835/36
Stewart, William, *cabinetmaker*
  D 1835/36, 1840
Stewart, William H., *ornamental painter, japanner,
    and gilder*
  D 1820, 1823
†Stewart, William H., *fancy chairmaker*
  D 1825, 1828–31, 1833, 1835/36
†Stewart & James, *chairmakers*
  U. S. Gaz., March 9, 1827; February 26, 1828
Stewart & Prall, *cabinetmakers*
  D 1823
†Stewart & Sanderson, *fancy chairmakers*
  D 1835/36, 1839–40

Stiles, George, *cabinetmaker*
    D 1823
Stiles, John, *portable desk and dressing case*
        manufacturer
    D 1825, 1828–31, 1833
        Unger Coll., December 16, 1825
        Wills, no. 38 (1829)
Stiles, Robert, *cabinetmaker*
    D 1820, 1823, 1837
Stillinger, Daniel, *pianoforte maker*
    D 1839–40
Stiner, Jacob, *looking glass framemaker*
    D 1829–31, 1833
Stites, George, *cabinetmaker*
    D 1820, 1831, 1833, 1837
Stittenger, Daniel, *cabinetmaker*
    D 1835/36
Stockel, Dewalt, *cabinetmaker*
    D 1839
Stockman, Adolphus, *framemaker*
    D 1839
Stoeckel, Theobold, *cabinetmaker*
    D 1837, 1839–40
Stoker, H. L., *turner*
    D 1835/36
Stokes, Samuel, *cabinetmaker*
    D 1825, 1829–31, 1833
Story, William, *chairmaker*
    D 1835/36, 1837, 1839
Stout, John L., *looking glass framemaker,*
        cabinetmaker
    D 1820, 1823, 1825, 1828–31, 1833
Stow, John, *turner*
    D 1820, 1825, 1828–31
Stretcher, Joseph, *ornamental painter*
    D 1833
Strieby, William, *cabinetmaker*
    D 1829–31, 1833, 1835/36
Stuart, Henry D., *cabinetmaker*
    D 1837
Stuhl, Joseph, *cabinetmaker*
    D 1835/36
Stull, Joseph, *framemaker*
    D 1840
Stumpkie, Charles, *cabinetmaker*
    D 1837
Stumps, Peter, *turner*
    D 1839–40
Stykes, George, *cabinetmaker*
    D 1825, 1828–31, 1833
Stylen, Charles, *cabinetmaker*
    D 1837
Sugden, J., *cabinetmaker*

    D 1840
Sugden, William, *cabinetmaker*
    D 1833, 1835/36, 1839–40
Summerell [Summervill] & Tyson, *furniture store*
        [proprietors]
    D 1837
        U.S. Gaz., March 31, 1837
Summers, Samuel, *cabinetmaker*
    D 1840
Summerset, Samuel, *cabinetmaker*
    D 1824
Summerville, Paul, *cabinetmaker*
    D 1839
Super, Jacob, *cabinetmaker*
    D 1820
Super, Jane (widow), *cabinetmaker*
    D 1823, 1825, 1829, 1833
Super, William, *cabinetmaker*
    D 1828–29, 1831, 1839–40
Suter, Joseph, *cabinetmaker*
    D 1820
Sutherland, James, *cabinetmaker*
    D 1840
Sutton, William, *cabinetmaker*
    D 1837
        Convict Docket, December 19, 1825
Sweed, Hiram, *cabinetmaker*
    D 1825
Sweet & Binder, *cabinetmakers*
    D 1825
Sweeten, William, *chairmaker*
    D 1820
Sweetzer, Simon, *cabinetmaker*
    D 1828–29
†Swift, William, *piano warehouse [proprietor]*
    D 1833, 1835/36
        U.S. Gaz., December 31, 1832; January 3,
        1833
Swift & Wilson, *pianoforte makers*
    D 1839
Swope, Benjamin, & Swope, Charles, *turners*
    D 1835/36, 1837, 1839–40
Swope, Walter, *turner*
    D 1829–31, 1833

Tage, Benjamin, *cabinetmaker*
    D 1835/36, 1839
Taggert, Robert, *cabinetmaker*
    D 1823
*Tash, Joseph, *cabinetmaker*
    1829 Const., p. 11
†Tatem, Allen, *cabinetmaker*
    D 1839–40

Tatem, Allen W., *chairmaker*
    D 1828–31, 1833, 1835/36, 1837
Tatem, Thomas J., *chairmaker*
    D 1829–31, 1833
Taws, Lewis, *organ builder*
    D 1831, 1833, 1835/36
Taxis, John, *cabinetmaker*
    D 1823, 1829
    Children's Register, August 24, 1825
Taxis, Samuel, *cabinetmaker*
    D 1839–40
Taylor, Benjamin, *chairmaker*
    D 1825
*Taylor, Enoch, *cabinetmaker*
    D 1835/36
    1829 Const., p. 11
Taylor, Francis J., *chairmaker*
    D 1835/36, 1837, 1839–40
Taylor, Malcolm W., *chairmaker*
    D 1840
Taylor, Rachael, *chairmaker*
    D 1822
Taylor, Samuel, *turner*
    D 1835/36
Taylor, William M., *chairmaker*
    D 1837, 1840
Teal, Jacob, *cabinetmaker*
    D 1823
Tees, Christopher, *cabinetmaker*
    D 1835/36
†Tees, Daniel, *spinning wheel and chairmaker*
    D 1820, 1828–29, 1831, 1833, 1835/36
Teil, Jacob, *cabinetmaker*
    D 1825, 1830–31, 1833, 1835/36
Tenbrick, William, *turner*
    D 1837
Teving, Lewis, *cabinetmaker*
    D 1839
Thackara, Benjamin, *cabinetmaker*
    D 1837, 1839–40
Thackery, Benjamin, *cabinetmaker*
    D 1831, 1833
*Theveny, Lewis, *cabinetmaker*
    1829 Const., p. 11
*Thomas, Enoch, *cabinetmaker*
    D 1820, 1822, 1824–25, 1828–31, 1833,
        1835/36
    1829 Const., p. 11
Thomas, Maybin, *cabinetmaker*
    D 1820
Thomas, Paul, *cabinetmaker*
    D 1840
Thomas, Stephen, *turner*

D 1837, 1839–40
Thomas, W. R., *cabinetmaker*
    D 1837
Thomas, William, *cabinetmaker*
    D 1825, 1828–31, 1833, 1835/36
Thomasson, Augustus, *chair painter*
    D 1835/36, 1837
Thompson, Alexander, *cabinetmaker*
    D 1820, 1825, 1829–31, 1833, 1835/36, 1837,
        1839–40
Thompson, Augustus, *cabinetmaker*
    D 1837
†Thompson, Benjamin, *cabinetmaker*
    D 1820, 1822, 1825, 1828–31, 1833, 1835/36,
        1837, 1839
    Girard Papers, reel 203, April 29, 1826
    HSP Indentures, April 14, 1831
Thompson, James, *cabinetmaker*
    D 1820, 1825
Thompson, John, *turner*
    D 1828–31, 1833, 1835/36, 1839–40
*Thompson, John G., *cabinetmaker*
    D 1835/36
    1829 Const., p. 12
Thompson, Mark, *cabinetmaker*
    D 1839–40
*Thompson, Moore, *cabinetmaker*
    Misc. bk. 3, pp. 658–65
Thorn, Richard, *turner*
    D 1837
Thorn, Thomas, *cabinetmaker*
    D 1837
Thorn, Thomas B., *cabinetmaker*
    D 1837
Thorne, Michael, *cabinetmaker*
    D 1840
*Tiel, Jacob, *cabinetmaker*
    D 1829, 1839–40
    1829 Const., p. 11
*Till, William, *cabinetmaker*
    D 1830–31, 1833
    1829 Const., p. 12
Timewell, William, *cabinetmaker and upholsterer*
    D 1835/36, 1837
Timmins, Silas, *cabinetmaker*
    D 1840
Tinewell, John, *cabinetmaker*
    D 1840
Tinewell, William, *cabinetmaker*
    D 1833
Tittermary, Robert, *cabinetmaker*
    D 1829–30, 1835/36, 1839–40
Toby, William, *turner*

D 1829, 1831, 1833
Todd, William, *turner*
    D 1830, 1835/36, 1839
†Tomlin, Enoch, *chairmaker, furniture warehouse*
    [*proprietor*]
    D 1823, 1825, 1828–31, 1833, 1835/36, 1837,
      1840
    Mayor's Court, January 6, January 15, 1825
    Indenture Papers, April 21, 1828
    Girard Papers, reel 202, June 19, 1824; reel
      210, June 22, 1824
Tomlinson, Richard, *looking glass framemaker*
    D 1825
*Tomlinson, Samuel S., *cabinetmaker*
    D 1835/36, 1839–40
    Misc. bk. 3, pp. 658–65
Town, Amos, *chairmaker*
    D 1833, 1835/36, 1837, 1839–40
Town, Benjamin, *chairmaker*
    D 1825, 1828–31, 1833, 1835/36, 1839–40
Townsend, John, *cabinetmaker*
    D 1820, 1825
Tracy, John, *turner*
    D 1828–30
Tracy, Patrick, *cabinetmaker*
    D 1824
Trader, Edward, *cabinetmaker*
    D 1839
Traechal [Treichel], George, *chairmaker*
    D 1823, 1825
Trapnell, Edward, *chairmaker*
    Men's Register, October 4, 1831
Tripp, John, *curled-hair manufacturer*
    D 1825
Trotter, William, *cabinetmaker*
    D 1823, 1825
Trotter, William, *cabinetmaker*
    D 1820
Trueman, Ephraim, *cabinetmaker*
    D 1825
Truman, Abraham, *cabinetmaker*
    D 1837
*Truman, Evan, *cabinetmaker*
    D 1824, 1829, 1831
    Misc. bk. 3, pp. 658–65
    1829 Const., p. 11
Tuller, Henry, *turner*
    D 1837
Tungardrecas, C., *pianoforte maker*
    D 1840
Turnbull, Alexander, *cabinetmaker*
    D 1820, 1833
Turnbull, George, *cabinetmaker*

D 1837, 1839–40
Turner, George, *chairmaker*
    D 1823, 1825, 1830–31, 1833, 1835/36, 1837,
      1839–40
Turner, Henry, *chairmaker*
    D 1829–31, 1833, 1835/36, 1840
Tweese, Daniel, *chairmaker, cabinetmaker*
    D 1829–31, 1833
Tyler, Charles, *cabinetmaker*
    D 1840
Tyson, James, *turner*
    D 1831, 1833

Ulmstead, David, *turner*
    D 1829, 1831, 1833
Umpleby, John, *sacking bottom manufacturer*
    D 1820, 1823
Underwood, John, Jr., *looking glass framemaker*
    D 1829, 1831, 1833, 1835/36, 1837, 1839–40

Valdez, John, *cabinetmaker*
    D 1839–40
Vallance, John H., *cabinetmaker*
    D 1840
*Vanaken, George, *cabinetmaker*
    D 1835/36, 1839–40
    1829 Const., p. 12
Vanaken, William, *cabinetmaker*
    D 1829–31, 1833, 1835/36, 1837, 1839–40
    Mechanics' Free Press, October 18, 1834
    Poulson's Advertiser, July 13, 1830
    U.S. Gaz., February 27, 1837
Van Brakle, Samuel, *cabinetmaker*
    D 1820, 1823, 1825, 1828–31, 1833, 1837,
      1839–40
Van Brakle & Davis, *cabinetmakers*
    D 1825, 1828–29
Vanbuskirk, Benjamin, *chairmaker*
    D 1837
Van Griffith, William, *cabinetmaker*
    D 1824
Vanhorn, Nathaniel, *windsor chairmaker*
    D 1820, 1823
Vannatta, James W., *cabinetmaker*
    D 1833
Vannosten, Edward, *fancy chairmaker*
    D 1823
*Vantilbergh, John, *cabinetmaker*
    1829 Const., p. 12
Veit, Clemens, *framemaker*
    D 1839–40
Verner, Robert, *framemaker*
    D 1835/36

Vernhes, J. V., *curled-hair manufacturer*
    D 1833
Viau, Benjamin, *cabinetmaker*
    D 1820
Vogelsang, Daniel, *cabinetmaker*
    D 1820, 1823
Vogle, John, *cabinetmaker*
    D 1839
Vonnieman & Garman, *cabinetmakers*
    D 1840

Waer, Thomas, *chairmaker*
    D 1840
Wagner, Otto, *cabinetmaker*
    Men's Register, February 27, 1833
Walker, Edward, *turner*
    D 1820
Walker, John, *cabinetmaker*
    D 1835/36, 1837, 1839
*Walker, Lewis, *cabinetmaker*
    1829 Const., p. 12
Wall, George, *chairmaker*
    D 1824–25, 1828–29
†Wall, John, *chairmaker*
    D 1820–21, 1824–25, 1828–31, 1833,
        1835/36
    Girard Papers, reel 202, October 20, 1824
Wall, Richard, *chairmaker, bellowsmaker*
    D 1820, 1823, 1825, 1828–29, 1835/36
Wallace, Thomas, *chairmaker*
    D 1823, 1831, 1833
Wallens, Jacob F., *cabinetmaker*
    D 1840
†Waln, John, *chairmaker*
    D 1829–31, 1833
Walpool, Thomas, *cabinetmaker*
    D 1829, 1831, 1833
Walraven, Joseph, *cabinetmaker*
    D 1825, 1828–31, 1833, 1835/36, 1839–40
    Mayor's Court, March 30, 1833
    Indenture Papers, August 22, 1831
Walton, Benjamin, *cabinetmaker*
    D 1823
Walton, Boaz, *cabinetmaker*
    D 1820, 1825, 1828–31, 1833, 1835/36, 1837,
        1839–40
Walton, Daniel, *looking glass framemaker*
    D 1820, 1825, 1828
Walton, George H., *cabinetmaker, framemaker*
    D 1837, 1840
Walton, Jeremiah, *cabinetmaker*
    D 1820, 1823, 1829–31, 1833, 1835/36, 1837,
        1839–40

Walton, John, *cabinetmaker*
    D 1822
Walton, Samuel, *cabinetmaker*
    Inventory, November 22, 1823, DMMC
Walton & Stout, *looking glass framemakers*
    D 1820
Ware, Thomas, *chairmaker*
    D 1823, 1829–31, 1833
Ware, William, *cabinetmaker*
    D 1820
Warner, Michael, *cabinetmaker*
    D 1820
Warner, William, *chairmaker*
    D 1835/36
Warner, William W., *chairmaker*
    D 1839
Warnick, Charles, *cabinetmaker*
    D 1829–31, 1833, 1835/36
Warnock [Warnick], Albert, *chairmaker*
    D 1823, 1828–31, 1833
    Men's Register, December 25, 1825
Warren, J. W., *cabinetmaker*
    D 1839
Warren, Michael, *cabinetmaker*
    D 1825
Warren, Philip, *cabinetmaker*
    D 1821–22, 1825, 1828–31, 1833
Warren, Philip, *cabinetmaker*
    D 1835/36
Warren, Philip, *cabinetmaker*
    D 1835/36, 1837, 1839
Warren, William J., *cabinetmaker*
    D 1835/36, 1839–40
    Pa. Inquirer, January 9, 1838
*Warwick, Edward, *pianoforte maker*
    D 1837
    1829 Const., p. 12
Waters, Daniel, *turner*
    D 1837, 1840
Watkins, M., *cabinet warerooms [proprietor]*
    U.S. Gaz., January 7, 1835
*Watkins, W., *cabinetmaker*
    Misc. bk. 3, pp. 658–65
Watson, Brock, *cabinetmaker*
    D 1840
Watson, F., *cabinetmaker*
    D 1835/36
†Watson, James, *cabinetmaker*
    D 1828–31, 1833, 1835/36, 1837, 1839–40
Watson, Samuel, *cabinetmaker*
    D 1825, 1828–31, 1833
Wayne, Caleb P., *looking glass and fancy store
        [proprietor]*

D 1820, 1828–29, 1833, 1835/36, 1840
Wayne, Jacob, *cabinetmaker*
    D 1820, 1823, 1825, 1828–31, 1833, 1835/36,
      1837
    Indenture Bk., June 21, 1824
Wayne, Samuel, *cabinetmaker*
    D 1828–31, 1833, 1835/36, 1837, 1839–40
Weaver, Christian H., *pianoforte maker*
    D 1839
Weaver, David, *cabinetmaker*
    Men's Register, May 15, 1839
Weaver, Isaac, *cabinetmaker*
    D 1839
Webb, A., *cabinetmaker*
    D 1837, 1839–40
Webb, John, *cabinetmaker*
    D 1840
Weber, Christian, *pianoforte maker*
    D 1840
Webster, William K., *cabinetmaker*
    D 1837, 1840
Wehrung, Nicholas, *cabinetmaker*
    D 1840
Weingartner, Jonathan, *cabinetmaker*
    D 1837, 1839
Weir, John, *chairmaker*
    D 1829–31, 1833, 1835/36
*Welch, George, *cabinetmaker*
    Misc. bk. 3, pp. 658–65
Welch, James H., *chairmaker*
    D 1823
Welden, Alexander, *framemaker*
    D 1837, 1839–40
Wells, James, *turner*
    Men's Register, July 1, 1833
Welsh, George, *cabinetmaker*
    D 1831, 1833, 1837, 1840
†Welsh, John, *cabinetmaker*
    D 1829–31, 1833
Wenzell, Samuel, *cabinetmaker*
    Mechanics' Free Press, October 18, 1834
    Pennsylvanian, March 30, 1833
Wenzell, S., & Wenzell, A., *cabinetmakers*
    D 1833
Werner, N. J., *pianoforte maker*
    D 1831, 1833
*West, Edward F., *cabinetmaker*
    D 1830–31, 1833
    1829 Const., p. 11
West, Edward J., *cabinetmaker*
    D 1828–29
†West, Robert, *cabinet- and sofamaker*
    D 1820, 1823–25, 1828–30
    Girard Papers, reel 210, January 2, 1821

    1820 Census, no. 533
    U.S. Gaz., March 29, 1830
    Wills, no. 133 (1871)
Weygant, Charles, *cabinetmaker*
    D 1835/36
Weymer, John, *cabinetmaker*
    D 1820
Wheaton, Amos, *chairmaker*
    D 1825, 1829–31, 1833
Wheeler, B[altis], *chairmaker*
    D 1829–31, 1833, 1835/36, 1837, 1839–40
Whitaker, James, *fancy chairmaker*
    D 1820
†White, Charles H., *cabinet- and chairmaker*
    D 1820, 1823–25, 1828–31, 1833, 1835/36,
      1837, 1839–40
    Unger Coll., February 26, 1830
    Mayor's Court, January 5, 1828; July 16,
      1836
    Poulson's Advertiser, January 2, 1823; Sep-
      tember 4, 1825
    U.S. Gaz., November 16, 1826
White, Francis, *cabinetmaker*
    D 1829–31, 1833
White, George, *chairmaker*
    D 1835/36, 1839–40
White, James, *cabinetmaker*
    Franklin Gaz., June 9, 1824
†White, John, *chairmaker*
    D 1823, 1829–31, 1833, 1840
    Franklin Gaz., June 9, 1824
White, John, *fancy painter*
    D 1825, 1830
†White, John F., *cabinet warerooms [proprietor]*
    D 1835/36, 1837, 1839
White, Joseph, *cabinetmaker*
    D 1829–31, 1833, 1839–40
    Men's Register, December 14, 1836
    Indenture Papers, November 29, 1830
    Children's Register, November 29, 1830
White, Richard, *chair painter*
    D 1835/36
White, William, *cabinetmaker*
    D 1840
White & Blummer, *turners*
    D 1828–31, 1833
White, C. H., & White, J. F., *cabinetmakers*
    D 1839–40
    Mayor's Court, July 16, 1836
Whitecar, Thomas, *chairmaker*
    D 1823–24
†Whitecar, Thomas, *cabinetmaker and mahogany
    dealer*
    D 1820

1820 Census, no. 527
Wills, no. 117 (1822)
*Whiteman, Richard C., *cabinetmaker*
1829 Const., p. 12
Whiteman, Windell, *turner*
D 1820
Wier, John, *chairmaker*
Men's Register, July 18, 1829
Wiggant, Charles, *cabinetmaker*
D 1833
Wildes, Joseph, *fancy chairmaker*
D 1823
Wile, George, *cabinetmaker*
D 1820, 1828–31, 1833, 1835/36, 1837,
1839–40
Wilhelm, Frederick, *cabinetmaker*
D 1820
†Wilkins, Jacob F., *cabinetmaker*
D 1820, 1822–23, 1825, 1828–31, 1833,
1835/36
Indenture of Silas Wilson, July 19, 1829,
DMMC
Mayor's Court, March 26, 1831
Wilkins, John, *cabinetmaker*
D 1820
Wilkins, Peter, *cabinetmaker*
D 1839
Wilkinson, James P., *framemaker*
D 1839–40
Wilkinson, John, *cabinetmaker*
D 1840
Wilkinson, Thomas, *chairmaker*
D 1828–30
Williams, James W., *ornamental painter*
D 1825, 1830, 1833
Williams, John, *cabinetmaker*
D 1839–40
*Williams, Lewis, *cabinetmaker*
1829 Const., p. 12
Williams, Mordecai, *cabinetmaker*
D 1833
*Williams, Reynear, *cabinetmaker*
D 1830–31, 1833, 1835/36
Unger Coll., November 24, 1840
Public Ledger, May 15, 1838
1829 Const., p. 12
Williams, Ryman, *cabinetmaker*
D 1840
Williams, Thomas, *chairmaker*
D 1820, 1823, 1829–31, 1833
Williams, Thomas, *cabinetmaker*
D 1825, 1828
Williams, Thomas R., *cabinetmaker*
D 1829–31, 1833

Williams, William, *cabinetmaker*
D 1829–31, 1833
Williams, H., & Williams, T. R., *cabinetmakers*
D 1820, 1822–23, 1825
Williamson, William, *turner*
Men's Register, September 16, 1831
Willis, M., *turner*
D 1823, 1829–31, 1833
Willis, Soloman, *turner*
D 1820
Willis, William, *chairmaker*
D 1823
Willis & Halverson, *cabinetmakers*
D 1823
Wilmer, Solomon, *turner*
D 1835/36
Wilson, Benjamin, *cabinetmaker*
D 1823
Wilson, Benjamin, *cabinetmaker*
D 1825, 1828–31, 1833, 1835/36
Wilson, Benjamin, *cabinetmaker*
D 1835
Wilson, J. P., *pianoforte maker*
D 1837
Wilson, J. P., *framemaker*
D 1837
Wilson, Jacob F., *cabinetmaker*
D 1820
Wilson, James, *cabinetmaker*
D 1820, 1823
Wilson, John, *cabinetmaker*
D 1839–40
Wilson, Samuel, *pianoforte maker*
D 1831, 1833
Wilson, Samuel, *cabinetmaker*
D 1833
Wilson & Leeds, *chairmakers*
D 1835/36
Wilson & Wilkins, *cabinetmakers*
D 1820–21
Wiltse, Benjamin, *cabinetmaker*
D 1820
Wimer, John, *cabinetmaker*
D 1820
Windle, William, *cabinetmaker*
D 1835/36
Winnemore, Andrew, *cabinetmaker*
D 1820
Winner, Joseph, *turner*
D 1839–40
Winner, Richard, *chairmaker*
Men's Register, May 24, 1834
Wintable, George, *chairmaker*
D 1829–31, 1833

Winter, Abraham, *cabinetmaker*
  D 1823
Winters, Abraham C., *cabinetmaker*
  D 1837
Winters, Anthony, *framemaker*
  D 1837, 1839
Wire, John, *chairmaker*
  D 1830–31, 1833
Wise, John, *cabinetmaker*
  D 1835/36, 1837
  Men's Register, September 15, 1838
Wiseman, John, *framemaker*
  D 1837
Wissinger, William, *chairmaker*
  D 1831, 1833, 1839
Wissinger, William, & Wissinger, Thomas,
    chairmakers
  D 1830, 1835/36
Witham, Thomas, *cabinetmaker*
  D 1825, 1829–31, 1833
Wohlien, William, *pianoforte maker*
  D 1835/36, 1837
Wolf, John F., *cabinetmaker*
  D 1829–31, 1833, 1839–40
Wolka, Charles, *cabinetmaker*
  Men's Register, April 25, 1835
Wolverton, Jacob, *cabinetmaker*
  D 1829–31, 1833
Wood, –, *cabinetmaker*
  D 1820
Wood, E. L., *cabinetmaker*
  D 1839
*Wood, Edward, *cabinetmaker*
  D 1837
  1829 Const., p. 12
Wood, Edward G., *cabinetmaker*
  D 1839–40
Wood, George C., *framemaker*
  D 1824
*Wood, Isaac, *cabinetmaker*
  D 1825, 1828–31, 1833, 1837, 1839–40
  Freeman's Jnl., April 5, 1825
  1829 Const., p. 11
Wood, John, *chairmaker*
  D 1840
Wood, Richard G., *chairmaker*
  D 1839
Wood, Thomas, *cabinetmaker*
  D 1837, 1839–40
Wood, William, *cabinetmaker*
  D 1829–31, 1833, 1835/36, 1839–40
Wood, William, *cabinetmaker*
  D 1837
Wood & Lukens, *cabinetmakers*

  D 1823
*Woodly, William, *cabinetmaker*
  1829 Const., p. 12
Woods, Richard, *chairmaker*
  D 1840
Woodside, John A., *ornamental painter*
  D 1825, 1828–31, 1833, 1835/36
*Woodside, Robert, *cabinetmaker*
  Misc. bk. 3, pp. 658–65
Worn, John, *cabinetmaker*
  D 1825, 1828
Worn & Shourds, *cabinetmakers*
  D 1824
Worrell, George, *pianoforte maker*
  D 1840
Worrell, George P., *cabinetmaker*
  D 1837
Wrame, Edward, *pianoforte maker*
  D 1840
Wright, Morris, *cabinetmaker*
  D 1839–40
Wright, William, *cabinetmaker*
  D 1823, 1825, 1828–31, 1833, 1835/36, 1837

†Yard, John, *cabinetmaker*
  D 1820, 1823, 1828–31, 1833, 1835/36
  U.S. Gaz., May 28, 1833
Yempee, Joseph, *cabinetmaker*
  Men's Register, May 21, 1835
Young, Daniel, *glass and furniture store*
    [proprietor]
  D 1820
Young, George, *chairmaker*
  D 1839
Young, James, *cabinetmaker*
  D 1833, 1835/36, 1837, 1839–40
Young, Jeremiah, *cabinetmaker*
  D 1820, 1822–23, 1825, 1828
  Wills, no. 78 (1827)
Young, Lewis, *cabinetmaker*
  D 1820, 1823
Young, Samuel, *cabinetmaker*
  D 1835/36
Young, Warren L., *chairmaker*
  D 1839
Young & Altmeyer, *cabinetmakers*
  D 1839

Zantzinger, Samuel F., *cabinetmaker*
  D 1839
Zeigler, Benjamin, *cabinetmaker*
  D 1837
Zipperer, John, *cabinetmaker*
  D 1839

Furnishing an Eighteenth-Century Tavern for Twentieth-Century Use

Constance V. Hershey

PHILADELPHIA'S "CONVENIENT AND elegant" City Tavern (fig. 1) flourished from 1774 to about 1800 as the most important public house in the most important city in North America.[1] Not simply a tavern, not solely a business exchange, not precisely a gentlemen's club, it was all three—and a concert hall and a ballroom as well. It also provided the model for a cluster of other establishments in the new nation, some of which acknowledged their indebtedness by borrowing its name.

In 1774 the new tavern had welcomed delegates to the First Continental Congress. For the next twenty-five years it was the city's unofficial center for the dissemination of news and the scene of many of the capital's parties and balls. The tavern remained the most important gathering place for Philadelphia's merchants and businessmen during the first decades of the nineteenth century, although many social events were held at newer and more fashionable establishments.

A quarter century ago, the National Park Service (NPS) began acquiring the land that would become Independence National Historical Park and making plans for the preservation, restoration, or reconstruction of historically significant structures. Within the new park's bounds had stood the City Tavern, which had been razed in the middle of the nineteenth century.

Reconstruction of the tavern would permit interpretation of an aspect of life that legislative halls such as the State House could not. Accordingly, plans were made for its inclusion in the park, and much of the research that made re-

construction possible was then conducted. Not until twenty years had passed did the NPS historians, historical architects, and curators receive the directive to begin preparing for actual reconstruction. But by the 1970s the concept of reconstructing demolished buildings was viewed with much less favor than it had been in 1950, and to the NPS team the reconstruction of a lively tavern in the form of an inanimate "house museum" seemed particularly inappropriate. Penelope H. Batcheler, the historical architect, voiced these reservations and suggested an alternative approach:

As a participation structure, the reconstruction of City Tavern is a valid project. But there are many who feel that our world has enough extant 18th century structures which need our undivided attention without diluting our efforts by adding a reconstruction to our maintenance schedules. I have much sympathy for this viewpoint. The National Park Service has suffered enough from imposed acceptance of structures which receive one-time injections of restoration money and inadequate funds for maintenance. But if City Tavern can absorb the activities which will allow free use of the reconstruction and its reproduction furnishings, it will in many ways serve to satisfy the visitor's need to be "in" a room and to "live" the 18th century for a short time. I believe this to be the overriding argument for the reconstruction.[2]

To reach the goal, the reconstructed building would have to encourage sensory involvement with the past, beyond that achieved by the park's other historic structures. Although this principle was accepted in theory, it proved difficult to up-

---

[1]*Pennsylvania Journal and the Weekly Advertiser* (August 11, 1773).

[2]Penelope H. Batcheler, "Historic Structure Report, Architectural Data Section, City Tavern, Independence National Historical Park," typescript (National Park Service, Denver Service Center, 1973), pp. 5–6.

Fig. 1. The City Tavern in 1800. Detail from William Birch, *Bank of Pennsylvania, South Second Street, Philadelphia*. Engraving; H. 14½″, W. 18″. (National Park Service.)

hold. At every step, past customs conflicted with present codes or conventions. For example, dogs and flies, the constant companions of eighteenth-century diners, are unacceptable in today's restaurants. But can one reconstruct an eighteenth-century tavern without them?

The countless instances in which twentieth-century requirements made the recreation of the eighteenth-century tavern difficult prompted the NPS team to evolve what may be called the principle of minimal intrusion: If you cannot duplicate another era, aim to approximate its effect, and, at the very least, keep the present from thrusting itself between the visitor and the past.

Fortunately, the past was sufficiently documented to provide a stable framework for both the refurnishing and reuse of the tavern. When examined, the documentation supports a few conclusions. Philadelphia's City Tavern, conceived for the benefit of the public as well as the merchants, was designed to be a meeting place, ballroom, and bourse more than a post station, hotel, or bar. It was furnished in the style of a London club or tavern and had a reputation for gentility and sophistication. And, within the quarter century that marked its period of greatest activity, it was redecorated several times with a combination of Philadelphia-made and imported English articles.

In August 1773, as the construction was nearing completion, the new property was first advertised:

To be lett, THE CITY TAVERN, Situate in one of the principal Streets, near the Center of the Town.——It has been built, at a great expence, by a number of gentlemen, and is the most convenient and elegant structure of its Kind in America: the front is fifty-one feet and forty-six feet in depth; the rooms are spacious, and the ceilings lofty. As the Proprietors have built this tavern without any view of profit, but merely for the convenience and credit of the city, the terms will, of consequence, be made easy to the tenant: The extensiveness of the undertaking, in superintending so capital a tavern as this is proposed to be, require some stock before hand, as well as an active, obliging desposition: A person so qualified, it is imagined, will find it in his interest to engage in it. The house is nearly finished, and may be entered into the First of September.[3]

The advertisement, perhaps with some exaggeration, presented the property attractively, dispelling the image (had it been in the reader's mind) of a rustic post station or cellar grogshop. The proprietors were quite specific; they had a substantial investment and wanted an experienced man to manage it. They found such a man in Daniel Smith, the City Tavern's first innkeeper.

Smith opened the tavern early in 1774 with the announcement that he had "completely furnished it, and at a *very great expense* . . . laid in every article of the first quality perfectly in the style of a London Tavern . . . fitted up several elegant bedrooms detached from noise . . . and fitted up a genteel Coffee Room well attended and properly supplied with English and American papers and magazines." He concluded by reminding the public that "the *City Tavern* in Philadelphia was erected at a great expense by a voluntary subscription of the principal gentlemen of the city for the convenience of the public, and is by much the largest and most elegant house occupied in that way in America."[4]

The validity of Smith's claim to be able to reproduce a successful London tavern in Philadelphia is substantiated by what is known of his life. A native of Ireland, he came to America as an adult and lived in the colonies for six years before moving to Philadelphia. Possibly he had prior firsthand knowledge of a London tavern. The in-

[3]*Pennsylvania Journal and the Weekly Advertiser* (August 11, 1773).
[4]*Dunlap's Pennsylvania Packet, or the General Advertiser* (February 14, 1774).

ference is strengthened by the fact that on his return to Europe in 1778 he settled near London and opened an inn rather than return to Ireland.[5] Undoubtedly, he could have learned "the London style" in another provincial city, but no record of his earlier residence has been found.

Smith advertised the tavern only once. The absence of any but specific announcements, like those posting the hour of a dinner meeting or admonishing against aiding a fugitive servant, suggest that the merits of the City Tavern spoke for themselves. Contemporaries soon referred to the tavern casually as "Smith's." It became Philadelphia's most fashionable public house and received the approbation of residents and visitors. The provincial capital's benevolent organizations adopted it for their meetings, numerous "dinner clubs" met in its private dining rooms, and the city's Dancing Assembly held weekly balls there.[6]

It was a few months after the building opened that the Long Room on the second floor was put to an unexpected use: "On Friday Evening the Letters brought by the Express from Boston were read to a great Number of respectable inhabitants, convened at the City Tavern. . . . A

Congress of Deputies from the several Colonies is thought to be absolutely necessary, to devise Means of restoring Harmony between Great Britain and the Colonies, and prevent Matters from coming to Extremities."[7] However, matters did come to "extremities," and in September 1774 the First Continental Congress convened in Philadelphia. Some of the arriving delegates were met at the outskirts of the city by numbers of Philadelphians, including members of the First City Troop, and escorted to the City Tavern. John Adams was among them. "[As] dirty, dusty, and fatigued as we were, we could not resist the Importunity to go to the Tavern, the most genteel one in America. . . . Here we had a fresh Welcome to the city of Philadelphia, and after some Time spent in Conversation, a curtain was drawn, and in the other Half of the Chamber a Supper appeared as elegant as ever was laid upon a Table."[8]

The First Continental Congress gave way to the Second; skirmishes gave way to war. In July 1777, according to Adams, the delegates celebrated the first anniversary of the publication of the Declaration of Independence with "festivity and ceremony becoming the occasion. . . . At three we went to dinner, and were very agreeable entertained with excellent company, good cheer, fine music from the band of Hessians taken at Trenton, and continued vollies between every toast, from a company of soldiers drawn up in Second-Street before the city Tavern."[9] The bill for these festivities was $832.47, including "the Expenses of Fire Works."[10]

Because there are no accounts to the contrary, it is probable that Smith, a prudent innkeeper, kept himself out of the debates as much as possible and served his patrons—whatever their opinions—the best way he could in the face of inflation and shortages. After the Battle of Quebec in the fall of 1775, a Colonel Prescott was taken to Philadelphia as a prisoner and placed under house arrest at the City Tavern. When a mob attempted to storm the building and seize

[5] The diary of Loyalist Samuel Shoemaker, former mayor of Philadelphia, provides an unexpected footnote to the account of Smith's career. Shoemaker, in London to press his claim for losses, met "little Smith," who, he wrote, "now keeps a tavern on the road to South Hampton." The two met a second time when the former was traveling by coach and halted at Smith's. "He was extreme glad to see me & pressd me very much to spend a few days there and said it should not cost me a farthing. He keeps a very genteel house indeed to which he has a very fine garden and wished to accommodate me with anything in his power. . . . On our getting into the coach he sent me a quantity of very fine Gooseberrys and currants which were very acceptable to refresh us on the road" (Diary of Samuel Shoemaker, Esq., of Philadelphia, November 7, 1783, to October 5, 1785, p. 432, Historical Society of Pennsylvania, Philadelphia).

[6] "Club dinners," or "supper clubs," were meals provided on a regular basis for a more or less regular number of gentlemen at a standard or group rate. The Annapolis gathering sketched by Dr. Alexander Hamilton and reproduced in his *Itinerarium* (Carl Bridenbaugh, ed., *Gentleman's Progress: The Itinerarium of Dr. Alexander Hamilton, 1744* [Chapel Hill: University of North Carolina Press, 1948]) was a supper club. George Read, delegate to the Continental Congress from Delaware, described a supper club at the City Tavern: "We sit in Congress generally till half-past three o'clock . . . and then dine at the City Tavern, where a few of us have established a table for each day in the week, save Saturday, when there is a general dinner. . . . A dinner is ordered for the number, eight, and whatever is deficient of that number is to be paid for at two shillings and sixpence a head, and each that attends pays only the expense of the day" (Edward Cody Burnett, ed., *Letters of the Members of the Continental Congress*, 8 vols. [Washington, D.C.: Carnegie Institute of Washington, 1921–36], 1:92).

[7] *Pennsylvania Gazette* (May 25, 1774).

[8] John Adams, *Diary and Autobiography of John Adams*, ed. L. H. Butterfield et al., 4 vols. (Cambridge, Mass.: Harvard University Press, Belknap Press, 1961), vol. 2, *Diary 1771–1781*, p. 114.

[9] John Adams to Abigail Adams 2d, July 5, 1777, *Adams Family Correspondence*, ed. L. H. Butterfield, 4 vols. (Cambridge, Mass.: Harvard University Press, Belknap Press, 1963), 2:274–75.

[10] Bill dated August 7, 1777, Journal of Treasury and Audit of Accounts, 1775–81, Record Group 39, National Archives, Washington, D.C.

him, Smith defended his guest and was rewarded by having some chairs broken. According to Smith's later testimony, the event forced him to take a stand that revealed his political convictions; from then on, the rebels of Philadelphia were against him. (His tavern, however, remained a popular gathering spot.) When Sir William Howe captured Philadelphia in September of 1777, Smith signed as a noncombatant who chose to remain in the city. He entertained the royal officers and, when the British troops left in June of 1778, Daniel Smith left with them.

The events during the fall and winter occupation provided Smith an occasion to make changes (and provided the curators with the first concrete evidence concerning specific furnishings of the tavern). On December 11, 1777, the following notice appeared in the *Philadelphia Evening Post:* "To be SOLD by public VENDUE, on Friday next, the twelfth instant, at nine o'clock, all that large and elegant assortment of HOUSEHOLD and KITCHEN furniture, in the CITY TAVERN, among which are feather beds, card tables, bureau tables, desks, chairs, Windsor chairs, window and bed curtains, pictures, table linen, carpets, glass, china and earthen ware, a neat assortment of plate, and irons, shovels, and tongs, open stoves, with sundry other articles too numerous to mention."[11] At first reading, it appears that Smith was closing down operations and converting his assets into cash in preparation for flight. However, in December he could not possibly have expected the debacle of May; the British officers sitting around his tables certainly did not. A December auction in preparation for a future British retreat is unlikely, particularly with the tavern's dining rooms and ballroom filled by a succession of suppers, parties, and dances. Nor, at the other extreme, was the auction a routine affair on the premises, for not until near the end of its long career did the tavern become an auction house. The most likely and consistent explanation is that Smith, far from pessimistic about the British success, was inspired by the frantic spirit of the occupied city. Departing from the practice of gradual replacement, he was clearing the tavern to decorate it in the latest style and make it a suitable and appealing resort for his English clientele. A letter from Rebecca Frank to Mrs. William Paca, dated February 26, 1778, corroborates the supposition. "You can have no idea

of the life of continued amusement I live in. I can scarce have a moment to myself. I have stole this while everybody is retired to dress for dinner. I am but just come from under Mr. J. Black's hands and most elegantly am I dressed for a ball this evening at Smith's where we have one every Thursday. You would not Know the room 'tis so much improv'd."[12]

Politically and militarily, matters did not proceed quite as Smith (and certainly not as Howe) had anticipated. In June the British troops withdrew, taking about 3,000 Philadelphians with them. Smith joined the flight, taking only what he could carry and leaving behind "the value of Eighteen Hundred pounds in effects."[13]

The tavern's fortunes rose and fell as the war progressed. Several innkeepers succeeded one another, and assembly balls and official banquets provided the only notices in the press. Then, at the end of the war, on July 23, 1783, the *Pennsylvania Packet* carried the following announcement:

Household Furniture for Sale
TO BE SOLD
At the City-tavern on thursday the 24th instant. by Public Auction, at nine o'clock in the morning, sundry Household and Kitchen Furniture; consisting of Tables, Chairs, Beds and Bedsteads, a variety of Tea and Table China, Tea spoons, Glasses and Decanters, Dessert and Jelly Glasses and Glass pyramids, an excellent large Jack compleat, a number of And-Irons, Shovels and tongs, Knives and Forks, Kettles, Candlesticks, Pewter, Pots &c, &c.

Although the advertisement did not specify that the sundry pieces were furnishings of the City Tavern, none of the objects listed are impossible tavern furnishings, and many, like the glasswares, are more likely to have been in a tavern than in a private home. The sale did not occur at a change of either managers or owners, so it may have been part of an effort to replace articles grown shabby after years of use.[14]

[11]*Pennsylvania Evening Post* (December 11, 1777).

[12]Rebecca Franks to Mrs. William Paca, February 26, 1778, as cited in Henry J. Thompson, ed., "A Letter of Miss Rebecca Franks, 1778," *Pennsylvania Magazine of History and Biography* 16, no. 2 (1892): 216.
[13]Petition of Daniel Smith late of Philadelphia, but now resident in London, Claims, American Loyalists, ser. 1 (1776–1831), 146 vols., Exchequer and Audit Department, vol. 102, fols. 82, 83, Public Record Office, London.
[14]A comparison of the 1783 list with the inventories of about a dozen other large taverns has indicated that none of the items listed in the advertisement is an unexpected tavern furnishing. Items such as the "Dessert and Jelly Glasses and Glass pyramids" augmented the generalizations in the 1777 list. *Pennsylvania Packet* (July 19, 1783).

The war's end brought increased prosperity to the city and the City Tavern. In 1785 the tavern acquired a new owner and a new innkeeper, Edward Moyston, who advertised in late April that he had "laid in a supply of liquors of the first quality" and had "engaged English and French cooks of approved abilities."[15] Formerly the steward of Robert Morris's household, Moyston had a sharp sense of how to run a fashionable tavern, and there is no doubt that he used to advantage his acquaintance with the prominent men he had met under Morris's roof.[16]

Moyston was probably the City Tavern's most accomplished innkeeper; he was certainly its best manager, and it was he who presided over its alteration from gentlemen's club to businessmen's club. In 1786, he established an ordinary, "dinner to be on the table precisely at 2 o'clock."[17] He annexed the small adjoining building to provide additional chambers and added stables to accommodate horses. But his most brilliant innovation was the creation of the "Merchants' Coffee-House and Place of Exchange," to which ship captains, merchants, and "other Gentlemen" could subscribe. Although merchants conducted their business out-of-doors in other American cities, Moyston persuaded Philadelphia merchants to move their negotiations indoors to the City Tavern. He reserved the two rooms fronting on Second Street for the subscribers at specified times of the day. Members observed regular exchange hours for buying and selling goods, posted notices of shipments to be bought or sold, and perused the bound books of public newspapers that were kept at the bar (kept there because they were secure from removal except with the knowledge of the barkeeper).

Although newer hotels, restaurants, and theaters had gradually captured the social audience, the City Tavern's hold on the businessmen grew even stronger, until the membership of the coffeehouse and exchange became too numerous for the small, old-fashioned quarters. The subscribers raised the funds for a new merchants' exchange, designed by William Strickland and erected a block west of the tavern in 1832. The tavern lingered as an auction house, a boardinghouse, and then a collection of offices. When it was finally pulled down in 1854, its passing was termed the "Demolition of a Relic of Olden Time . . . to make room for a splendid improvement."[18]

The comments of contemporaries shed more light upon the tavern's atmosphere than upon its physical appearance. Reconstruction required more specific information, and for this the NPS team turned to specialized documents such as the 1773 insurance survey and generalized records such as cartoons. The information from these was combined with data in the NPS files in an effort to achieve an accurate reconstruction.

Pictorial materials revealed that the Second Street brick facade was high and rather severe, relieved only by central marble steps that rose to the pedimented door. The exterior elaboration was focused on the entrance. The insurance survey, made when the completed building was unfurnished, mentions a "frontespiece," and the single brief account sheet kept by Gen. John Cadwalader, who disbursed funds in the name of the subscribers, contains the entry, "Bill of Carving. 5.12.16," paid to Martin Jugiez.[19] Jugiez carved some of the city's finest woodwork, including elements of Cadwalader's own townhouse. Because the amount is comparatively modest, the NPS architects concluded that Jugiez's work had not been extensive. It suggested that a carved and molded frontispiece was a likely treatment for the new City Tavern, and they detailed a door and frontispiece based on designs in James Gibbs's 1728 *Book of Architecture* and on several Philadelphia buildings. Other details of construction and finishing, when unspecified by the survey, were duplicates of elements of comparable age, elaboration, and scale in Philadelphia (fig. 2).

The building's interior arrangement, as described in the insurance survey, was straightforward: a central hall, flanked by four rooms on the basement and main floors, three on the second, and five on the third (figs. 3, 4, 5). A staircase that rose from the middle of the main hall ascended to the rear of the second and third floors. Doors connected the dining rooms on both the main and second floors. In the new City Tavern, these are augmented by doors on two floors between the main building and the reconstructed annex to the south.

[15] Ibid. (August 27, 1785).

[16] "The enclosed is to Edward (I do not know his Surname) who formerly lived with Mr. R. Morris, but now, I am informed, keeps the City Tavern, to see if he can be instrumental in procuring me a House Keeper" (George Washington to Clement Biddle, August 17, 1785, Clement Biddle Papers, Historical Society of Pennsylvania).

[17] *Pennsylvania Packet* (June 14, 1786).

[18] Unidentified newspaper clipping dated January 1854, Poulson Scrapbooks, Free Library of Philadelphia, 7:95.

[19] Gen. John Cadwalader Section, Cadwalader Papers, Historical Society of Pennsylvania.

Fig. 2. East facade (Second Street) of the reconstructed City Tavern in 1975. The adjoining building, annexed in 1786, was reconstructed to provide service facilities. (National Park Service.)

The secondary entrance, from the innyard, had a two-story balustraded porch which was probably one of the crowded building's more welcome features. The porch masked deliveries to the basement kitchens and provided a sheltered entrance to the main hall. Moreover, its roof, accessible from one of the second-floor private dining rooms, afforded a balcony that allowed guests to take the air during balls and concerts (fig. 6). Nowhere were the details of the porch described, so the balusters and rails on both levels of the porch were copied from those that had been used at Port Royal, Edward Stiles's home built in Frankford, north of Philadelphia, in 1770.

Acting on the official recommendations from the park's professional staff, the administration had agreed that the tavern should be constructed to house a functioning restaurant despite the ways in which its presence would complicate the reconstruction.[20] Initially, the most obvious prob-

lems were those of the architects. The building's interior would have to look like one century but be workable in another. The NPS architect and the firm responsible for the construction worked in a tedious problem-by-problem, baluster-by-cornice effort to limit the number of modern encroachments without rendering the structure incapable of functioning. The government determined to offer the restaurant's operation to a concessionaire rather than operate the facility with its own personnel. Yet the restaurant planning staff would not enter the picture until the structure was nearly complete, so the architects were forced to anticipate the concessionaire's needs in lighting, plumbing, ventilation, access—while conforming to the confinements of an eighteenth-century structure within a historic area. Recognizing that they would be forcing the restaurateur to live with their decisions, the park architects agonized over every question. There were instances in which one century clearly won over the other. Much of the modern kitchen equipment was special-ordered and shipped in pieces for assembly after it had passed between the building's narrow eighteenth-century door frames. And, despite the principle of minimal intrusion, the bar was visibly equipped with a mod-

[20]Four reports were submitted to the NPS administration: Miriam Q. Blimm, "Historic Structure Report, City Tavern, Historical Data, Part I" (1962); Penelope H. Batcheler, "Historic Structure Report, Architectural Data Section, City Tavern" (1973); John D. R. Platt, "Historic Resource Study, City Tavern" (1973); Constance V. Hershey, "Historic Furnishings Plan, City Tavern" (1974).

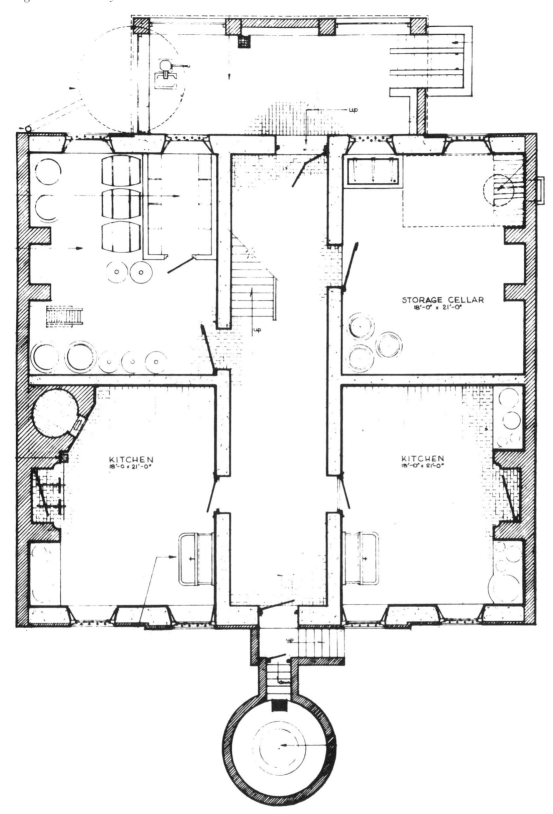

Fig. 3. Cellar plan of the City Tavern as originally constructed. Accessories are placed according to documentation or conventional usage. (National Park Service.)

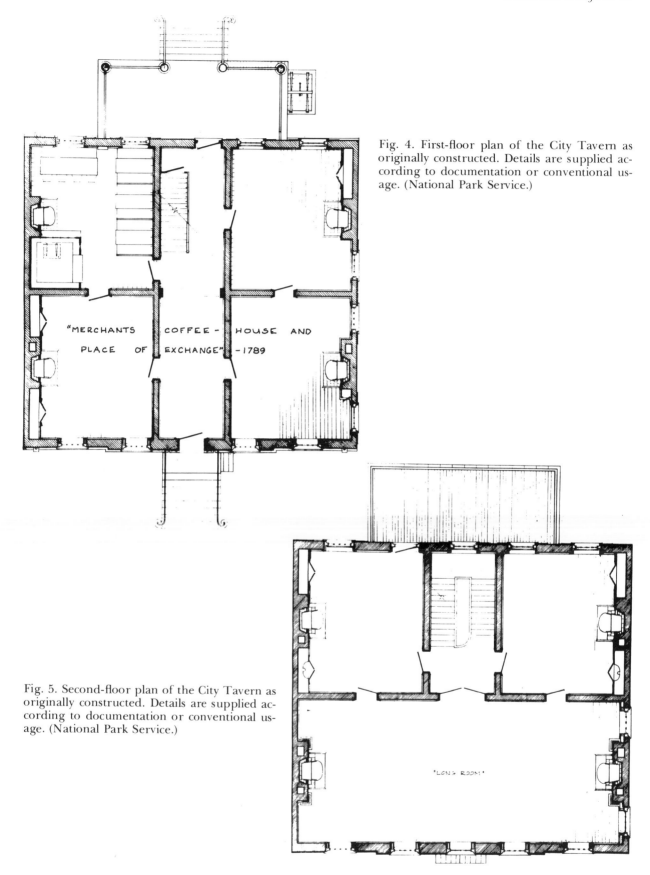

Fig. 4. First-floor plan of the City Tavern as originally constructed. Details are supplied according to documentation or conventional usage. (National Park Service.)

"MERCHANTS COFFEE-HOUSE AND PLACE OF EXCHANGE" -1789

Fig. 5. Second-floor plan of the City Tavern as originally constructed. Details are supplied according to documentation or conventional usage. (National Park Service.)

"LONG ROOM"

Fig. 6. Side elevation of the City Tavern as originally constructed. Details are supplied according to documentation or conventional usage. (National Park Service.)

ern sink, modern liquor bottles, and, ultimately, a modern cash register.

In their attempts to reconstruct a workable version of the City Tavern, the curators and architects confronted many problems jointly. They used every aid from eighteenth-century cartoons to twentieth-century engineering consultants to find answers to the countless questions. Was there a single most appropriate style of bar enclosure for an urban tavern of the 1770s? Could it be made functional for a modern bartender? Which windows would have been curtained, which shuttered, and which closed with blinds? Could any of the fireplaces be made to function without raising the already staggering construction costs too greatly? And where could a model be found from which to cast a 1770 open stove? What could be done to avoid having the twentieth century flash across an eighteenth-century candle-lit dining room as a waiter opened the kitchen door? Were the number and location of exits not only accurate but in accordance with fire codes? Could the small kitchens provide sufficient refrigerator space to save the restaurateur from the authentic but time-consuming need for daily marketing? And where would the waiters change?

The lighting of the tavern's rooms brought historical architect, construction architect, curator, and engineers together over sheets of specifications in what was possibly the most trying aspect of the reconstruction. Contemporary illustrations are quite detailed in their depictions of the means by which men saw to dine in the eighteenth century, from the candlestick tumbling to the floor in a brawl to the ambitious Adamesque sconce lifting its spidery arms over the heads of dancers. Cartoons, written descriptions, and inventories confirm that the number of fixed lights was dismayingly low by modern standards. The curators and historical architects were not surprised; the engineers and restaurateur were. The engineers maintained that the low light level was a safety hazard; the restaurateur claimed it would make his food appear unpalatable. Only the unanimity of the evidence convinced them that reliance on ambient light was necessary to the presentation of the original circumstances of dining in the tavern. The engineer wired the whole building with parallel circuits, one carrying standard voltage, one supplying twenty-five volts to fixtures that had so-called candelabra-base bulbs. Rather than drill antique fixtures and wire them to carry electricity, the

curators decided to find reproductions. They quickly discovered, however, that in reproduction fixtures the range of styles is limited, the degree of authenticity is low, and the several brands are made with different sizes of bulb bases, wall mounts, and types of finish. On-site installation was complicated, and the master electrician earned every penny of his contract. The very act of installation raised a whole new set of questions. How high on a wall were candle sconces placed when candles were changed by hand (although these would not be)? Where would hurricane shades have been necessary to combat drafts (although there would be none)? How many candles were provided per room in an establishment in which the number of candles burned was figured into a dining party's bill? The level of make-believe rose higher in the lighting of the tavern than in any other aspect of the reconstruction, and it was a source of great friction. The engineer contended that the curators were demanding an unrealistic standard of accuracy; the curators felt the engineer was asking too many departures from documentable fact.

The illustrations of contemporary English taverns and descriptions and inventories from American ones, amplified by the newspaper accounts, advertisements, insurance surveys, and personal papers mentioning the City Tavern, allowed the NPS team to infer a great deal about the specific articles of furniture in the building and the ways in which they could have been arranged (see figs. 3, 4, 5).

The insurance surveys were of little direct use to the curators. However, they did permit inference from the level of architectural elaboration to the style of furniture that would be appropriate. Using the initial advertisements placed by Smith and the proprietors, the curators established the bon ton for which to aim. The two auction lists combined with the information sources produced a sufficiently comprehensive body of information; this prompted the NPS decision to confine the style of the refurnishing to the tenure of Daniel Smith (1773–78).

Lacking both detailed bills for the interior furnishings and objects with a history of having been in the tavern, the staff chose to furnish with representative rather than landmark objects. Using tavern inventories, they created a generalized urban sample inventory and then specified the Philadelphia equivalents of those objects. The resulting inventory included not only the forms listed in the tavern's advertisements but also those depicted in the more urban of the English cartoons. Because the tavern's dining rooms would receive hard treatment and because the restaurant consultants decried the use of antique furniture, except as accessories, in such a busy facility, the curators decided to use only reproduction tables and seating furniture. Serving pieces, occasional objects, and wall furniture (prints, maps, looking glasses) would be antique.

Assistance in locating and acquiring reproduction furnishings to match the articles in the contemporary sources was offered by the National Home Fashions League, a professional organization of women in the design industry. Their initial effort was to find manufacturers willing to accurately reproduce appropriate objects from Independence National Historical Park's collections. It was hoped that the firms would absorb the cost of manufacture of the few pieces needed for the tavern in return for permission to market the line. They hoped, too, to induce these twentieth-century merchants and gentlemen to become subscribers to the new tavern, as their predecessors had been 200 years ago.

Changing market conditions, however, made manufacturers reluctant to add to their line any costly or untried new reproductions. Many claimed they could see no difference between their reproduction furniture and the antique furniture shown them and responded: "We already make a chair that looks just like yours. Order those, and we'll give you two free." Or "we'll upholster them in anything you want." Or, "we'll give them to you at our cost plus a few dollars." Those who could see a difference claimed that their production costs would be prohibitively high. Only a few firms were interested in creating reproductions from objects which they themselves had not selected. Consequently, some of the objects that were once cheap enough to be purchased frequently by Daniel Smith rank among the most costly reproductions in the new tavern. Other objects remained unobtainable, for the techniques of their manufacture have been lost since the eighteenth century.

Finally, the effort to replicate the variety of styles characteristic of even the most fashionable inns, clubs, and taverns became the most difficult aspect of the redecoration. Simply put, most public houses had unmatched furnishings. Simulating this process of natural selection became one of the most challenging of curatorial problems.

Tavernkeepers purchased furniture in small quantities from a variety of suppliers over a period of years and replaced them as they were destroyed with purchases from still other suppliers. The NPS found their range of possibilities limited by current availability of reproductions, minimum order numbers, manufacturers' production schedules, and durability of the finished product under commercial usage. In short, the task became almost impossible.

As difficult as the project was for the curators, it was perhaps more so for the designers of the National Home Fashions League. They were forced to abandon some of the cardinal principles of decoration as practiced in the third quarter of the twentieth century in order to approximate the third quarter of the eighteenth. This was complicated by the discovery that the curators and designers used many of the same terms very differently, and each was forced to translate to the other very carefully. Even so, a residual mutual concern survived until the curators became convinced that the designers were, indeed, doing their utmost to find suitable manufacturers and funds, and the designers became convinced that the curators were not trying to make fools of them.

Contemporary sources had provided planners of the new tavern with a clear picture of the ways in which the building operated. The four rooms of the cellar were described in the initial insurance survey with the words, "Stairs down to the kitchen." Fortunately, the *Pennsylvania Gazette* was more specific: "two large kitchens and every other convenience for the purpose."[21] Assuming there was also one room beneath the bar for the storage and dispensing of bottled and decanted liquors, the cellar was left with a fourth room for dry storage. Although a nineteenth-century excavation of the area beneath the sidewalks obliterated any traces of a possible ice pit, the tavern, like many Philadelphia homes, had its own cold storage (see figs. 3, 6). Deliveries of casks, barrels, and beeves came through the bulkhead doors beneath the innyard porch.

In the new City Tavern, all modern kitchen facilities are in the adjoining building (reconstructed solely as a service area), which frees the four basement rooms for other uses. The his-

[21]November 2, 1773, Survey Book no. 1, p. 54, Contributionship Insurance Company of Philadelphia; *Pennsylvania Gazette* (April 7, 1773).

torical architect suggested dining rooms in which schoolchildren could be served with foods resembling those of the eighteenth century. The curator envisioned functional tavern kitchens and cellars to which visitors could descend to see an approximation of the methods of preparing the foods they had eaten in the dining rooms upstairs. However, the restaurateur clamored for a sales area, and the architect reminded everyone that basement toilet facilities were the only alternative to constructing a necessary behind the building. In compromise, one quarter of the space was given over to such utilities as toilets, a janitor's closet, and plumbing access. Two of the remaining rooms were assigned to school dining; and the fourth, against the wall that had been fitted with fireplace ducts, was designated the "restored kitchen." The school dining rooms proved unsuccessful and eventually were closed. The partially completed kitchen, left without ovens and stovetop when construction funds ran out, did double duty as a gift shop. Subsequently, monies have been found to renew work on the demonstration kitchen.

Most guests have always entered the tavern from Second Street. The central hallway and four rooms that comprise the main, and most public, floor served for all of the tavern's functions except that of dancing and concerts.

As early as 1774 the two rooms fronting on Second Street were somewhat distinct from the rest of the building. Initially the subscribers who built the tavern retained proprietary rights over the two rooms and used them for the conduct of daily private business. But the rooms were not closed to others. Evidence suggests that the shareholders expected and received special treatment, but ship captains, merchants, travelers, and others had equal claim on tables there. In 1786, the subscribers' rights became both more specific and more restricted. They had lost their control over the tavern but maintained their organization and their responsibility for one of the two front rooms. In 1789, public notices announced the establishment of trading hours in the two front rooms. Advertisements welcomed merchants and captains from other cities, while reminding local businessmen that only members of the merchants' exchange could exercise the right to trade, advertise, or consult the newspapers available there. The tavernkeeper submitted his bill for maintaining and redecorating the front rooms to members of the exchange. The

merchants and businessmen conducted their business in these rooms until the 1830s, when they finally moved, name and all, to larger quarters which they had built a block away.

The bills that survive make clear that the City Tavern's front rooms were plain, almost austere. With American and English practice as precedent, the curators recommended windsor chairs and settees, plain tables, and tin and brass lighting fixtures. The floors of such public spaces were almost invariably left bare, with rugs thrown down as needed in wet weather. Windows were shuttered, hung with blinds, or given only the most perfunctory ornamentation. Walls were plain but hung with maps and charts, notices, or political prints. And the atmosphere was predictably heavy with smoke, the sounds of earnest conversation, and the odor of hot punch (fig. 7).

In one of the two front rooms of the new City Tavern, the anticipated usage coaxed a slightly higher level of elaboration from the reluctant NPS staff. The restaurant needed a room in which guests could wait to be seated in the dining rooms. The northeast room was chosen, for it was not only the nearest to the front door but also connected to the bar. The room's windsor furniture was augmented by two wing chairs—a curatorial concession on the grounds that they were comfortable, reasonably accurate copies, and supplied free of charge by their manufacturer. Because there could be no dining tables in that room, the designers insisted that the curators permit the introduction of small tables and candlestands to afford a place for guests to set their drinks. Regrettably, twentieth-century editions of the "principal Papers published throughout the United States, and the most interesting of those from Europe, etc." that provided news to enliven the conversation in the first City Tavern are not supplied, for the tavern's managers fear the newspapers would be carried off.

The location of the barroom was not specified in the 1773 insurance survey, but custom and subsequent advertisements strongly suggest that it was one of the two rear rooms on the main floor. Having found no evidence in favor of either, the architect chose the northwest room because service lines could be run to it with greater ease.

The bar was very much the center of any eighteenth-century tavern, and the newspaper notices placed by each City Tavern innkeeper confirm this. Naturally beverages were served

Fig. 7. *Good News.* London, 1783, published by Thomas Macklin. Stipple etching; H. 13⅞″, W. 16⅝″. (Library of Congress Print Collection.)

from the bar. Probably it had an opening directly into cellar storage facilities, so that locking the bar also secured the tavern's supply of wines and spirits. But the bar was the distribution point for more than just drink. "Tea, Coffee, Soups, Stews, Jellies, Ice Creams and a variety of French Liquors, together with the usual Refreshments, will at all times be procured at the Bar" advertised the City Tavern innkeeper in 1796.[22] This was a customary practice in England and America, and the barkeeper in many taverns kept either a small stove or a brazier warming the soup du jour or a hot dish left from the day's ordinary. The bar's cellar also stored the ices and chilled jellies, while bags of oysters and wheels of cheese were stored and disbursed from the enclosed area behind the bar.

[22]*Claypoole's American Daily Advertiser* (May 26, 1796).

The furnishings of the barroom were as predictable as its service: frequently, booths; often, running benches fastened to the walls; invariably, windsor and ladderback chairs and small, very portable tables. Using English prints as models (fig. 8), the curators curtained the booths of the barroom by installing a wooden rod above the back of each booth and hanging green baize curtains from it (fig. 9). These provide greater sound absorption and cut down the drafts.

The tavern was given three "private dining rooms," one on the first floor, two on the second. It was to those that the "dinner clubs" and fraternal organizations repaired, and there the care and quality of furnishings would have been most evident: the floors carpeted, the windows hung with curtains, and the walls ornamented with looking glasses and colored prints (fig. 10). Various walnut and mahogany chairs and tables

Fig. 8. *The Contrast.* England, ca. 1800. Mezzotint engraving. (Library of Congress Print Collection.)

would have approximated, to a degree, the comfort of a small parlor, and the "table linen, . . . glass, china, and . . . neat assortment of plate" would have been the foundation of the tavern's appeal for men who, when they dined at home, dined well.[23]

Unfortunately, many twentieth-century restaurants are furnished with adaptations of eighteenth-century styles, although not always accurately. Because of this, some of the effect of a diner's progress from the painted pine tables and turned chairs of the new City Tavern's public rooms to the dark wood tables covered with white linen and set with china of the private rooms is lost. The fascination with the adaptations of eighteenth-century styles created conflicts between the park staff and the designers who were

[23]*Pennsylvania Evening Post* (December 11, 1777).

assisting them. Even with the use of hardwood furniture and antique accessories, the private dining rooms at the City Tavern are considerably less colorful, less ornate, and less opulent than the dining rooms of many so-called colonial restaurants. Dismayed that they could not order colored linens, elaborate window hangings, and ornamental picture frames, the designers reminded the park staff that potential contributors to the cost of the furnishings would be more likely to pay for rooms that expressed in vivid terms the cost of their furnishing. The curators responded that they would be delighted to include in their furnishings plan such articles as oriental carpets, silver tablewares, and porcelain—all of which could be justified by the first City Tavern's records. None of these had been permitted because of initial cost, fragility, or the likelihood of theft. Because the staff prevailed on the designers, they

Fig. 9. Barroom of the City Tavern showing bar enclosure and curtained booths. The windsor armchair was made by Saybolt and Cleland, the ladderback chair by the Robert Treate Hogg Cabinet Shop, and the tavern table by the Robert C. Whitley Studio. The latter two are reproduced from originals in the Independence National Historical Park collections. (Photo, Robert B. Grubb.)

Fig. 10. *The Country Club.* London, 1788, published by William Dickinson. Engraving; H. 17⅝″, W. 22½″. (Library of Congress Print Collection.)

had to resign themselves to the loss of some anticipated contributions.

The Long Room, the front room on the second floor, alone had interior ornamentation
which was sufficiently elaborate and costly that
the insurance surveyor detailed it carefully. It
also is the only room in the tavern that the survey
located and described beyond a doubt. Like the
smaller rooms on the first and second floors, its
end or fireplace walls were paneled from ceiling
to floor. Unlike the smaller rooms, the Long
Room was embellished with paired pilasters sup-
porting a full entablature that encircled the room
at the cornice level. It was entered by double
doors that opened onto its fifty-foot width and
that faced the seven windows that looked onto the
street below.

The Long Room was the scene of an unend-
ing round of concerts, banquets, and balls, with
only changes of uniform permitting one to identify the players. Using Rebecca Franks's letter as a
point of departure, the staff attempted to reproduce a provincial Georgian room that had
been updated with a few modern accessories.
This is the only room in the tavern whose wall
fixtures are augmented by chandeliers. These are
reproductions of one that had hung in the ballroom of Gadsby's Tavern in Alexandria, Virginia.
The room's woodwork is painted the light gray-
green "stone" color that paint analysis had revealed was the first finish coat on the entrance

and stair halls of Cliveden, Benjamin Chew's
1770 residence in Germantown, Pennsylvania.
This color stands in sharp contrast to the stronger
colors used on the woodwork throughout the rest
of the tavern. Those were taken from documented colors found in other park structures and
belong to the more vivid palette that was becoming old-fashioned by the 1770s. Augmenting the
portable tables and benches that facilitate the
room's conversion to a ballroom are pier tables,
looking glasses, and a number of upholstered
backstools.

Using descriptions and illustrations of American and English banquets and surviving examples
of Delaware Valley furniture, the curators provided the tavern with what is possibly its least expected and certainly most controversial furniture.
Even given the eighteenth century's limited standards of comfort, 200 guests could only have
been accommodated in a fifty-foot dining room
by being seated on benches at long tables (fig. 11).
An entry in William C. Ellery's diary provided the
necessary corroboration. He described the celebration of the second anniversary of independence at the Long Room of the City Tavern:

The entertainment was elegant, and well conducted.
There were four Tables spread, two of them extended
the whole length of the Room, the other two crossed
them at right angles. At the end of the Room opposite
the upper Table, was erected an Orchestra. . . . As soon
as the Dinner began, the Musick consisting of Clarinets,

Fig. 11. Untitled cartoon of a banquet (caricature of William Pitt, Charles Fox, and several others). London,
1770s. Etching with watercolor; H. 10 11/16″, W. 21 3/16″. (Library of Congress Print Collection.)

Haut-boys, French horns, Violins and Bass Viols, opened and continued making proper pauses until it was finished. Then the Toasts followed each by a discharge of Fieldpieces, were drank, and so the afternoon ended. In the evening there was a cold collation and a brilliant exhibition of Fireworks.[24]

The tables were doubtless boards on sawhorses that were capable of being broken down and stacked in an attic storeroom with the benches laid over them. For a brief time the curators persuaded the restaurateur that benches and banquet tables could be made part of a diverting dining experience, and the Long Room was furnished with them. The restaurateur also agreed to the purchase of a reproduction harpsichord and eighteenth-century music stands for the planned reinstatement of the Long Room's "City Concerts," at which eighteenth-century Philadelphians listened to the music of Bach, Corelli, and Stamitz. Later, the restaurant's manager insisted on replacing the benches and long tables with chairs and smaller tables. The harpsichord was moved downstairs and is now played for the guests waiting to be seated in a dining room as well as those who are enjoying an after-dinner drink (fig. 12).

Among the variety of eighteenth-century furniture needed in the new City Tavern, the easiest to duplicate were the turned and joined furniture: windsor chairs and settees, ladderbacks, tavern tables, and the barroom's painted pine tables and benches. Even so, the curators were forced to ignore most commercially produced turned furniture. They ordered from small firms whose ideas of eighteenth-century furniture had been less affected by "early American modern" and whose production was sufficiently small that an offending detail could be eliminated. The most satisfactory turned furniture was produced by cabinet shops, although high expenses forced them to charge premium prices. The tavern could afford to turn to the shops only for special orders, like for the turned tables.

The fixed wooden bar furniture and the collapsible tables and long benches for the Long Room were made by the shop at the park, as were the tables and benches for the basement school dining rooms and such other wooden accessories as the cistern and wet-sink in the demonstration

Fig. 12. Musicians rehearsing in the Subscription Room of the City Tavern. The harpsichord was built by William Dowd of Boston, the reproduction music stand is by Robert C. Whitley, and the windsor furniture is by Saybolt and Cleland. The framed print is William Faden's 1777 engraving, *Plan of the City and Environs of Philadelphia*. (Photo, Robert B. Grubb.)

kitchen. The NPS has a small core of master carpenters, many of whom have worked on eighteenth- and early nineteenth-century sites for a quarter of a century. These men can copy a set of specifications or even a reasonably careful sketch with complete fidelity.

An unexpected obstacle to accurate furnishing sprang from the changed taste in the finish of windsor furniture. The curators found themselves repeating tiresomely that eighteenth-century turned furniture was painted in a limited, predictable range of colors. Furthermore, the green-black paint on one piece need not be coordinated to the blue used on another. In several instances, the curators finally had paint specifications written up from the park's records of windsor paint colors, and, in a few cases, the paint was actually mixed in the park's shop. These were supplied to the various manufacturers and finishers.

The eighteenth-century tables, with gate legs, drop leaves, and varied dimensions, also contributed to the visual variety of tavern dining rooms. But, as the curatorial staff was reminded, such tables also play havoc with a room's seating capacity, and the new tavern would have to survive in an area that has an average of three restaurants on every block. The curators agreed to let the restaurateur specify the height, width, and

[24]William C. Ellery, "Diary June 28 to July 23, 1778," *Pennsylvania Magazine of History and Biography* 11, no. 4 (1887): 477–78.

depth of the tables, and the restaurateur let the curators specify types of legs and finish. The curators selected a firm that manufactures office furniture of high quality. The firm, a small and highly personal one, is descended from a cabinet shop, and its president engaged in the project for the challenge it presented. The park staff provided sections and elevations of the most common variations on the Philadelphia Marlborough leg, and the firm's designers selected three that they felt would stand up under hard use. The effort to include tables with cabriole legs was abandoned when manufacturers and designers alike insisted that they would be costly and fragile. The staff was mollified when analysis of cartoon tables showed that the great majority were square or rectangular, with legs that were straight, stationary, and dismayingly unadorned. Stains were mixed under the park's supervision, and models were approved before being put into production. The resulting mix of table shapes, sizes, and finishes, while not so varied as the curators wished, is less predictable than the "deuces" or "doubles" in most modern chic restaurants. Grateful for the restaurateur's concessions, the staff added in the bar a few small turned and painted tables reproduced from a tavern table in the park's collection (see fig. 9).

A similarly enthusiastic response to the problem of creating a durable, attractive, and relatively inexpensive reproduction chair was evoked from another very different organization. That company, one of the country's largest manufacturers of reproduction furniture, expressed interest in the project to the National Home Fashions League. One of the park's chairs was taken to the company's factory to serve as a model. In later conversations, the curators learned that it became the subject of great interest. Every workman in the plant examined it, and the firm's subsequent sample was made with such care that the curators had to suggest only minor alterations (figs. 13, 14).

The City Tavern also was able to take advantage of the Bicentennial urge that had led a few companies to produce reasonable facsimiles of accessories: mirrored tin candle sconces, brass candlesticks, pewter cutlery and drinking vessels. These instances were few, and, in general, the dearth of interesting and accurate reproductions was striking. The high cost added an unforeseen obstacle; the restaurateur had been reluctant but willing to use museum reproductions, although

they would be "attractive nuisances" for both his staff and his guests. But when he learned the cost, his reluctance hardened to opposition. The curators spent fruitless hours searching restaurant supply catalogues in an effort to assemble table settings that did not mock the rest of the reconstruction. They realized that, no matter how accurate the paneling, paint, tables, and chairs, their efforts would succeed or fail at the level of the table top (fig. 15). It was cruelly disappointing to discover that the inexpensive wares of the eighteenth century are virtually impossible to duplicate today.

In 1770, Philadelphia had been a major market for English decorative goods. Local merchants advertised English ceramics, Irish glass, and London pewter and brasswares. The numerous archaeological excavations of the past few years have retrieved household wares of astonishing variety and modernity, corresponding to the range of wares advertised in the city's newspapers. The curators were particularly anxious that the tavern's ceramics be chosen carefully, since one of the city's major importers of china, Joseph Stansbury, was a patron of Smith's. (Stansbury came to history's attention when he jeopardized his safety by rising to his feet in one of the tavern's dining rooms and crying, "God Save the King!" at an inopportune moment.) Today's Joseph Stansburys sell restaurants heavy plates with rolled edges and bright glazes, thick cups with ring handles, and dull glasses with bottle-like bottoms. True earthenwares and oriental porcelains are too fragile for rough handling by busboys and dishwashers.

One local supplier, with admirable patience and resourcefulness, assisted the staff in assembling a table setting from among diverse sources and unlikely forms: cream-colored ware with a less lustrous glaze, thinner glasses from a French firm, handleless soup cups for the service of tea. Pewter, silver, and common redwares were beyond reach. The restored tavern used facsimile pewter tablewares until government regulations forced their abandonment, and it is still searching for redware dishes that are neither cute nor costly.

The curators have discovered that the more successful the effort to achieve a quality reproduction, the greater the problem: wares that are accurate are expensive, or fragile, or available in limited quantity. And any that survive the dishwasher succumb to pilferage. Out of frustra-

Fig. 13. Side chair, Philadelphia, 1760–85. Walnut, leather upholstery; H. 39¾". W. 20½". (Independence National Historical Park Collection, no. 8173: Photo, National Park Service.)

Fig. 14. Reproduction of side chair shown in figure 13. Pennsylvania House, "Independence Hall Chair." (Photo, George Eisenman.)

Fig. 15. Private, second-floor dining room of the City Tavern. The piazza is visible through the doorway. The furnishings are reproductions. The table is by Knipp and Company, the pretzel-back chairs by the Kittinger Furniture Company, the cabriole-leg chair at the left by Henkel-Harris, and the one at the right by Pennsylvania House (shown in figure 14). The carpet is by Scalamandre. (Photo, Robert B. Grubb.)

tion, the restaurateur has resorted to ordering replacements without consulting the curatorial staff, although this violates his contract with NPS. Likewise, the curators are frustrated by the discovery of the new wares when they visit the tavern on other business. They are told, "We needed replacements and couldn't wait. Now we've spent the money and have to use what we've bought."

From the curatorial standpoint, if any aspect of the new City Tavern can be said to have been an unqualified success, it is the ornamentation of the windows and walls. The covering of windows in the eighteenth century, especially in public buildings, was dictated by comfort as much as by fashion. And, although the tavern's internal climate would be controlled by dials and switches, its appurtenances simulate those of a building subject to the weather. The windows of the east facade (the Second Street side of the building) are shuttered on the inside, eliminating the need for blinds. And the strong morning sun is held off by the large canvas awnings stretched from the beltcourse above the first floor to poles sunk into the ground near the curb (see fig. 2). Its west wall is exposed to harsh light, and there is no record of shutters having been placed there. Consequently, the windows of the barroom that occupied the northwest corner are closed by venetian blinds patterned after a lone eighteenth-century survivor discovered in the attic of a nearby Quaker meetinghouse. Private dining rooms demand somewhat more ornamental window coverings. Documents indicate that the style of curtains used in taverns and similar buildings fell within a narrow range; their ornamentation was sparse and their yardage as limited as possible. They covered the window fully when extended, they kept out sun and drafts, and they had to be manipulable by hand from below by a waiter or innkeeper who would not be likely to spend great care on their arrangement.

When curators attempted to make cloth models for the drapery house that had volunteered to fabricate the curtains, they found that "what you see" is not always "what you get." Venetian curtains were relatively simple to reproduce, and suggestions from the staff of Winterthur Museum saved hours of trial and error. However, not even Winterthur's seamstresses had needed to construct a movable festoon curtain. Days of experimentation with muslin, pins, rings, and cords eventually produced two movable varieties: one that parts in the center and draws to each side

and one that gathers across the window in a single festoon. Both the curators and the manufacturers were jubilant when the cords proved sufficiently simple to operate so that the curtain's positions could be altered during the course of a day. Once the movable festoons had been mastered, the finished window hangings in document fabrics duplicated eighteenth-century curtains to a satisfying degree.

The maps and prints ornamenting the walls of the new tavern do not replicate those in the original building, but the range of subjects, artists, and media illustrates the considerable variety available to provincial Englishmen in the 1770s. A few of the cartoons that the NPS staff used as sources of information had detail sufficient to permit identification of subject matter. They showed English history, contemporary politics, maps, sporting scences, genre subjects, and landscapes (fig. 16). Acting on the stated interpretive purpose of the tavern, the curators attempted to select prints typical of the eighteenth century by including popular artists and subjects. The rich variety of eighteenth-century graphic arts has diminished with time, of course, but it is still impressive. And the walls of the City Tavern present an exciting range of works, from John Montresor's splendid folio map of New York City and its environs to a colored mezzotint of Copley's *A Youth Attacked by a Shark*.

City Tavern was very much an English tavern in Philadelphia. The entry area of the building presents portraits of some Englishmen popular with the colonists and plans of some major colonial cities. The two front rooms, once used to conduct business, are hung with subjects of interest to merchants: maps and charts, recognition views of the ports with which Philadelphia ships traded, scenes from some European cities, and the most current information about areas under exploration in the 1770s.

The barroom, of course, is given over to comic subjects, political cartoons, and topical prints. Notices and cartoons no longer timely were scrapped, then as now, and depictions of taverns show them to have been tacked hastily onto walls and torn off when they had done their duty. But time and scarcity have lifted them from artifact to art, and their greater rarity is reflected in tighter security, so that the eighteenth century's casually driven nail gave way to glass, frames, and specially fabricated hooks.

The tavern's private dining rooms contain

Fig. 16. J. Barlow after Samuel Collings, *An English Ordinary*. London, 1786. Etching; H. 10″, W. 14⅝″. (Library of Congress Print Collection.)

landscapes, genre scenes, and—in one room—the building's only reference to the war that enveloped it. Interpreters and curators agreed that emphasizing the Revolution would be unwise; the Irish loyalist innkeeper had patrons ranging from Washington to Cornwallis. However, one of the City Tavern's more interesting entries into American history occurred in 1784, when the Society of the Cincinnati met there and elected Washington its commander-in-chief. The Pennsylvania Line of the society is still very active and expressed an interest in the new tavern even before it was rebuilt. The group contributed funds toward furnishing one of the private dining rooms, asking only for first opportunity to reserve it for dinner meetings. Consequently, the walls in that room have a somewhat martial character, for they are hung with portraits of revolutionary leaders, battle maps, and wartime cartoons. The contribution of the Pennsylvania Line also made possible the purchase of antique accessories for the room, most notably a large serving table with a top of King of Prussia blue marble.

In other rooms, antique accessories complete the furnishings and meet some of the needs of the tavern staff. The waiters were given chests of drawers and serving tables instead of collapsible metal tray stands and stainless steel racks. The restaurateur initially was not enthusiastic about this, but for a time, he conceded that the tavern was surviving without metal racks. However, as heavy usage took its toll on the chests, he introduced folding wooden stands with web straps.

The creation of the City Tavern as a functioning restaurant tested preconceptions on all sides. And, at every stage of its reconstruction, at least one of the parties concerned was sure that it could not—should not—be done. It proved far more difficult than the NPS staff, the curators, the designers, or the contracting restaurateur expected. The result is probably somewhat less satisfactory than any of them hoped. Moreover, unlike a "house museum," its interpretive problems are ongoing: the supplier of a good line of glassware goes out of business; the new shipment of waiters' shirts has elastic cuffs; the manager slips chicken à la king onto the menu. Because this is a commercial establishment, it must be permitted to function without such rigid controls as those that can be imposed on a "living history" installation. But every day the tavern presents a slightly different view of itself to its guests. The change and accommodation that are essential to its survival could never have been approximated in the most perfect museum setting.

The new City Tavern, by the continually vary-ing nature and degree of its interpretive prob-lems, has taught every museum professional as-sociated with it an important lesson: The person who aims to present a past that lives must be pre-pared to cope with the past as vigorously as he copes with the present.

Wares and Chairs

A Reappraisal of the Documents

Deborah Dependahl Waters

S OUTH JERSEY TURNED CHAIRS, particularly the slat-backed, rush-bottomed type (fig. 1) associated with Maskell Ware of Roadstown and his descendants, have excited collectors of American furniture aesthetically for more than fifty years. As examples of the persistence and longevity of traditional craft forms, such chairs have also interested furniture historians. Yet the extent of Ware family involvement in the chair and furniture trades of Cumberland, Salem, and Cape May Counties from 1790 into the 1940s and the relationship of the Wares to other retailers and manufacturers of seating furniture supplying their markets have been little explored. Like many craftsmen, this family of chairmakers left few direct records, but surviving census, probate, and land-transfer records; newspapers; genealogies; and account books provide guideposts necessary for such exploration. When charted, these points map the accommodations made by one group of traditional craftsmen to modernizing society.[1]

Maskell Ware (1766–1846) was the first of twenty-three Ware family members active in some phase of the chair and furniture trades (fig. 2). He was the third son of Marcy Moore and Elnathan Ware and was apprenticed to John Laning (1738–1826), a Greenwich, New Jersey, chairmaker and farmer. Maskell Ware married Hannah Simpkins in 1789 and settled in Roadstown, a village of twenty dwellings "peopled principally by the cultivators of the soil" located five miles west of Bridgeton, Cumberland County, on land purchased from Laning. Like traditional craftsmen in other areas, he found the local market for his chairs insufficient to support a family of eleven children. Farming was a necessity.[2]

Although occasionally he sold chairs in quantity for resale, Maskell Ware worked in an econ-

---

[1] My interest in the Wares began with the 1974 Loan Exhibition of South Jersey Turned Chairs, 1775–1925, organized by Mrs. Richard D. Wood at the Museum of Glass, Wheaton Village, Millville, New Jersey, for the Cumberland County Historical Society. Benno M. Forman, who spoke about the Wares in conjunction with the exhibition, encouraged that interest, and the discussions and field photography trips in which he and I participated jointly over the subsequent two years have been most helpful in the development of my knowledge of the Wares and their work. See Mabel Crispin Powers, "The Ware Chairs of South Jersey," *Antiques* 9, no. 5 (May 1926): 307–11; Margaret E. White, *Early Furniture Made in New Jersey* (Newark, N.J.: Newark Museum, 1958), p. 19.

[2] The Ware family genealogy is detailed by Franklin Ware, *Genealogy of the Descendants of Joseph Ware of Fenwick Colony, England, 1675*, ed. John D. Ware, rev. ed. (1891; Tampa: privately printed, 1969), pp. 16 ff. Mabel Crispin Powers, following Dan Ware's narrative of 1888 published in ibid., p. 105, asserted that Maskell Ware learned chairmaking from John Laning in Salem. However, the marriage record of John Laning and Rhoda Izard, May 20, 1773, listed both as residents of Cumberland County. See New Jersey Historical Society, *Documents Relating to the Colonial, Revolutionary, and Post-Revolutionary History of the State of New Jersey*, 1st ser., 42 vols. (Newark, 1900), 22:36. Laning's residence in Greenwich, Cumberland County, is substantiated by a manuscript map of his landholdings on Greenwich Street dated September 16, 1786, as cited in *New Jersey Genesis* 20, no. 3 (April 1973): 885. See also William J. S. Bradway, "Journeys around Jericho: Journey the Thirty-seventh—Maskell Ware, Noted Chair Maker of Roadstown," in *How Dear to My Heart: A Collection of the Photographs and Writings of William J. S. Bradway,* comp. and ed. William B. Vanneman (Salem, N.J.: Township of Lower Alloway's Creek, 1976), p. 177; Thomas Francis Gordon, *Gazetteer of the State of New Jersey* (Trenton, N.J., 1834), p. 227; Bruce R. Buckley, "A Folklorist Looks at the Traditional Craftsman," in *Country Cabinetwork and Simple City Furniture,* Winterthur Conference Report 1969, ed. John D. Morse (Charlottesville: University Press of Virginia for the Henry Francis du Pont Winterthur Museum, 1970), pp. 272–73. Ware's agrarian pursuits included raising hogs. *Washington Whig* (Bridgeton) (March 26, 1825).

Fig. 1. Maskell Ware, side chair. Roadstown, Cumberland County, New Jersey, ca. 1790–1800. Maple, ash seat lists, rush seat; H. 42¾″, W. 18¼″, D. 14⅝″, SH. 16 15/16″. (Collection of Mrs. Hamilton D. Ware: Photo, Benno M. Forman.) This chair descended in the family of the maker's son Dan. Members of Richard Ware's family owned others of the set in 1922.

omy based more on barter and liberal extension of credit than on cash. In transactions with the Greenwich store operated by Richard Wood, Jr., and his successors, Ware exchanged farm commodities and chairs for textiles and grocery staples. He paid for purchases of sundries, pocket handkerchiefs, and calico on June 17, 1791, with a set of chairs, presumably of his own manufacture, valued at 27s. Cash, bushels of seed, and a "chair left to sell" valued at $1.25 on May 19, 1819, covered in part purchases of shingles, lime, salt, spirits of turpentine, and sundries recorded

on the store's books between 1804 and 1819. Not until December 25, 1827, was the account settled by cash and seven chairs, one valued at 87½¢, and the other six at $5.00 the set.[3]

Of Maskell Ware's seven sons, five actively followed their father's trade during portions of their adulthood. Thomas (1792–1867), the eldest, followed tradition and combined chairmaking with farming his acreage along the Roadstown-Jericho road in Stow Creek Township. Tools and furniture in his shop as inventoried after his death included:

Turners Lathe	[$]1.00
Drawing knife	1.00
¾ Inch Augur	.20
Wide chizel for turning No. 1	.30
Do. No. 2	.30
Do. No. 3	.20
one large Gouge	.25
one Small do.	.25
1½ inch Augur	.15
one inch Augur	.15
Do Do	.15
Two thread cutters at 10¢ each	.20
one Reamer	.15
one Clamp	.20
Lathe Strings (rawhide)	.15
Work Bench, and vise attached	3.00
one set of gauges	.25
4 paint brushes at 6¼ ct.	.25
3 Iron wrenches	.40
Lot of Frames & nose basket	.10
Iron Square & Seine Corks	.25
One broad axe	.50
One Rivetting Hammer	.20
large Pincers	.20
Frows & hold fast	.50
2 Boxes at 10 cts	.20
2 stools at 25 cts	.50
one Rock chair	.15
Slats & rounds for chairs	.05
Shaving horse	.25
Framing bench	1.25
Two wood saws (Best 50 cts, the other 30 cts)	.80
Lot of Bits	.25
Lot of drawers & contents	3.00
chair posts, Slats & lists	1.00
½ dozen new Chairs	5.00
7 chair frames at 40 cts	2.80
Lot of rounds & posts	1.00
4 Stools at 10 cts	.40

[3]Wood & Bacon, Store Ledgers D & E, Day Book (1815–), Historical Society of Pennsylvania, Philadelphia.

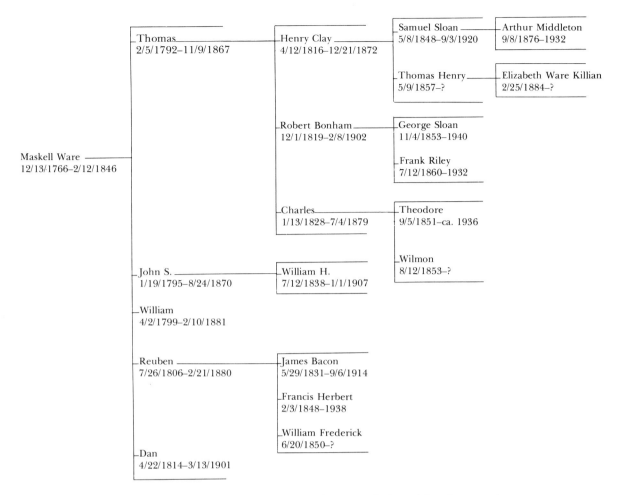

Fig. 2. Descendants of Maskell Ware involved in the South Jersey chair and furniture trades.

lot of old worn out chisels	.25
4 Saws at 10 cts	.40
Hand saw	1.00[4]

Both the low valuation assigned to the lathe, necessary for turning of posts and rounds, and the rawhide lathe strings included in the shop inventory suggest that it was probably a pole lathe, with a spring pole and treadle drive. However, a foot lathe with a treadle-activated flywheel mounted directly beneath the pulley also would have allowed the turner to operate the lathe without assistance. All the components of slat-backed chair frames—posts, slats, rounds (stretchers), and seat frame lists, as well as completed frames—appear among the shop's contents. Missing, however, is any mention of rush for chair seats. Perhaps Thomas Ware employed another craftsman to weave seats. With seats, his "½ dozen new chairs" were worth more than twice as much as finished frames. Two other forms of seating furniture were listed in the shop—stools and one "rock" chair. Other chairs and stools were scattered throughout various outbuildings and the main dwelling, including the garret, where "6 Rock Chairs" valued at $1.40 each were stored.[5]

Although Thomas made detailed provisions in his will for the disposition of his real estate holdings, it mentioned neither his shop nor his

[4] Inventory E-460, Surrogate's Office, Cumberland County, N.J. (hereafter cited as CC Inventory).

[5] The wholesale price of straight-back chairs ranged from $4.00 to $5.00 for a set of six, while that of bent backs was from $5.00 to $6.00 per half dozen, according to William H. MacDonald (*Central New Jersey Chairmaking of the Nineteenth Century* [n.p., 1959], pp. 16–17). The absence of racks (crimps) for bending posts in Thomas's shop inventory suggests that the "new chairs" listed in the same inventory were straight backed.

tools. They may have passed to his son Charles (1828–79), whose 1879 inventory included "Lot Chair-makers Tools [valued at] $2.50," or to his eldest son Henry Clay Ware (1816–72), who was working as a chairmaker in Stow Creek Township by 1850. Henry's estate, when inventoried by his chairmaking son Samuel Sloan Ware and two disinterested freeholders on March 5, 1873, included lathe, shaving horse, framing bench, and a lot of tools worth $10. A half dozen rush-bottomed chairs, a large "rock" chair, and a "small D[itt]o," with a total value of $9.00, were also listed.[6]

Maskell Ware's sons, John S. (1795–1870) and William Ware (1799–1881), left Roadstown for Bridgeton, the county seat, where, by 1826, they established a chair manufactory. A thriving industrial town, Bridgeton boasted an extensive rolling mill, a foundry and nail factory, a grist mill, a woolen manufactory, and "some very good houses" by the 1830s. Through an advertisement in *The Bridgeton Observer and Cumberland Cape-May and Salem Advertiser* (fig. 3), the partners announced the removal of their factory to the stand formerly occupied by Stephen Miller, a Bridgeton cabinetmaker active from about 1788 to 1822. Simultaneously, they expanded their product line to include cabinet wares. To supply such goods, they hired "good steady workmen" and bought walnut, cherry, and gum boards and maple and poplar scantling, the latter probably intended for bedstead rails, for their products. The brothers purchased adjoining lots on the south side of Broad Street in the same year. How long the partnership continued remains unclear, but by 1840 it had dissolved.[7]

Following the dissolution of the partnership, John S. Ware continued chairmaking in Bridgeton. *Kirkbride's New Jersey Business Directory . . . for 1850 & 1851* listed only one other chairmaker in

the town, Moses Reiley (Riley), who produced painted fancy chairs until his death in the fall of 1850. In addition to the customary chairmaker's tools as found in Thomas Ware's shop, Reiley's estate inventory listed a paint stone for grinding colors, and cauls and glue kettle, perhaps for applying veneers. Raw material for chairs, including a "lot of Chair Stuff," rushes, and a "lot of Painted rushes" as well as "2 Doz fancy Chairs" valued at $12, also appeared in Reiley's inventory. Unlike Reiley, John S. Ware and his two male hands produced "rush Bot Chairs" finished only with varnish, in 1849–50. His plant and equipment, valued at $400, turned lumber worth $150 into chairs which sold for $600. Ten years later, the value of the shop itself had been halved, but the two employees increased output to an annual rate of 100 dozen chairs worth $800.[8]

By 1860, John S. Ware had also expanded his business dealings to include the sale of coal from a yard at the foot of Broad Street in Bridgeton. In this enterprise, he was joined by his eldest son Benjamin Thackara Ware (1819–1904), who had moved to Bridgeton from Allowaystown (Alloway), Salem County, about 1853 to keep a variety store in Prosperity Row, a few doors west of the Bridgeton bridge.[9]

While John S. Ware did not mention his trade in his will, the 1870 census recorded the firm "John S. Ware & Son" as operating a chair manufactory which employed one male hand. Utilizing hand power, the firm took wood and rush valued at $300 and produced rush-bottomed chairs worth $800, the value of output in 1860. Although the coal yard used the same firm name as did the chair factory, it is not clear if the junior partner was the same in both. While Benjamin T. Ware sold such items as wallpaper and paints in his variety store, his youngest brother, William H. Ware (1838–1907), was listed as a chairmaker in Bridgeton and Cumberland County business and farm directories from 1893 through 1903. An extant invoice indicates that William H. Ware wove chair bottoms in addition to rushbottoming, re-

[6]CC Inventory G-206; Manuscript Population Schedule, Stoe Creek Township, Cumberland County, N.J., 7th U.S. Census (1850), Archives and History Bureau, New Jersey State Library, Trenton (unless otherwise specified, all 1850–70 manuscript census returns hereafter cited are available in the New Jersey State Library); CC Inventory F-211.

[7]White, p. 71; Gordon, p. 108; Manuscript Population Schedule, Hopewell Township, Cumberland County, N.J., 6th U.S. Census (1840), National Archives, Washington, D.C.; Deeds 47/117 (February 22, 1826) and 47/139 (February 25, 1826), Clerk's Office, Cumberland County, N.J. (hereafter cited as CC Deed). For a similar advertisement by Bridgeton cabinetmaker Josiah Fithian for a quantity of maple and poplar bedstead stuff, see *Washington Whig* (March 6, 1824).

[8]*Kirkbride's New Jersey Business Directory . . . for 1850 & 1851* (Trenton, N.J.: Stacy B. Kirkbride, Jr., 1850), p. 158 (hereafter cited as *Kirkbride's*); CC Inventory C-238; CC Deed 83/219 (December 20, 1851); Manuscript Census Schedule 5, Cohansey Township, Cumberland County (1850, 1860). Inconsistencies in the reported census data make it difficult to compare productivity.

[9]*Salem Sunbeam and Democratic Journal* (February 4, 1853); *West-Jersey Pioneer* (Bridgeton) (March 24, 31, 1855; February 23, 1856).

JOHN S. & WILLIAM WARE.
Cabinet & Chair Makers,

RESPECTFULLY inform their friends and the public, that they have *REMOVED* their CHAIR Manufactory to the stand formerly occupied by Stephen Miller, in Market Street, where they will carry on, in addition to Chair Making and Turning,

CABINET MAKING,

In its various branches;—having employed good steady workmen, they hope to give general satisfaction.

** The highest price will be given for Walnut, Cherry and Gum boards; also for Maple and Poplar Scantling.

Bridgeton, March 17, 1826—63tf

Fig. 3. Advertisement, *The Bridgeton Observer and Cumberland Cape-May and Salem Advertiser* (March 18, 1826). (From the original in the collections of the New Jersey Historical Society.)

pairing, and dealing in cane and caning materials.[10]

After dissolving his partnership with his brother John S. Ware, William Ware left Bridge-

ton but did not abandon chairmaking. He continued making, or supervising the manufacture of, rush-bottomed chairs at least as late as 1876, working from a Roadstown shop which local historian William J. S. Bradway recalled as being located on the north side of his dwelling, facing the street. By 1859–60, William's four male employees used hand-powered tools to turn lumber and other raw materials valued at $400 into "100 Doz. chairs" worth $700. His eldest brother Thomas and Thomas's son Charles were also actively making chairs in Roadstown in 1860, for all three were listed as "chair manufacturers" in the annual South Jersey business directory. The centennial edition of *The Mercantile Agency Reference Book*, predecessor to the modern Dun and Bradstreet's listings, rated William as having an estimated pecuniary strength of between $1,000

[10]Will F-62, Surrogate's Office, Cumberland County, N.J. (hereafter cited as CC Will); Manuscript Census Schedule 4, 3d Ward, Bridgeton, Cumberland County, N.J. (1870); *Boyd's Cumberland County, N.J., Directory 1893–94* (Philadelphia: C. E. Howe Co., 1893), p. 441; *Boyd's Cumberland County, N.J., Directory, 1895–96* (Philadelphia: C. E. Howe Co., 1895), p. 191; *Boyd's Directory of Cumberland and Cape May Counties, New Jersey, 1897–98* (Philadelphia: C. E. Howe Co., 1897), p. 444; *Boyd's Directory of Cumberland County, New Jersey, 1899–1900* (Philadelphia: C. E. Howe Co., 1899), p. 469; *Boyd's Directory of Cumberland County, New Jersey, 1901–1902* (Philadelphia: C. E. Howe Co., 1901), p. 490; *Boyd's Directory of Cumberland County, New Jersey, 1903–1904* (Philadelphia: C. E. Howe Co., 1903), p. 492; "Study Shows Ware Chairs Were Made without Nails or Glue—Just Pegs," *Evening Bulletin* (Philadelphia) (December 3, 1970).

and $2,000, and "fair" general credit. When he sold the family homestead in 1878, William probably disposed of his tools, for none of the specialized equipment used by a chairmaker appeared in the inventory of his personal property taken on October 24, 1881. The inventory did list a half dozen "Rush chairs" valued at $8.00, six unspecified chairs appraised at $6.00, and three rockers, two small and one large.[11]

Yet another of Maskell Ware's sons, Reuben Ware (1806–80), was actively engaged in chairmaking in Cumberland County in 1850. His shop was located in Cedarville, Fairfield Township, eight miles southeast of Bridgeton. The village, "scattered a mile and a half on the road," contained in 1844 "2 Presbyterian a Methodist, and a Baptist church, 2 stores, an oakum factory, a tannery," sawmill, and about 100 dwellings. Working with Reuben in 1850 was his son James Bacon Ware (1831–1914).[12]

It is unclear what prompted Reuben's move to Bridgeton by 1863, when he and his brother John S. purchased nearly eight acres of maple swamp in Deerfield Township on the east side of the main arm of Cohansey Creek. Possibly the lure was the greater concentration of potential purchasers for his rush-bottomed chairs and cabinetware available at the county seat. In 1870, his manufactory, which employed his son William Frederick Ware (1850–?), converted wood and rush valued at $300 into rush-bottomed chairs worth $1,200. The factory's output was valued at 50 percent more than John S. Ware and Son's shop in the same year. Despite the volume of production, Reuben Ware apparently was less successful financially than either his younger brother Dan (1814–1902) or his older brother William. *Bradstreet's Commercial Reports* for January 6, 1870, rated Dan Ware's business as CCC— "a house of moderate capital, yet with means sufficient for the business done, prudent, careful,

and economical, regarded safe for business requirements." Reuben's rating was DE—"not to be refused credit in all cases, but caution is advised in selling." Six years later, *The Mercantile Agency Reference Book* gave no credit rating for Reuben and estimated his pecuniary strength as less than $1,000, one rating below that of his brother William Ware.[13]

Francis Herbert Ware (1848–1938), another son of Reuben, continued the family tradition. He began his career in a furniture and undertaking firm in Millville, New Jersey. After a brief stint in the furniture business, he became a traveling salesman for a Philadelphia coffee firm, then Millville's postmaster, and finally conducted a grocery business which he transferred to Ocean City, New Jersey, in 1889. Although he could cane or rush chair seats, he made no chairs.[14]

Mabel Crispin Powers's statement that Maskell Ware's fifth son, Maskell, Jr. (1811–1905), did not continue chairmaking after reaching maturity cannot be affirmed or denied. However, his brother Dan, a chairmaker, worked for him briefly during the 1830s. Maskell's will and inventory contain no mention of rush-seat chairs, although a "long mahogany case Eight day clock" and the "large oaken chair" given him by his sister Elizabeth Reeve's children are specified.[15]

Dan Ware, the youngest of the active chairmakers in the second generation, combined chairmaking with house painting and was listed under both occupational headings in South Jersey business directories for 1850/51 and 1860. After working for his brother Maskell, Jr., prior to 1839, he had moved to Woodstown, Salem County, where he established an independent shop by December 1841. Although listed in the 1870 census as a painter of houses who employed four painters and glaziers, he continued chairmaking until his retirement in 1897. According to

[11]CC Deed 77/64 (March 22, 1847); Bradway (n. 2 above), p. 178; Manuscript Census Schedule 5, Stoe Creek Township, Cumberland County (1860); *Boyd's Business Directory of the Counties of Atlantic, Camden, Cape May, Cumberland, Gloucester, Monmouth, Ocean, and Salem, N.J. 1860* (Philadelphia and New York: William H. Boyd, 1860), p. 57; R. G. Dun & Co., *Mercantile Agency Reference Book* (New York, 1876); CC Inventory G-488.

[12]Manuscript Census Population Schedule, Fairfield Township, Cumberland County, N.J. (1850); *Kirkbride's*, p. 158; John W. Barber and Henry Howe, *Historical Collections of the State of New Jersey*, rev. ed. (1844; Newark, N.J.: Justus H. Bradley, 1855), p. 143.

[13]CC Deed 101-392 (November 1, 1863); *Mercantile Agency United States Business Directory for 1867* (New York: R. G. Dun & Co. and John F. Trow, 1866), p. 536; Manuscript Census Schedule 4, 3d Ward, Bridgeton, Cumberland County, N.J. (1870); Manuscript Census Schedule 1, 1st Ward, Bridgeton, Cumberland County, N.J. (1870); *Bradstreet's Commercial Reports*, vol. 26 (January 6, 1870); R. G. Dun & Co. (n. 11 above).

[14]Alfred M. Heston, ed., *South Jersey: A History 1664–1924*, 4 vols. (New York: Lewis Historical Publishing Co., 1924), 3:46; interview with Dr. Carl N. Ware, grandson of Francis Herbert Ware, August 27, 1975.

[15]Liz Smith, "Metal Box Holds Bygone Days," *Today's Sunbeam* (Salem County, N.J.) (August 9, 1976); CC Will P-243; Inventory O-654, Surrogate's Office, Salem County, N.J. (hereafter cited as SC Inventory).

Dan's will, written in 1896, all his "shop, fixtures, tools, etc., together with all unframed work that may be on hand" were to be given to his son Harold Maskell Ware (1853–?). The 1901 inventory of Dan's personal property included unspecified tools in his shop valued at $5.00, "Framed chairs in shop $3.00," "Finished chairs $30.00," and paint, oil, whiting, and cans appraised at $4.50.[16]

table) and nearly equaled the value of output of their rivals. Through informal apprenticeships, their sons and grandsons were taught the chairmaking skills which they practiced into the twentieth century.

Robert Bonham Ware (1819–1902), Thomas Ware's son, worked in Roadstown during the same period in which his cousin William H. Ware was active in Bridgeton. The 1870 census and

Production of Seating Furniture in
Cumberland County, 1860

Firm	Quantity	Value ($)
Whitaker and Newcomb	1,000 Chairs	500
	100 Settees	400
John S. Ware	100 Dozen rush chairs	800
Webster Newcomb	90 Dozen chairs	675
William Ware	100 Dozen chairs	700

SOURCE.—8th U.S. Census (1860), manuscript, Products of Industry Schedule, Archives and History Bureau, New Jersey State Library, Trenton.

Although Powers reported that Richard Moore Ware (1816–97), Maskell Ware's youngest son, learned to make chairs, he did not follow the trade. Instead, he studied law in the offices of James B. Dayton and ex-Governor Peter D. Vroom, at Trenton, and then established a practice at Mullica Hill, Gloucester County, New Jersey.[17]

Maskell Ware's five chairmaking sons perpetuated the Ware chairmaking tradition not only in Roadstown, but also in Woodstown, Bridgeton, and Cedarville. By 1860, two of their shops dominated production of seating furniture in Cumberland County in terms of quantity (see

Cumberland County business directories from 1893 through 1901 listed him as a chairmaker.[18]

More widely known than Robert Bonham Ware is his son George Sloan Ware (1853–1940), who worked with his father and brothers Warren and Frank in a shop located in front of the family home in Roadstown. Although listed in *The Farm Journal Farm Directory of Cumberland County New Jersey* (1913) as a carpenter, he manufactured rush-bottomed chairs of the same pattern and by the same processes as those used by his great-grandfather. His one concession to modernity was the substitution of motor for foot power to operate his lathe. According to family tradition, George Sloan Ware sold a portion of his output wholesale to the Van Sciver furniture store of Camden, New Jersey. In his will written in 1935, a year after his retirement, George mentioned specifically only three chairs. Of these one had been made by his uncle Henry Clay Ware. George left in his shop, in addition to the motor for his lathe, a tool chest and tools, six planes, two saws, a drawing knife, square, lathe and fixtures, "shaft

[16]According to the autobiographical sketch which Dan Ware prepared in 1888 and published in the 1891 edition of the family genealogy, he moved to Woodstown in 1839, but *The Biographical, Genealogical and Descriptive History of the First Congressional District of New Jersey* (2 vols. [New York: Lewis Historical Publishing Co., 1900], 2:105) states that he moved to Woodstown in 1843. *Kirkbride's*, p. 158; *Boyd's* (1860), p. 57; Deed XX-520, Clerk's Office, Salem County, N.J. (hereafter cited as SC Deed); Manuscript Census Schedule 4, Pilesgrove Township, Salem County, N.J. (1870); Will K-561, Surrogate's Office, Salem County, N.J. (hereafter cited as SC Will); SC Inventory N-713.

[17]Thomas Cushing and Charles E. Sheppard, *History of the Counties of Gloucester, Salem, and Cumberland, New Jersey, with Biographical Sketches of Their Prominent Citizens* (Philadelphia: Everts & Peck, 1883), pp. 133–34.

[18]Population Schedule, Stow Creek Township, Cumberland County, N.J., 9th U.S. Census (1870), National Archives; *Boyd's* (1893, 1895, 1897, 1899, 1901).

Fig. 4. Detail of photograph, "Edward Keely's Segar Manufactory, No. 381/S.S. Ware. CHAIRMAKER," ca. 1875. (Collection of Dorothy T. Stables: Photo, Benno M. Forman.)

& hanger" valued at $3.00, chair rounds worth 50¢, a crosscut saw, patent beam, grindstone, vise, box of bits, hacksaw, crowbar, block and pulley, and assorted junk.[19]

Others of Maskell Ware's line also have been mentioned as chairmakers. Samuel Sloan Ware (1848–1920), son of Henry Clay Ware, worked in Salem County. Although recorded as a resident of Stow Creek Township, Cumberland County, in 1870 and 1874, he worked subsequently above Edward Keely's store and cigar manufactory which moved from Bridgeton to Alloway, Salem County, in the mid 1870s. A granddaughter remembers visiting his workshop when he lived in the Burden Hill area of the Pine Barrens and seeing him turn chair parts on a lathe. Powers

stated that he used the heavy ball-turned front stretchers favored by his cousin George Sloan Ware; however, the two chairs shown in a surviving photograph (fig. 4) have simply turned front stretchers.[20]

Arthur Middleton Ware (1876–1932), son of Samuel Sloan Ware, may be the Arthur Ware of Salem who wove rush seats in the 1920s. Family members recall him and his father going out the Walnut Street Road from Salem to Elsinboro to cut rush. They stored the cured and bundled rush at Arthur M. Ware's home.[21]

Thomas Henry (Harry) Ware (1857–?), second son of Henry Clay Ware, settled at Marlboro, where he bottomed chairs and made axe handles.[22]

Harry's daughter, Elizabeth Ware Killian

[19]Ware, p. 101; CC Inventory U-419; Sara Carlisle Watson and Richard Joslin King, *American Craftsmen: The Ware Chairmakers* (n.p., n.d.), p. 8; Losada Carlisle, "The Wares' Famous Chairs," *Bridgeton Evening News* (April 11, 1970); CC Will 44-382; the Van Sciver firm has no purchase records available prior to 1940; CC Will 44-382; the five-slat armless rocker together with a card from George Sloan Ware stating that it was made by Henry C. Ware in 1853 was bequeathed to Ella J. Elwell. It was shown as no. 96 in the 1974 Wheaton Village exhibition.

[20]*Salem Sunbeam* (September 10, 1920); Carlisle, "The Wares' Famous Chairs"; SC Deed 77, 100 (March 30, 1893); R. G. Dun & Co.; Population Schedule, Stow Creek Township, Cumberland County, N.J., 9th U.S. Census (1870), National Archives; William C. Haskett included N. Mildred Hitchner's notes on Ware genealogy in a letter to Waters, April 24, 1978.

[21]Powers (n. 1 above), p. 308; Hitchner notes.

[22]Carlisle, "The Wares' Famous Chairs."

(1884–?), retained her father's shop and tools and engaged in chair repair work.[23]

Frank Riley Ware (1860–1932) of Roadstown, George Sloan Ware's brother, has been mentioned as one of "the last of the four generations of chairmakers."[24]

Theodore, son of Charles Ware (1851–ca. 1936), lived in Roadstown at the time of his death. Seven rush-bottomed chairs, two chair frames, and two rockers were included in his household furnishings. Other chairs in the house were listed as cane seated. However, no chairmaker's tools appear in his inventory. According to Bradway, Theodore worked at chairmaking until he was twenty-seven and had in daily use before his death a chair which he had made nearly sixty years previously.[25]

Wilmon Ware (1853–?), Theodore's brother, may merit the distinction of being the last of the Ware chairmakers. A truck farmer raising peppers in Newport, New Jersey, in 1913, Wilmon completed a curled maple chair of excellent design and workmanship in the mid-1930s, according to Bradway. He continued to bottom chairs, if not make them, as late as 1942.[26]

Although no account books kept by members of Maskell Ware's immediate family are known, those of two craftsmen related to the family survive. The variety of tasks performed by a rural craftsman, as recorded in the accounts of Maskell's nephew, Samuel Fithian Ware of Cape May County (1800–77), contrast markedly with those of a craftsman resident in a county seat—Salem's William G. Beesley.

That Samuel Fithian Ware's shop equipment included a lathe is evident from his charges for turning such diverse items as "two Augur handles," "30 sein[e] corks," "62 Balls for Biliard Table," several dozen clothespins, a "whirl to wheel," and a "handle to winnowing mill." For making rocking chairs in 1822 and 1828, he charged customers $1.50. Three chairs of unspecified type cost $3.00 in 1823. Ware also made a "bonnet box for Harriet," "splints for J. Stevens arm," hanging

shelves, tables, cupboards, grain cradles, and plows. A significant portion of his craft activity was devoted to repairing or altering existing furniture. In 1824, he charged $2.25 for "bottoming 6 Chairs." His standard charge for adding rockers to a chair was 25¢, but for "bottoming rockers varnishing 1 Chair," he charged 75¢. He also painted and mended a variety of chairs. In addition, he performed chores more commonly executed by a wheelwright, such as rimming a wheelbarrow wheel and mending sulky chairs and other vehicles. A portion of his income came from house carpentry, in which he was assisted by his younger brother Wilmon W. Ware (1818–86). On occasion he did heavier work; once, on June 3, 1830, he billed Joseph B. Hughes $11 for "moving house." Besides craft-related work, Ware also recorded charges for performing agricultural chores like a day's mowing, cradling rye, and raking. He received payment for these services, and for chairmaking, in goods such as "1 load of brush," "gum stick," a "smoothing plain," and an oil stone; in services such as "horse hire to go to Roadstown"; or in foodstuffs like quarters of veal and beef.[27]

From the latter 1830s until his death in the 1870s, an increasing segment of Samuel Fithian Ware's income came from coffin sales and undertaking services. In his workshop at the time of his death were a variety of cabinetmaker's tools; walnut, mahogany, and poplar boards; seven completed coffins valued at $4.00 each; coffin hardware; fabrics and trimmings for lining coffins; and an icebox. According to his inventory, he had a half interest in a "Taylor's Corpse Preserver," as well as a half interest in a hearse, shafts, pole, one pair of undertaker's stools, and one pair of grave straps. His son-in-law, H. Rutherford, owned the other half interest in those items. Apparently, undertaking was more profitable than chairmaking and farming, for Samuel Fithian Ware's total personal estate, including numerous small sums of money out on loan, was valued at nearly $21,000, while the personal property of Charles Ware (Maskell's grandson), including chairmaking tools and livestock, was worth only $438 just two years later in 1879.[28]

[23]Watson and King, p. 5.

[24]Ware, p. 101; Losada Carlisle, "Chairmakers' Homes of the Past," *Bridgeton Evening News* (April 18, 1970).

[25]Watson and King, p. 3; Carlisle, "Chairmakers' Homes of the Past"; CC Inventory T-439.

[26]*Farm Journal Farm Directory of Cumberland County, New Jersey, 1913* (Philadelphia: Wilmer Atkinson Co., 1913), p. 66; *Fenwick's Colony: Salem County Pictorial 1675–1964* (Salem, N.J.: Salem County Tercentenary Committee, 1964), p. 53.

[27]Samuel Fit[h]ian Ware, Account Book, Joseph Downs Manuscript and Microfilm Collection, 74 × 366, Winterthur Museum Library, Winterthur, Del.

[28]Will and Inventory 1756E, Archives and History Bureau, New Jersey State Library, Trenton; CC Inventory G-206.

While the diversity of assignments under-taken by a townsman might rival that of his country counterpart, he rarely engaged in noncraft work. This distinction is evident in the entries made by chairmaker and ornamental painter William G. Beesley in his daybook between March 29, 1828, and December 1841. Beesley, first employer and then employee of Elijah Ware (1814–93), worked in Salem, "a snug little, out-of-the-way town—the market of a rich and widely-cultivated tract; with a goodly number of substantial families of Swedish and English descent."[29]

Beesley's daybook records sales of a number of seating-furniture forms with types of ornamentation not generally associated with Ware chairs. Not only are rocking chairs listed, priced between $1.25 and $3.00 with a majority at the same $1.50 charged by Samuel Fithian Ware, but also children's rocking chairs, a "hieback rocking chair" priced at $3.50 in 1828, and a "scroll back rocking chair" for $2.00 in 1830. In 1831, the fee for painting a fancy rocking chair was 75¢, the sum charged for "putting rockers on a large chair" the previous year. For altering a chair by adding rockers, putting on a "writing bord," and painting it, Beesley charged $1.50 in 1832. Stools of various types, including a countinghouse stool at 75¢, appear in the entries, as do sewing chairs and settees with or without ornamentation. Other chairs were available in "plain" or "ornamented" versions with either straight or bent backs. For bent backs, constructed with a definite backward bend to the rear posts above the seat rail, Beesley generally charged one dollar more per half dozen than he did for straight-back chairs. "Ball-back chairs," perhaps similar to the chair illustrated in John S. and William Ware's 1826 advertisement (see fig. 3), and scroll-back chairs were the most expensive, $8.50 per half dozen in 1829 and 1830. Beginning in 1834, sales of "broad top chairs" at $7.50 per half dozen and charges for ornamenting "broad tops" are recorded.

Although Beesley sold several chairs specified as "hie back," such a description is insufficient to clearly define the form.[30]

Beesley was primarily an assembler and decorator of chairs. He purchased chair parts from several sources. One supplier was Nathaniel G. Swing (1798–?) of "Swing's Corner," Salem County, who sold Beesley quantities of "st. back" and bent-back stuff, settee stretchers, chair bows, stumps for arms, and "100 Ball sticks" between 1829 and 1834. Swing manufactured such turnings as well as carriage wheel hubs and spokes in the horsepowered mill which he had erected in 1825. William Major, in 1831, and Jacob Anderson, in 1832, sawed off chair seats for Beesley's plank-seated chairs. Other craftsmen, like cabinetmakers Hezekiah Hews, Thomas McDonnol, and George W. Conarroe (better known as a painter), exchanged case furniture and bedsteads for Beesley's chairs, putty, varnish, cash, or credit.[31]

The first references in Beesley's records to Elijah Ware, Maskell's relative, appear in March 1830, when a customer was charged for "four days work painting by Elijah $4.00." On August 2, 1834, Beesley recorded the transfer of his stock-in-trade to Ware. Little more than seven months later, on March 25, 1835, he agreed to tend Elijah's shop and ornament his chairs at $1.00 per week. Thereafter he charged Ware for "streaking," "ornamenting," "shading," and "mapoling" a variety of chairs; for painting and glazing window lights and sash; for painting and gilding a tin sign; and for lettering twenty-one fire badges.[32]

Continuing the business after Beesley's death in 1842, Elijah Ware advertised a "large lot of Picture and Window Glass" in thirty-five different sizes for sale, "very cheap," in July 1848. Both the 1850 census returns and *Kirkbride's Business Directory* listed him as a house and sign painter. The census also indicated that two apprentices, David Ware and John Harris, resided with his family in that year. Within three years, Ware transferred the painting and glazing segments of his business to Harris and one William N. Davis. The sale

[29] Beesley Day Book, MN-52, Salem County Historical Society, Salem, N.J.; Elijah Ware, whose home and chairmaking shop were at 255 East Broadway, Salem (White [n. 1 above], p. 86), probably was the son of Job Ware and his third wife Mary Beesley Ware. The will of this Elijah Ware was proved on December 1, 1893 (SC Will J-79). Elijah's grandfather, John Ware, Jr. (1722–73), was the half-brother of Elnathan Ware, Maskell Ware's father; Charles Joseph Latrobe, *The Rambler in North America*, 2 vols. (London: R. B. Seeley & W. Burnside, 1836), 2:87.

[30] Beesley Day Book.

[31] Gilbert S. Swing, *Events in the Life and History of the Swing Family* (Camden, N.J.: Graw, Garrigues & Graw, 1889), pp. 117–18; Beesley Day Book.

[32] Beesley Day Book; *Freeman's Banner* (Salem, N.J.) (December 24, 1834).

permitted him to focus on merchandising paints, pigments, glass, brushes, and the "good assortment of chairs and settees" kept "constantly on hand." Ware severed completely his connection with the chair trade in August 1859, when he sold his stock and fixtures to Salem competitor William P. Chattin.[33]

Whether working in Cumberland County or Salem County, the Ware chairmakers confronted regional as well as local competition for sales. The low transportation costs and frequent shipping departures that had directed South Jersey farmers to the Philadelphia market in the colonial period continued and expanded in the nineteenth century with the development of stage lines, steamboats, and railroads. Philadelphia manufacturers and retailers advertised widely in South Jersey newspapers. Both cabinet- and chairmaker A. I. Bowen and Thomas Nossitter, proprietor of a cabinet, chair, and sofa warehouse located on North Front Street in Philadelphia, sought Bridgeton clients in the 1820s. Nossitter appealed to potential customers by noting that goods purchased from his firm would be packed for shipping and put aboard any vessel. Salem Countian John Simpson bought eight fancy chairs at $2.62 each and one "maple rock chair" at $9.00 from the fancy chair wareroom of Stephen H. Simmons located at 122 South Second Street in 1836. Philadelphia merchant and chairmaker Dell Noblit, Jr., offered counting house chairs and camp stools at his carpeting, bedding, and furnishing warerooms, 83 South Second Street, in 1849, while the 1852 consumer could select from the "large and fashionable stock of Cane seat, Rush seat and Windsor chairs, Arm chairs, large and small rocking chairs, Settees," lounges and stools manufactured at N. F. Wood's chair factory, 131 North Sixth Street, opposite Franklin Square. Other Philadelphians who sought South

Jersey sales included George W. Allen, proprietor of a wholesale and retail fancy chair manufactory and H. F. Hoover, 126 South Second Street, who packed goods for Cumberland County customers with "care and dispatch."[34]

Nor can the Ware family's long period of craft activity be attributed to a dearth of local competition. In the 1820s John S. and William Ware shared the Bridgeton market with Richard Hand, producer of first-quality "fancy and Windsor chairs equal to those made in Philadelphia," and with veteran cabinet- and chairmaker Josiah Fithian, among others. Although the "ball-backed" fancy chair in the 1826 Ware advertisement was probably a stock printer's ornament, the brothers may have produced or sold rush-bottomed chairs, as did Hand, who advertised "an assortment of common Rush-bottomed chairs, for sale," in 1827.[35]

In Salem, William P. Chattin (ca. 1823–ca. 1887), among others, challenged and then succeeded Elijah Ware. Chattin, a house and sign painter, took over the stand previously occupied by cabinetmaker Elijah Gilmore on Market Street in 1847. There he offered for sale painting supplies and "an assortment of chairs and cabinet furniture." The following year, he sought an apprentice to the housepainting and chairmaking business between the ages of fourteen and seventeen. By 1850, Chattin and two assistants, William Davis and Joseph S. Dubose, both nineteen, were producing chairs valued at $750 and miscellaneous cabinetware worth $1,200 annually. After a brief partnership with William Sparks at the West Jersey Furniture Warerooms in 1851, he continued independently, offering "an assortment of substantial and neat-made Furniture . . .

[33]William N. Davis may be the William Davis who was listed in William P. Chattin's household in 1850 as a house painter; the Davis and Harris partnership dissolved on December 19, 1855, with Davis continuing the house and sign painting and glazing business at the stand formerly occupied by the firm (which was nearly opposite the Friends Meeting House); John Harris joined William B. Smith in a new house and sign painting firm which operated from the basement of James Brown's new building on Broadway in Salem. SC Will D-352; SC Inventory E-219; *National Standard and Salem County Advertiser* (July 26, 1848); Manuscript Census Population Schedule, Salem, Salem County, N.J. (1850); *Kirkbride's*, p. 263; *National Standard and Salem County Advertiser* (December 30, 1853.)

[34]John F. Walzer, "Colonial Philadelphia and Its Backcountry," in *Winterthur Portfolio 7*, ed. Ian M. G. Quimby (Charlottesville: University Press of Virginia for the Henry Francis du Pont Winterthur Museum, 1972), p. 163; *Washington Whig* (November 20, 1820; April 3, 1824); Simmons to Simpson, March 29, 1836, typescript, Margaret E. White files, Newark Museum, Newark, N.J.; *Sunbeam* (November 16, 1849; October 8, 1852); *West-Jersey Pioneer* (March 3, May 5, 1855).

[35]The same cut appears in N. W. Burpee's advertisement in the *Canadian Courant* (September 9, 1828) (reproduced in *Antiques* 105, no. 5 [May 1974]: 1134] and in the advertisement of chairmakers Mullen and Cowperthwaite (*Cincinnati Directory for 1834* [Cincinnati, 1834]; *Washington Whig* [January 23, 1823]; *Bridgeton Observer and Cumberland Cape-May & Salem Advertiser* [March 25, 1826]; *Washington Whig and Bridgeton Observer and Cumberland, Cape May & Salem Advertiser* [November 3, 1827]).

consisting of our own make of Chairs," tables, case pieces, and bedsteads. On August 31, 1859, Chattin advertised that he had purchased Elijah Ware's interest in the paint, glass, and chair business and moved the stock and fixtures to his own paint and furniture store. Advertising as a house and sign painter, grainer, and paperhanger in 1861, Chattin operated from his shop on Fenwick Street. Fifteen years later, *The Mercantile Agency Reference Book* listed Chattin as a painter and cabinetmaker, with an estimated pecuniary strength between $2,000 and $5,000 and a fair credit rating. Elijah and Maskell Ware, Jr., listed no lathe when they appraised his estate, including the contents of his paint shop, after his death.[36]

Even in Cedarville, Reuben Ware was not alone. Competitors A. F. and E. F. Bateman advertised the availability of all kinds of furniture, willow cradles, window sash and frames, doors, shutters, and revolving blinds, as well as undertaking services, at their shop in 1856. Chairmaker Webster Newcomb in 1859/60 produced ninety dozen chairs valued at $675 from $250 worth of planks and turned chair stuff.[37]

A writer for *The West-Jersey Pioneer,* surveying the Cumberland County chair industry in 1856, reported "until within a short time since, but few or no chairs and settees were manufactured in this part of the state, except rush bottom chairs." The establishment of two windsor (plank-seated) chair and settee manufactories, one conducted by Whitaker and Newcomb, first in Cedarville and subsequently in Bridgeton, and the other by Johnson and Tatem, near the corner of Broad and Franklin streets in Bridgeton, altered the situation by the mid-1850s. Ephraim E. Johnson and E. S. Tatem advertised that "dealers in CHAIRS will find it to their advantage to call on the subscribers as they intend to wholesale chairs and settees at city prices. N.B. the chairs and settees we sell are made by us and we warrant them to give satisfaction. Old chairs repaired, re-painted and ornamented to look as well as new." The *Pioneer* reporter noted that the

partners were "young men who understand their business and sell goods on the right terms." Whitaker and Newcomb, according to the *Pioneer,* "by personal application and good workmanship," filled their shop with articles at fair prices and "had more orders than they could fill." When they announced the opening of their furniture store at No. 4 Carl's Building in Bridgeton in March 1859, they featured a self-rocking cradle, "A Sure Remedy for Cross Babies," fancy chairs, and "a large lot of windsor chairs and settees of our own make, which have always taken the premium for durability and finish." According to the 1860 census figures, their manufactory assembled 1,000 chairs valued at $500, and 100 settees at $400, from chair and settee stuff and sundries costing $320 in 1859/60.[38]

Given the alternative sources and types of seating furniture available to potential Ware customers, why did some choose the locally made rush-bottomed product? As a factor, fashion was irrelevant. Widely popular among Delaware Valley households of all economic levels during most of the eighteenth century, the rush-bottomed chair was no longer considered suitable for the reception areas of stylish South Jersey homes by mid-nineteenth century. *The West-Jersey Pioneer*'s reporter summarized the shift in taste:

Twenty or thirty years since, when people cared more for comfort and less for show than they do at the present day, they could sit in rush bottom chairs, and without a blush, offer one to a friend who might chance to call in their parlor, but show us a parlor now-a-days furnished with rush bottom chairs, and we will show you a person of but little pretensions to fashion or show. It is a question with some, what kind of chairs are the most comfortable, and not a few are in favor of the old rush, but modern fashions and customs have placed them nearly all in the kitchen or up in the loft. Occasionally we see in an ancient farm house or at a vendue, a set of the primitive style, which are relics of the past, fast passing away to give place to the windsor and more fashionable styles.[39]

As the reporter suggested, consideration of comfort may have favored the purchase of rush-

[36]*National Standard and Salem County Advertiser* (March 8, May 10, 1848; August 31, 1859; June 19, 1861); White, p. 57; Manuscript Census Schedule 5 and Population Schedule, Salem, Salem County, N.J. (1850); *Sunbeam and Democratic Journal* (February 21, October 3, 1851); R. G. Dun & Co. (n. 11 above); SC Inventory L-167.
[37]*West-Jersey Pioneer* (May 24, 1856); *Boyd's* (1860), p. 57; Manuscript Census Schedule 5, Fairfield Township, Cumberland County, N.J. (1860).

[38]*West-Jersey Pioneer* (September 13, 1856; October 27, 1855; August 2, 1856; March 26, 1859); Manuscript Census Schedule 5, Bridgeton, Bridgeton Township, Cumberland County, N.J. (1860).
[39]Nancy Goyne Evans, "Unsophisticated Furniture Made and Used in Philadelphia and Environs, ca. 1750–1800," in Morse (n. 2 above), pp. 162–67; *West-Jersey Pioneer* (September 13, 1856).

bottom chairs. Low unit cost was also a consideration. When a bent-back rush-bottomed chair retailed at from $1.25 to $1.50, a windsor chair cost $3.75 or more in Bridgeton shops. In its consistency of design concept, the rush-bottom chair also may have appealed to a conservative clientele wishing to retain familiar furnishing forms.[40]

For more than 150 years, local demand encouraged the chairmakers of the Ware family, working in Cumberland, Salem, and Cape May counties, to produce large quantities of turned chairs for the South Jersey region. Despite competition from other suppliers of seating furniture, they maintained their share of the market while continuing to produce chairs of traditional form. Through informal apprenticeships within the family, the craft skills necessary for chairmaking survived and thrived for four generations.

[40]MacDonald, pp. 16–17; *West-Jersey Pioneer* (March 31, 1855).

A Cabinetmaker's Price Book

Martin Eli Weil

PRICE BOOKS of cabinet- and chairmakers came into popular use in the late eighteenth century and today are a major source of information on the conduct of the furniture-making business during its handicraft phase. They are especially useful for the insights they provide into the terminology used by the craftsman himself as opposed to the terminology invented in subsequent years by collectors and dealers. The presence or, indeed, the absence of certain furniture forms can suggest the preferences of customers within the area served by the cabinetmaker. Most of all, perhaps, the price books reveal the economics of the trade. Their very existence suggests the need to establish stable and uniform prices, which in turn suggests that the trade was disturbed by competitive pricing practices. Costs were an essential part of the problem—perhaps the major problem—because the wages of journeymen are often the object of detailed attention. It is surely no coincidence that journeymen began forming their own organizations, thereby separating their interests from those of the masters, at about the same time that price books were introduced.

Most American price books for cabinet- and chairwork derive from English examples. The first printed English price book known was published in 1788. The first printed American example extant, of which only six pages survive, was published in Hartford, Connecticut, in 1792. The first major American printed price book was produced in Philadelphia in 1794. It is known only through the revised edition published in the following year. Significantly, the book was published on behalf of the Federal Society of Chair Makers, an organization of journeymen engaged at the time in a dispute with masters over wages. Two other price books followed in rapid succession, with the second, *The Cabinet-Makers Philadelphia and London Book of Prices of 1796,* basing its rate structure precisely on a 1793 London book. It represented a compromise worked out between the masters and the journeymen.[1]

That there were earlier attempts to agree on prices for cabinet- and chairwork is indicated by the several price lists that survive in manuscript form. The earliest known American example is "Rule and Price of Joyners Work—A Table of Joyners Work," an agreement signed in 1757 by six Providence, Rhode Island, craftsmen. By far the most useful and extensive of such lists is the manuscript in the Historical Society of Pennsylvania entitled "Prices of Cabinet & Chair Work/Binjamin Lehman January 1786." Selections from this document were published in 1904, and a complete transcription was published in 1930. Lehman was thought to be a cabinetmaker at first, but William Macpherson Hornor, Jr., could only find evidence that he was a lumber dealer and keeper of a livery stable.[2]

Recently another manuscript price list was discovered in the library of the Tyler Arboretum in Lima, Pennsylvania. This thirteen-page, handwritten, bound booklet is in poor condition, but it throws open to question the whole matter of when price books were introduced in America and, for that matter, England. Although in-

[1]Charles F. Montgomery, *American Furniture: The Federal Period* (New York: Viking Press, 1966), pp. 19–26.
[2]"The Furniture of Our Ancestors," *Pennsylvania Magazine of History and Biography* 28, no. 1 (1904): 78–83, and no. 2, pp. 199–200; Harrold E. Gillingham, "Benjamin Lehman, A Germantown Cabinetmaker," *Pennsylvania Magazine of History and Biography* 54, no. 4 (1930): 288–306; William Macpherson Hornor, Jr., "Fancy versus Facts," *Antiquarian* 15, no. 5 (November 1930): 76, 108, 112.

complete because of damage or deterioration, the title contains significant information. It reads "Prices of Cabinet & Chair . . . /Philadelphia printed by James Hum . . . / at the loer Corner of Black hors Aley / M,DCCLXXII Copied out of. . . ." Here is clear evidence that a *printed* price book was published in Philadelphia in 1772 by the well-known printer James Humphreys. No such book is known nor have any other references to it been found. Barring the possibility that the anonymous scribe erred in the date, it appears that a price book existed sixteen years prior to the earliest known English printed example and twenty-two years before *The Philadelphia Cabinet and Chair-Makers' Book of Prices* (1794).[3]

The Tyler manuscript price book closely resembles the Lehman manuscript in content. With a few exceptions, it lists the same forms in the same order. Both have three columns of figures, which might pose a mystery except the columns in the Lehman manuscript are titled mahogany, walnut, and journeyman. The prices are the same in both documents. The similarities between the two documents suggest a common source, probably the book whose existence is so strongly implied in the Tyler manuscript.

The differences between the two documents are also instructive. The Lehman list was executed by a better hand, its entries are more complete, it includes some additional furniture forms, it is dated, its ownership seems clear, and it explains the three columns of figures. The Tyler list is written in a less precise hand, has omissions, and its original ownership is uncertain.

The Tyler manuscript bears no relation to the Providence example of 1756 and 1757, the oldest known American price list. Neither is there any resemblance in format, content, or vocabulary to the earliest known published British list, *The Cabinet-Makers' London Book of Prices and Designs of Cabinet Work,* published in 1788 and the presumed model for the various American price books of the 1790s. There are some similarities between the Tyler manuscript and the fragmentary 1792 Hartford price book. While the individual entries differ, both price lists use a common vocabulary and describe similar furniture forms. As in the case of the Lehman price book, a common source for both is a possibility.

The history of the Tyler price book remains obscure. The manuscript was discovered among the family papers in the library of the John J. Tyler (Painter) Arboretum. The Minshall, Tyler, and Painter families are all descendants of Thomas Minshall (1652–1727) and his wife Margaret who in 1682 settled the land in Upper Providence Township, Delaware County, now occupied by the arboretum. Although it is not known how the price book came into the collection, it seems likely that it belonged originally to a member of the Minshall family. Possibly it belonged to Thomas Minshall (1708–83), grandson of the original settler, who was a farmer and wheelwright. In addition to farming and general merchandising, he or his employees provided numerous services which included cabinetmaking, carpentry, toolmaking, weaving, shoemaking, and carting. Minshall's accounts for the 1740s and 1750s reveal that he sold rocking chairs, tables, clock cases, bedsteads, cupboards, as well as coffins, apple mills, cider mills, cheese presses, dough troughs, and salt boxes. His son, Jacob Minshall (1738–1818), continued in the tradition of the versatile country craftsman, and his accounts include the making and repairing of furniture. The inventory of his estate in 1818 contained a wide range of woodworking tools. However, there is no evidence that Thomas or Jacob Minshall owned the price list, beyond its presence among the family papers.[4]

Turning to evidence in the price list itself, there is the intriguing reference in the title to James Humphreys as the printer of the book from which this manuscript was apparently copied. James Humphreys learned the printing trade from William Bradford. In 1772, the same year the mysterious source book was published, he set out on his own. His advertisement of July 6, 1772, in *The Pennsylvania Packet* announced that "having furnished himself with a general and

---

[3] I wish to express my deep appreciation to Mrs. Virginia Willis, former archivist at the Tyler Arboretum, Lima, Pa., for bringing the Tyler manuscript to my attention.

[4] The papers of the Minshalls, Painters, and Tylers were scrupulously maintained by succeeding generations of the families. These documents along with the furniture, structures, and landscaped grounds are preserved by the Tyler Arboretum. The following documents in the archives of the arboretum were used in the preparation of this paper: AV2 1735–55, Thomas Minshall Account Book; AV2 1746–91, Account Book Thomas Minshall and Son Jacob; AV2 1733–1809, Jacob Minshall Account Book; AV2 1775–79, Thomas Minshall or Jacob Account Book Weaving; AV2 1789–91, Jacob Minshall Account Book; AV2 1791, Jacob Minshall Account Book Records of Importing Goods; AV2 1791–1816, Enos Painter Account Book cost of Imported Dry Goods; AV2 1799–1800, Jacob Minshall Account Book Wages Payment for farm Labour; and AV2 1799–1818, Jacob Minshall Administrator for John Tyler and Agness.

neat assortment of Printing Materials, [he] has opened an Office at his father's house, at the lower corner of Black-Horse Alley, in front-street, where he purposes carrying on the Printing Business in a most extensive manner."

Between 1775 and 1778 he published the *Pennsylvania Ledger; or the Virginia, Maryland, Pennsylvania & New-Jersey Weekly Advertiser.* As a loyalist he found himself increasingly at odds with local patriots. Late in 1776 he ceased publication but resumed after the British occupation of Philadelphia in 1777. On May 23, 1778, shortly before British forces evacuated Philadelphia, Humphreys ceased publication of the *Pennsylvania Ledger* for good. Subsequently, he went to New York, England, and Nova Scotia before returning to Philadelphia in 1797 where he carried on the printing business until his death in 1810.[5]

Except for the information in the Tyler manuscript, no other evidence has been discovered to suggest that Humphreys printed a price book for Philadelphia cabinet- and chairmakers. Such a book would, in all probability, have been produced in a small edition and because of its semisecret nature would not have been advertised. All copies may have perished with time. It might be of interest to note that Humphreys printed what might be considered related material: *Rules and Constitutions of the Society of the Sons of St. George* (1772) and a broadside entitled "The Rates of Porterage and Carriage, &c to any parts of the City and Suburbs, proper to be stuck up in taverns, stores, shops, &c" (1774).[6]

Why should manuscript copies survive when the printed source does not? The reason in this case may be the special role of price books in eighteenth-century America. As early as 1732 the carpenters of Philadelphia had organized for the purposes of regulating prices charged for their

work and establishing standards of workmanship. The lists of prices were limited to the use of members, who were subject to fines or expulsion for divulging this information to outsiders. The Carpenters Company of the City and County of Philadelphia made occasional exceptions, as when the company permitted carpenters in Boston and Baltimore to borrow its price book to aid them in preparing their own.[7]

The practice of the Philadelphia carpenters suggests two conclusions that might also apply to Philadelphia cabinet- and chairmakers. First, the carpenters had manuscript price books long before they had printed ones. (The first one known printed was in 1786.) Second, the secrecy surrounding prices was relaxed when it came to fellow craftsmen not working in Philadelphia and who, therefore, did not represent potential competition. Possibly Philadelphia cabinet- and chairmakers permitted out-of-town craftsmen the privilege of copying their price books as well, and perhaps that is why the Tyler and Lehman manuscripts exist.

The content of the Tyler manuscript corroborates currently held views regarding the variety and sophistication of Philadelphia furniture in the third quarter of the eighteenth century. There are 84 entries for tables, 61 for case furniture, 37 for chairs, 24 for sofas, 10 for beds, and 3 for firescreens. Windsor chairs and looking glasses are not listed. One anachronistic and puzzling item is the entry for joint stools "with a drawer and sliding top 3 feet long." Otherwise the price list represents a wide range of furniture forms with high-style Queen Anne and Chippendale characteristics. These two terms are not used in the document; the stylistic character of each piece is determined by the description of the details. Chairs, for example, were available with "crooked legs" (i.e., cabriole legs) having either "plain" or claw feet. (A "plain" foot may be what is now called a pad foot.) The alternative was Marlborough legs with or without "bases" and "brackets." What this and similar information in the list suggest is the simultaneous availability of Queen Anne and Chippendale characteristics. Since most of the furniture was offered in either

[5] Isaiah Thomas, *The History of Printing in America*, ed. Marcus A. McCorison (2d ed., 1874; reprint ed., Barre, Mass.: Imprint Society, 1970), pp. 397–99, 439–40; "William McCulloch's Additions to Thomas's History of Printing," *Proceedings of the American Antiquarian Society*, n.s. 31, pt. 1 (April 1921): 133–34; Douglas C. McMurtrie, *A History of Printing in the United States*, vol. 2, *Middle and South Atlantic States* (1932; reprint ed., New York: Burt Franklin, 1969), pp. 60–61; and Charles Evans, *American Bibliography*, 13 vols. (1903; reprint ed., New York: Peter Smith, 1941–42), see esp. vol. 4 for 1772. For additional imprints of Humphreys, see also Roger P. Bristol, *Supplement to Charles Evans' American Bibliography* (Charlottesville, Va.: University Press of Virginia for the Bibliographical Society of America and the Bibliographical Society of the University of Virginia, 1970).

[6] Evans, 4: no. 12528, and 5: 13563.

[7] The Housewrights of Boston to the Carpenters' Co. (of Philadelphia), June 13, 1804, Papers of the Carpenters' Company, vol. 32, p. 36, Library of the American Philosophical Society, Philadelphia; December 15, 1773, Wardens Book No. 2, February 1, 1769 to July 16, 1781, Papers of the Carpenters' Co., p. 77.

walnut or mahogany, attempts to date Philadelphia furniture by these criteria alone must be regarded as meaningless speculation.

Some terminology is momentarily confusing. It is clear from the context, however, that "'bannister" is the eighteenth-century cabinetmaker's term for splat. An "open" or "cut through" banister is a pierced splat, and "relieving the bannister" meant carving the splat. "Fluted or ogee back" refers not to the entire chair back but to the decorative treatment of the front surface of the stiles.

Extra features abound on large case furniture. Tops of desks and bookcases are described as having either "squair heads," pitch pediments, or scroll pediments. They might also include a "shield," "roses," and "blazes" or, in modern parlance, a cartouche, rosettes, and flame finials. A corner cupboard could have "common sash dores," a "plain pannel dore," "scalloped dores and flat pannels," or "Chinese dores." In desks one could chose between shell drawers, scalloped drawers, and column drawers, in addition to "sliding prospects," the central drawer in the working section of most desks.

A "folding stand" does not immediately suggest a familiar form, but further reading in the entry offers enough information to make a positive identification. A "stand 22 inches with a box" available with claw feet, leaves on the knees, and fluting on the pillar reveals the familiar tilt-top table with the so-called bird cage. They were available in a smaller diameter as "stands fixed." "Dum waiteres with four topes" are pole stands with graduated circular shelves.[8]

Some design features commonly associated with Philadelphia furniture of the period are not mentioned in the Tyler manuscript. These include the trifid foot, the hairy-paw foot, and the carved "spit curls" on the crests of arm and side chairs. Perhaps these features are covered by the phrase found in the section on chairs: "for Any Extraordinary Work Ad in proporsion."

While most entries quote prices for both mahogany and walnut, occasionally prices are specified for one material only. Low chests of drawers are priced only in walnut, but card tables with round corners, commode dressing tables,

china tables, certain frames for marble slabs, and dumbwaiters are priced only in mahogany.

Four woods other than mahogany and walnut are mentioned in the price book. Pine is noted in connection with a kitchen table and a clothespress. Red cedar was an option for lining a clothespress, and poplar is mentioned in conjunction with beds. Extrapolating from the Lehman list (because of damage to this portion of the Tyler list), oak is the wood designated for a stool. Other materials mentioned include "stuffing" for the backs and seats of chairs; leather, damask, and "hair bottoms" for chairs and settees; "cloath" and "green cloth" for card tables; cording for bedsteads; and casters for sofas.

While the descriptive entries provide an excellent source of information concerning the design choices and materials favored by the Philadelphia cabinet- and chairmakers, the list of prices is especially valuable for the insight into the prices that were charged for the furniture and the wages that were paid to the journeyman. Prices for individual pieces of furniture varied from 5s. for an oak stool to £22 for a mahogany chest on frame. Within this spectrum the most expensive items were case pieces that cost from £4 to £21. Next in value were sofas and settees (£4.0.0–£10.10.0), tables (£1.17.6–£10.0.0), chairs (£1.0.0–£3.15.0) and bedsteads (£0.5.0–£0.12.0).

Furniture made in mahogany generally cost about one-third more than when it was made in walnut, although the difference could range from 25 percent to 40 percent. Only two entries in the price book indicate the availability of a third wood other than mahogany or walnut. The clothespress made in pine and the stool made in oak were approximately one-third cheaper than walnut and one-half the price of mahogany.

The third column in the price book was reserved for indicating the amount of money due the journeyman. Neither the Tyler nor the Lehman manuscript indicates whether the price charged the customer was the amount listed in the first two columns or if the total cost was the sum of the first or second column and the amount in the third column. It was assumed for the purpose of this paper that the price charged for a piece of furniture was the figure listed in either the first or second columns. The guideline set forth in the price book guaranteed journeymen the same wage whether the furniture was made of mahogany or walnut. Journeymen's wages gener-

---

[8] I am indebted to Benno M. Forman, research fellow and teaching associate, Education Divison, Winterthur Museum, Winterthur, Del., for assistance in identifying some of the period terminology used in the Tyler manuscript.

ally amounted to 25 percent of the cost of mahogany furniture, 30 percent of the cost of walnut furniture, and 40 percent of the cost of pine furniture. Journeymen's wages varied somewhat according to the form of the furniture. Usually, they accounted for 35 percent of the cost of case furniture and tables, 32 percent for chairs, and 25 percent for sofas and beds. As one would expect, the more elaborate furniture forms or those pieces constructed entirely of exposed wooden elements required greater labor, and thus journeymen's wages represent a larger percentage of the total cost.

The appearance of journeymen's wages in the Tyler price book is strong evidence that by the 1770s there was sufficient difference of interest between the masters and the journeymen concerning equitable remuneration for work to warrant the preparation of comprehensive guidelines. While it is not known at this time if the document was drawn up by the masters or the journeymen, it is reasonable to assume that the associations that existed in the furniture-making trade at the end of the eighteenth century had their roots in prerevolutionary Philadelphia. The price books published in Philadelphia in the 1790s were clearly the result of sophisticated negotiations between the two groups in the industry. Each of the price books was published either by a group of journeymen or master craftsmen in response to the wage negotiations then in progress. The existence of the Tyler manuscript suggests that an association had formed within the furniture industry during the third quarter of the eighteenth century. Certainly, a printed book of prices published in 1772 must alter our view of cabinetmaking in Philadelphia in the late colonial period.

Prices of ____ of ____ Chair ____

Philadelphia printed by James ____

at the ____ corner of Black hors Alley

M,DCCLXXII   Copied out of

1772

	L	s	d	L	s	d	L	s	d
Desk winged	14	0	0	10	0				
Ditto with Scolloped drawers below									
& Shell drawers above	13	10	0	9	10	0	4	0	
Ditto with Collomd drawers	12	10	0	8	10	0	3		
& Sliding prospect	13	0	0	9	0	0	4		
Ditto with two Rows of ____	11	15	0	8	0	0			
Ditto with out A prospect ____	10	0	0	7	0	0			
Ditto with A prospect ____	10	0	0	7	10				
Book Cases with dentels									
& fret work	7	10	0	5					
Ditto Squair hed pannel									
or Sash dores & Sliding Shelves	0	0	0	4					
Ditto pitch pederment hed without									
denteles & fret & plain balls	7	10	0	5	0	0			
Ditto with dentels fret & Shield	10	0	0	0	0	0			
Ditto with Arch drawers	10	10	0	7					
Ditto with Scolloped drawers	11	0		8	0	0			
Ditto with Chine ____	12			9	0				
Ditto ____ hed ____									
nel dores Chine	15	0	0	10	0				
____									

High Chest of Drawers

	£	s	d	£	s	d	£	s	d
Chest on a frame of square hed & corni	13	0	0	9	0	0	3	10	0
Table to Suit ditto	4	10		2	5	0	1	5	0
Ditto Chest on Chest & Sweld Broget	13	0	0	9	0	0	3	10	0
Table to Suit ditto	5	0	0	3	5	0	1	7	0
Ditto Drawers on a frame Claw feet And quarter Collums	15	0	0	11	0	0	4	0	0
A Table to Suit ditto	5	0	0	3	15	0	1	7	6
Drawers Chest on Chest & Sweled Bragetes	15	0	0	10	10	0	4	0	0
A Table to Suit ditto	6	0	0	4	0	0	1	10	0
Ditto Drawers pitch pedement Head, Squair Corners plain fal with out dentels or fret plain balls	16	0	0	11	10	0	4	0	0
Table to Suit ditto with plain	4	0	0	2	15	0	1	5	0
Ditto Drawers Chest on Chest	16	0	0	11	10	0	4	0	0
Table to Suit with Strait Bragets	5	0	0	3	0	0	1	5	0
Ditto Drawers with quarter Collums	17	0	0	12	10	0	4	10	0
Table to Suit dito	6	0	0	4	0	0	1		
Ditto Drawers with dentels fret & shel	19	0	0	14	0	0	5	0	
Ditto Drawers Chest on Chest	20	0	0	13	0	0	4	0	
Chest on a frame Claw feet & Leaves on the knees & Shel drawer ing fram	20	0	0	15	0	0			
Ditto Drawers Scroul pedement the Carved work	21	0	0	16	0	0	5		

	L	S	d	L	S	d	L	S	d
Low Chest of drawers with Three Long & 5 Small drawers				4	10	0	1	12	6
Ditto with four long and five small				5	0	0	1	15	0
Ditto on a frame 12 Inch high without drawers				5	10	0	1	17	6

Chairs with Crooked legs

	L	S	d	L	S	d	L	S	d
Chair with plain feet & banniter with leather Bottoms	1	14	0	1	5	0	0	9	0
Arm ditto	2	18	0	2	5	0	0	16	0
Ditto with Cut through banniter	1	16	0	1	7	0	0	10	0
Arm ditto	3	0	0	2	12	0	0	17	0
Ditto with Claw feet	2	0	0	1	10	0	0	10	0
Arm ditto	3	3	0	2	19	0	0	17	0
Ditto with Shels on the knees & front Rail	2	3	0	1	13	0	0	10	0
Arm ditto	3	7	6	2	16	0	0	17	6
Ditto with Leaves on the knees	2	6	0	1	15	0	0	10	0
Arm ditto	3	11	0	2	18	0	0	17	0
Ditto with fluted or Ogee Backs	2	10	0	1	14	0	0	10	0
Arm ditto	3	15	0	3	0	0	0	17	

for Releiving the Bannesters
Do According to the work on them
for Any Extraordinery work
Do in proportion
Do for Any Arm Chair
maid for a Close Stool
ditto not fram

Chairs Malbro.^{ugh} feet

	£ s d	£ s d	£ s d
Chair plain open bannester with out bases or braget leather Bottom	2 12 0	1 5 0	0 0 0
Arm Ditto	2 18 0	2 5 0	0 16 0
Ditto with fluted or Ogee Back Bases and Brageles	2 5 0	1 15 0	0 10 0
Arm Ditto	3 10 0	2 15 0	0 17 0
Do for Reliving the Bannesters and for Damask or hair bottoms or a Close Stool, as in Crooked leg Chairs			

Corner Chairs for Close Stool

Corner Chair plain feet and ban	2 10 0	2 0 0	0 12 6
Ditto Claw feet & open banisters	3 10 0	2 15 0	0 14 0
Corner Chair with the upper part of the Legs worked Crook'd	3 15 0	3 10 0	0 16 6
For commode frant, add	0 12 0	0 10 0	0 5 0

Easy Chairs

Easy Chair frame, plain feet and knees, without Casters	2 10 0	2 5 0	0 18
Ditto with Claw feet	2 15 0	2 10 0	0 1
Ditto, with Claw feet & leaves on	3 5 0	3 0 0	0
Ditto Marlborough feet bases & bracket	2 10 0	2 5 0	
Chair frame for stuffing over back and seat with marlborough feet	1 5 0	1 0 0	0
Arm Ditto	2 0 0	1 10 0	0
folding cabbin chair frame for stuffing	1 5 0	1 0 0	0 8 0
Ditto	0 12 0	0 5 0	0

	£ s d	£ s d	£ s d
Add for brackets to any Chair	0..2..6	0..2..6	0..1..3
And bases to any chair is	0..2..6	0..2..6	0..1..3
Add for carved mouldings	0..12..0	0..12..0	0..1..3

Soffas Marlborough Feet.

Soffa, plain feet & rails without Casters	4..10..0	4..0..0	1..0..0
Ditto with bases and brackets	5..0..0	4..10..0	1..5..0
Ditto with a fret on the Feet	7..10..0	7..0..0	1..15..0
Ditto with a fret on feet & rails and carved mouldings	10..10..0	9..10..0	2..10

Soffas with crooked Legs.

Soffa, plain feet and knees without Casters	5..0..0	4..10..0	1..5..0
Soffa Claw feet	5..10..0	5..0..0	1..5..0
Ditto with leaves on the knees	6..10..0	6..0..0	1..5..0
Ditto with carved mouldings	7..10..0	7..0..0	1..7..6
Add for casters, 10s			

Settees.

Settee, plain crooked legs feet & banisters without casters with hair or Damask bottom	6..10..0	5..0..0	
Ditto Marlborough with bases and brackets cut through banisters	6..10..0	5..0..0	
Ditto with claw feet and knees cord	8..0..0	5..15..0	1..
Ditto with fretted or ogee backs	8..10..0	6..5..0	1..

Add for carved moulding 2o⁵
And to the journeyman

	£ s d	£ s d	s
			0..2..0
Couches with Crooked Legs			
Couch frame, plain knees feet			
and banisters without bottom or Casters	4..10..0	3..0..0	1..4..0
Ditto with claw feet and open Ban⁵	5..5..0	3..15..0	1..4..0
Ditto with leaves on the knees	6..0..0	4..10..0	1..4..0
Ditto with flutted or ogee backs	6..5..0	4..13..0	1..5..0
Ditto with Marlborough feet			
without bases or Brackets	4..10..0	3..10..	1..4..0
Ditto with bases and Brackets			
Ditto with fluted or ogee backs	5..5..0	3..13..	1..6..0
Add for carved moulding 2o⁵			
and to the Journeyman			0..2..0

Dining Tables

Dining table plain feet crook-			
=ed or Marlborough with bases			
3 feet in the bed	3..5..0	1..17..6	0..17..6
Ditto 3 feet 6 Inches	4..10..0	2..15..0	1..2..
Ditto 4 feet	4..10..0	2..15..0	1..2..
Ditto 4 feet 6 Inches	5..0..0	3..10..0	1..
Ditto 5 feet with 6 Inch Legs	6..10..0	4..10..	
Ditto 5 feet 6 Inches with 8 legs	8..0..0	5..15..0	

For tables with claw feet add
2..6d ⅌ Claw for tables with straight
Legs without bases Deduct 5 ⅌ 35

Card table plain feet & knees	3 10 0	2 5 0	0 17 6
Ditto with Claw feet	4 0 0	2 15 0	0 17 6
Ditto with Carved knees & moldings	5 0 0	3 15 0	0 18 0
Add for Covering without finding			
the Cloath 7/6 & to the Jurney			
man 2/6 for sinking the top			
Card tables with Malbrough feet			
Card table with a drawer without			
braces or brackets —— ——	3 0 0	2 0 0	0 15 0
Ditto with baces & bragetes ——	3 10 0	2 5 0	0 17 6
Ditto with Carved moldings ——	4 0 0	2 15 0	0 17 6
Add for Champing the Tops 10/			
& to the Jurney Man — 5/ —			
Card tables with Round Corners			
Claw feet & plain knees ——	5 0 0		1 2 6
Ditto lined with Green Cloath	6 10 0		1 10 0
Ditto leaves on Knees & Carved mo	8 0 0		1 10 0
Ditto with Carved Rales —— ——	10 0 0		2 0 0
Pembroke Tables			
Break fast Table plain ——	2 15 0	1 15 0	0 12
Ditto with a drawer ——	3 0 0	2 0 0	0 14
Ditto with baces & bragetes —	3 5 0	2 5 0	0 1
Ditto with A plain Strecher	3 10 0	2 10 0	0 1
Ditto with open Strecher & drah	4 0 0	3 0 0	
Ditto with Claw feet ——	3 15 0	2 15 0	0 15 6
Add for Scolloping the top 4/			
& to the Jurney man — 2/			0

Corner Tables
Corner Table Cruked legs or
marlbro feet with bases 3 feet square
Ditto Claw feet

Tea Tables
plain top & feet
plain Tea table with Claw feet
Ditto Leaves on the knees
Add for fluting the piller 5 & Turney

folding Stands
Stand 22 Inches with A box plain top & feet
Ditto plain top & Claw foot
Ditto with leaves on the knees
Ditto fixed 18 Inches
Add for fluting the piller 5 & to Turney man

Sidebord Tables
Side bord Table with bases &
bragdes Six feet by 2 feet 6 Inch
fine feet by 2 feet 6 Inches
four feet by 2 feet 6 Inches
Three feet 6 In by 2 feet 3 Inches
Add for Carved moldings 2 per foot &
for fret Round the Rales 5 per feet
& to the Turney man

Tea Kettle Standes
Tea Kettle Stand with Gallery top
& plain feet

Tea Kettee Stand with Claw feet
leaves on Knees Carved & fluted pillers   £ d £ £ d £ £ d
with turned banesters — — — — — —   3 10 0   2 10 0   1 10 0
Bason Stand with three pillers
& 2 drawers — — — — — — — — — —   2 10 0   1 15 0   0 15 0
Ditto Squair with 2 drawers   1 10 0   1 2 6 0   12

        Squair Tea Tables

Tea Table Squair top plain
feet & Rail — — — —   3 0 0   2 5 0 1 5 0
Ditto Claw feet — — — — — —   3 10 0   2 15 0 1 8 0
Ditto leaves on the Knees — —   4 10 0   3 10 0 1 5 0
Ditto with Carved Rales —   6 0 0   1 5 0

      Commode Dresing Tables
Dresing Table with 4 long draw ers
with out Adresing Drawer   14 0 0   4 10 0
Add for Adresing Drawer 30 Shi
to 80 & for Turney mans
wages in pewrporshon

      Writing Tables
Writing Table with one
top to Rase on one Side only frunt
to draw out — — — — —   7 0 0   5 0 0
Ditto with one top to Rase on both Side   7 10 0   5 10 0
Ditto with 2 tops to Rase on both Side   8 0 0   6 0 0
work in the draw ers excluded

Bureau Tables
Bureau Table with prospect
fore And Squair Corners   7 10 0 | 6 0 0 | 2 . 7 6
Ditto with Qarter Callome   8 10 0 | 7 0 0 | 2 . 15 0

Chinea Tables
Chinea Table with plain legs
3 feet long Strecher with bases
Brageles & fret top ————   4 10 0 | | 1 15 0
Ditto open Strecher top 3 feet long
bases & brageles ————   5 0 0 | | 1 16 0
Ditto with fret frame ———   8 0 0 | | 3 10 0
the for Commode Ditto £ . 10 s
to Jurney Man ——— | | 1 15 0

Plain Night Table ———   4 0 0 | 3 5 0 | 1 5 0

frames for marble Stands
frame for Marble Slab
malbro fee about 4 feet long   2 10 0 | 1 10 0 | 0 12 0
Ditto with bases & brageles   3 10 0 | | 0 15
Ditto with plain knees & Claw   4 0 0 | | 1 0
Ditto with Leaves on the knees
with Carved Moldings ———   5 0 0 | |

Pine Kitchen Tables

Tables full framed with 2 Leaves, hung with Rule Joynt 4 feet long with 2 Drawers		1	16	0	18
Ditto with one Leaf with one drawer		1	10	0	12
Ditto 3 feet 6 In long with 2 Leaves		1	10	0	12
Ditto with one Leaf — —		1	5	0	10
Ditto Single frame 3f 6 J with a drawer —		0	16	0	7
Ditto with out A drawer		0	12	0	5

Joynd Stooles
With A drawer & Shoinglop

3 feet long —		0	12	0	5	6
Ditto with out A drawer		0	10	0	4	6
Ditto fixed with A drawer		0	10	0	4	6
Ditto fixed with out A drawer		0	16	0	3	3
five Screenes with plain feet	1	15	0	1	5	0	11	0
Ditto with Claw feet —	2	2	6	1	12	0	9
Ditto with Leaves on the knee	2	10	0	2	0	0	11
Dum Waiters with four tops	5	0	0		
Ditto with Claw feet —	5	10	0		1
Ditto with Leaves on the knee	6	0	0		

Cloaths preses

Cloath press in two partes
About 4 feet Square in y frunt
the dore hung with Rule Joynt
& Sliding Shelues with 3 drawers

	£ s d	£ s d	£ s d
in the Lowr part inside of Red Seader	15 0 0	11 0 0	8 10
Ditto in Sid work Not Red Seader	13 10 0	9 10 0	3 10 0
Ditto inside not Red seader	10 10 0	7 10 0	2 10 0
Ditto 2 drawers below insid and pine aboue with bore hung in a mon	8 10 0	6 0 0	2 0
Ditto of pine		4 0 0	1 1

Corner Cuberds in 2 partes
about 7 feet high 9 gare hed
& Straught panneles

& Straught panneles	9 10 0	6 10 0	2
Ditto with Common Sash dore	9 10 0	6 10	2 0
Ditto with Square hed denteles & fret work plain pandor	10 10 0	7 10 0	2 10
Ditto with Common Sash dores	10 10 0	7 10 0	2 0
Ditto with Scroul pediment hed denteles Cornice fret Sheild Roses & Glases with plain pannel dor	15 0 0	10 10 0	3
Ditto with Common Sash dores	14 0 0	10 10 0	3

Corner Cubbords
with Scolloped dores & flat pann ek

with Scolloped dores & flat pann ek	16 0 0	11 10 0	3 10 0
Ditto with Chinese dores	15 10 0	11 10 0	

deduct in a pitk pederment for
any of the aboue Coberds 15 s
& to the Jurney Man 7 s 6

Single Cobered About 4 feet high
& 3 feet wide. Square hed & Sash d ——— 4 15 0 | 3 15 0 | 1 5 0
Ditto with panneles ———————— 4 15 0 | 3 15 0 | 1 5 0
Ditto with Dentel Cornice plain pannel 5 10 0 | 4 0 0 | 1 10
Ditto with Common Sash dores — 5 10 0 | 4 0 0 | 1 10
    Clock Cases with Sqare hed & Corner 6 0 0 | 4 0 0 | 1 15
Ditto with Scrol pedment hed ——— 8 0 0 | 5 0 0 | 2 5
Ditto with Cllom Corners ———— 10 0 0 | 7 0 0 | 3 0
Do With fret Denteles Shel Roses
 & Cases — — — — 12 0 0 | 9 0 0 | 4 0
Do Without fret or Denteles ——— 11 0 0 | 8 0 0 | 3 5
Are Above prices with Out glass
Cradeles without Carving ———— 2 15 0 | 1 10 0 0 | 12 6
Popler bedstids Corded ———— 0 18 0 | 0 5 0
Col Ditto ——————— 0 18 0 | 0 5 0
Ditto Low post with Serus 4 1 5 0 | 0 7 0
Ditto Claw feet & posts 2 0 0 | 0 9 0
Ditto high posts plain turned 1 17 6 | 0 9 0
Ditto with Braces & Capes Claw feet 2 12 6 | 12 6
Popler field bedstids Canopy Rales — 2 15 0 | 13 0
Do for fluting the feet post
Do to the Jurney m — 7 6

A Methodological Study in the Identification of Some Important Philadelphia Chippendale Furniture

Philip D. Zimmerman

FEW PIECES of American furniture have received as much attention or have been the focus of as much argument as the Winterthur Museum's saddle seat chair (fig. 1). Although probably familiar to the small coterie of important dealers and collectors of the early 1900s, the chair did not become widely known until it was publicized by Samuel W. Woodhouse, Jr., in a 1927 issue of the magazine *Antiques*. Woodhouse identified the chair as one of six different "sample chairs" whose relationship to each other was confirmed by an old wives' tale. Tracing ownership of five of these six chairs through descendants of Philadelphia cabinetmaker Benjamin Randolph's stepson, Nathaniel Fenimore, he then attributed all six to Randolph. Woodhouse furthered the Benjamin Randolph sample chair theory in a second article in 1930.[1] Although his hypothesis gained popular acceptance, it was greeted with skepticism in some quarters. Both before and after the publication of his articles, controversy over the manufacture of the six chairs continued among such noted antiquarians as Herbert Cescinsky, Luke Vincent Lockwood, Henry W. Erving, and William Macpherson Hornor, Jr.[2]

Between the 1930s and the early 1970s, the identification of the saddle seat chair remained unresolved. In 1973 a set of five chairs, seemingly identical with the Winterthur sample chair were found in England and scheduled for a January 1974 sale at Sotheby and Company in London. They were catalogued and advertised as "a fine set of five late George II mahogany chairs in the manner of Thomas Chippendale." However, the agent in charge of Americana at the New York office subsequently recognized that these five chairs were like the Winterthur example. The auction house withdrew them from the London sale and sent them to its New York subsidiary, Sotheby Parke Bernet, for its fall Americana sale. The catalogue entry, rewritten for the New York sale, included both an attribution to Benjamin Randolph and the following observation: "A careful comparison and analysis of both this set of five hairy-paw foot chairs and the famous sample chair in . . . Winterthur Museum . . . reveals that the chairs are virtually identical and although probably not from the same set, they were certainly made by the same joiner and carver." It also noted that the woods and "clamp marks on the

[1] Samuel W. Woodhouse, Jr., "Benjamin Randolph of Philadelphia," *Antiques* 11, no. 5 (May 1927): 366–71; Woodhouse, "More about Benjamin Randolph," *Antiques* 17, no. 1 (January 1930): 21–25. Both articles are reprinted in John J. Snyder, Jr., ed., *Philadelphia Furniture and Its Makers* (New York: Universe Books, 1975), pp. 33–43.

[2] For a discussion of some of the six sample chairs, see Herbert Cescinsky, "An English View of Philadelphia Furniture," *Antiques* 8, no. 5 (November 1925): 272–75, and his written exchange with *Antiques* editor Homer Eaton Keyes in *Antiques* 9, no. 1 (January 1926): 11, in which he specifically denied a Randolph attribution to the easy chair. Three of the six samples are pictured together in *Pennsylvania Museum Bulletin* 19, no. 86 (May 1924): 153, 155, pl. 2. They are identified

as "indisputably English made" but were thought to be imported from England as three of the six sample chairs. An argument for the English origin of one of the chairs is in Luke Vincent Lockwood, *Colonial Furniture in America*, 2 vols., 3d ed., enl., (New York: Charles Scribner's Sons, 1926), 2:93–94, fig. 556. In a letter to Henry Francis du Pont, antiques dealer Albert Collings stated: "Both he [Lockwood] & Mr. Erving agreed with me on the origin of all the Reifsnyder so-called 'Randolph sample chairs' and Mr. Erving has one of them that he pronounces English himself" (Collings to Henry F. du Pont, June 11, 1931, Dealer Correspondence Files, Registrar's Office, Winterthur Museum). Hornor's skepticism regarding the Woodhouse theory is found in *The Blue Book of Philadelphia Furniture* (Philadelphia: privately printed, 1935), p. 94n.

Fig. 1. Saddle seat chair, Philadelphia, ca. 1770. Mahogany and arborvitae; H. 36⅞", W. 23¾". (Winterthur Museum.)

tradict the Woodhouse argument which affirms the Winterthur saddle seat chair as one of the sample chairs. To conform to Woodhouse's theory, and to preserve the Randolph attribution, the auction house cataloguers departed from accepted identification procedures and unconvincingly advanced the suggestion that, although the six chairs were identical, they were not of the same set. The deep-rooted problems with the identification of these chairs did not unduly affect their sale at the auction. Each was sold into a major collection of American furniture at an average price of $40,500.

The deficiencies apparent in the auction catalogue entry for the saddle seat chairs have not been corrected in subsequent interpretations of any of these six chairs. Although no consensus has emerged, a reluctance to disavow the Woodhouse theory likewise typifies recent efforts. The conclusions of these authors have either contradicted historical facts or simply heightened the ambiguous relationship between the Winterthur saddle seat chair and the five Sotheby Parke Bernet examples.[4]

In light of the confusion surrounding these chairs, consideration of all pertinent data is necessary before a reasonably certain explanation can be advanced. Important, too, are the byproducts of such an examination—the development of an analytical methodology and some general observations pursuant to the study of eighteenth-century American furniture.

underside of the seat rails" were identical among the six saddle seat chairs.[3]

The unwillingness to synthesize the new information with both the traditional interpretation and the Randolph attribution assigned by Woodhouse is evident in the sale catalogue entry. Under ordinary circumstances, the likenesses detailed in the Sotheby Parke Bernet catalogue would provide more than sufficient grounds for considering all six chairs as representing a single set. Yet such a declaration would directly con-

Methodology

Modern furniture scholarship demands that all sources of information relevant to an object be explored in order to recover as much data about the object as possible. One way of approaching this is to divide the entire body of furniture data into two categories. The first contains intrinsic data which identify the properties of the object through direct examination. Construction techniques, materials, workmanship, design (or plan), and alterations to the object are among the types of information belonging to this group. The sec-

---

[3]*Catalogue of Fine English Furniture, Rugs and Carpets,* Sotheby and Company, January 25, 1974, lot 68. The London sale of the five chairs was advertised in *Country Life* 154, no. 3991 (December 20, 1973): 32, suppl.; Janet Green, "Superb American Chippendale Chairs Discovered by Sotheby Parke Bernet," *Early American Antiques* 3, no. 2 (February 1975): 17; *The American Heritage Society Auction of Americana,* Sotheby Parke Bernet sale no. 3691, November 12–16, 1974, lots 1477–79. Despite the caution expressed in the SPB catalogue entry, no two carved Philadelphia Chippendale chairs that appear to be identical have ever been shown to be from different sets.

[4]See Charles F. Hummel, *A Winterthur Guide to American Chippendale Furniture: Middle Atlantic and Southern Colonies* (New York: Crown Publishers, 1976), p. 89; and Beatrice B. Garvan, "Side Chair," *Philadelphia: Three Hundred Years of American Art* (Philadelphia: Philadelphia Museum of Art, 1976), pp. 114–15, no. 90.

ond category includes all information extrinsic to the object, such as the history of ownership, any information conveyed by accompanying bills or manuscripts, and the interpretation and evaluation of the various intrinsic data. In the latter category, judgment is required to associate a particular fact or idea with the object. Together, the characteristics of intrinsic and extrinsic data suggest a general procedure for the identification of furniture and other objects.

An initial mechanical and often tedious recovery of intrinsic data results in a body of precise information, free of interpretive biases. Object measurements, microanalysis of woods, identification of the use of templates, and recognition of patterns governing construction are established or verified by simple comparisons of these object data to known indexes. The quantitative information is less susceptible to argument over matters of degree and can be compared and contrasted with great exactness. For example, a chair may be constructed with its side rails tenoned through the rear stiles or only partially into them and not visible from the rear. Likewise, a front rail may measure eighteen inches in length to the nearest one-eighth inch. Such properties can be compared with those of other chairs to yield results that are highly reliable. In an analytical framework that is designed to minimize subjective comparisons or associations, intrinsic data can also yield a more complex, but equally reliable, level of information. Identification of a particular construction technique employed in an object may be expanded to include the frequency of its use among all similar objects. The relative significance of this particular property emerges from simple quantification. Moreover, such quantification improves the foundation for subsequent interpretations of data, and it may suggest relationships among objects that are otherwise not apparent. Similarly, it may identify those potentially misleading traits that are insignificant because they are too common or even too rare (e.g., unique properties by definition have nothing in common with anything else).

Intrinsic data alone are seldom sufficient to reach a desired conclusion concerning an object and must be given meaning or context through interpretation or analysis. The mere fact that a specific species of wood is used in a piece of furniture is of little use without a statement of its importance to the problem at hand. Extrinsic data can provide these vital links between an object and its cultural context. Names and dates appearing in family and public records can save an object from historical anonymity, even transform it into a significant document of its culture.

As with intrinsic data, extrinsic data have shortcomings in the context of identifying objects. First, extrinsic data survive haphazardly. Often they are vague or incomplete, requiring some interpretation simply to produce a clear and usable historical statement. Second, because extrinsic information must be applied to an object, the possibility of error from misapplication is significant. Finally, the variety of forms in which extrinsic data survive mitigates against comparison of similar types of information. Even such similar data as furniture descriptions and valuations obtained from household inventories and shop accounts may not be compatible for some purposes because of differing terms and the use of retail as opposed to wholesale valuations.

Although the advantages and disadvantages of both intrinsic and extrinsic data can be explored separately when casting a model, the empirical application of them to a specific object may blur the theoretical edges. Frequently, the two categories exist in such close juxtaposition that to discuss them individually is impractical. Extrinsic data often amplify intrinsic data. An evaluation of style, for instance, must include comment upon many intrinsic properties of the object. Nevertheless, for purposes of evaluating any such statements about an object, separation of the statement into these two components is helpful in determining the source and quality of the information. In so doing, it is crucial to remember that intrinsic and extrinsic information cannot stand in contradiction to each other, because both categories represent alternative ways of describing the same object. The existence of any contradiction is an indication of an error somewhere in the identification process.

Application: Object Examination

A careful examination of each of the saddle seat chairs revealed that they are sufficiently alike in construction and design details to be regarded as from the same set and their design is unlike that of any other known chairs. The secondary wood, rounded rear legs, and through tenons suggest a Philadelphia origin, yet these characteristics are so common among all Philadelphia chairs of this period that they are of no use in isolating a particular maker.[5] However, with the exception of these six chairs, the use of a splat joined to the rear stiles is unknown in any other Philadelphia side chair. Unusual, but not unknown, are the hairy paw feet, half-upholstery (upholstery covering half of the rails), asymmetrically carved side rails, and the use of the saddle seat. The combination of all these characteristics in a single object renders it so unusual that no patterns governing their use can be identified.

The first clue that the Winterthur saddle seat chair (and by implication the five additional saddle seat chairs) might have a specific relationship to any other Philadelphia chair in particular emerged from the results of a comparative analysis of over 100 different Philadelphia Chippendale chairs. In this study many intrinsic properties of each chair were itemized, including specific measurements, construction techniques, and the use of certain design motifs (with no qualitative assessment of the execution). The frequency of recurrence for each property was then measured against the entire bank of information. This comparative operation revealed that some chairs can be grouped tentatively as products of the same shop on two assumptions: (1) common elements have a common origin and (2) the shop owner's control over the manufacture of his various products is reflected in the significant recurrence of some of the properties among similar furniture forms, which is sufficient to isolate them from all others.[6]

The Winterthur saddle seat chair was among a small number of chairs rejected from the comparative study because so few points of comparison could be established. However, chance inspection of the chair revealed that the shoe (the element at the base of the splat and resting on the top of the rear rail) might help provide a link to other chairs made in Philadelphia in this period. This particular element of a chair is quite inconspicuous in the context of the overall design, yet it varies considerably among all of the chairs examined in the comparative study. Using terminology employed in the study, the shoe on the

Fig. 2. Detail showing shoe of the saddle seat chair. (Winterthur Museum.)

Winterthur saddle seat chair (fig. 2) can be described as an "overhanging quarter-round with nine gadroons." This mechanical description of a very rare design treatment for a shoe also describes the shoe on another chair which is one of four straight-front side chairs owned by Winterthur Museum (figs. 3, 4).[7] The importance of this focus upon the shoes is not in the discovery of an element which might become an identifying trait or signature of a shop but merely as a first step in which these chairs can be separated for further study from other chairs of Philadelphia origin.

The two chairs were examined for more common denominators in keeping with the guidelines set forth in the comparative study. Despite obvious differences in the decorative plan and details, their construction techniques are the same. Although many of these techniques are common among almost all Philadelphia Chippendale style chairs, three points of comparison establish a relationship between these chairs and set them apart from the others. First, the sequence of pins holding the rails into the legs is identical on both chairs. Each has one pin securing the front and rear tenons of the side rail into the front leg and rear stile, respectively. No pins are visible on the front rail. One pin secures each

---

[5] The corner blocks of the Winterthur saddle seat chair have been identified by microanalysis as arborvitae (Atlantic white cedar), a wood commonly found in eighteenth-century Philadelphia furniture.

[6] Philip D. Zimmerman, "A Comparative Study of Philadelphia Chippendale Chairs" (M.A. thesis, University of Delaware, in progress).

[7] The curvature required to fit the shoe to the back of the saddle seat is ignored in this comparison.

Fig. 3. Straight-front side chair, Philadelphia, ca. 1770. Mahogany and arborvitae; H. 38″, W. 23⅝″. (Winterthur Museum.)

Fig. 4. Detail showing shoe of the straight-front side chair. (Winterthur Museum.)

side of the rear rail to a stile. Given that at any of the four joints, one, two, or no pins could have been used, exact duplication of this pattern suggests a relationship. Second, the rails of both chairs are 3 inches high—among all of the chairs examined in the comparative study this dimension varied from 2½ inches to over 4 inches. Third, microanalysis of the corner blocks reveals that arborvitae is used in both chairs.[8] While none of these likenesses alone is sufficient to establish a relationship based upon shop practices, the combination represents a convincing argument for origin in a common shop.

The postulated relationship is strengthened by two obvious design features common to both sets of chairs and rare among Philadelphia chairs—each has hairy paw feet and half-upholstery. These features would have been selected by the eighteenth-century customer at a greater cost to him, which suggests that they were made for an integrated setting (i.e., en suite) or at least in awareness of each other. This hypothesis introduces the possibility that the two sets of chairs were part of a larger group of related furniture. One of these additional pieces of furniture is identified throughout the body of literature in which the saddle seat chair is discussed. Woodhouse was the first of many writers to equate the design similarities of the saddle seat chair with a card table (fig. 5) that has long been identified as having been owned by General John Cadwalader of Philadelphia. The table appears in Charles Willson Peale's portrait of the John Cadwalader family painted in the early 1770s (fig. 6) and is still owned by direct descendants.[9]

The interrelationship of the saddle seat chair (see fig. 1), the straight-front side chair (see fig. 2), and the card table (see fig. 5) becomes compelling with the recognition that, like the saddle seat chair, the straight-front side chair also matches a card table (fig. 7). Both have hairy paw feet, display the same carved motif on the knees, and have gadrooning underneath a smooth, planar surface. Furthermore, as with the two chairs, the few construction details of the card tables that are suitable for comparison manifest a favorable re-

[8]Wood identification by microanalysis (see n. 5 above).

[9]Woodhouse, "Benjamin Randolph," pp. 370, 371; Joseph Downs, *American Furniture: Queen Anne and Chippendale Periods* (1952; reissued, New York: Viking Press, 1967), no. 138; Nicholas B. Wainwright, *Colonial Grandeur in Philadelphia: The House and Furniture of General John Cadwalader* (Philadelphia: Historical Society of Pennsylvania, 1964), p. 118.

Fig. 5. Commode card table, Philadelphia, ca. 1770. Mahogany, pine, white oak, poplar; H. 28″, L. 39½″. (Privately owned: Photo, Philadelphia Museum of Art.)

Fig. 6. Charles Willson Peale, portrait of the John Cadwalader family. Philadelphia, 1771. Oil on canvas; H. 51½″, W. 41¼″. (Privately owned: Photo, Philadelphia Museum of Art.)

Fig. 7. Straight-sided card table, Philadelphia, ca. 1770. Mahogany, pine, white oak; H. 28½″, W. 32″. (Winterthur Museum.)

lationship. Each is made of richly figured mahogany and has a hard pine back rail as well as a white oak rail supported by the rear swinging leg.[10] Each card table has an opening in the rear pine rail for a drawer which is concealed by the swinging oak rail. Most important, however, is the fact that Henry Francis du Pont acquired the straight-front card table from Joe Kindig, Jr., who had purchased it earlier from a collateral descendant of John Cadwalader.[11] Thus, a matrix of furniture emerges in which chairs and matching card tables are related in design and construction to each other. In addition, two separate family histories suggest that John Cadwalader owned all the objects.

The relationships established above rely heavily upon intrinsic data. Absent as a source of information is discussion or analysis of carved workmanship (distinguished from design which is considered in its abstract sense of being a plan). Omission of this physical property of the object requires brief explanation and, at the same time, provides an opportunity to review some of the underlying principles governing this process of relating these pieces of furniture.

Carving has long been a focus of much discussion of furniture. Such focus is not only justified but often necessary to measure the quality and aesthetic importance of a piece of furniture. However, no satisfactory study of American eighteenth-century furniture carving exists that outlines a methodology or procedure for using carving as a tool for identification of the object. Although some regional expressions of carving have been identified, elements of carving attributable to any particular hand have not been determined with any degree of reliability.[12] Identification of the properties of carving, such as depth, fineness of detail, quality of line, and organization of individual motifs, are determinations of degree rather than of kind. Objective measures of these have not been formulated. Assessments of carving rely upon judgment, not simple empirical observations. Identification of each property, and eventually of the whole, is a matter of locating that trait on a sliding scale of values. Both the location on the scale and the scale itself are constantly open to reexamination, making conclusions unstable.

A second problem plaguing the use of carving as a tool of identification is that very few surviving examples of Philadelphia carving can be documented to a specific craftsman. Most of the one-half dozen or so examples are architectural carvings for which carvers have been identified through bills rendered to the owners of the buildings.[13] Research into the practices of the furniture-making craft has suggested that carvers did not always affiliate with only one shop but worked on a piece basis for several furniture makers.[14] In sum, attributions based on techniques and abilities evidenced in only one or two identified examples are tenuous at best.

This examination of objects employs a proce-

---

[10]Garvan, "Pair of Card Tables," *Philadelphia,* p. 115, no. 91. The woods in the straight-front card table have been identified by microanalysis.

[11]The table, described as a "Philadelphia small Chippendale hairy paw card table with gadrooned skirt, ca.1760," was purchased from Joe Kindig, Jr., on January 2, 1950, for $12,500 (Purchase Records, Registrar's Office, Winterthur Museum). Wainwright identifies Anne Cadwalader as the last owner of the table before Kindig purchased it (p. 120).

[12]For the best discussion to date of regional differences in carving, see John T. Kirk, *American Chairs: Queen Anne and Chippendale* (New York: Alfred A. Knopf, Inc., 1972); see also William R. Johnston, "Anatomy of the Chair: American Regional Variations in Eighteenth Century Styles," *Metropolitan Museum of Art Bulletin* 21, no. 3 (November 1962): 118–29.

[13]The one important exception is a looking glass now at Winterthur Museum (acc. no. 52.261) which was made for John Cadwalader by James Reynolds and two other small looking glasses at Cliveden in Philadelphia, made by Reynolds for Benjamin Chew.

[14]Although no monograph exists which addresses itself to this question directly, there is repeated reference to this idea in Hornor, pp. 13, 93, 100–101, 207.

dure that focuses on quantifiable physical and structural relations, thereby minimizing disputes over matters of degree. The procedure is also designed to conform to the current theories of cabinetmaking in mid-eighteenth-century Philadelphia which emphasize the complexity of shop production and the movement of workers among many shops. The physical data from any one object can be measured against the larger body of data. Positive correlations suggest the possibility of common origins, yet the correlations may not reflect historical relationships. The common denominators may be accidental—the product of limited and haphazard survival. Until the pieces of furniture in question can be grounded in a more secure historical context, the relationships must remain tentative.

Application: Accompanying Manuscripts

One of the most completely documented examples of Philadelphia Chippendale furniture surviving today is the card table (see fig. 5) that matches the saddle seat chair. Now known to be one of a pair, this table has never left family ownership.[15] In addition to being pictured in the Peale portrait of the John Cadwalader family, it is also described in a bill found among John Cadwalader's papers. On January 2, 1771, Thomas Affleck, Philadelphia cabinetmaker, billed Cadwalader for "2 Commode Card Tables @ £5" apiece.[16] In this eighteenth-century context, the term "commode" refers to the serpentine shaping of the frame—perhaps showing some stylistic dependence upon French furniture forms for this detail.[17] Although Affleck's bill was published by Wainwright in 1964 and cited by Garvan in 1976,

neither writer linked it to this table. One explanation of this oversight lies in the reluctance to reject the Randolph sample chair theory. The obvious visual relationship between the Winterthur saddle seat chair, presumed to have been made by Randolph, and the commode card table required that Randolph be the maker of the table too. When he wrote his book, Wainwright was unaware of the existence of the second commode card table and the five additional saddle seat chairs and decided that the Affleck bill referred to the straight-sided card table (see fig. 7), which he thought was one of a pair.[18]

At the bottom of Affleck's bill, the names of James Reynolds and the partnership of Bernard and Jugiez appear beside the notation "Carving the Above." Unfortunately, individual carvers cannot be assigned to a particular work; specific objects enumerated in the bill are not linked with the names. However, the appearance of the three names on this bill provides an explanation for the slight variations in design and execution which exist between the two commode card tables. For instance, the digits of the hairy paws on the one still owned by the Cadwalader family are slightly separated, revealing a ball between them, while the digits on its mate are not separated.[19] Variations of similar degree exist among the six known saddle seat chairs. Nevertheless, these differences are not sufficient to suggest that the chairs represent more than a single set.

Construction techniques among all the saddle seat chairs are the same. In the elaborate over-engineered splat, three pieces of wood with the grain running perpendicular to one another are held together with long mortise and tenon joints. The piercings in the splat, which separates the many intricate joints, required a considerable expenditure of time in their fabrication. The ex-

---

[15]The second card table of the pair, with its central peanut motif facing the opposite direction, is rumored to have been found in Canada before it was sold by Charles Woolsey Lyon to a private collector in the late 1960s.

[16]All of the bills cited in this study are reproduced as halftones in Wainwright's excellent book; the bills are among the Cadwalader papers at the Historical Society of Pennsylvania, Philadelphia (Affleck to Cadwalader, October 13, 1770, in Wainwright, p. 44).

[17]The eighteenth-century use of this term is discussed in Gilbert T. Vincent, "The Bombé Furniture of Boston," in *Boston Furniture of the Eighteenth Century* (Charlottesville: University Press of Virginia for the Colonial Society of Massachusetts, 1974), pp. 143–44. Vincent refers to Thomas Chippendale's *The Gentleman & Cabinet-Maker's Director* (1754) when drawing a link between the terms "commode" and "bombé." He does not mention that serpentine fronts are

shown in half of the first edition plates showing commode furniture and are predominant among those in the third edition of 1762; for examples, see Chippendale (1762; reprint ed., New York: Dover Publications, 1966), pls. 62, 64–71, 130, 131, and annotations. Vincent's Boston inventory references to commode chairs again refer to serpentine shaping of the front—in this case the front rail. The *Oxford English Dictionary* (1971) cites an 1851 quotation as the first recorded use of commode as meaning a close- or potty-stool.

[18]Wainwright, pp. 120–21; Garvan, "Pair of Card Tables," pp. 115–16, no. 91.

[19]The pair of card tables was separated for a considerable length of time, which contributed to other differences, particularly in the rate of erosion of the carved highlights and in the repairs.

traordinary work, coupled with structural problems revealed by subsequent repairs to the joints
in the splat, suggests that the maker had not fully
resolved the construction problems created by the
new design. Both the use of this embryonic construction technique on all six chairs and the unqualified rarity of design attests to their being of a
single set. Additional evidence lies in the Roman
numerals stamped into the top of the rear rail
underneath the shoe of each chair. Philadelphia
Chippendale style chairs within a set are almost
always numbered consecutively, each in the same
place. The six surviving saddle seat chairs are
stamped II, VII, VIII, IX, X, XI.[20]

If the assumption of consistent construction
practices within a shop is correct, the use of
stamped numbers to indicate members of a set
also should be found in the same place on the
four straight-front side chairs at Winterthur (fig.
2). Removal of the shoes and upholstery from the
rear rails of all four side chairs produced two
findings that seemed to deny their already
established relationship to the saddle seat chairs.
The shoes are replacements, and no numbers are
visible on the top of the rear rails. However, an
old photograph shows one of the straight-front
side chairs upholstered but without a shoe. Lacking evidence of age on any of the existing four
shoes, the only plausible conclusion is that du
Pont purchased all four chairs without shoes, the
element that had suggested a relationship between the two sets of chairs. A search through the
manuscript materials provided evidence that resolved the issue and strengthened the
hypothesized interrelationship.

Among Henry F. du Pont's correspondence
with antique dealers are three letters with Joe
Kindig, Jr., of York, Pennsylvania:

Dec. 10, 1947

Dear Harry,

I find that Sam only gave me the pieces from 2 of
the chairs in the Blackwell room. It was really my fault
as I only spoke about the 2 that were out in the center
of the room.

But please have him send me the other 2 as there is
enough wood in there to carve them out of the same

ones. And it is good old mahogany. So we wont make
new ones, but just have your 4 carved.

With best wishes,

Sincerely,
Joe Kindig, Jr.

December 16, 1947

Dear Joe:

Thank you for your letter about the pieces from the
chairs. Sam has sent the other two pieces to you and will
you let Mr. du Pont know when they are received by
you?

Very truly yours,
Secretary [to Mr. du Pont]

December 29, 1947

Dear Joe:

The bases for the splats arrived safely, and I am
delighted to have them and couldn't have a nicer
Christmas present. How lucky it was that you found
that other chair.

We had a very nice Christmas, and though it wasn't
a white one it made up for it on Friday.

With all kinds of best wishes for the New Year, and
with renewed thanks,

Sincerely yours,
[H. F. du Pont][21]

While open to different shades of interpretation,
the letters unmistakably refer to making shoes for
four chairs. The combined evidence of the room
location, the number of chairs, and the recent
discovery that the four straight-front side chairs
have new shoes is convincing. Most tantalizing is
du Pont's reference to finding "that other chair."
It could not have been the well-known Winterthur saddle seat chair located in the same
room. The most logical conclusion is that it was a
fifth representative of the same set, complete with
its original shoe.

Further research revealed that Kindig had
sold an identical straight-front side chair to a private owner in 1948, shortly after he had the shoes
made for du Pont's four chairs. That chair has
since been given to Stratford Hall Plantation,
Westmoreland County, Virginia, the ancestral
home of the Lee family.[22] Recently, Stratford sent
it to Richmond for reupholstery by the firm of
Jones and Ivie, Inc. Inquiries to the upholsterers
about any identifying marks brought a prompt

[20]The Winterthur saddle seat chair is stamped II, which by
itself suggests that this chair was not a sample but part of a
larger set. Garvan incorrectly identifies the saddle seat chair at
Colonial Williamsburg as stamped XIII. The two vertical
slashes which follow the XI are longer and not as deeply cut;
they are not part of the original stamping. Colonial Williamsburg has catalogued the number as XI.

[21]Kindig file, 1946–47, Dealer Correspondence, Registrar's Office, Winterthur Museum.
[22]The chair (G. 1978.1) is now owned by the Robert E. Lee
Memorial Association (Thomas E. Bass III to Zimmerman,
January 11, 1978).

Fig. 8. Detail of straight-front side chair (prior to restoration) showing recessed lip. (Winterthur Museum.)

response: the chair is stamped IIV on the rear rail.[23] This established yet another common denominator between the two sets of chairs.

The absence of any visible numbers on the four Winterthur straight-front side chairs is probably the effect of wear and tear. Measurement of the inside height of all the chair rails (the horizontal structural members of the chair seat) shows the back rail on each is approximately one-quarter inch less than the other rails. The difference conforms to the depth of a lip extending along the upper rear edge of the back rail on each (fig. 8), indicating that the upper front surface of this rail was recessed by the removal of a one-quarter inch layer of wood. This would also have removed any evidence of a chair number. An upholsterer may have decided to recess the rails to allow layers of fabric to lay flush with the rear lip to improve the appearance of the chairs after reupholstery without the original shoes. Or, perhaps this part of each chair was damaged by nail holes from too many reupholsterings, and the splintered wood was removed to provide a more secure anchor for the nails used with a new seat cover.[24]

[23]Allan Denny Ivie III to John A. H. Sweeney, June 30, 1976. Photographs and clay impressions document the existence of the number. The shoe is stamped III on the underside, indicating that it originally came from another chair of this set. This mix-up probably occurred during one of the many reupholsterings of the set. The author did not personally inspect these marks. (Copy of letter, photographs, and impressions are in my possession.)

[24]When this most recent upholstery was removed from the backs of these four chairs, three sets of nails securing the webbing, a muslin liner, and the damask outer covering were removed from the crumbling rear rail. Conservation measures have been taken by the Winterthur Museum.

The family histories of the chairs and tables continually reinforce the hypothesis that they are related to each other. One of the commode card tables is still owned by direct descendants of John Cadwalader. The straight-sided card table and a matching side chair were purchased by Kindig from a collateral descendant of Cadwalader.[25] Du Pont purchased the table in 1950 while, two years earlier, another individual purchased the chair which eventually was given to Stratford. No history of the second commode card table is available except that it was recently sold to an anonymous buyer by dealer Charles Woolsey Lyon. But in 1931 it was Lyon's father, also a dealer, who sold du Pont "4 Chippendale chairs claw feet similar to Randolph chairs" for $20,000.[26] Possibly the reference to "claw feet" was incorrect; if so, four details suggest the chairs may be the four side chairs in question: (1) the high price indicates a rare feature like hairy paw feet; (2) at that time hairy paw feet (not claw feet) and the particular splat design used on these chairs were both interpreted as Randolph characteristics; (3) a memorandum dated November 7, 1932, indicates that four "paw foot" chairs were in the Breakfast Room; and (4) in du Pont's purchase records, no other references to chairs with hairy paw feet have come to light.[27] That both the four chairs and the second commode card table

[25]Telephone conversation between Joe Kindig III and author, January 30, 1977.

[26]Purchased on June 15, 1931, from J. H. O'Brien through C. W. Lyon (Purchase Records, Registrar's Office, Winterthur Museum).

[27]Chairs file, History of Objects drawer, cabinet 51, Winterthur Estate Archives.

Fig. 9. Charles Willson Peale, portrait of Lambert Cadwalader. Philadelphia, 1771. Oil on canvas; H. 51″, W. 41″. (Privately owned: Photo, Winterthur Museum Library.)

passed through the same antiques firm may be coincidence, but it also may be the result of related sources for the purchase of each.

Unlike the card tables and straight-front side chairs, none of the saddle seat chairs has a firm family history. No line of descent was ever established by Sotheby and Company or Sotheby Parke Bernet to explain their presence in England. The Winterthur chair from this set had been located and purchased by Thomas A. Curran, a prominent Philadelphia antiques dealer, sometime in the first quarter of the twentieth century. It was sold out of Curran's private collection to du Pont in 1942.[28] The history ascribed to this

chair in the Woodhouse articles must be regarded as suspect, not only because of the recent discovery of chairs related to the sample chairs but also because of errors in logic. Woodhouse conceded that Randolph had stated in his will, "there was a verbal agreement between me and my [second] wife . . . that neither of us would claim any right in any property of the other . . . therefore I bequeath to my said wife, Mary, £20."[29] Despite this statement and despite the lack of any mention of such chairs in the probate records of Randolph, his second wife, and her descendants, Woodhouse nonetheless threaded an attribution to Randolph. Furthermore, no manuscript evidence suggests that eighteenth-century Philadel-

[28]Purchased from Mrs. T. A. Curran on December 28, 1942, for $7,000 (Purchase Records, Registrar's Office, Winterthur Museum).

[29]Woodhouse, "Benjamin Randolph," p. 369.

phia furniture makers ever used such samples. Of the six samples Woodhouse identified, the sixth chair (a photograph is the only known evidence of the actual chair) is identical with a set of six chairs owned by the Philadelphia Museum of Art, and Winterthur Museum owns the armchair to this set.[30] Thus, even if the old wives' tale of six sample chairs were true, Woodhouse failed to identify the correct sample chairs.

No family histories exist to substantiate or deny Cadwalader's ownership of the six saddle seat chairs, but sufficient historical data survive to verify the hypothesis. In addition to the appearance of the commode card table in the Peale portrait of the John Cadwalader family, another portrait shows Lambert Cadwalader, John Cadwalader's younger brother, leaning against the crest rail of one of the saddle seat chairs (fig. 9).[31] These two portraits are among five including Cadwalader's mother, father, and sister which Peale painted for John Cadwalader between 1770 and 1772. Wainwright used the bills and room inventories (1778 and 1786) for John Cadwalader's household furnishings to best advantage and determined that all five portraits, fitted in frames carved by James Reynolds and Hercules Courtney, hung in the large, elaborate front parlor. The rich and conspicuous display of material advantages suggested by these portraits in the same room with the saddle seat chairs and commode card tables would have been consistent with Cadwalader's wealth and status in eighteenth-century Philadelphia.[32]

A documentary framework for his ownership of half-upholstered saddle seat chairs is given by an upholstery bill from Plunket Fleeson to Cadwalader. In October 1770, Fleeson charged: "To

covering over rail finish'd in Canvis 32 chairs." In January 1771, other pieces of furniture were enumerated, to wit: "a Large Sopha," "1 smaller Do," "an other Do," and "an Easy Chair." Like the thirty-two chairs, these four pieces of furniture were half-upholstered in canvas. The canvas provided the undercovering, over which were tied removable seat covers, such as the set made of "51 yds. of fine Saxon blue Fr. Chk [French check]" with "blue and white fringe."[33]

The thirty-two chairs cited in the Fleeson bill are not specifically identified anywhere else in the surviving Cadwalader papers. The only furniture bill mentioning framed chairs (as opposed to turned chairs) is one from William Savery listing six "Walnut lether Bottom Chairs" and twelve "Walnut Chairs stuff'd & Canvas'd." The wording indicates that Savery assumed responsibility for the upholstery work himself, which eliminates these walnut chairs from consideration as part of the unspecified thirty-two in the Fleeson bill. That the thirty-two chairs in Fleeson's bill included the saddle seat chairs is suggested not only by the description of the unusual upholstery scheme but also by his mention of the sofas and easy chair. These additional pieces of furniture are clearly recognizable as the same "2 Mahogany Commode Sophias for the Recesses," "one Large ditto," and "Easy Chair to Sute ditto," listed just above the pair of commode card tables on Affleck's bill. The commode card tables, made en suite with the saddle seat chairs, were also made en suite with the pair of small commode sofas, the large sofa, and the easy chair. With the possible exception of the easy chair, all were intended for the large front parlor. Although no floor plan for the Cadwalader house survives, the architectural recesses into which the pair of small sofas fit had to have been in this room. Two of the three sofas were still located in the front parlor when the 1786 inventory was taken (the easy chair had been relegated to the garret).[34] This evidence strengthens the probability that the saddle seat chairs were among the thirty-two chairs upholstered by Fleeson.

Thirty-two chairs can be divided into two or three sets in a number of ways. When Wainwright

[30]Philadelphia Museum of Art, acc. nos. 68.70.1–.6. The author examined chairs stamped II, III, IV, VI. The armchair at Winterthur Museum is stamped II (acc. no. 61.805).

[31]The stile of the chair in the portrait is fluted, while those on the actual chairs are foliated. This difference has caused many writers to believe that the chair in the portrait is not from the set represented by the six known saddle seat chairs but documents the existence of more chairs exactly like that in the painting. No other evidence supports this claim. In light of the information available regarding the known saddle seat chairs, this writer believes the difference is inconsequential and should be understood as painter's license.

[32]Affleck to Cadwalader, October 13, 1770, and Reynolds to Cadwalader, n.d. (paid June 29, 1771), in Wainwright, pp. 44, 46. The provisional tax of 1774 for the city of Philadelphia lists Cadwalader as having nine servants, more than anyone else in the city. Such men as Governor John Penn, Samuel Powell, John Stamper, and Benjamin Chew paid a greater tax (Pennsylvania Archives, *Proprietary Tax of City of Philadelphia, 1774*, ed. William Henry Egle, 3d series, vol. 14 [Harrisburg, Pa.: n.p., 1897], pp. 149–220).

[33]Fleeson to Cadwalader, n.d. (paid August 1, 1771), in Wainwright, pp. 40–41.

[34]Savery to Cadwalader, August 27, 1770, and Affleck to Cadwalader, October 13, 1770, in Wainwright, pp. 49, 44. The recesses may have been created by the pilasters carved by Bernard and Jugiez and billed to Cadwalader, October 1770 (Wainwright, p. 29). A composite of three inventories taken in April 1786 is given in Wainwright, pp. 72–73.

confronted the problem of determining the sizes of the sets of chairs owned by John Cadwalader, he relied upon the 1786 inventory taken a month and a half after Cadwalader's death. Among the objects listed in the downstairs rooms are ten mahogany chairs, a card table, and both a large and a small settee in the large front parlor; ten mahogany chairs and a card table in the back parlor; and a card table with no chairs in the small front parlor. Wainwright's conclusion that there were two sets of ten chairs is contradicted by the 1778 inventory in which the chairs are divided 15, 6, and 6 among the three parlors. Simple arithmetic fails to resolve the confusion, but the locations of the other related pieces of furniture provide a number of clues. The three card tables in the 1786 inventory are the pair of commode card tables and the straight front one. By 1786 only one small settee or sofa is listed in the front parlor; the second one is in the upstairs entry, not in one of the front parlor recesses for which it was made. Similarly, only one card table is in the large front parlor where, in 1778, "two mahogani tables" had been and where the five family portraits hung.[35] Since one of each pair of sofas and card tables had been moved to separate rooms, the accompanying set of side chairs also may have been divided. Most likely, the ten mahogany chairs mentioned in each of the front and back parlors in 1786 constituted a single set of twenty. A single set of this size is large enough to include the fifteen chairs listed in the front parlor in 1778. The set of twenty may be identified further as the saddle seat chairs because the more ornate chairs owned by John Cadwalader would have been placed in his best parlor. Finally, the survival of a saddle seat chair stamped XI demonstrates that the set was larger than ten chairs.

This division of the set of twenty chairs into two smaller sets of equal size fits exactly a second upholstery bill of January 1772 rendered by John Webster. In it he charged John Cadwalader for making cases for twenty chairs and three sofas. The contents of a trunk in the garret listed in the 1786 inventory indicate half of the chair cases were of blue damask and the others were of yellow, the same as the paint colors used in the front and back parlors, respectively.[36]

John Cadwalader's apparent intention in 1772 to alter or scale down the furnishings of his front and rear parlors so soon after his order had been filled is puzzling. The Affleck bill (1770) placed the pair of commode sofas in one room, which stands in marked contrast to later room inventories and to the Webster bill for making cases of different colors for each sofa. Similarly, the "2 green covers for card tables" stored in a trunk in the garret reinforces the hypothesis that the pair of card tables were once used together.[37] Although insufficient evidence exists to explain fully this shift in usage, two observations aid in understanding it. First, the sets of blue and yellow cases were made in addition to the cases provided earlier by Fleeson. Second, social occasions or the change of seasons may have warranted a different arrangement of furniture in the Cadwalader household. Together, these two considerations suggest a possible fluidity of object usage and movement that simply cannot be identified in the few pieces of surviving data which only mark moments in time.

The twelve chairs remaining from the thirty-two chairs upholstered by Fleeson were most likely the straight-front chairs. Originally these twelve chairs and their matching card table probably were arranged in the back parlor, where they would echo the more fully furnished grand front parlor. The six chairs in the 1778 inventory in the back parlor and the six in the small front parlor may have constituted this set. Their disposition among the furnishings listed in 1786 is impossible to determine. Since the third card table was in a room with no chairs whatsoever, it is possible the twelve chairs had been removed from the house by that time. Of this set of twelve, the one at Stratford stamped IIV (presumably seven) and the four chairs at the Winterthur Museum with their numbers removed are the only examples currently known.

Without bills for the manufacture of either set of chairs or the third card table, an attribution to a maker depends upon interpretation of related sources of information. Often sufficient data have perished, but in this case enough survives to warrant such an investigation. Three well-known Philadelphia craftsmen, Affleck, Randolph, and Savery, billed John Cadwalader for furniture during the time he was furnishing his house. Wil-

---

[35]Wainwright, pp. 72–73, 66–67. Neither of the small sofas is identifiable in the wartime inventory. As these inventories illustrate, names of furniture forms were not standardized in the eighteenth century.

[36]Webster to Cadwalader, January 1772, in Wainwright, p. 51. The material was bought from Rushton & Beachcroft,

---

London mercers, August 9, 1771 (Wainwright, p. 69). Wainwright's conclusions on the colors are on p. 30.

[37]Wainwright, p. 73.

liam Savery, whose bill included making eighteen walnut chairs, provided John Cadwalader with a considerable amount of furniture. All of it, however, appears to have been for upper and service rooms. Walnut chamber tables, a walnut chest of drawers, a painted clothespress, a pine corner cupboard, and kitchen furniture are among the items mentioned in two bills covering the period from August 1770 to October 1772.[38] There is nothing in these bills suggesting anything comparable in description or price to the furnishings known to have been in the two parlors. On the other hand, the serviceable furniture of rather common form listed in these bills is well documented as being the type of furniture most representative of Savery's work.

Distinguishing John Cadwalader's fine sets of chairs and straight-front card table as products of the shops of either Randolph or Affleck is more difficult. In addition to manuscript evidence indicating that these cabinetmakers made furniture of the highest quality for leading Philadelphia families, labeled and otherwise documented examples survive, further attesting to their capabilities. Unfortunately, the variety of forms which constitute this body of identified furniture has so far prevented any reliable determination of a Randolph or an Affleck trait that can serve as a standard or gauge against which the Cadwalader furniture can be measured. For instance, the construction of a desk does not illuminate how its maker would construct a card table, because the problems of the fabrication of each form are different, thereby precluding any common ground for comparison or study. Similarly, the common denominators that can be drawn among these various examples are too general for use in identification. Design, proportion, and properties of carved work were traits shared among the products of various cabinetmaking establishments. Likewise, the positive identification of the maker of the commode card tables does little to secure the identification of the two sets of Cadwalader chairs on the basis of construction because they differ in form. Comparison of these tables to the third card table does not provide sufficient evidence of Affleck's manufacture. Although similar in form, the physical properties common among these objects are not sufficiently distinctive to attribute manufacture to one cabinetmaker or shop. The common de-

nominators among all of these related objects that are most useful are their intangible historical circumstances.

The timing of bills and other events signaling when these objects were made, combined with the assumption that John Cadwalader ordered them from either Randolph or Affleck, ultimately suggests that Thomas Affleck was responsible for the two sets of Cadwalader chairs. The appearance of the three carvers on the Affleck bill which describes the pair of card tables provides an avenue of investigation. The identity of both the overall design and the plan of specific carved details between these tables and the matching side chairs suggests that these same three craftsmen also carved the saddle seat chairs.

No concrete evidence survives to support the possibility that other carvers contributed their skills to carving these matching pieces of furniture.[39] To suggest otherwise, even for the sake of argument, requires belief in a degree of cooperation among eighteenth-century entrepreneurs that conflicts with the vigorous competition expressed in their advertisements of their individual abilities.

A search for the names of the three carvers and two furniture makers among the surviving shop account books of any of these craftsmen may provide the connections between objects and shop which are left indeterminate by missing bills. The mechanics of this inquiry are simple. For example, Thomas Affleck billed John Cadwalader for furniture including separate charges for carving by Reynolds and by Bernard and Jugiez. At about the time of this billing, Affleck's own books must have shown a disbursement of cash in the amount of the carving charges to these individuals. The commercial activities evidenced by bills may also be identified through other sources. Unfortunately, no account books for any of the carvers or of cabinetmaker Thomas Affleck are known. However, two Randolph account

---

[38] Savery to Cadwalader, August 27, 1770, and n.d. (ca. December 1772), in Wainwright, pp. 49, 62.

[39] Hummel (n. 4 above) states that the Winterthur example from this set "could have been made by a number of excellent Philadelphia cabinetmakers and carvers" (p. 89). Garvan, on the other hand, attributes manufacture of the set to Randolph and identifies John Pollard as the carver. Her reasoning is as follows: "The carved detail on this chair is more like Pollard's work on the pier table at the Metropolitan than that on the card tables [fig. 5], probably carved by Hercules Courtney, which the set was designed to match." Garvan attributes the carving on the pier table to Pollard because "the hint of Chinoiserie in the central figure on the Metropolitan's table would be appropriate for a carver soon to hang up his 'Sign of the Chinese Shield'" (n. 4 above, "Side Chair," pp. 114–15, no. 90).

books survive, both of which cover the years when John Cadwalader was furnishing his house. A search through Randolph's ledger book (1768–86) yields one reference in 1779 to James Reynolds. In the other account book, which records disbursements from 1763 to 1775, the following entry appears: "Philadelphia 4th August 1771. Received of Mr. Benjn. Randolph a note of hand for forty— Pounds payable in Six mounths wen paye—shall Be in full of all acc. p. Nich. Bernard."[40] Although the timing of the entry is late, the possibility that the Bernard entry provides the needed documentation is enticing. But the inadequacy of this reference alone is demonstrated by two reasons. First, the appearance of Bernard in this account book is not sufficient to establish that he or his partner Jugiez carved these chairs for Randolph or even worked for him on the occasion of this debt. An entry such as this one could arise as a result of any labor charge, a sale of goods, or a settlement of accounts involving other parties. The entry exists as a debt to Bernard only. Neither the partnership nor Reynolds can be associated with this transaction, and it was not posted in the rather detailed business ledger. As such, this particular entry cannot be presumed to be the connecting link between the carvers and the cabinetmaker. In addition to the difficulties of identifying this debt, its timing represents a second problem. Randolph's total furniture charges of £94.15 were billed to John Cadwalader on September 26, 1769, and paid in full two weeks later. If his bill included the chairs, over a year elapsed before Fleeson upholstered them, and sixteen months passed before Randolph paid Bernard for carving them.[41]

Few manuscripts describing Thomas Affleck's shop and business activities have survived, making a similarly detailed investigation impossible. However, enough data remain to allow reconstruction through interpolation of a hypothetical timetable of the manufacture of the two sets of chairs and the third table. The timetable is useful as a test of whether Affleck *could* have made this furniture.

With the exception of the 1769 Randolph bill for unspecified furniture, bills for the remainder of John Cadwalader's interior furnishings date from after 1770.[42] Fleeson's upholstery bill indicates the two sets of chairs were made by October 18, 1770. Peale's portrait of Lambert Cadwalader painted that fall confirms that October was the latest possible date of manufacture of the saddle seat chairs. The three sofas and the easy chair listed on Affleck's bill under the date December 20, 1770, were upholstered by Fleeson on January 15, 1770, twenty-six days later. Using the time differential between these two steps in the production of this furniture as a gauge, the thirty-two side chairs were probably constructed during September 1770. The initial entry on the only surviving Affleck-Cadwalader bill is dated October 13, 1770, so possibly the thirty-two chairs were listed on a preceding bill which is now lost.

The evidence suggesting that Thomas Affleck made these two sets of chairs in the early fall of 1770 is not beyond question, yet it is strong enough to support this conclusion with reasonable certainty. Such a conclusion does not contradict manuscript evidence or shop practices, including settlement of debt. Moreover, an attribution to Affleck follows logically from the relationships based on intrinsic data drawn between the two sets of chairs and the pair of commode card tables by Affleck. In contrast, a Randolph attribution for the furniture requires that exceptions be made to the historical patterns which characterize the eighteenth-century cabinetmaking industry in Philadelphia. The relatively complete survivals of Cadwalader and Randolph manuscripts covering the time this furniture was made also suggest that at least one clear connection should exist between Randolph and these chairs if Randolph were responsible for them.[43]

The single straight-front card table cannot be

[40] Philadelphia Merchant's Account Book, 1768–86, New York Public Library (microfilm copy on deposit at Winterthur Museum Library); Account Book of Benjamin Randolph, 1763–75, Joseph Downs Manuscript and Microfilm Collection, Winterthur Museum Library.

[41] Wainwright, p. 38. Neither the bill nor the ledger book recording this transaction could be located at the Historical Society of Pennsylvania in the spring of 1977. Fleeson billed Cadwalader for upholstering the chairs on October 18, 1770. Randolph's note to Bernard was payable on February 4, 1772.

[42] Wainwright, p. 38. For a sampling of goods purchased, see p. 35 (John Elliott, looking glasses), p. 38 (Daniel King, brassware), p. 46 (James Reynolds, looking glasses and frames), and pp. 49, 62 (William Savery, furniture).

[43] Preliminary findings from a comparison of these Cadwalader chairs with three labeled Randolph chairs do not show a set of common denominators among the five different examples that is sufficient to identify them as products of the same shop. The labeled chairs examined were: Yale University Art Gallery, acc. no. 1930.2495 (two unlabeled chairs from the same set are at the Winterthur Museum, acc. nos. 61.1200.1–.2); Museum of Fine Arts, Boston, acc. no. 41.602a (careful examination of the chair at the MFA revealed that it is a period chair; arguments questioning the authenticity of the label are incomplete because the criteria demanded of this chair have not been tested against other examples of labeled furniture); and a chair in a private collection.

clearly identified in any of the surviving Cadwalader manuscripts. Therefore, identification of the circumstances of its manufacture depends entirely upon the findings pertaining to the two sets of chairs and the pair of commode card tables. Intrinsic properties alone of the single card table are not sufficient to ascribe its manufacture to any particular maker. However, if this table is considered in its context as a member of a suite of furniture made for John Cadwalader, it can be described more completely. The same grounds for identifying this table as part of the suite may be extended to support an attribution of its manufacture to Affleck. It seems reasonable to speculate that this table was made in the late summer or early fall of 1770, about the same time as the chairs, since it is not listed on the Affleck bill (and the Cadwaladers began moving into their new house that winter).[44]

Conclusion

Specific attributions, especially when they disagree with prevailing notions, offer dramatic conclusions to studies of furniture. However, the primary importance of this study does not lie with the assignment of a maker to this furniture, or even with the implied failure of the Benjamin Randolph sample chair theory, but in the presentation and use of a methodology. This methodology allows any object to be examined and interpreted in the full cultural context of which maker identification represents only a part. In addition, the methodology stresses the need to ensure that the intrinsic and extrinsic properties of the objects reinforce each other; it also enables them to clarify one another. Further, by widening the context of the object through its comparison with many other similar objects, the methodology allows a greater degree of accuracy in assessing likenesses and differences.

Particular findings, including maker attributions, cannot be ignored, and many in this study have general application to the understanding of eighteenth-century American furniture; for example, the identification of objects made by Thomas Affleck aids in efforts to recognize his other work. Other findings have more comprehensive effects on the field of furniture history. The fact that the Cadwalader furniture provides an early dated example of furniture made

en suite is not only important to the study of taste in the eighteenth century but also provides another tool for furniture identification. Careful attention to designs or plans of decoration on various forms of chairs and case pieces may help reassociate objects made en suite which may otherwise have been irretrievably lost in a maze of intermarriage and haphazard inheritance patterns. Once considered together, these objects may benefit from the kind of synergism effected with the Cadwalader furniture.

In addition, this study has also shown the need to exercise caution in using carving as a means of furniture identification. The suite of Cadwalader furniture provides unequivocal evidence of collaboration among individual carvers in a single task and, at the same time, demonstrates the difficulty, indeed the impossibility, of identifying the individual work of these carvers. Yet another caution arises regarding the practice of attributing furniture to a maker solely on the basis of its ownership in a family that once patronized that maker. John Cadwalader employed three prominent Philadelphia cabinetmakers at much the same time (although the type of object commissioned may have dictated his selection of individual craftsmen).

Undoubtedly, the most exciting result of this study is the completeness with which the Cadwalader furniture can be described. What, when, for whom, by whom, and much of the how are known. While the relative merits of the design of these objects will continue to undergo constant reassessment among aestheticians, the fact that John Cadwalader owned this furniture identifies it as among the most ambitious and style-conscious products of eighteenth-century Philadelphia. He was one of the wealthiest inhabitants of the city, he apparently spared little expense in both his house and furnishings, he was young, and he was prepared to impress. "Dear Brother," writes Richard Bennett Lloyd from London in 1769. "I cannot let this opportunity slip without writing you a few lines. Your chariot is at last completed: it is elegant, but in my eye heavy. Were my advise asked in a carriage for America, I would have it as light and free from carv'd work as possible. Such chariots as these are only used from the Palace to the house of Lords."[45]

[44]Wainwright, p. 37.

[45]Richard Bennett Lloyd to John Cadwalader, June 26, 1769, folder 1, Cadwalader Papers, Incoming Correspondence (June–October 1769), Historical Society of Pennsylvania.

Mitchell and Rammelsberg

Cincinnati Furniture Manufacturers 1847–1881

Donald C. Peirce

CINCINNATI, located at the midpoint of the Ohio River, was the sixth largest American city in 1850 and the vigorous commercial and industrial center of the West.[1] Since the early years of the nineteenth century, furniture making had been a significant aspect of the city's economic profile, and the introduction of steam-powered machinery combined with the rapid settlement of the prosperous Midwest had provided the means and the market for expansion. As the Cincinnati chamber of commerce explained: "The great reduction in price caused by the introduction of steam, has attracted a large trade from the western and southern country, and Cincinnati furniture is now purchased for the most distant portion of the States bordering on the Ohio, Mississippi, Missouri, Illinois, Cumberland and Tennessee rivers. Considerable quantities are also sent out by canals and railroads, and indeed, we may say there is a demand from every section." Of the city's nine steam-operating furniture factories in 1850, the firm of Mitchell and Ram-

melsberg emerged over the following three decades as the largest and most successful.[2]

The company had been formed in 1847 when Robert Mitchell (fig. 1) and Frederick Rammelsberg (fig. 2), two Cincinnati cabinetmakers, agreed "to become co-partners together under the name and style of Mitchell and Rammelsberg, in the business of manufacturing all kinds of cabinetware, buying, selling, vending and retailing all sorts of goods and commodities belonging to said business." Each partner contributed $10,000 to the enterprise.[3] Beyond entries in Cincinnati directories, nothing is known about the training of either man or the success of any endeavors before

I gratefully acknowledge my indebtedness to Kenneth L. Ames, Donald L. Fennimore, Elizabeth H. Hill, Catherine E. Hutchins, and Deborah D. Waters, Winterthur Museum; Carol Macht, Cincinnati Art Museum; Laura Chace, Cincinnati Historical Society; and Dianne H. Pilgrim, Brooklyn Museum, for their suggestions, encouragements, and cooperation during the preparation of this article.

[1]Cincinnati, with a population in 1850 of 115,435, followed New York, Philadelphia, Boston, Baltimore, and New Orleans in size. St. Louis was the closest western rival with a population of 77,860. Rivalry between the western cities during the first third of the nineteenth century is discussed and documented in Richard Wade, *The Urban Frontier* (Chicago: University of Chicago Press, 1959). Cincinnati viewpoints are revealed in Charles Cist, *Sketches and Statistics of Cincinnati in 1841* (Cincinnati: Printed and published for the author, 1841), and a decade later in Charles Cist, *Sketches and Statistics of Cincinnati in 1851* (Cincinnati: Wm. H. Moore & Co., 1851).

[2]The Cincinnati furniture industry during its formative years is fully documented in Donna Streifthau, "Cincinnati Cabinet- and Chairmakers, 1819–1830" (Ph.D. diss., Ohio State University, 1970). Information in this dissertation may be found in abbreviated form in Streifthau, "Cincinnati Cabinet- and Chairmakers, 1819–1830," *Antiques* 99, no. 6 (June 1971): 896–905. See also Richard Smith, *A Review of the Trade, Commerce and Manufactures of Cincinnati for the Commercial Year Ending August 31, 1850* (Cincinnati, 1850), p. 9. For discussion of the development of steam-powered furniture manufacture in Cincinnati, see Polly Anne Earl, "Craftsmen and Machines: The Nineteenth-Century Furniture Industry," in *Technological Innovation and the Decorative Arts*, Winterthur Conference Report 1973, ed. Ian M. G. Quimby and Polly Anne Earl (Charlottesville: University Press of Virginia, 1974), pp. 307–29.

[3]Exhibit 1: Articles of copartnership between Robert Mitchell and Frederick Rammelsberg, in Charles Rammelsberg et al. v. Robert Mitchell and William Lape, Cincinnati, 23416 (Super. Ct. 1870), p. 218 (hereafter cited as Rammelsberg v. Mitchell). Five years after the death of Rammelsberg and the sale of his business interests, his heirs—Charles Rammelsberg, Robert G. and Sarah Maria Rammelsberg Johnson, Charles H. S. and Catherine Francis Rammelsberg Schultz, and Henry Kessler, the guardian for Emma F., Harry, Clara Louise, and Oscar Rammelsberg, who were minors—brought suit against the executors of the estate, Robert Mitchell and William Lape. During the course of the lawsuits, many of the legal documents and records of the Mitchell and Rammelsberg enterprises were presented as evidence and were printed in the court record. These court transactions were used extensively in researching the firms.

Fig. 1. Robert Mitchell (1811–99). From *Cincinnati Past and Present; or, Its Industrial History as Exhibited in the Life Labors of Its Leading Men* (Cincinnati: M. Joblin & Co., 1872), facing p. 188.

Fig. 2. Frederick Rammelsberg (1814–63). (Photo, Cincinnati Historical Society.)

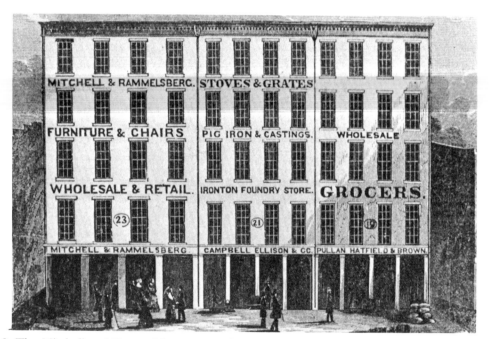

Fig. 3. The Mitchell and Rammelsberg store, 1851. Robert Mitchell used this building as his wareroom in the 1840s. After the merger with Frederick Rammelsberg in 1847, the new firm utilized the building, first as a retail then as a wholesale store until the early 1860s. From *Williams' Cincinnati Directory and Business Advertiser, for 1851–52* (Cincinnati: C. S. Williams, 1851), frontispiece.

the partnership. Within two months of signing the agreement, the partners were advertising "the largest and best assortment of all the varieties and kinds of Cabinet Ware, Chairs, Looking Glasses, &c. &c." for sale at "R. Mitchell's old stand on Columbia Street [also called Second Street]" (fig. 3). They also opened a furniture factory with "facilities for manufacturing superior to any establishment in the western country" on the southwest corner of Second and John streets.[4]

Before signing articles of copartnership, Mitchell and Rammelsberg had paid $8,240 to secure a perpetual lease for the corner lot. If the four-story factory was standing when the lease was secured, it was not recorded in the document. Less than two years later, on December 29, 1848, the factory burned. Immediately after the fire, Mitchell and Rammelsberg issued a "particular notice" in the *Cincinnati Gazette* offering furniture "at very reduced prices for cash or good paper, on short time in order to raise means to rebuild."[5]

In October 1849, the firm announced the opening of a new manufactory, built on the old site, producing "furniture at lower prices, than . . . has ever been offered in the West." Within a year the factory, equipped with steam-powered machinery, employed 150 workers and manufactured "all possible variety of furniture and chairs" worth $145,000 annually. All stages of production were handled there. Beginning from rough lumber which was cut and shaped by steam-driven saws on the lower floors, each piece progressed toward the top floors of the building where the assembled furniture received final dressing and finishing for market.[6] In 1854, the Englishwoman Isabella Lucy Bird visited the expanded factory. Her recorded impressions provide evidence of the

expanded size and scope of operations in the factory: "There is a furniture establishment in Baker Street, London, which employs perhaps eighty hands, and we are rather inclined to boast of it, but we must keep silence when we hear of a factory as large as a Manchester cotton-mill, five stories high, where 260 hands are constantly employed in making chairs, tables, and bedsteads." The workers were "native Americans and Germans, the English and Scotch being rejected on account of their intemperance" and earned them "twelve to fourteen dollars a week." Common chairs, turned out at a weekly rate of 2,500, were the principal manufacture, but other products included rocking chairs ("only made to perfection in the States"), chests of drawers, and rocking baby cribs "in which the brains of the youth of America are early habituated to perpetual restlessness."[7]

Throughout the 1850s, rapid market expansions and extensive facility improvements underscored the success of Mitchell and Rammelsberg. With a market in the South and the Midwest, the firm began establishing branch stores in other cities. On July 2, 1855, Robert Mitchell and Frederick Rammelsberg signed articles of copartnership with William Mitchell, Robert's brother, "for the purpose of carrying on the furniture business" in St. Louis, Missouri. William Mitchell managed the Mitchell and Rammelsberg investment of $30,000 for an annual salary of $1,500 plus one-third of the profits. The manager's share of the profits was reinvested until it equaled those of his partners. Probably Mitchell, Rammelsberg and Company, St. Louis, was predominantly stocked with products fabricated at the Cincinnati factory, however, the copartnership agreement allowed William Mitchell to purchase elsewhere those arti-

[4]The 1836 Cincinnati directory gives the first documented evidence for both Robert Mitchell and Frederick Rammelsberg living and working as cabinetmakers in the city. Directories from the eleven years following indicate that both men worked in various partnerships and each on his own account. See also *Cincinnati Gazette* (April 22, 1847).

[5]Summary of deeds and leases, in Rammelsberg v. Mitchell, p. 112. See J. Leander Bishop, *A History of American Manufactures 1608–1860*, 3 vols. (Philadelphia: Edward Young & Co., 1866), 3:385; *Cincinnati Gazette* (December 30, 1848; January 1, 1849). The *Gazette* reported that one of the results of the conflagration was "upwards of a thousand men" thrown out of employment. The number seems exaggerated since in the new and enlarged factory Mitchell and Rammelsberg employed only 150 workers in 1850.

[6]Cincinnati Gazette (October 4, 1849); Manuscript Census of Industry, Sixth Ward, Hamilton County, Ohio, 1850. Only the firm, Clawson and Mudge, manufacturing $150,000 in

bedsteads, exceeded the annual production of Mitchell and Rammelsberg in Cincinnati. Yet that firm invested only $45,000 compared to the Mitchell and Rammelsberg reported 1850 investment of $100,000. Among the furniture manufacturers in Cincinnati, Mitchell and Rammelsberg employed the greatest number of workers. In the census, annual production of the Cincinnati furniture manufacturers was generally itemized according to form for each firm. The recorded "all possible variety of furniture and chairs" in the Mitchell and Rammelsberg entry suggests the broad scope of the firm's manufacture. The manuscript returns for Ohio 1850–70 are available at Winterthur Museum Library, Winterthur, Del.; see also Cist, *Cincinnati in 1851*, p. 203.

[7]Isabella Lucy Bird, *The Englishwoman in America* (1856; reprint ed., Madison: University of Wisconsin Press, 1966), pp. 122–23.

cles "which Mitchell and Rammelsberg of Cincinnati do not make."[8]

Within a year, the St. Louis store offered extensive and varied wares which included "a large STOCK of beautiful and new styles of PARLOR, CHAMBER, DINING ROOM AND HALLL Furniture in Rosewood, Mahogany, Walnut and Oak." It also stocked "looking glasses and plain furniture of every variety." A single April 1856 steamboat shipment consigned to the St. Louis store contained 141 packages of furniture from Cincinnati, and in all probability most of these came from the Mitchell and Rammelsberg factory. The success of Mitchell and Rammelsberg and other Cincinnati firms discouraged St. Louis-based industries. An 1856 trade and commerce report published in St. Louis bemoaned: "Furniture by the piece, package and cargo still pours in from Cincinnati."[9] By 1859, Mitchell, Rammelsberg and Company, St. Louis, had moved to larger quarters, and reportedly "a large share of their stock" was then being manufactured in that city. Although Mitchell and Rammelsberg did its own extensive upholstery work, the evidence for a furniture factory in St. Louis is inconclusive.[10]

While the St. Louis branch prospered during the 1850s, Mitchell and Rammelsberg continued to expand and improve merchandising and man-

ufacturing facilities at the headquarters in Cincinnati. Here, their interests and talents complemented each other: Robert Mitchell directed merchandising, stores, and general business; Frederick Rammelsberg supervised the factory production operations.[11]

Expanded production at the factory probably made "R. Mitchell's old stand" inadequate for exhibiting the range of the firm's manufactures. In 1856, the partners paid $30,000 to acquire title to "land on Fourth Street" next to the Customs House and paid another $30,000 or $35,000 to build a new store. By 1858 the new store at 99 West Fourth Street was open for business. The seven-story, 100-foot-tall building extended from Fourth Street to Burnet Street. Its design allowed the firm to use new display techniques which Cincinnati promoter Charles Cist described. "Each story is divided into two sections, the stairs in the centre approaching alternately first to one end of the building and then to the other. This is a novel and desirable arrangement, and affords to the visitor a view of the furniture on three different sections at any stand point, and this plan also admits light to much better advantage than the ordinary form, and as the customer passes up only half a story at a time, it is less fatiguing."[12]

Mitchell and Rammelsberg used the new store as a sample room and exhibited one piece or set of each kind of furniture produced. A loft in the store was equipped as an upholstery room. The old store on Second Street became the wholesale warehouse, filled with manufactured work ready for the market, although bottoms for stools and chairs were also caned there.[13] The building served as a warehouse until the early 1860s when the wholesale warerooms were moved to the factory.

By 1859 the factory complex at John and Second streets had also been improved and enlarged. Two buildings were in use, one for machinery and one for varnishing operations. The structures, linked at each floor by enclosed bridges, were sep-

[8]Exhibit 36A: Articles of copartnership of Mitchell, Rammelsberg and Company, St. Louis, in Rammelsberg v. Mitchell, p. 900.

[9]*Daily Missouri Republican* (April 9, April 27, 1856). W. B. Baker, secretary of the chamber of commerce, expressed the bewilderment over the St. Louis industrial situation: "It is difficult to understand why it is that with the best raw material, such as sand for glass, rags for paper, iron for nails, and other articles, and forests of diversified timber we should be dependent on Cincinnati" (*Annual Statement of the Trade and Commerce of St. Louis for the Year 1856* [St. Louis, 1856], pp. 4, 5).

[10]Charles Cist, *Sketches and Statistics of Cincinnati in 1859* (Cincinnati, 1859), p. 295. Mitchell, Rammelsberg and Company first advertised an address at 81–82 Second Street (*Daily Missouri Republican* [April 9, 1856]), but in 1859 Cist reported that the firm was located at Fourth and Washington. St. Louis directories of 1860 and 1863 list Mitchell, Rammelsberg and Company, St. Louis, as furniture manufacturer. A bedstead, now in the John Wornall House in Kansas City, bears a stenciled label with the firm's name and address (134 and 136 North Fourth Street). The label identifies the company as "Manufacturers & DEALERS." The 1864 inventory of the St. Louis stock designates St. Louis-made goods. Whether these wares were produced by a Mitchell, Rammelsberg and Company factory in St. Louis or purchased from a local factory is not indicated. The large amount of upholstery material included in the 1864 inventory suggests that a large volume of upholstery work was carried on in the St. Louis store; Exhibit 36C: Appraised Inventory of Stock, Mitchell, Rammelsberg and Co., St. Louis, Mo., in Rammelsberg v. Mitchell, pp. 919–49.

[11]Joseph R. Hewitt, head of the wholesale department for the firm during the 1860s, recalled in 1868 that Rammelsberg had general superintendence of the factories and that "he did not know the price of a piece of furniture without looking at the catalogue" (Testimony of Joseph R. Hewitt, Rammelsberg v. Mitchell, p. 156); see also George Mortimer Roe, *Cincinnati: The Queen City of the West* (Cincinnati: Times-Star, 1895), p. 2.

[12]Summary of deeds and leases, and testimony of Truman B. Handy, in Rammelsberg v. Mitchell, pp. 111, 167; Cist, *Cincinnati in 1859*, p. 294.

[13]Cist, *Cincinnati in 1859*, p. 294.

arated by a narrow alley. As a fire precaution, the enclosed boilers were beneath the alley.

The basement or first story of the machinery building housed two steam engines for driving all the construction machinery. Also in the basement were "sixteen turning lathes, a tin punching machine presumably used for punching inset tin panels on food safes, three of Bettgemen's patent machines for cutting dovetails on bedrails, two of Wright's patent machines for turning bedspring discs, and in one end . . . a large blacksmith shop, for the exclusive use of the establishment."[14] Rough boards were cut and smoothed on the second and third floors: Daniels's planing machines, two Woodworth's cut saws, and three scroll saws, all powered by steam, were on the second floor; one Daniels's patent planer, two tenoning machines, two friezing machines, three scroll saws, one molding machine, one miter saw, three fine rip saws, three fine crosscut saws, one grooving machine, four boring machines, and four jointing machines were on the third floor. Boards cut to specification on the second and third floors were transported to the upper floors for assembly. Meanwhile, on the fifth floor, thirty-six carvers fabricated crest rails and ornaments for the nearly finished furniture.

Adjacent to the machinery building stood the varnishing building, eighty-feet-square and eight stories high. Mahogany, walnut, and rosewood veneers, looking-glass plates, and marble tops were stored throughout the building. Furniture in various stages of completion were transported from floor to floor by a steam-driven elevator. This elevator also opened onto the roof where much of the finished work could dry outside. Except for the caning of seats and upholstering, all Mitchell and Rammelsberg manufacturing took place in the two factory buildings. The woods—black walnut, cherry, oak, pine, ash, maple, solid mahogany, and rosewood—were stored in a 75,000-square-foot lumberyard adjacent to the factory. By 1859 the woods were turned into furniture products worth $500,000, more than three times the value of the 1850 output.[15]

The mass production and distribution methods used by Mitchell and Rammelsberg had enabled the firm to manufacture and sell great quantities and enormous varieties of furniture, as surviving pieces of furniture and the firm's 1863

and 1864 wholesale price lists illustrate. The 1863 price list included sixty-three different categories of furniture and 483 patterns. Nearly 71 percent of the offerings were priced at $30 or less. Prices of beds ranged from $3.25 for a poplar low post bed to $150.00 for a French bedstead with two oval panels in the headboard. Dressing bureaus varied in price from $9.50 for a "Misses'" solid front in walnut, cherry, imitation rosewood, or ash, to $175.00 for an "Eagle pattern" dresser with a serpentine front, round ends, and doors in mahogany, rosewood, or oak. Etagères were available in a wide variety from a one-shelf hanging corner type priced at $2.25 to a "fine" parlor étagère with French mirror at $125.00. Mitchell and Rammelsberg supplied sideboards ranging from a plain example in ash, walnut, or mahogany for $14 to extra fine étagères priced between $125 and $250. Common and standard forms were also manufactured. Kitchen tables were priced between $1.75 and $2.50 according to size. Painted slat-back chairs cost $4.50 a dozen. Mitchell and Rammelsberg products were not limited to domestic wares; they also sold saloon tables, office tables, and a wide variety of office chairs.[16]

Supplementing the price lists is a March 1864 inventory of stock in the Cincinnati buildings which confirms the availability of the wide range of stock manufactured and offered by the firm. A comparison of the inventory and the price lists reveals that great quantities of lower priced goods were kept in stock and indicates that the more expensive items perhaps were more often made to order. Some of the unusual entries were willow chairs valued from $2.50 to $3.60; a gilt fancy chair appraised at $10.00; two "bent-rim" chairs, worth $2.00 apiece; and "childs wagons" appraised at $18.00 each. The diversity of goods listed in the inventory confirms that Mitchell and Rammelsberg could supply entire interiors while continuing to manufacture "furniture from the plainest to the most elegant and fashionable."[17]

Surviving common and standard furniture forms manufactured by Mitchell and Rammelsberg tend to be less identifiable than most

---

[14]Ibid.

[15]Ibid., pp. 292–94, 295.

[16]Exhibit 17: List of prices for furniture manufactured by Mitchell and Rammelsberg, 1863, in *Rammelsberg v. Mitchell*, pp. 721–38. The entire price list for 1863 was placed as evidence in the lawsuits. This price list is reproduced as part of the court transactions, and the terms and prices quoted in the text of this article are taken from this source.

[17]Exhibit 6: Inventory and appraisement of the assets and liabilities of Mitchell and Rammelsberg of Cincinnati, in *Rammelsberg v. Mitchell*, pp. 238–312.

expensive lines. Labeled common tables and chairs have not yet been located, and possibly such furniture was unlabeled. Throughout history, most common furniture has had a low survival rate because it has received greater abuse than more expensive chamber and dining room sets. This pattern seems to fit Mitchell and Rammelsberg products: chamber sets and case pieces are the most frequently found pieces. Few upholstered pieces have survived, although upholstery work was a major aspect of the firm's trade.[18] Perhaps reupholstery destroyed Mitchell and Rammelsberg labels.

The simpler line of Mitchell and Rammelsberg chamber furniture was simply constructed. The small chests had ordinary turned wooden knobs and lacked ornamentation. Some walnut pieces were stained red, possibly to create the imitation rosewood finish mentioned in the 1863 price list. The West Fourth Street address stenciled on one such red-stained walnut chest (fig. 4) places the date of its manufacture as sometime after 1857. Both this chest and an earlier one have wooden knobs and the firm's name and address stenciled on the bottom of the top drawer. The carved and applied decorations on the drawer fronts seem to have been standard forms that were used on a number of Mitchell and Rammelsberg pieces.[19]

The outbreak of the Civil War in 1861 depressed the Cincinnati furniture trade because secession had removed the affluent and demanding southern market.[20] However, by 1863, new customers were ordering Cincinnati furniture which the chamber of commerce quickly explained.

The superior character of the cabinet ware turned out of the Cincinnati factories attracted the attention from districts of the West which had previously bought at the East, and this, with a demand for "fashionable" furniture from the thousands who had been placed in posses-

Fig. 4. Mitchell and Rammelsberg, chest of drawers. Cincinnati, 1851–57. Walnut stained in imitation of rosewood; H. 29″, W. 30″, D. 17″. (Private collection: Photo, Donald C. Peirce.)

sion of large amounts of money by the war, created a brisk market, and all the factories were taxed to their utmost capacity during the year, so that business is again active and profitable, as in years before the rebellion. . . . The advance in all kinds of material, and in labor, together with the tax, resulted in much higher prices, but this seems to have had no influence on the demand.[21]

Mitchell and Rammelsberg were among the firms that strove to meet the demand for "fashionable" furniture from suddenly wealthy westerners. A mahogany lady's worktable (fig. 5) probably dates from this prosperous period. The 1863 price list included a lady's workstand "with silk bag and scroll leg, carved" available in mahogany or rosewood at $35 wholesale. A rosewood desk and bookcase (fig. 6) probably was also made in the early 1860s. The carved decoration around the keyhole of the fall front is similar to that on the chest in figure 5. The shaped fall front may link this desk and bookcase with the "O. G. fall secretary and bookcase" in the 1863 price list. A similar but larger secretary and bookcase (fig. 7) with identical carved decoration on the lower doors, corners of the bases, and ogee fall fronts illustrates the use of interchangeable parts and the adaptability of form in Mitchell and Rammelsberg products. Despite the enormous size of these desks, mass production techniques

[18]The recapitulation of the 1864 inventory of the Cincinnati building showed Mitchell and Rammelsberg had in stock $45,302.23 worth of upholstery goods. This amount reflected just over half the total worth of goods in the retail store on Fourth Street—$89,663.16. The total value of all goods and equipment in the Cincinnati buildings was $302,172,62; Exhibit 6: Inventory, in *Rammelsberg v. Mitchell*, p. 312.

[19]Similar or identical carvings decorate a chamber set in the Indiana State Museum, a dressing bureau now in the collection of the Jackson County Historical Society and exhibited in the Wornall House, and a desk and bookcase in the Newark Museum (fig. 6).

[20]William Smith, *Annual Statement of the Commerce of Cincinnati for the Commercial Year Ending August 31, 1862* (Cincinnati, 1862), p. 26.

[21]William Smith, *Annual Statement of the Commerce of Cincinnati for the Commercial Year Ending August 31, 1863* (Cincinnati, 1863), p. 27.

Fig. 5. Mitchell and Rammelsberg, worktable. Cincinnati, 1857–68. Mahogany; H. 31″, W. 20″, D. 18″. The blue silk bag may be original. (Cincinnati Art Museum, bequest of Nan C. Sheerer: Photo, Winterthur Museum Library.)

Fig. 6. Mitchell and Rammelsberg, desk and bookcase. Cincinnati, 1857–68. Rosewood; H. 120″, W. 54″. (Newark Museum, gift of Archdiocese of Newark: Photo, Winterthur Museum Library.)

Fig. 8. Mitchell and Rammelsberg, desk. Cincinnati, 1857–68. Mahogany; H. 72″, W. 32″, D. 16″. (Private collection: Photo, Donald C. Peirce.)

Fig. 7. Mitchell and Rammelsberg, desk and bookcase. Cincinnati, 1857–68. Rosewood; H. 120″, W. 72″. The stenciled label is on the back of the upper section. (Executive Mansion of Missouri, Jefferson City: Photo, courtesy of Lynn Springer.)

enabled them to be manufactured as part of the firm's standard offerings.

The mass production methods of Mitchell and Rammelsberg and other Cincinnati manufacturers gave keen competition to eastern firms. An unsigned essay on home furnishings in Samuel Sloan's 1861 edition of *Homestead Architecture* published in Philadelphia gives the easterners' perspective.

An immense trade has sprung up in the last few years in a cheap and showy class of furniture, of mongrel design and superficial construction. The location of many dealers in the different cities and town South and West has increased the demand for this class of goods to so great an extent that a number of large steam factories are engaged in this trade exclusively. They make furniture of a showy style, with but little labor on it, and most of that done with the scroll saw and turning-lathe. The dealers both south and west, find this work very profitable, as the showy appearance gives an erroneous idea of value, and purchasers pay more profitable prices for it than they do for good but less pretentious goods. This furniture is easily detected by examination, as it consists mostly of broad, flat surfaces, cut with scroll-saws into all imaginable and unimaginable shapes, and then by a moulding machine the edges are taken off uniformly; this gives it a showy finish. The principal articles thus produced are etageres, or whatnots, fancy tables, hat-racks, bookshelves, music stands, bedsteads, cribs and fancy reception chairs. There is not much of this class of goods that will exist as long as the manufacturer, but will no doubt outlive his reputation as a cabinetmaker. This is not to depreciate the value of the goods of any person, but is truthful matter, properly belonging to a work of this kind.[22]

The author may well have had Mitchell and Rammelsberg in mind, for the factory was equipped with scroll saws, molding machines, and turning lathes and produced quantities of étagères, hat racks, music stands, bedsteads, and cribs. The desk unit in figure 8 is a simple box secured to the shelves by columns which were probably turned on a steam-powered lathe. The shelves have had their "edges taken off uniformly" giving the desk "a showy finish." The shapes for the scroll work on top of the desk unit

and the top shelf were probably roughed out on a scroll saw. In short, the Mitchell and Rammelsberg desk seems to epitomize the kind of work critized in Sloan's book. It was not without just cause that eastern manufacturers looked askance at the burgeoning furniture factories of Cincinnati.

By 1862, with prosperity beginning to return to the Cincinnati furniture market, Mitchell and Rammelsberg again considered expansion. In the summer of 1862, J. and M. Flaherty, a furniture store in Memphis, Tennessee, which was also a distributor of Mitchell and Rammelsberg goods, closed for financial reasons. The owners sent head clerk John P. Hoffman to Cincinnati "to offer the balance of the stock of J. and M. Flaherty, to Mitchell and Rammelsberg, to be sold to them and credited to the account of J. and M. Flaherty, or to take up such of J. and M. Flaherty's acceptance or notes due Mitchell and Rammelsberg as far as their stock would go." In July 1862, Mitchell and Rammelsberg accepted these terms and granted Hoffman power of attorney to purchase the Flaherty stock in the firm's name. The three men also agreed to reopen the old Flaherty store under the name and management of Hoffman. He received an annual salary of $1,200 and retained an option of becoming a partner after one year.[23]

On January 30, 1863, less than a year after Hoffman began managing the Memphis store, Frederick Rammelsberg died of lung disease. During the next several years a number of business transactions occurred as a direct result of Rammelsberg's demise. In September 1863, Hoffman approached Robert Mitchell seeking a full partnership in the Memphis branch. On October 22, 1863, Robert Mitchell, his brother George, and Hoffman signed articles of copartnership in the Memphis store which was renamed Mitchell, Hoffman and Company. Each partner invested $10,000. For his share, Hoffman borrowed $8,000 from Robert Mitchell which he repaid within a year, suggesting the immediate success of the new firm. John Hoffman and George Mitchell managed the store. The stock was inventoried prior to the change in ownership and name. The inventory, which is simply a list of goods, offers no evidence for the appearance or size of the store in Memphis, but it reveals a stock that included all varieties of furniture forms, car-

[22]Samuel Sloan, *Homestead Architecture* (Philadelphia: J. B. Lippincott & Co., 1861), p. 328. It has been suggested that George Henkels, a prominent Philadelphia cabinetmaker, was responsible for the furnishing sections of Sloan's book. Sloan was primarily an architect and tastemaker. Certainly Henkels, for professional reasons, might have had reason to criticize the competitive Cincinnati manufacturers. See Kenneth Ames, "George Henkels, Nineteenth-Century Philadelphia Cabinetmaker," *Antiques* 104, no. 4 (October 1973): 641–50.

[23]Exhibit 26: Deposition of John P. Hoffman in Rammelsberg v. Mitchell, pp. 799–800.

pets, window shades, and caskets. Much of the furniture apparently came from Mitchell and Rammelsberg of Cincinnati, while burial cases, carpets, and curtain materials were supplied by other manufacturers. The total value of goods at the Memphis store was $30,300 in 1863.[24]

Shortly after Mitchell, Hoffman and Company was founded, Mitchell, Rammelsberg and Company, St. Louis, underwent a number of changes. After Rammelsberg's death in January 1863, his estate, Robert Mitchell, and William Mitchell shared equally in the expenses and profits of the St. Louis branch. Early in January 1864, William Mitchell paid the estate $59,111.33 for Rammelsberg's interest in that business. Within a month, Robert Mitchell purchased half of Rammelsberg's former share from William Mitchell, making the brothers equal partners in the St. Louis business. The store was renamed R. & W. Mitchell of St. Louis and continued to sell "Furniture, Pianos, & house furnishing goods."[25]

The inventory taken prior to the transfer of ownership of the St. Louis business reveals a wide variety of stock. Merchandise on five floors, in a cellar, and in an upholsterer's room were listed as being Cincinnati-, St. Louis-, or eastern-made goods. Cincinnati manufactures constituted the bulk of the stock, valued at $19,027.80. Eastern goods were considered worth $8,495.46 and St. Louis products, $8,024.95. The Cincinnati-made wares consisted almost exclusively of furniture in a wide variety of forms. Over half the value of eastern goods ($4,365.10) was in upholstery materials. The remaining eastern manufactures were furniture. Locally made items included furniture forms, stepladders, mattresses, upholstery goods, and mosquito net frames.[26]

Under the terms of Rammelsberg's will and the original copartnership agreement, Robert Mitchell continued to operate the Cincinnati factories and stores for a year after his partner's death. Profits were divided equally between Mitchell and the Frederick Rammelsberg estate. On March 2, 1864, following the completion of an inventory of the Cincinnati buildings, Robert Mitchell signed a nine-month note for $336,846.71 to purchase the Rammelsberg

share from the estate. Although unable to comply with the time limit in the note, by June 21, 1866, Mitchell completed payment to William Lape who with Mitchell was co-executor of the Rammelsberg estate, and the note was canceled. At that time Robert Mitchell became the sole owner of the lucrative Mitchell and Rammelsberg business in Cincinnati.[27]

Within six months, Mitchell established a third branch store, Mitchell, Craig and Company of New Orleans, to distribute Mitchell and Rammelsberg furniture in the delta region. By 1871, John and James Craig had been replaced by George Mitchell, and the store was renamed the Mitchell and Rammelsberg Furniture Company of New Orleans.[28]

After the fall 1866 opening of the New Orleans branch, Robert Mitchell had moved to incorporate his Cincinnati properties. On April 26, 1867, he deeded all the holdings of Mitchell and Rammelsberg to the Mitchell and Rammelsberg Furniture Company for $393,000. Mitchell was president of the new joint-stock corporation, and his son Albert was secretary-treasurer. Foremen and some of the employees were offered shares of stock in the reorganized firm. Robert Mitchell continued to manage the business aspects rather than the manufacturing operations of the firm. William Stossmeister, who had worked under Rammelsberg for about twenty-five years, had been promoted to foreman of the factory building in 1863 not long after Rammelsberg's death. At about the same time, Frederick Unnewehr was put in charge of the varnishing building.[29] The manufactory remained at the southwest corner of Second and John. By this time, the varnishing building adjacent to the assembling plant also

[24]*Cincinnati Gazette* (February 3, 1863); Exhibit 26: Deposition of Hoffman, and Exhibit 26B: Inventory of Memphis stock, in Rammelsberg v. Mitchell, pp. 804, 816–40.

[25]Exhibit 36: Deposition of William Mitchell, and Exhibit 62: Second deposition of Mitchell, in Rammelsberg v. Mitchell, pp. 896, 969.

[26]Exhibit 36C (see n. 10 above).

[27]Exhibit 1 (see n. 3 above); Exhibit 2: Will of Frederick Rammelsberg, pp. 221–24; Exhibit 20: Promissory note from Robert Mitchell to William H. Lape, p. 768; Testimony of Thomas B. Smith, p. 140, all in Rammelsberg v. Mitchell. In his testimony, Smith, a Cincinnati furniture manufacturer in business with W. Meader and Co., implied that the goodwill in trade built up by Mitchell and Rammelsberg at the time of Rammelsberg's death added to the real value of the business. Mitchell may have retained Rammelsberg's name after assuming sole ownership because the firm was established and well known under the double name.

[28]*Daily Picayune* (November 28, 1866); New Orleans Directory (1871), p. 435.

[29]Exhibit 19: Indenture transferring all the holdings of the firm Mitchell and Rammelsberg to the Mitchell and Rammelsberg Furniture Company in Rammelsberg v. Mitchell, p. 763; *Cincinnati Past and Present; or Its Industrial History as Exhibited in the Life Labors of Its Leading Men* (Cincinnati: M. Joblin & Co., 1872), p. 188; Testimony of William Stossmeister, and Testimony of Frederick Unnewehr, in Rammelsberg v. Mitchell, pp. 161, 153.

served as a chair factory. The upholstery work which had been done in a loft of the retail store on Fourth Street in 1859 had been moved to a newly constructed wholesale warehouse on the southeast corner of Second and John opposite the factory (fig. 9).[30]

The reorganized company continued to expand. In 1870 the gross annual product of the Mitchell and Rammelsberg Furniture Company was $700,000. Six hundred employees—550 men, 10 women, and 40 children—transformed 3,000,000 feet of lumber into furniture by the firm in that year.[31]

In 1873 the *Cincinnati Enquirer* devoted an entire page to a feature article on the Mitchell and Rammelsberg Furniture Company operations. By then, the factory complex consisted of five structures—the manufactory, the varnishing building, two wholesale warehouses, and a residence building for 250 workers. From this com-

pound the factory produced "most of the best furniture in the West and South, and not a little in the East." Even the use of steam power which Mitchell and Rammelsberg had used since the late 1840s was defended and praised in the article. "The taste it [steam-powered manufacturing] creates and fosters, the difference in comfort it causes and the almost illimitable employment into which it branches off in every direction is a matter of which any city might boast. . . . By it, and it alone, the cheapness is the only means of bringing it into thousands of homes to add to their attractions, and thereby . . . to lend its powerful aid in preserving unharmed the mainstay of our national strength, the homelife of our people."[32]

The article in the *Enquirer* coincided with the completion of a new Mitchell and Rammelsberg retail store (fig. 10), located on Fourth Street a few doors west of the 1857 store. James K. Wil-

[30]Testimony of Joseph R. Hewitt, in *Rammelsberg v. Mitchell*, pp. 155–56.

[31]Manuscript Census of Industry, Second Ward, Hamilton County, Ohio, 1870.

[32]*Cincinnati Enquirer* (August 27, 1873), p. 10. The extent of Mitchell and Rammelsberg trade in the eastern states has not been documented. Most nineteenth-century accounts define the firm's (and Cincinnati's) sphere of trade as the southern and western states.

Fig. 9. The Mitchell and Rammelsberg Furniture Company factory complex, ca. 1875. The company's wholesale warerooms were in the building on the left. The manufacturing building was on the right at the corner of Second and John Streets. Directly behind was the varnishing building. From D. J. Kenny, *Illustrated Cincinnati* (Cincinnati: Robert Clarke & Co., 1875), p. 157.

Fig. 10. The Mitchell and Rammelsberg Furniture Company store, post-1873. (Photo, Cincinnati Historical Society.)

son, a Cincinnati architect, had designed the new store in the style of the "French Renaissance, adapted to strictly business purposes." Each of the six stories of the building had an area of 15,000 square feet. The first floor was divided into two rooms while each of the upper floors was one large room. Elevators carried both merchandise and customers from floor to floor. Platforms were constructed at the rear of the building on Baker Street so that wagons could easily deliver goods from the factory to the store.[33]

Large show windows constituted the new store's facade. At the time of the 1873 opening, the large windows on the ground floor displayed sets of furniture "for the drawing-room, the library, or the bedroom precisely as if in actual present use in the house of some wealthy and judicious citizen."

On the second floor in the front position, is a raised platform extending the whole length of the building,

100 feet, on which is tastefully arranged as elegant a stock of furniture as can be seen in the country, comprising the finest American and imported cabinet wares, artistic in design, highly ornamented, and very substantial furniture for use. It is composed of Chairs, Parlor Cabinets, Jardiniers, Card Receivers, Sofas, Writing Tables, Secretaries, Fire Screens, Buffets, Bouquet and Flower Stands, Pedestals for Statuary and Bronzes, Japanese Card Stands, Tables and numerous other articles . . . the whole forming an exhibition of the finest work that can be produced in this line, embracing Tarsia work or Marquetry; Inlaid Buhl work in Brass and Ebony, as well as Porcelain work of the most elegant description.[34]

The 1859 Mitchell and Rammelsberg retail store had served as a sample wareroom for the display of representative examples of their furniture. The larger 1873 store allowed the company to suggest entire room arrangements of their furniture and, at the same time, a wide variety of accessories and imported objects. The increase in inventory and new display methods suggest that the firm had expanded beyond its role as supplier of furniture and upholstery goods and that by the 1870s it could supply a buyer with an entire interior.

The Mitchell and Rammelsberg Furniture Company continued to mass-produce furniture of all kinds as well as the expensive furniture filling the windows of the new retail store. For example, the simple walnut bureau in figure 11 bears the stenciled label of the Mitchell and Rammelsberg Furniture Company and could not have been made earlier than 1868 when the corporation was founded. Its small scale and lack of ornament suggest that it was among the plainest lines of the firm's manufacture. Even imposing pieces like a massive sideboard (fig. 12) have the same rough interior construction characteristic of the firm's earlier and plainer work. A comparison of this sideboard with another (fig. 13) illustrates the company's continued use of interchangeable parts even in elaborate furniture. The bases and mirrored tops are separate sections. The bases of the two sideboards are identical, yet each has a distinct top section. Another distinguishing feature is the marble top on the base of the sideboard shown in figure 12. Undoubtedly such variations reflected costs, availability of materials, and personal taste. Mechanization and use of interchangeable parts had enabled the Mitchell

[33]James K. Wilson was also the architect for the Isaac M. Wise Temple in Cincinnati. For further information on Wilson, consult Glenn Patton, "James Keys Wilson (1828–1894): Architect of the Gothic Revival in Cincinnati," *Journal of the Society of Architectural Historians* 26, no. 4 (December 1967): 285–93.

[34]*Cincinnati Enquirer* (August 27, 1873), p. 10.

Fig. 11. Mitchell and Rammelsberg, dressing bureau. Cincinnati, 1868–81. Walnut; H. 72″, W. 41″, D. 19″. (Private collection: Photo, Donald C. Peirce.)

Fig. 12. Mitchell and Rammelsberg, sideboard. Cincinnati, 1868–81. Walnut; H. 72″, W. 60″, D. 21″. (Hillforest Historical Foundation.)

Fig. 13. Mitchell and Rammelsberg, sideboard. Cincinnati, 1868–81. Walnut; H. 114″, W. 60″, D. 21″. (Rutherford B. Hayes Library.)

Fig. 14. Mitchell and Rammelsberg Furniture Company exhibit of an oak sideboard and hallstand at the Philadelphia Centennial Exposition of 1876. From *Gems of the Centennial Exhibition* (New York: D. Appleton & Co., 1877), p. 141.

and Rammelsberg Furniture Company to meet the demands of a broad and varied market.[35]

In the 1870s the company not only increased manufacturing and merchandising facilities but also helped introduce and popularize new styles of furniture. The Mitchell and Rammelsberg Furniture Company "contributed the only examples of furniture designed rigidly after the canons of Eastlake" shown at the Centennial Exposition. The firm's display (fig. 14) consisted of an oak sideboard with burnished steel mounts and an oak hall stand. In the nineteenth-century exhibitions, furniture manufacturers often designed and fabricated cabinets and sideboards specifically for a particular exhibition.[36] Although the company may have designed this furniture especially for the exposition, it soon was offering identical and adapted pieces to its more affluent customers.

Less than a year after the close of the exposition, Abram Gaar, a successful and wealthy businessman and farmer, began furnishing his newly completed $20,000 home near Richmond, Indiana. Gaar had purchased furniture from Mitchell and Rammelsberg in the 1850s, and he once again turned to the firm.[37] Two surviving bills of sale in a private collection dated May 30 and May 31, 1877, prove that the Mitchell and Ramelsberg Furniture Company provided the bulk of furnishings for the new Gaar home. The furniture was purchased in Cincinnati at a cost of $3,865.50 and was probably shipped by railroad to Richmond.

Included in Gaar's purchase was "1 Walnut Eastlake sideboard bronze trimmings" (fig. 15), made to order at a cost of $325.[38] The central pointed pediments with pineapple finials and Gothic crockets clearly link it to the centennial sideboard, but there are some differences. In the upper section of the Gaar sideboard, the center is open, the side shelves are enclosed, and mirrors have been added. In the lower section, drawers were added and the canted corners were squared off. The Gaar sideboard is made of walnut instead of oak and is fitted with bronze rather than with steel mounts. Gaar probably specified these changes to make the piece more practical for domestic use. In contrast to the sideboard, the hall rack (fig. 16), which Gaar purchased along with a Japanese vase for $260, is nearly identical in detail to that exhibited at the exposition. Like the sideboard, the Gaar hall rack is walnut rather than oak, and it is fitted with bronze hooks not illustrated on the exhibition piece, and ceramic tiles.

Gaar paid $200 for the ten walnut "Eastlake" dining chairs, an armchair (fig. 17), and an "Eastlake Tea Chair"; and $75 for an extension dining table, also of walnut, which with seven leaves expands to fourteen feet (fig. 18). The chairs are upholstered in red embossed leather

---

[35]I am indebted to Kenneth Ames for bringing these sideboards to my attention.

[36]George T. Ferris, *Gems of the Centennial Exhibition* (New York: D. Appleton & Co., 1877), p. 133; Kenneth Ames, "The Battle of the Sideboards," in *Winterthur Portfolio 9*, ed. Ian M. G. Quimby (Charlottesville: University Press of Virginia, 1974), pp. 1–27.

[37]*Richmond Telegram* (April 20, 1877). A small worktable survives in a private collection with Mitchell and Rammelsberg stenciled on the inside bottom of the drawer. The label gives the address for the firm at 23 and 25 Second Street. The firm's retail store was at this address between 1851 and 1857 when Gaar undoubtedly purchased the table.

[38]I am indebted to Judith A. Barter for bringing a private collection of Gaar furniture to my attention. The documentation for the Gaar furniture consists of a bill of sale dated May 30, 1877, and a second bill of sale which may be a shipping order dated May 31, 1877. Throughout the discussion of the Gaar furniture, style terms and prices are taken from the May 30 bill of sale.

Fig. 15. Mitchell and Rammelsberg, sideboard. Cincinnati, ca. 1877. Walnut; H. 105″, W. 63″, D. 23″. (Private collection: Photo, Ralph Pyle.)

Fig. 16. Mitchell and Rammelsberg, hall rack. Cincinnati, ca. 1877. Walnut; 97½″, W. 50¾″, D. 19″. (Private collection: Photo, Ralph Pyle.)

Fig. 17. Mitchell and Rammelsberg, side chair and armchair. Cincinnati, ca. 1877. Walnut; side chair, H. 38½″, W. 18″, D. 18½″; armchair, H. 38″, W. 22¾″, D. 21½″. (Private collection: Photo, Ralph Pyle.)

Fig. 18. Mitchell and Rammelsberg, extension table. Cincinnati, ca. 1877. Walnut; H. 29½″, W. and L. (closed) 54″. (Private collection: Photo, Ralph Pyle.)

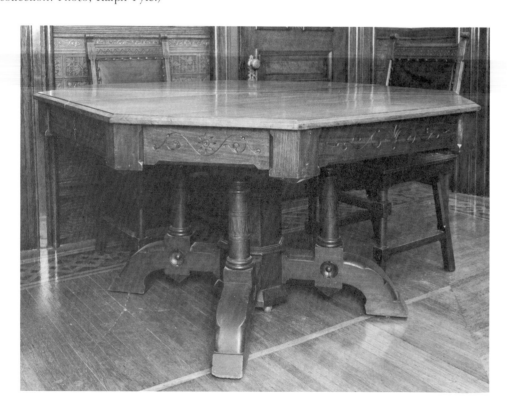

Fig. 19. Mitchell and Rammelsberg, bedstead. Cincinnati, ca. 1877. Ash and mahogany with marquetry decoration; H. 97″, W. 65½″, L. 86½″. (Private collection: Photo, Ralph Pyle.)

Fig. 20. Mitchell and Rammelsberg, dresser. Cincinnati, ca. 1877. Ash and mahogany with marquetry decoration; H. 101″, W. 67½″, D. 16″. (Private collection: Photo, Ralph Pyle.)

and black velvet gimp and have scroll terminals on the side stiles that match the finials above the cupboards in the sideboard.

Abram Gaar's bedroom furniture illustrates his diverse taste, the varied offerings of the Mitchell and Rammelsberg Furniture Company, and the overlapping popularity of furniture styles in the 1870s. Compared with the impressive massiveness of the chamber furniture selected by Gaar, the Eastlake style dining room furniture seems almost delicate. The largest bedroom set included a bedstead (fig. 19), a dresser (fig. 20), a commode (fig. 21), a pair of side chairs (fig. 22), and a rocker (fig. 23). The bedstead and case pieces were executed in ash and mahogany and decorated with inset marquetry panels. The side chairs are ash ornamented with mahogany, and the rocking chair is entirely ash. All three were originally upholstered in "blue wool satine." If the Mitchell and Rammelsberg Furniture Company manufactured rather than merely sold the marquetry set, the quality of construction and

Fig. 21. Mitchell and Rammelsberg, commode. Cincinnati, ca. 1877. Ash and mahogany with marquetry decoration; H. 31″, W. 18½″, D. 16½″. (Private collection: Photo, Ralph Pyle.)

Fig. 22. Mitchell and Rammelsberg, side chair (one of a pair). Cincinnati, ca. 1877. Ash with mahogany decoration; H. 33″, W. 18″, D. 17″. (Private collection: Photo, Ralph Pyle.)

Fig. 23. Mitchell and Rammelsberg, rocker. Cincinnati, ca. 1877. Ash; H. 39½″, W. 21″, D. 17″. (Private collection: Photo, Ralph Pyle.)

execution of decorative details distinguish this furniture as an example of the firm's best lines.[39] Except for the rocker which was priced separately on the bill of sale at $30, this bedroom furniture seems to have been considered a set and sold for $400.

In addition to the marquetry bedroom set, Gaar ordered a walnut bedroom set which consisted of a bedstead (fig. 24), a dresser (fig. 25), and a commode (fig. 26). Similar in scale to the marquetry set, the less elaborate walnut bedroom furniture sold for $245. The dresser is the only piece in the Gaar collection known to bear the

stenciled label of the Mitchell and Rammelsberg Furniture Company. The label is on the top of the base beneath the "Formosa" marble slab. The stylized flowers in the crests of the walnut bedstead and dresser are similar to those on the marquetry set. Commodes in each set are of similar construction.

Among the parlor furnishings selected by Abram Gaar was a $200 walnut center table with "Tarsia work or Marquetry" (fig. 27). The Mitchell and Rammelsberg Furniture Company exhibited such pieces in their retail store. Possibly another firm supplied the marquetry and inset panels. But the gross carvings on the legs and stretcher are similar to those on other known Mitchell and Rammelsberg products (see figs. 12, 13).

Abram Gaar required simple as well as elaborate furniture. Included in the 1877 order was a

[39]Thomas B. Smith testified that Mitchell and Rammelsberg "kept a pretty good force of draughtsman, and they keep a pretty good supply of eastern furniture." The quality of workmanship on the marquetry bedroom set seems superior when compared to other Mitchell and Rammelsberg products; see Testimony of Smith, in Rammelsberg v. Mitchell, p. 132.

Fig. 24. Mitchell and Rammelsberg, bedstead. Cincinnati, ca. 1877. Walnut; H. 96″, W. 55″, D. 23¾″. (Private collection: Photo, Ralph Pyle.)

Fig. 25. Mitchell and Rammelsberg, dresser. Cincinnati, ca. 1877. Walnut; H. 93″, W. 55″, D. 23¾″. (Private collection: Photo, Ralph Pyle.)

Fig. 26. Mitchell and Rammelsberg, commode. Cincinnati, ca. 1877. Walnut; H. 32″, W. 20¼″, D. 17″. (Private collection: Photo, Ralph Pyle.)

Fig. 27. Mitchell and Rammelsberg, center table. Cincinnati, ca. 1877. Walnut with marquetry decoration; H. 27½″, W. 32″, L. 53¼″. (Private collection: Photo, Ralph Pyle.)

Fig. 28. Mitchell and Rammelsberg, library table. Cincinnati, ca. 1877. Walnut; H. 31½″, W. 32½″, L. 57½″. (Private collection: Photo, Ralph Pyle.)

bedroom set apparently painted blue and gray. The set consisted of a dressing case, a wardrobe, a table, two chairs, a rocker, a towel rack, and a bedstead, all of which cost $90. (This set is no longer with the rest of Gaar's furniture.) For his library, Gaar purchased one "wal[nut] Flat Top Liby Table with cloth top & brass trimngs" for $45 (fig. 28). The simple construction and ornamentation are predictable features of the sturdy but plain lines of the Mitchell and Rammelsberg manufactures. Four cane seat walnut chairs, like the example in figure 29, were also supplied by the Cincinnati firm at a price of $13.

No parlor furniture, except for the marquetry center table mentioned earlier, has survived. Gaar had selected three sets of parlor furniture for the new house. The most expensive set consisted of a "French Sofa," two French armchairs, and four French parlor chairs, "all tufted in Satin Damask" and cost $675. Another set in "Raw Silk Tapestry & plush border" included one "Stuff over Sofa," two stuffed armchairs, and four stuffed parlor chairs priced at $270. At $170, a group of walnut "Queen Anne" chairs upholstered in "bronze raw silk" was the least expensive parlor furniture ordered by Gaar. In the set were two small chairs, an odd armchair, an armchair, and a corner chair. In addition to the furniture, the Mitchell and Rammelsberg Furniture Company also supplied Gaar with three pairs of "Brussels Lace Curtains" with "Boxing About" at a combined cost of $279.

About two years after furnishing the Gaar home, the Mitchell and Rammelsberg Furniture Company changed the display rooms in the Cincinnati retail store. Perhaps as a consequence of the firm's well-received Eastlake exhibit at the Centennial Exposition, the company "brought over from England an artist in household decoration." This unidentified decorator "supervised the fitting up in the store of three rooms illustrative of the dispensation of aestheticism . . . at a cost of thousands of dollars." And, according to one account, "that innocent suite of rooms quietly revolutionized the interior decoration of the homes of wealth in the valley of Ohio."[40] The series of mock rooms provided what were considered to be furniture of the company's manufacture or in its inventory. Mitchell at this time became increasingly confident of his reputation and

by 1881 dropped the Rammelsberg name. His firm continued to prosper into the 1930s.

In the thirty-four years between 1847 and 1881, the Mitchell and Rammelsberg enterprise had measurably demonstrated successful business practices. This period was marked by continuing expansion and improvement in manufacturing and distribution facilities. While providing common and utilitarian furniture for the masses, the firm also introduced new furniture styles and influenced the taste of broad segments of the population in the South and Midwest during the last half of the nineteenth century.

Fig. 29. Mitchell and Rammelsberg, cane chair. (Cincinnati, ca. 1877. Walnut; H. 36″, W. 20½″, D. 17½″. (Private collection: Photo, Ralph Pyle.)

[40]*The Week: Illustrated* (Cincinnati) (December 15, 1883), p. 242.

Notes on Contributors

Robert Blair St. George is a Ph.D. candidate in folklore and folklife, University of Pennsylvania.

William L. Dulaney is a professor of journalism, Pennsylvania State University, State College.

Cathryn J. McElroy is curator of decorative arts, William Penn Memorial Museum, Harrisburg, Pennsylvania.

Kathleen M. Catalano is curator, National Park Service, Longfellow National Historic Site, Cambridge, Massachusetts.

Constance V. Hershey is curator of a private collection in Pennsylvania.

Deborah Dependahl Waters is librarian, Decorative Arts Photographic Collection, Winterthur Museum.

Martin Eli Weil is chief, Restoration Services Division, Department of Indian and Northern Affairs, Ottawa.

Philip D. Zimmerman is a Ph.D. candidate in American and New England studies, Boston University.

Donald C. Peirce is assistant curator of decorative arts, Brooklyn Museum.

Index

[EDITOR'S NOTE.—^{r} = illustration, ^{t} = table. See also alphabetical listing of Philadelphia cabinetmakers and related craftsmen, pp. 91–138.]

Abigail, ship, 41

Accessory reproductions, 156, 158

Account books: of William G. Beesley, chairmaker and painter, 169, 170; of Samuel Fithian Ware, chairmaker, 169, 170

Adams, John, on City Tavern, Philadelphia, 141

Adventure, ship, 68

Advertisement: for City Tavern, Philadelphia, 140, 141; of James Humphreys, Philadelphia printer, 176–77; of Ware chair manufactory, 164, 165^r, 170, 171

Affleck, Thomas, Philadelphia cabinetmaker, furniture for John Cadwalader, 200, 204, 205, 206, 207, 208

Aldis, John, colonial joiner-carver, 41, 42, 43

Aldis, Mrs. John (Sarah Eliot), 42

Aldis, Nathan, 3, 41, 42

Alexandria, Virginia, Gadsby's Tavern, 154

Allen, George W., Philadelphia chairmaker, 171

Allen, Nathaniel, 64

American furniture: Centennial Exhibition (1876) display, 222^r; Cincinnati industry, 209–29; mass production, 213, 214, 217, 220; New Jersey industry, 161–73, 167^t; Philadelphia industry, 81–138, 177–79; *see also furniture entries; individual craftsmen and objects*

Anderson, Jacob, New Jersey chairmaker, 170

Annapolis, supper club, 141n

Antique collector, Wallace Nutting as, 47, 58–60

Apprenticeship: in furniture industry, 87, 89–91; joinery, 12, 20; school attendance and, 90–91; style dissemination and, 28–29

Architect, role in reconstruction, 144, 148, 150

Architectural drawing, City Tavern, Philadelphia, 145^r, 146^r, 147^r

Architecture: artifactual language of, 20, 24; church, 1, 5, 12; domestic, 27, 67; factory, 212, 219^r; French Renaissance style, 220; furniture store, 210^r, 219–20^r

Armchair: colonial Philadelphia, 66^r; decoration, 11–12; Dedham, Massachusetts, joinery, 25^r, 26^r, 36^r; design, 12; first American dated, 25, 26; by John Houghton, 9, 10^r, 11, 36^r; by Mitchell & Rammelsberg, 222, 224^r; Wallace Nutting reproduction, 48, 49^r, 50; in Philadelphia inventories, 65; social rank and, 64; with storage cupboard, 25–26

Artifact study: accompanying manuscripts, 200–208; extrinsic data, 195; furniture carving in, 199, 200, 206–7, 208; intrinsic data, 194–195; language of, 4–5, 12, 20, 25n; methodology, 194–95; microanalysis, 197; object comparison, 196; object examination, 195–200; Philadelphia Chippendale furniture identification, 193–208; style dissemination and, 27–29, 44

Art Institute of Chicago, box by John Thurston, 18^r, 19, 33^r

Ashurst, Richard, furniture merchant, 86

Assheton, Ralph, japanned furniture, 69

Auction, Benjamin Randolph "sample chairs," 193–94

Awnings, City Tavern, Philadelphia, 158

Bachelor, John, 40

Baker, John, colonial carpenter, 41, 43, 46

Baker, Mrs. John (Abigail Fisher), 46

Baker, Samuel, colonial carpenter, 46

Balcony, City Tavern, Philadelphia, 144

Balusters, church architecture, 7

Balustrade: City Tavern, Philadelphia, 144; Edward Stile's home, 144

Banister back chair, in Philadelphia inventories, 65

Barber, Edward, 38

Barber, George, colonial carpenter, 3, 12, 28, 38, 39, 40, 42

Barber, Mrs. George (Elizabeth Clarke), 38

Barber, John, 38

Barlow, J., *An English Ordinary* (after Collings), 159^r

Barroom: City Tavern, Philadelphia, 150–51, 153^r, 158; eighteenth century, 150–51

Bass-bottomed chair, in Philadelphia inventories, 65

Batchelor, Penelope H., on reconstruction of City Tavern, Philadelphia, 139

Bateman, A. F., New Jersey furniture merchant, 172

Bateman, E. F., New Jersey furniture merchant, 172

Baxter, Joseph, colonial clergyman, 1

Beake, William, Jr., Philadelphia joiner, chest of drawers, 61, 73^r, 79

Beardsley, Margaret: bedsteads, 63; chamber furnishings, 74

Bed (bedsteads): feather, 64; flock, 64; gum, 63, 64; by Mitchell & Rammelsberg, 225^r, 226, 227^r; in Philadelphia inventories, 62–64, 74; price book listing, 177, 178; textile for headboard, 64; types, 64

Bedding, colonial, 63

Bedroom furniture, by Mitchell & Rammelsberg, 225–26, 229

Bed screws, 63

Bee, J. Simmons, Charleston furniture merchant, 85

Beesley, William G., New Jersey chairmaker and painter, account book, 169, 170

Behrend, B. A., box by John Thurston, 19

Bermuda chair, 64

Bernard, Bartholomew, colonial builder, 24

Bernard, Nicholas, Philadelphia furniture carver, 207

Bernard & Jugiez, Philadelphia furniture carvers, 200, 206, 207

Bettgemen's furniture machinery, 213

Biles, Johanna, case furniture, 71

Binder, Daniel, 89

Bingham, Josephine, 27n

Bingham, Zacheus, 27n

Bird, Isabella Lucy, on Mitchell & Rammelsberg, 211

Blockfront secretary, Wallace Nutting reproduction, 53

Blue Book (Hornor), 61

Blythborough, Suffolk, Holy Trinity pulpit, 7, 8[r], 15, 26, 30[r]

Bookcase: colonial Philadelphia, 77[r]; design features, 178; by Mitchell & Rammelsberg, 214, 215[r], 216[r]; in Philadelphia inventories, 77–78

Book of Architecture (Gibbs), 143

Boston: first townhouse, 24; King's Chapel, 24

Bosworth, Benjamin, 42

Bousquet, Peter, Philadelphia furniture merchant, 82

Bouvier, Michel, Philadelphia cabinetmaker, 82; exports, 82

Bowen, A. I., Philadelphia cabinetmaker, 171

Box, by John Thurston, 13, 18[r], 19, 33[r]

Boyden, Thomas, colonial joiner, 44–45, 46; furniture for William Gilson, 45

Boyden, Mrs. Thomas (Frances), 45

Boyden, Mrs. Thomas (Hannah Morse), 44

Boyden, Thomas, son of Thomas, colonial joiner, 45

Bradford, William, Philadelphia printer, 176

Bradway, William J. S., New Jersey historian, 165

Brasses, for furniture, 74, 80

Bridgeton, New Jersey, furniture manufacture, 164, 166, 167, 171, 172

Bristol, Rhode Island, meetinghouse pew door, 5n

Brock, Henry, 3

Brockton, Charles, imported furniture, 68

Brooks, John, cabinetmaker apprentice, 91

Bullen, Samuel, 12, 41

Bureau, by Mitchell & Rammelsberg, 220

Burge, James, furniture shipper, 87

Cabinetmakers: journeymen's marketing cooperative, 88–89, 90[t]; labor organization, 88; Philadelphia, 79, 81–138; Philadelphia checklist, 91–138; price books, 175–92, 180[r]–92[r]; tools, 82, 84

Cabinet-Makers' London Book of Prices and Designs of Cabinet Work, The, 176

Cabinet-Makers Philadelphia and London Book of Prices of 1796, The, 175

Cabriole-leg chair: by Henkel-Harris, 157[r]; by Pennsylvania House, 157[r]

Cadwalader, John, Revolutionary officer: card table, 197, 199–208; card table by Thomas Affleck, 200; carved picture frames, 204; City Tavern, Philadelphia, and, 143; family portrait by Charles Willson Peale, 197, 198[r], 200, 204; furniture by Thomas Affleck, 200, 204, 205, 206, 207, 208; furniture distribution, 201–3; furniture en suite, 199, 204–5, 208; furniture by Benjamin Randolph, 205, 206, 207, 208; furniture by William Savery, 205–6;

household furnishings, 204–5; interior design, 204, 205; saddle seat chairs, 199, 204; upholstery by Plunket Fleeson, 204, 205; upholstery by William Savery, 204; upholstery by John Webster, 205

Cadwalader, Lambert, Charles Willson Peale portrait, 203[r], 204, 207

Campion, Joseph H., Philadelphia cabinetmaker, 82

Candlestand, in Philadelphia inventories, 79

Cane furniture: by Mitchell & Rammelsberg, 229[r]; in Philadelphia inventories, 65, 69

Cape May County, New Jersey, furniture industry, 161–73

Card table: of John Cadwalader, 197, 199–208; colonial Philadelphia, 197, 198[r], 199[r], 200, 204; commode, 200; identification, 197, 199, 200–208; matching chairs, 199–208

Carpenter, Samuel, Pennsylvania merchant, chamber table, 69

Carpenters: labor organization, 177; price books, 177

Carpenters Company of the City and County of Philadelphia, 177

Cart, Joshua, Philadelphia brewer, chest of drawers, 79

Cartoon: banquet scene, 154[r]; as reconstruction source, 143, 148

Carus, Thomas, colonial joiner, escritoire, 79

Case furniture: design feature, 69, 71, 72–73; 178; English design, 76–77; by Mitchell & Rammelsberg, 225–26; in Philadelphia inventories, 69, 71–74; price book listings, 177, 178

Caswell, Albert, 54n

Caswell, Mrs. Albert (Mariet Griswold), 54n

Catalano, Kathleen M., 81–138

Catalogue: ironwork by Wallace Nutting, 54; Wallace Nutting reproductions, 51, 54

Cedar chest, in Philadelphia inventories, 69, 71, 73, 80

Cedarville, New Jersey, furniture manufacture, 166, 167, 172

Cellar, City Tavern, Philadelphia, 149

Centennial Exposition (Philadelphia, 1876), Mitchell & Rammelsberg display, 222[r]

Cescinsky, Herbert, antiquarian, 193

Chair: artifact comparison, 196; artifact object examination, 195–200; artifact study methodology, 194–95; Bermuda, 64; for City Tavern, Philadelphia, 156; design, 170; hairy paw feet design, 196, 197, 202; half-upholstery design, 196, 197, 204; matching card table, 199–208; microanalysis, 197; by Mitchell & Rammelsberg, 211, 222, 224[r], 229; Wallace Nutting reproductions for Colonial Williamsburg, 48, 50; ornamentation, 164, 170; Philadelphia design features, 65–67, 195–96; in Philadelphia inventories, 64–67, 79; pin design, 196–97; price book listing, 177, 178; rail design, 196, 197, 202[r]; set numbering, 201, 202; shoe design, 196, 197[r], 201; social rank and, 64; South Jersey slat-backed, rush-bottomed, 161–73, 167[t]; South Jersey turned chairs, 161–73, 167[t]; splat-rear stiles joining, 196, 200–201; style changes, 172; textiles, 66; turkey-work, 64; *see also specific designs*

Chair cases, for John Cadwalader, 205

Chairmakers: Philadelphia craftsmen (checklist), 91–138; price books, 175–92, 180[r]–92[r]; tools, 162–63, 164, 167–68

Chair seat, rush, 163, 168

Chair-table, 26n

Chamber-table, 26n

Chamber suite, by Mitchell & Rammelsberg, 214

Chamber table, 69, 79

Chamfering, chest, 14, 15, 16

Charleston, South Carolina, furniture imports, 82

Charter of Privileges (1701), 61

Chattin, William P., New Jersey cabinetmaker, 171–72

Chest: artifactual language of, 20, 24, 25; bottom board design, 9, 11, 12, 14, 16, 19, 20, 29; Connecticut Valley design, 11; conceptualization and construction, 20, 21^r, 22–24; Dedham, Massachusetts, joinery, 26^r, 36^r; Dedham-Medfield school, 28; without drawers, 16, 19; Hadley chest, 59; Hedges family chest, 15n; by John Houston, 9, 10^r, 11, 20, 22, 23^r, 24, 26, 34^r; lid construction, 11, 16; Merwin family chest, 28; Milford, Connecticut, design, 6^r, 35^r, 37^r; by Thomas Mulliner, 7n, 28; New Haven school, 28; Wallace Nutting reproduction, 50^r; ornamentation, 7, 11, 14, 15, 16, 19, 21^r, 22, 24; in Philadelphia inventories, 73–74; Pierce family chest, 3n; for Jonathan Rudd, 26; Suffolk tradition, 7; by John Thurston, 13^r–18^r, 19, 20, 21^r, 22, 24, 26, 30^r–33^r

Chestnut, in colonial furniture, 46

Chest of drawers: by William Beake, 61, 73; colonial Philadelphia, 72^r, 73^r; by John Crosswhite, 79; Dedham chests, 3; by Edward Evans, 77; Fairbanks house, 3n; inlaid, 73; by Mitchell & Rammelsberg, 214^r; Philadelphia design features, 73, 74; in Philadelphia inventories, 69, 71–74, 79; scarves, 72

Chest-on-frame: colonial Philadelphia, 74^r; Wallace Nutting reproduction, 51, 52^r

Chest with one drawer, 13–15, 16

Chew, Benjamin, Germantown house, 154

Chick, James, Philadelphia joiner, 74

Chickering, Francis, 4

Chickering, Henry, 4

China: for City Tavern, Philadelphia, 156; for tea service, 71–72

Chippendale style, 177; furniture set numbering, 201; Philadelphia chair comparison analysis, 196; Philadelphia furniture, 61, 193–208

Church architecture: Dedham, Massachusetts, meetinghouse, 12, 46; Holy Trinity, Blythborough, 7, 15, 26; King's Chapel, Boston, 24; Malden, Massachusetts, meetinghouse, 7, 24; Medfield, Massachusetts, meetinghouse, 1, 5, 7, 9^r, 13, 27, 43, 44; Puritan meetinghouse, 7; Salisbury, Massachusetts, meetinghouse, 7; Sudbury, Massachusetts, meetinghouse, 7

Church decoration, *see* Ecclesiastical decoration

Church of the Holy Trinity, Blythborough, pulpit, 7, 8^r, 15, 26, 30^r

Cigar manufactory, 168^r

Cincinnati: furniture industry, 209–29; furniture markets, 209, 211

City Tavern, Philadelphia: 130–60, 140^r; accessory reproductions for, 156, 158; architect / curator / designer / engineer roles in reconstruction, 148–52; 154–56, 158; barroom, 150–51, 153^r, 158; business facilities, 150; cellar, 145^r, 149; during Continental Congress, 139, 141; demolition, 143; description, 140; design function, 140; dining rooms, 154–55, 157^r, 158–59; east facade, 144^r; eighteenth- and twentieth-century compromises, 148; exterior design, 143, 144; floor plan, 143, 145^r, 146^r, 149–50; frontispiece, 143; front rooms, 150, 158; furnishings, 157^r; furniture sale, 142; historical importance, 139; interior design, 139–60; kitchens, 150; lighting, 148, 154; Long Room, 141, 154, 155; Merchants' Coffee-House

and Place of Exchange, 143, 150; Edward Moyston as innkeeper, 143; musical entertainment, 155^r; private dining rooms, 151–52; reconstruction, 139–60; reconstruction sources, 143, 148; as restaurant, 144; service area, 159–50; side elevation, 147^r; Daniel Smith as innkeeper, 141–42; subscribers' rights, 150; tableware, 156, 158; utilities area, 150; wall decoration, 150, 151, 158–59; during War of Independence, 141–42; window decoration, 158

Civil War, furniture industry and, 214

Clark, Benjamin, colonial wheelwright, 41, 45

Clark, Mrs. Benjamin (Dorcas Morse), 45

Clark, Joseph, 45

Claypoole, George, 75

Claypoole, James, Philadelphia merchant, 61; furniture, 64; writing cabinet, 75

Claypoole, Joseph, Philadelphia joiner, 79–80

Cliveden, Germantown, Pennsylvania, 154

Clock: colonial Philadelphia, 78^r; in Philadelphia inventories, 78

Clothespress, 72, 79

Club dinners, 141n

Coane, Robert T., Philadelphia cabinetmaker, 89

Coffeehouse, City Tavern, Philadelphia, 143, 150

Coffin manufacture, 169

Cold storage, City Tavern, Philadelphia, 149

Collings, Samuel, *An English Ordinary*, 159^r

Colonial Williamsburg: colonial Philadelphia fall-front desk, 76^r; Flemish armchair by Wallace Nutting, 49^r; Wallace Nutting reproductions for, 47–50

Commode, by Mitchell & Rammelsberg, 225^r, 226, 227^r

Commode card table, 198^r, 200, 204

Commode sofa, 204, 205

Communion table: Medfield, Massachusetts, meetinghouse, 7; by Joseph Moyce, 40; Puritan meetinghouse, 7; Salisbury, Massachusetts, meetinghouse, 7; Sudbury, Massachusetts, meetinghouse, 7

Conarroe, George W., New Jersey cabinetmaker-painter, 170

Connecticut sunflower chest, by Wallace Nutting, 50^r

Connecticut Valley, chest decoration, 11

Connelly, John, 89

Continental Congress, City Tavern, Philadelphia, and, 139, 141

Contrast, The, 152^r

Cook, Arthur, 64

Cook & Parkins, Philadelphia cabinetmakers, 82

Copeley, John Singleton, *A Youth Attacked by a Shark,* 158

Copson, John, Philadelphia clockmaker, 78

Corner cupboard: design features, 178; in Philadelphia inventories, 79

Cottey, Abel, Philadelphia clockmaker, 78; bass-bottom chairs, 65

Couch, in Philadelphia inventories, 63, 65

Country Club, The, 153^r

Court cupboard, Prence-Howes, 58

Courtney, Hercules, carved frames for John Cadwalader, 204

Cradle, South Jersey furniture, 172

Craftsmen, Philadelphia colonial, 61; Philadelphia checklist, 91–138; *see also specific trades*

Craig, James, New Orleans furniture merchant, 218

Craig, John, New Orleans furniture merchant, 218

Crosswhite, John, Philadelphia joiner: chest of drawers, 79; clothespress, 79

Culver, Edward, colonial wheelwright, 38
Culver, Mrs. Edward (Anne), 38
Cumberland County, New Jersey, furniture industry, 161–73
Cupboard: in Philadelphia inventories, 78–79; Prence-Howes, 58[r]
Curator, role in reconstruction, 148–52, 154–56, 158
Curled-hair manufacture, Philadelphia (checklist), 91–138
Curran, Thomas A., Philadelphia antiques dealer, saddle seat chair, 203
Cushions, for furniture, 65

Daniels's furniture machinery, 213
Davis, William, New Jersey chairmaker, 171
Davis, William N., New Jersey painter-glazer, 170
Day, John, Philadelphia merchant, desk, 75
Daybed, colonial, 63
Dayton, James B., New Jersey lawyer, 167
Declaration of Independence: 1777 festivities cost, 141; 1778 celebration, 154–55
Decorative arts, Wallace Nutting influence, 47
Dedham, Massachusetts: English craftsmen origin, 4[r]; English cultural heritage, 3; Fairbanks house, 3; founding, 3; linguistic subculture, 4; meetinghouse, 12, 40, 41, 42, 43, 46; sawmill, 13, 41; subdivision, 3
Dedham, Massachusetts, joinery: 1–46; armchair, 25[r], 26[r], 36[r]; chest, 26[r], 36[r]
Dedham chest, 3
Dedham Covenant, 27, 39
Dedham Historical Society: armchair with storage cupboard, 25; John Houghton armchair, 11; Metcalf chair, 26n
Delaware Art Museum, chest by John Thurston, 16, 19
Dennis, Thomas, colonial joiner, 5
Designer, role in reconstruction, 148–50, 152, 156
Desk: colonial Philadelphia, 75[r], 76[r]; design features, 75–78, 178; by Edward Evans, 61, 76; by John Goddard, 47; by Mitchell & Rammelsberg, 216[r], 217; in Philadelphia inventories, 75–78
Desk-and-bookcase: colonial Philadelphia, 77[r]; by Mitchell & Rammelsberg, 214, 215[r], 216[r]; in Philadelphia inventories, 77–78
Desk box: Southold, Long Island, joinery, 29[r], 35[r]; of William Wells, 28
Desk-on-frame, colonial Philadelphia, 75[r]
Deuser, William F., Wallace Nutting reproductions, 51n
Dickinson, Caleb, mahogany trade, 72
Dickinson, Jonathan, Philadelphia merchant: clothespress, 79; escritoire, 76; furniture, 65, 72; tea service, 71–72
Diligence, ship, 77
Dining room: City Tavern, Philadelphia, 151–52, 154–55, 157[r], 158–59; colonial Philadelphia furnishings, 67; Mitchell & Rammelsberg furniture, 222, 225
Dining table, by Mitchell & Rammelsberg, 222
Dinner clubs, 141
Donnelly, Ernest John, Wallace Nutting associate, 59n
Donnelly, Marian Card, on Puritan meetinghouse design, 7
Door knockers: by Edward Guy, 57; Wallace Nutting reproduction, 57[r]
Down, William, harpsichord, 155[r]
Drapery, for City Tavern, Philadelphia, 158
Drawer design, Philadelphia case furniture, 69, 71, 72–73
Dresser: by Mitchell & Rammelsberg, 225[r], 226, 227[r]; in Philadelphia inventories, 79
Dressing box, in Philadelphia inventories, 74

Dressing bureau, by Mitchell & Rammelsberg, 221[r]
Dressing table: colonial Philadelphia, 70[r], 71[r]; in Philadelphia inventories, 69, 71
Dubose, Joseph S., New Jersey cabinetmaker, 171
Dulaney, William L., 47–60
Du Pont, Henry Francis: John Cadwalader furniture, 199, 201, 202; chest by John Thurston, 19; Chippendale chair purchase, 202; Joe Kindig, Jr., correspondence, 201; Wallace Nutting and, 59; saddle seat chair, 203; straight-front side chairs, 201
Dutch tables, in Philadelphia inventories, 67

Eames, Samuel, 40
Eames, Thomas, colonial carpenter-joiner, 40
Eames, Mrs. Thomas (Mary Paddlefoot), 40
Eastlake style: dining room furniture, 225; furniture by Mitchell & Rammelsberg, 222, 225, 229; sideboard by Mitchell & Rammelsberg, 222, 223[r]; tea chair, 222
Easy chair: colonial Philadelphia, 67[r]; in Philadelphia inventories, 66–67
Ecclesiastical decoration, 7
Eckley, Sarah, bedstead, 63
Elbow chair, in Philadelphia inventories, 64, 65
Elevator: for furniture factory, 213; for furniture store, 220
Ellery, William C., on City Tavern, Philadelphia, 154
Engineer, role in reconstruction, 148
England, Thomas, Philadelphia upholsterer, 63
Engraving: *The Contrast,* 152[r]; *The Country Club,* 153[r]; *An English Ordinary* (Barlow after Collings), 159[r]; *Good News,* 151[r]; *Plan of . . . Philadelphia* (Faden), 155[r]; untitled banquet cartoon, 154[r]
Entablature, City Tavern, Philadelphia, 154
Erving, Henry Wood, antiquarian, 193; Hadley chest and, 59; Wallace Nutting and, 58
Escritoire, in Philadelphia inventories, 75–78, 79
Evans, Edward, Philadelphia, 76–77; chest of drawers, 77; desk 61, 76–77; fall-front desk, 76[r]; oval table, 77; stand, 77
Evans, William, 76
Exchange, Philadelphia, 143, 150
Exhibitions, Centennial Exposition (Philadelphia, 1876), 222[r]
Exports: Philadelphia furniture, 81–87, 83[t], 84[t], 91; Philadelphia furniture materials, 82, 84
Eyre & Massy, Philadelphia furniture merchants, 82

Facade: City Tavern, Philadelphia, 143, 144[r]; Mitchell & Rammelsberg furniture store, 220
Factory architecture, Mitchell & Rammelsberg furniture factory, 212, 219[r]
Faden, William, *Plan of . . . Philadelphia,* 155[r]
Fairbanks, John, colonial wheelwright-turner, 38, 39, 41, 42, 43; house, 27
Fairbanks, Jonathan, colonial joiner, 4, 9, 37, 41
Fairbanks family, oak chest by John Houghton, 9, 11, 20
Fall-front desk, colonial Philadelphia, 76[r]
Farrington, Jessie, armchair by John Houghton, 11
Farrington, John, armchair by John Houghton, 11, 26, 27
Federal Society of Chair Makers, 175
Fellows, John, Philadelphia joiner, 63, 79
Fenestration, City Tavern, Philadelphia, 143, 144, 158
Fenimore, Nathaniel, 193
Ferniside, John, colonial joiner, 45
Fisher, Anthony, 4, 42

Fisher, Cornelius, colonial carpenter, 4, 42–43

Fisher, Daniel, 42

Fisher, Joshua, colonial carpenter, 4, 41, 42

Fisher, Mrs. Joshua (Mary Aldis), 41

Fisher, Lt. Joshua, 41, 42, 43

Fisher, Thomas, colonial carpenter, 27, 28, 38–39

Fisher, Mrs. Thomas (Elizabeth), 38

Fithian, Josiah, New Jersey chairmaker, 171

Fleeson, Plunket, Philadelphia upholsterer, work for John Cadwalader, 204, 205, 207

Flemish armchair: for Colonial Williamsburg by Wallace Nutting, 49[r]

Fling, Bennet, Philadelphia cabinetmaker, 82

Fling, William B., Philadelphia cabinetmaker, 82

Floors, tavern, 150, 151

Floral design: armchair, 12; chest, 11, 15

Ford, Henry, Wayside Inn and, 59

Foster, Thomas, 44

Fowle, Harriet A., 1; Medfield Historical Society gift, 2[r]

Fowle, Mary Baxter, 1

Fox, Charles, caricature, 154[r]

Fox, James, Philadelphia baker, dining room furnishings, 67

Framemakers, Philadelphia (checklist), 91–138

Frampton, William, Philadelphia merchant, Bermuda chair, 64

Francis, ship, 44

Frank, Rebecca, on City Tavern, Philadelphia, 142, 154

Frankfort, Pennsylvania, Port Royal, 144

French, Nathaniel, colonial wheelwright, 45–46

French, Mrs. Nathaniel (Mary Tisdale?), 46

French, Stephen, colonial builder, 24

French Renaissance style, in store design, 220

French style, in furniture, 229

Frontispiece, City Tavern, Philadelphia, 143

Furniture: artifact comparison, 196; artifact object examination, 195–200; artifact study methodology, 194–95; by Thomas Boyden, 45; brasses for, 74, 80; Chippendale style, 61, 177, 193–208; for City Tavern, Philadelphia, 148–52, 154–56, 159; colonial imports, 62; cushions, 65; en suite, 197, 204–5; exports, 81–87, 83[t], 84[t], 91; French style, 229; imports, 64, 65, 66, 68, 69, 74, 76; inlaid, 68, 73; japanned, 68–69, 75, 79; Mannerist style, 12; marquetry, 225–26; microanalysis, 197; Wallace Nutting collection, 47; Philadelphia colonial, 61–80; post-Restoration style, 62; Queen Anne style, 61, 79, 80, 177, 229; set numbering, 201, 202; style changes, 172; terminology, 177–78; textiles, 64, 66; veneering, 62; William and Mary style, 68, 79, 80; windsor style, 155; wood, 46, 62–80, 178, 213; wood-price relation, 178; *see also individual craftsmen and objects*

Furniture carving: in artifact study, 199, 200, 206–7, 208; Mitchell & Rammelsberg products, 213; Philadelphia furniture, 199, 200; seventeenth-century Massachusetts, 7, 11, 14, 15, 16, 19, 21[r], 22, 24

Furniture catalogue, of Wallace Nutting, 51, 54

Furniture manufacture: apprenticeships, 87, 89–91; auction sales, 85; barter in, 162; in Cincinnati, 209–29; Civil War and, 214; commission merchants, 84–85; consignment sales, 84–85, 86; consignment to ship's captain, 86; custom work, 87; distribution, 171; domestic trade, 81–82; hours of work, 88; interchangeable parts, 214, 220; journeymen, 87–88, 175, 178–79; journeymen's marketing cooperative, 88–89, 90[t]; labor disputes, 87–88, 89; labor

organization, 88, 175, 179; machinery, 209, 211, 213; markets, 81–82, 171, 209, 211, 214; mass production, 213, 214, 217, 220; merchandising, 84, 87; merchant-exporters, 82; in New Jersey, 161–73, 167[t]; Pennsylvania interstate trade, 86; in Philadelphia, 81–138, 177–79; piecework, 88; power, 209, 211, 219; price books, 175–92, 180[r]–92[r]; price competition, 87, 88; production methods, 211, 213, 214, 217, 220; regional competition, 214, 218; retail sales (shop work), 87; shipping, 84; varnishing, 213; volume of shipments, 87; wage rates, 88, 175, 178–79, 211; wholesale, 87, 213; work force, 211

Furniture markings: Chippendale sets, 201; Wallace Nutting reproductions, 51; Mitchell & Rammelsberg products, 213–14, 220, 226

Furniture merchants, Philadelphia (checklist), 91–138

Furniture of the Pilgrim Century (Nutting), 16, 54, 57, 59

Furniture ornamentation: 155, 156, 164, 170; Philadelphia craftsmen (checklist), 91–138; *see also* Furniture carving

Furniture reproductions: chest by Wallace Nutting, 50[r]; chest-on-frame by Wallace Nutting, 52[r]; for City Tavern, Philadelphia, 149, 155–56; colonial Philadelphia side chair, 157[r]; lowboy by Wallace Nutting, 52[r]; National Park Service, 155–56; by Wallace Nutting, 47, 50–53; Wallace Nutting labeling, 48[r], 51; Wallace Nutting styles, 53n; secretary by Wallace Nutting, 53[r]; windsor chair by Wallace Nutting, 50[r]

Furniture showroom, Mitchell & Rammelsberg, 220

Furniture store, Mitchell & Rammelsberg, 219–20

Furniture Treasury (Nutting), 16, 47, 48, 54, 59

Gaar, Abram, Indiana businessman, Mitchell & Rammelsberg furniture, 222, 225–26, 229

Gadsby's Tavern, Alexandria, Virginia, 154

Gallery, in church architecture, 7

Garvan, Francis P., antique collector, 51

Gateleg table, colonial Philadelphia, 68[r]

Gee, Noah, Philadelphia cabinetmaker, 91

George, Daniel, colonial painter, 15n

Georgian style, in interior design, 154

Gibbs, James, *Book of Architecture,* 143

Gilbert, Charles M., 89

Gilmore, Elijah, New Jersey cabinetmaker, 171

Gilson, William, colonial miller, 44

Glassie, Henry, on object structure, 20

Goddard, John, blockfront desk, 47

"Goddard School," blockfront secretary, Wallace Nutting reproduction, 53[r]

Good News, 151[r]

Grant, Thomas, colonial clergyman, desk, 77

Griffith, William V., 89

Guardianship, colonial, 45

Guilloches, Salisbury, Massachusetts, communion table, 7

Guy, Edward, American ironmaster, 54, 57; door knockers, 57; statement on Wallace Nutting ironwork promotion, 56[r], 57

Hadley carving, 5, 11, 14, 15

Hadley chest, 59

Hairy paw feet design, 196, 197, 202

Hall rack, by Mitchell & Rammelsberg, 222, 223[r]

Hall stand, by Mitchell & Rammelsberg, 222[r]

Halzel, Philip, Philadelphia chairmaker, 82

Hamilton, Alexander, 141n

Hamilton, Andrew, colonial governor, furniture by Edward Evans, 77

Hammock, colonial, 63

Hand, Richard, New Jersey chairmaker, 171

Harding, Abraham, box by John Thurston, 19

Harpsichord, by William Dowd, 155ʳ

Harris, John, New Jersey painter-glazer, 170

Harrison, James, steward to William Penn, 62

Harvey, R. Wistar, colonial Philadelphia dressing table, 70ʳ

Hatch & Kinsey, furniture merchants, 82

Hatfield chests, 11

Haydon, William, Philadelphia chairmaker, 82

Hayne, W. A., South Carolina banker, furniture, 84

Hayward, John, 40

Heath, Richard, escritoire, 79

Hedges family, chest, 15n

Henkel-Harris, cabriole-leg chair, 157ʳ

Hershey, Constance V., 139–60

Hews, Hezekian, New Jersey cabinetmaker, 170

High chest, colonial Philadelphia, 71ʳ

Hinges: armchair cupboard, 26; box, 19; chest, 11, 16, 19

Historical Society of Pennsylvania, "Prices of Cabinet & Chair Work / Binjamin Lehman January 1786," 175

History of the Town of Medfield (Tilden), 1

Hoffman, John P., Memphis furniture merchant, 217

Holebrook, John, colonial builder, 24

Holland, immigrants from, 64

Homestead Architecture (Sloan), 217

Hooper, Abraham, Philadelphia joiner, mahogany stock, 72

Hooton, Thomas, Jr., Philadelphia merchant, dining room furnishings, 67

Hoover, H. F., Philadelphia furniture merchant, 171

Hornor, William Macpherson, Jr., antiquarian, 175, 193; *Blue Book*, 61; on Philadelphia cabinetmaking, 81

Houghton, John, colonial joiner, 40, 41; apprenticeship, 12; armchair, 9, 10ʳ, 11, 36ʳ; armchair for John Farrington, 26, 27; biographical data, 41–42; chest, 9, 10ʳ, 11, 20, 22, 23ʳ, 24, 26, 34ʳ; comparison with John Thurston, 20; Medfield, Massachusetts, meetinghouse joinery, 5, 7, 13; Medfield pulpit, 2ʳ, 5, 7, 9ʳ, 11, 12, 19, 27, 35ʳ, 36ʳ, 43; technique, 20, 26; tools, 11

Houghton, Mrs. John (Beatrix Buckminster), 42

Houghton, Robert, 42

House architecture, Jonathan Fairbanks house, 27

Housing, Philadelphia colonial, 61–62

Howe, Abraham, box by John Thurston, 19

Howe, Adam, box by John Thurston, 19

Howe, Sir William, 142

Howes, Abby: Wallace Nutting and, 58; Prence-Howes court cupboard, 58

Hughes, Joseph B., 169

Humphreys, James, Philadelphia printer, 176–77

Humphries, Letitia, colonial Philadelphia gateleg table, 68ʳ

Huneker, John, Philadelphia chairmaker, 82

Immigration, from Holland, 64

Imports: bedsteads, 64; English decorative goods, 156; furniture, 62, 65, 66, 68, 69, 74, 76

Independence National Historical Park, 139

Inlaid work: chest of drawers, 73; colonial Philadelphia dressing table, 70ʳ; table, 68

Insurance survey, as reconstruction source, 143, 148

Interchangeable parts, in furniture manufacture, 214, 220

Interior design: Georgian style, 154; London tavern style, 140–41; maps in, 74–75; tavern, 139–60; *see also specific structures*

Inventory: John Aldis, joiner-carver, 42; George Barber, carpenter, 38; John Cadwalader, 205; Benjamin Clark, wheelwright, 45; John Fairbanks, wheelwright-turner, 41; Jonathan Fairbanks, joiner, 37; Cornelius Fisher, carpenter, 43; Mrs. Elizabeth Fisher, carpenter's widow, 38–39; William Gilson, miller, 45; Robert Houghton, joiner, 42; Mitchell & Rammelsberg, furniture manufacturers, 213; Mitchell, Hoffman & Co., furniture merchants, 217–18; Jeremiah Morse, wheelwright, 46; of Philadelphia furniture, 61–80; Daniel Pond, carpenter, 43; John Pratt, carpenter, 46; R. & W. Mitchell, furniture merchants, 218; Moses Reiley (Riley), chairmaker, 164; Seth Smith, carpenter-joiner, 43; John Thurston, joiner, 40–41; Joseph Thurston, carpenter-joiner, 44; Thomas Thurston, colonial carpenter, 44; Ware family, chairmakers, 162–63, 164, 166, 167–68

Ironwork catalogue, of Wallace Nutting, 54

Ironwork reproductions, by Wallace Nutting, 54, 56ʳ, 57ʳ; statement by Edward Guy, 56ʳ, 57

James, Charles W., Philadelphia chairmaker, 86–87

J. and M. Flaherty, Memphis furniture manufacturers, 217

Japanning, 68–69, 75, 79

Jenkins & Milton, furniture merchants, 82

John, Philip, Philadelphia joiner, 78

Johnson, Ephraim E., New Jersey furniture manufacturer, 172

Johnson, John F., Philadelphia cabinetmaker, 86; exports, 82

John S. Ware & Son, chair manufactory, 164, 166

Joiners: apprenticeship, 12, 20; artifactual language of, 4–5, 12, 20, 24–25; in colonial Philadelphia, 79; colonial prices, 39, 40; cost determination, 22; Dedham, Massachusetts, 1–46; Lancashire, England, joinery tradition, 5, 14–15; Medfield, Massachusetts, 1–46; style dissemination, 27–29, 44; Suffolk, England, joinery tradition, 5, 7, 12, 14, 25, 26, 27–28; technique, 20, 26, 28; tools, 11, 12, 19, 20, 22; workmanship standards, 24

Jones, John, Philadelphia merchant, 63

Jones & Ivie, Inc., Richmond upholsterers, 201

Journeymen, furniture industry, 87–88, 175, 178–79

Joy, Thomas, colonial builder, 24

Jugiez, Martin, Philadelphia woodcarver, frontispiece for City Tavern, 143

Keely, Edward, New Jersey cigar manufactory, 168ʳ

Killian, Elizabeth Ware, 168–69

Kindig, Joe, Jr., John Cadwalader card table, 199; John Cadwalader furniture, 201; Henry Francis du Pont correspondence, 201

King of Prussia blue marble, 159

Kingsbury, Joseph, 40

King's Chapel, Boston, 24

Kitchen, City Tavern, Philadelphia, 150

Kite, James, Philadelphia cabinetmaker, 87

Kittinger Furniture Company, pretzel-back chair, 157ʳ

Knipp & Company, table, 157ʳ

Labor dispute, in furniture industry, 87–88, 89, 175

Labor organization, in furniture industry, 88, 175, 177, 179

Ladderback chair, by Robert Treate Hogg Cabinet Shop, 153[r]
Lancashire, England, joinery tradition, 5, 14–15
Lane, Job, colonial joiner, 7, 24
Laning, John, New Jersey chairmaker, 161
Lape, William, 218
Latin American, furniture imports, 82
Latour, John, Philadelphia furniture merchant, 82
Lawton, Herbert, chest by John Thurston, 19
Laycock, Isaac H., Philadelphia chairmaker, 84
Leader, Isaac, colonial mariner, furniture, 65
Leaf design, chest, 11
Lehman, Binjamin, Pennsylvania lumber dealer, 175
Lévi-Strauss, Claude, on historical intent, 29
Library table, by Mitchell & Rammelsberg, 228[r], 229
Lighting, City Tavern, Philadelphia, 148, 154
Lindsley, Thomas, imported furniture, 68
Linguistics, Massachusetts subcultures, 4
Lloyd, Richard Bennet, 208
Lloyd, Thomas, colonial governor, 64; cane chair, 65
Lockwood, Luke Vincent, antiquarian, 51, 193
Logan, James, Philadelphia merchant: bed by Thomas Stapleford, 63; furniture by Edward Evans, 77; furniture imports, 65, 66, 68, 69, 71, 74, 76
Logan, Peter, Philadelphia furniture merchant, 82
London tavern style, in interior design, 140–41
Looking glass, in Philadelphia inventories, 71, 74; Philadelphia manufacturers (checklist), 91–138
Lothrop, John, colonial clergyman, 44
Loud, John, Philadelphia pianoforte maker, 86
Loud & Bros., Philadelphia piano manufacturers, 82, 86n
Lowboy, Wallace Nutting reproduction, 52[r]
Lozenge design: armchair, 11–12, 26 chest, 7, 26; panels, 1, 7, 11, 12, 36[r]–37[r]
Lunette design, chest, 7
Lusher, Eleazer, 4, 43, 46
Lyon, Charles Woolsey, antique dealer, John Cadwalader card table, 202

McDonnol, Thomas, New Jersey cabinetmaker, 170
McDonough, Abraham, Philadelphia chairmaker, 90
McElroy, Cathryn J., 61–80
Mahogany: colonial Philadelphia furniture, 72; furniture reproductions, 53; Philadelphia exports, 82; Philadelphia joiner stock, 72
Major, William, New Jersey chairmaker, 170
Malden, Massachusetts, meetinghouse, 7, 24
Mannerist style: chest, 16, 24; furniture, 12
Manuscript, in artifact study, 200–208
Map: in interior design, 74–75; by John Montresor, 158
Marble, table, 159
Marblehead, Massachusetts, meetinghouse seats, 5n
Markham, William, on court appearance, 64
Marquetry, Mitchell & Rammelsberg furniture, 225–26
Mason, Robert, 43
Mason, Thomas, colonial joiner, 43–44
Mason, Mrs. Thomas (Margery Partridge), 43
Massachusetts: colonial joinery, 1–46; English immigrants, 3
Mass production, in furniture manufacture, 213, 214, 217, 220
Master, Thomas, Philadelphia merchant, desk and bookcase, 78
Mather, Richard, colonial clergyman, 46
Mattress, colonial, 63

Maynard, Henry P., on Wallace Nutting, 60
Mayo, Edward, colonial merchant, chest of drawers by John Crosswhite, 79
Measuring tools, joinery, 20, 22
Medfield, Massachusetts: Seth Clark House, 3n; English craftsmen origins, 4[r]; English cultural heritage, 3; founding, 3; linguistic subculture, 4; meetinghouse, 1, 5, 7, 9, 11, 12, 13, 19, 27, 38, 39, 40, 43, 44; sawmill, 38
Medfield, Massachusetts, joinery, 1–46; pulpit panels by John Houghton, 1, 2[r], 9[r], 35[r], 36[r]
Medfield Covenant, 38, 39, 40
Medfield Historical Society: Harriet A. Fowle gift, 2[r]; pulpit panels, 1, 2[r]
Meetinghouse: Bristol, Rhode Island, 5n; Dedham, Massachusetts, 12, 46; Malden, Massachusetts, 7, 24; Marblehead, Massachusetts, 5n; Medfield, Massachusetts, 1, 5, 7, 9[r], 13, 27, 43, 44; Salisbury, Massachusetts, 7; Sudbury, Massachusetts, 7
Memphis, furniture business, 217
Mercantile Agency Reference Book, The, 165, 166
Merchants' Coffee-House and Place of Exchange, Philadelphia, 143
Merchants' exchange, Philadelphia, 143, 150
Merwin family, chest, 7, 28
Metcalf, Michael, colonial weaver, armchair, 25, 26
Metcalf family, 26n
Metropolitan Museum of Art, box by John Thurston, 18[r], 19, 33[r]; chest from Milford, Connecticut, 6[r], 37[r]
Mezzotint, *The Contrast,* 152[r]
Microanalysis, in artifact study, 197
Milford, Connecticut, chest, 6[r], 35[r], 37[r]
Miller, Stephen, New Jersey cabinetmaker, 164
Minimal intrusion principle, in reconstruction, 140
Minshall, Jacob, furniture craftsman, 176
Minshall, Thomas, 176
Minshall, Mrs. Thomas (Margaret), 176
Minshall, Thomas, grandson of Thomas, colonial furniture craftsman, 176
Mirrible, Joseph, brickmaker apprentice, 40
Mitchell, Albert, Cincinnati furniture manufacturer, 218
Mitchell, George, furniture merchant, 217, 218
Mitchell, Robert, Cincinnati furniture manufacturer, 209, 210[r], 217, 218
Mitchell, William, St. Louis furniture merchant, 211–12, 218
Mitchell & Rammelsberg, Cincinnati furniture manufacturers, 209–29; armchair, 222, 224[r]; bedroom furniture, 225–26, 229; bedstead, 225[r], 226, 227[r]; bureau, 220; cane chair, 229[r]; capital investment, 209, 211; case furniture, 225–26; Centennial Exposition (Philadelphia, 1876) display, 222[r]; chair production, 211, 229; chamber furniture, 214; chest of drawers, 214[r]; commode, 225[r], 226, 227[r]; desk, 216[r], 217; desk and bookcase, 214, 215[r], 216[r]; dining room furniture, 222, 225; dresser, 225[r], 226, 227[r]; dressing bureau, 221[r]; Eastlake style products, 222, 225, 229; factory design, 212, 219[r]; factory site, 211; furniture carving, 213; Abram Gaar furniture purchases, 222, 225–26, 229; hall rack, 222, 223[r]; hallstand, 222[r]; incorporation, 218; interchangeable parts, 214, 220; interior design, 229; library furniture, 228[r], 229; machinery, 213; markets, 211, 214; marquetry, 225–26; Memphis store, 217; New Orleans branch, 218; output, 211, 213, 219; parlor furniture, 226, 229; power, 209, 211, 219; product identification, 213–14, 220, 226; production

methods, 211, 213, 214, 217, 220; retail store, 210ʳ, 219, 220ʳ, 229; rocker, 225, 226ʳ; secretary and bookcase, 214; sideboard, 220, 221ʳ, 222ʳ, 223ʳ; side chair, 224ʳ, 225, 226ʳ; stock inventory, 213; table, 224ʳ, 228ʳ; upholstered furniture, 212, 214, 222, 225, 229; wages, 211; wholesale pricing, 213; window decoration, 229; work force, 211, 219; work table, 214, 215ʳ

Mitchell, Craig & Company, New Orleans furniture merchants, 218

Mitchell, Hoffman & Company, Memphis furniture merchants, 217–18

Mitchell, Rammelsberg & Company, St. Louis furniture merchants, 211–12, 218

Mitering, 14, 15

Moll, John, painted chest, 74

Montresor, John, New York City map, 158

Moore, Thomas H., Philadelphia cabinetmaker, 82

Morgan, J. P.: Wallace Nutting and, 58; Wadsworth Atheneum gift, 13

Morris, Lydia Thompson: colonial Philadelphia dressing table, 71ʳ; colonial Philadelphia high chest, 71ʳ

Morris, Robert, steward of, 143

Morris family, Philadelphia case furniture, 69

Morse, Daniel, 44

Morse, Jeremiah, colonial wheelwright, 45, 46

Morse, Mrs. Jeremiah (Elizabeth Hamant), 46

Morse, Joseph, 45

Moyce, Joseph, colonial joiner, 7n, 39–40; Salisbury, Massachusetts, communion table, 40

Moyston, Edward, Philadelphia innkeeper, 143

Mullan, Thomas, Philadelphia joiner, cane chair, 79

Mulliner, Thomas, colonial joiner, chest, 7n, 28

Museum of Fine Arts, Boston: chest, 3n; chest by John Houghton, 9, 11

Musical entertainment, City Tavern, Philadelphia, 155ʳ

Music stand, by Robert C. Whitley, 155ʳ

Nash, John, colonial builder, 24

National Historical Parks, Independence, 139

National Home Fashions League, 149, 156

National Park Service: City Tavern, Philadelphia, reconstruction, 139–60; furniture reproductions, 155–56

Newcome, Webster, New Jersey chairmaker, 172; production, 167ᵗ

New England: artifact style dissemination, 27–29; socioreligious factor in community organization, 27–28

New Haven, chests, 28

New Jersey, furniture industry, 161–73, 167ᵗ

New Orleans, furniture business, 218

New York, artifact style dissemination, 44

New York City, map by John Montresor, 158

Noblit, Dell, Jr., Philadelphia furniture merchant, 171

Norman, John, colonial carpenter, meetinghouse seats, 5n

Norris, Isaac, furniture by Edward Evans, 77

Nossitter, Thomas, Philadelphia furniture merchant, 171

Nutting, Wallace, 47–60, 48ʳ; American decorative arts and, 47; as antique collector, 47, 58–60; auction of collection, 47; chest by John Thurston, 16; chest-on-frame reproduction, 51, 52ʳ; Connecticut sunflower chest reproduction, 50ʳ; correspondence, 60; Henry Francis du Pont and, 59; eighteenth-century mahogany furniture collection, 59; Henry Wood Erving and, 58; evaluation, 47; Flemish armchair for Colonial Williamsburg, 49ʳ; furniture catalogue, 51, 54; furniture for Colonial Williamsburg, 47–50; furniture for William F. Deuser, 51n; *Furniture of the Pilgrim Century*, 16, 54, 57, 59; furniture reproductions, 47, 50–53; furniture reproductions labeling, 48ʳ, 51; furniture reproductions styles, 53n; *Furniture Treasury*, 16, 47, 48, 54, 59; Edward Guy statement on, 56ʳ, 57; handtinted photographs, 47, 53–54, 55ʳ; Abby Howes and, 58; ironwork reproductions, 54, 56ʳ, 57ʳ; lowboy reproduction, 52ʳ; J. P. Morgan and, 58; Prence-Howes court cupboard and, 58; products, 53; promotional material, 54n, 57; publications, 47, 54, 58; Israel Sack and, 59; as scholar, 60; secretary reproduction, 53ʳ; trenchers reproduction, 51n; windsor chair collection, 59; windsor chair reproduction, 50ʳ, 51; workshop, 51

Nutting, Mrs. Wallace (Mariet Griswold Caswell), 47, 54; death, 59n

Oak, millsawn, 41

Ohl, John, Philadelphia furniture merchant, 82

Old Lyme Historical Society, Metcalf chest, 27n

Old Saybrook Historical Society, chair-table, 26n

Organ builders, Philadelphia (checklist), 91–138

Owen, Edward, colonial physician, desk, 76; leather chairs, 66

Painted furniture, 15, 19, 155, 156, 164

Painted woodwork, 154

Pallet bedstead, colonial Philadelphia, 63

Paneling, City Tavern, Philadelphia, 154

Panels: armchair, 2; box, 19; chest, 9, 11, 15, 16, 19, 22, 24, 26; Holy Trinity, Blythborough, 7, 15, 26; Medfield, Massachusetts, meetinghouse, 1, 2ʳ, 5, 7, 9, 11, 12, 19, 27, 35ʳ, 36ʳ, 43

Parke-Bernet, Wallace Nutting collection auction, 47; *see also* Sotheby Parke Bernet

Parlor suite, by Mitchell & Rammelsberg, 226, 229

Pasa, Mrs. William, 142

Patterson, John, Philadelphia chairmaker, 82

Peale, Charles Willson: John Cadwalader family portrait, 197, 198ʳ, 200, 204; Lambert Cadwalader portrait, 203ʳ, 204, 207

Peirce, Donald C., 209–29

Penn, Letitia, chest of drawers by Edward Evans, 77

Penn, Thomas, cane chairs, 79

Penn, William: household furnishings, 62; report on Philadelphia, 61

Pennsbury Manor, 62; bed inventory, 62, 63; furniture, 79

Pennsylvania House, cabriole-leg chair, 157ʳ

Pennsylvania Ledger . . ., 177

Pews: Dedham, Massachusetts, meetinghouse, 12; Medfield, Massachusetts, meetinghouse, 13

Philadelphia: cabinetmaking, 81–138; checklist of cabinetmakers and related craftsmen, 91–138; Chippendale style furniture, 193–208; Chippendale style furniture numbering, 201; City Tavern, 139–60, 140ʳ; colonial cabinetmakers, 79; colonial craftsmen, 61; colonial furniture, 61–80, 157ʳ; colonial housing, 61–62; furniture exports, 82, 83ᵗ, 84ᵗ; furniture industry, 81–138; 177–79; furniture inventories, 61–80; furniture price book, 175–92; furniture style characteristics, 195–96; merchants' exchange, 143, 150; social life, 139, 140, 141, 142, 154; in War of Independence, 141–42

Philadelphia Cabinet and Chair-Makers' Book of Prices, The, 176

Philadelphia Marlborough leg, 156

Philadelphia Museum of Art: chest of drawers, 72; desk-and-bookcase, 77ʳ; dressing table, 70ʳ, 71ʳ; gateleg table, 68ʳ; high chest, 71ʳ; saddle seat chairs, 204; tall-case clock, 78ʳ

Phillips, John, colonial clergyman, 4

Photographs, Wallace Nutting productions, 47, 53–54, 55ʳ

Pianoforte makers, Philadelphia (checklist), 91–138

Pickering, Charles, Philadelphia merchant, desk, 75

Pierce family, chest, 3n

Pilasters, City Tavern, Philadelphia, 154

Pipe tongs, Wallace Nutting reproduction, 57ʳ

Pitt, William, caricature, 154ʳ

Pittsburgh Transportation Line, furniture shipments, 87

Plan of . . . Philadelphia (Faden), 155ʳ

Plumley, Charles, Philadelphia joiner, 63, 79; cherry chest of drawers, 73; furniture, 66

Pond, Daniel, colonial carpenter, 41, 43, 46

Pond, Mrs. Daniel (Abigail Shepard), 43

Pond, Mrs. Daniel (Ann Shepard), 43

Pond, Robert, colonial carpenter, 1, 43

Porch, City Tavern, Philadelphia, 144

Portable desk makers, Philadelphia (checklist), 91–138

Portraits, *see individual artists and subjects*

Port Royal, Edward Stile's home, 144

Post-Restoration style, in furniture, 62

Powell, Samuel, desk import, 76

Pratt, John, colonial carpenter, 46

Pratt, Phineas, colonial joiner, 12n

Prence-Howes cupboard, 58ʳ

Prescott, Colonel, British prisoner, 141

Pretzel-back chair, by Kittinger Furniture Company, 157ʳ

Price book: *Cabinet-Makers' London Book of Prices and Designs of Cabinet Work*, 176; *The Cabinet-Makers Philadelphia and London Book of Prices of 1796*, 175; cabinetmaking, 175–92, 180ʳ–92ʳ; of carpenters, 177; of English cabinetmakers, 175; *The Philadelphia Cabinet and Chair-Makers' Book of Prices*, 176; "Prices of Cabinet & Chair . . . / Philadelphia . . . ," 175–92, 180ʳ–92ʳ; "Prices of Cabinet & Chair Work / Binjamin Lehman January 1786," 175; role of, 177; "Rule and Price of Joyners Work—. . . ," 175

Price List, of Mitchell & Rammelsberg, furniture manufacturers, 213

"Prices of Cabinet & Chair . . . / Philadelphia . . . ," 175–92, 180ʳ–92ʳ

"Prices of Cabinet & Chair Work / Binjamin Lehman January 1786," 175

Pritchard, Barbara, clocks, 78

Providence, Rhode Island, furniture industry, 175

Puckle, Nathaniel, Philadelphia merchant, chamber furnishings, 74

Pulpit: Holy Trinity, Blythborough, Suffolk, 7, 8ʳ, 15, 26, 30ʳ; Medfield, Massachusetts, meetinghouse, 1, 2ʳ, 5, 7, 9ʳ, 11, 12, 19, 27, 35ʳ, 36ʳ, 43; Puritan meetinghouse design, 7; sounding board, 7

Puritanism, meetinghouse design, 7

Pyle, Howard, chest by John Thurston, 16

Quakers, influence on furniture, 61–62

Quary, Sarah: bedsteads, 63; case furniture, 71

Queen Anne style, in furniture, 61, 79, 80, 177, 229

Quervelle, Anthony, Pennsylvania cabinetmaker, 84

Rabbeting, chest, 14

Rammelsberg, Frederick, Cincinnati furniture manufacturer, 209, 210ʳ; death, 217

Randolph, Benjamin, Philadelphia cabinetmaker: chair design, 202; furniture for John Cadwalader, 205, 206, 207, 208; saddle seat chairs (sample chairs), 193, 200, 203–4; will, 203

Randolph, Mrs. Benjamin (Mary), 203

R. & W. Mitchell, St. Louis furniture merchants, 218

"Rates of Porterage and Carriage, . . . ," 177

Read, George, 141n

Reconstruction: architect/curator/designer/engineer roles, 148–52, 154–56, 158; cartoon sources for, 143, 148; of City Tavern, Philadelphia, 139–60; eighteenth- and twentieth-century compromises, 148; insurance survey source for, 143, 148; minimal intrusion principle, 140, 144; sources for, 143, 148

Redman, Joseph, Philadelphia merchant, desk, 77

Reed, Elias, 89

Reiley (Riley), Moses, New Jersey cabinetmaker, 164

Religious factor, in New England community organization, 27–28

Restaurant, City Tavern, Philadelphia, 139–60

Reynolds, James, Philadelphia furniture carver, 200, 206, 207; carved frames for John Cadwalader, 204

Richards, Philip, Philadelphia merchant, chest of drawers, 73

Richardson, Francis, Philadelphia merchant-silversmith, tea table, 71

Richardson, Francis, Jr., Philadelphia goldsmith-clockmaker, 78; tall-case clock, 78ʳ

Richardson family, Philadelphia, desk, 76

Richmond, ship, 65

Riddle, Crawford, Philadelphia cabinetmaker, 82, 88

Riley, William, 89

Roadstown, New Jersey, furniture manufacture, 161, 165, 167, 169

Robert C. Whitley Studio, tavern table, 153ʳ

Robert Treate Hogg Cabinet Shop, ladderback chair, 153ʳ

Robinson, Patrick, court appearance, 64

Rocker, 163, 170; by Mitchell & Rammelsberg, 225, 226ʳ

Roper, John, colonial joiner, 12, 27, 28, 39, 41

Roper, Mrs. John (Alles [Alice]), 39

Rudd, John, 26n

Rudd, Mrs. John (Mary Metcalf), 26n

Rudd, Jonathan, chest, 26

Rudd, William, 26n

Rudd, Mrs. William (Eunice Bingham), 26n

"Rule and Price of Joyners Work—. . . ," 175

Rules and Constitutions of the Society of the Sons of St. George, 177

Rulon, John W., furniture merchant, 85

Rush, for chair seats, 66, 163, 168

Rush-bottomed chairs, 161–73, 167ᵗ; popularity of, 172–73

Russian leather, 66

Rutherford, H., 169

Rutland, John, cabinetmaker apprentice, 91

Sack, Israel, Wallace Nutting and, 47, 59

Saddle seat chair: of John Cadwalader, 199; card table comparison, 197–208; colonial Philadelphia, 194ʳ, 196ʳ, 200; hairy paw feet design, 196, 197, 202; half-upholstery design, 196, 197, 204; identification, 193–208; numbering, 201; pin design, 196–97; rail design, 196, 197; shoe design, 196ʳ; splat-rear stiles joining, 196, 200–201

Sage, Mrs. Russell: box by John Thurston, 18ʳ, 33ʳ; Milford,

Connecticut, chest, 6^r, 37^r
St. George, Robert Blair, 1–46
St. Louis, furniture industry, 211–12, 218
Salem, New Jersey, furniture manufacture, 171
Salem County, New Jersey, furniture manufacture, 161–73
Salisbury, Connecticut, communion table, 40
Salisbury, Massachusetts, meetinghouse, 7
Salter, Anna, chairs, 64
Sauer, John Christopher, bedstead, 64
Savery, William, Philadelphia cabinetmaker, furniture for John Cadwalader, 204, 205–6
"Savery School" lowboy, Wallace Nutting reproduction, 52^r
Sawmill: Dedham, Massachusetts, 13, 41; Medfield, Massachusetts, 38; Wrentham, Massachusetts, 46
Saybolt & Cleland; windsor armchair, 153^r; windsor furniture, 155^r
Schuylkill Navigation Company, furniture shipments, 87
Scituate, Massachusetts, windmill, 44
Scottow, Joshua, colonial joiner, 45
Screens, in Philadelphia inventories, 72, 79
Searle, William, colonial joiner, 5
Secretary, Wallace Nutting reproduction, 53^r
Secretary and bookcase, by Mitchell & Rammelsberg, 214
Settee: price book listing, 178; South Jersey, 172
Sharp, Thomas, imported furniture, 68
Shelburne Museum, Fairbanks house chest of drawers, 3n
Shepard, Edward, 43
Shippen, Edward, japanned cabinet, 69, 75
Shoe: saddle seat chair, 196^r; straight-front side chair, 196, 197^r, 201
Shoemaker, Samuel, colonial Loyalist, 141n
Shutters, City Tavern, Philadelphia, 158
Sideboard, by Mitchell & Rammelsberg, 220, 221^r, 222^r, 223^r
Sideboard table, in Philadelphia inventories, 67
Side chair: colonial Philadelphia, 67^r, 157^r, 196, 197^r, 201, 202^r; by Mitchell & Rammelsberg, 224^r, 225, 226^r; in Philadelphia inventories, 65; rail design, 202^r; by Maskell Ware, 162^r
Simmons, Stephen H., Philadelphia furniture merchant, 171
Simpson, John, furniture, 171
Slat-backed chair, 161–73, 167^t; components, 163
Slate, table, 67
Sloan, Samuel, *Homestead Architecture,* 217
Smith, Daniel, Philadelphia innkeeper, 140–42, 148, 149
Smith, Henry, colonial joiner, 12, 28, 38, 39, 40, 43
Smith (Smythe), John, chest by John Thurston, 19
Smith, Seth, colonial carpenter-joiner, 43
Social life, Philadelphia, 139, 140, 141, 142, 154
Social rank, armchair and, 64
Society for the Preservation of New England Antiquities, 59–60
Society of Cincinnati, Pennsylvania Line, 159
Society of Journeymen Cabinetmakers, 88, 91; marketing cooperative, 88–89, 90^t
Socioreligious factor, in New England community organization, 27–28
Sofa: of John Cadwalader, 204, 205; price book listing, 177, 178
Sotheby & Company, London, 193, 203
Sotheby Parke Bernet, 203: on Benjamin Randolph "sample chairs," 193–94
South, furniture imports, 82
Southard, Samuel L., secretary of the Army, furniture, 84

Southold, Long Island, desk box, 29^r, 35^r
South Jersey turned chairs, 161–73, 167^t
Spanish table, in Philadelphia inventories, 67
Sparks, William, New Jersey furniture merchant, 171
Spaulding, Philip L., chest by John Thurston, 16
Spice boxes, in Philadelphia inventories, 72, 75
S-scroll design, 7n, 30^r–35^r; chest, 7, 11, 15, 20, 28; desk box, 28; pulpit panel, 7, 11; style dissemination, 28
Stand: design features, 178; by Edward Evans, 77; in Philadelphia inventories, 79
Stansbury, Joseph, Philadelphia china merchant, 156
Stanton, Edward, Philadelphia joiner, 63
Stapleford, Thomas, Philadelphia joiner, 77; beds for James Logan, 63; furniture, 79
Starr, Comfort, colonial carpenter, 1
Sterling, Henry, Pittsburgh furniture merchant, 87
Stevenson, J. H., furniture merchant, 84–85
Stiles, Edward, Port Royal home, 144
Stool, 163; with drawer and sliding top, 177; in Philadelphia inventories, 65
Store architecture, Mitchell & Rammelsberg, 210^r, 220^r
Stossmeister, William, Cincinnati furniture craftsman, 218
Straight-front side chair: colonial Philadelphia, 196, 197^r, 201, 202^r; rail design, 202^r; shoe design, 196, 197^r, 201
Straight-sided card table, 199^r, 200
Stratford Hall, John Cadwalader straight-front side chair, 201–2
Stretch, Peter, Philadelphia clockmaker, 78
Strickland, William, American architect, merchants' exchange, Philadelphia, 143
Sudbury, Massachusetts, meetinghouse, 7
Suffolk, England: joinery tradition, 5, 7, 12, 14, 25, 26, 27–28; Massachusetts immigration, 3
Supper clubs, 141n
Svenson, Esther, Wallace Nutting associate, 59n
Swing, Nathaniel G., New Jersey turner, 170

Table: for City Tavern, Philadelphia, 155; colonial Philadelphia, 68^r; with drawers, 68, by Edward Evans, 77; inlaid, 68; King of Prussia blue marble, 159; by Knipp & Company, 157^r; by Mitchell & Rammelsberg, 224^r, 228^r, 229; Philadelphia design features, 67–69; in Philadelphia inventories, 67–69, 71, 72, 77; price book listing, 177, 178; slate, 67; with sliding stool, 69; Wallace Nutting reproduction, 50
Tableware, for City Tavern, Philadelphia, 156, 158
Tall-case clock, colonial Philadelphia, 78^r
Tatem, E. S., New Jersey furniture manufacturer, 172
Tatham, John, Philadelphia merchant: bedstead, 64; inlaid furniture, 68; japanned furniture, 68
Tatham, Mrs. John (Elizabeth), 64, 68
Tavern: City Tavern, Philadelphia, 139–60, 140^r; interior design, 139–60
Tavern table, by Robert C. Whitley Studio, 153^r
Taylor, Christopher, Phladelphia merchant, furniture inventory, 62
Taylor, Licard & Company, furniture merchants, 84
Tea chair, Eastlake style, 222
Tea service, in colonial Philadelphia, 71–72
Tea table, in Philadelphia inventories, 71–72, 79
Tea tray, 71, 72
Textiles: for bedstead headboard, 64; for furniture, 64, 66; turkey work, 64

Thurston, John, colonial joiner, 4, 12, 28, 38, 39, 44; biographical data, 40–41; box, 13, 19, 33ʳ; chest, 13ʳ–16ʳ, 17ʳ, 18ʳ, 19, 20, 21ʳ, 22, 24, 26, 30ʳ–33ʳ; comparison with John Houghton, 20; Dedham, Massachusetts, meetinghouse pews, 12; Dedham, Massachusetts, schoolhouse joinery, 12; Medfield, Massachusetts, meetinghouse pews, 13; technique, 20, 26, 28; tools, 12, 22
Thurston, Mrs. John (Margaret), 40
Thurston, Joseph, colonial carpenter-joiner, 40, 44
Thurston, Mrs. Joseph (Anne Foster), 44
Thurston, Thomas, colonial carpenter, 38, 44
Thurston, Mrs. Thomas (Sarah Thaxter), 44
Thurston, Thomas, son of Thomas, colonial joiner, 40
Tibby, Elizabeth, bedstead, 63
Tilden, William S., *History of the Town of Medfield*, 1
Till, William, Philadelphia joiner, 73, 79; mahogany stock, 72
Tools: chairmaker, 162–63, 164, 167–68; joiners, 19, 20, 22; *see also* Inventory
Transportation, furniture marketing and, 86–87, 171
Trencher, Wallace Nutting reproduction, 51n
Trent, William, colonial shipbuilder, 77
Turkey-work chair, in Philadelphia inventories, 64
Turners, Philadelphia (checklist), 91–138
Tyler Arboretum, "Prices of Cabinet & Chair . . . / Philadelphia . . . ," 175–92, 180ʳ–92ʳ

Undertaking service, 169
Unnewehr, Frederick, Cincinnati furniture craftsman, 218
Upholstered furniture: half-upholstered chairs, 196, 197, 204; leather, 65, 66ʳ; by Mitchell & Rammelsberg, 222, 225, 229
Upholsterers, Philadelphia (checklist), 91–138

Van Sciver, New Jersey furniture merchant, 167
Varnishing, in furniture manufacture, 213
Vaughan, John, Philadelphia furniture merchant, 82
Veneering, colonial Philadelphia furniture, 62
Venetian blinds, City Tavern, Philadelphia, 158
Vroom, Peter D., New Jersey governor, 167

Wadsworth Atheneum: chest by John Thurston, 16, 19, 26; Wallace Nutting furniture collection, 16, 19; Prence-Howes court cupboard, 58; Salisbury communion table by Joseph Moyce, 40
Waite, Martha, case furniture, 71
Wallace Nutting Chain of Colonial Houses, 59
Wallace Nutting Collectors Club, 54n
Wall decoration, tavern, 150, 151, 158–59
Wanamaker, John, Wallace Nutting furniture, 59, 60
Warder, John, Philadelphia pipemaker, case furniture, 69
Ware, Arthur Middleton, New Jersey chair-seat maker, 168
Ware, Benjamin Thackara, New Jersey storekeeper, 164
Ware, Charles, New Jersey chairmaker, 164, 165, 169
Ware, Dan, New Jersey chairmaker, 166–67
Ware, David, 170
Ware, Elijah, New Jersey merchant, 170–71, 172
Ware, Elnathan, 161
Ware, Mrs. Elnathan (Marcy Moore), 161
Ware, Francis Herbert, New Jersey chairmaker, 166
Ware, Frank, New Jersey chairmaker, 167
Ware, Frank Riley, New Jersey chairmaker, 169
Ware, George Sloan, New Jersey chairmaker, 167
Ware, Harold Maskell, New Jersey chairmaker, 167

Ware, Henry Clay, New Jersey chairmaker, 164, 167
Ware, James Bacon, New Jersey chairmaker, 166
Ware, John S., New Jersey chairmaker, 164, 166, 170, 171; production, 167ᵗ
Ware, Maskell, New Jersey chairmaker, 161–62; side chair, 162ʳ
Ware, Mrs. Maskell (Hannah Simpkins), 161
Ware, Maskell, Jr., New Jersey chairmaker, 166, 172
Ware, Reuben, New Jersey chairmaker, 166
Ware, Richard Moore, New Jersey lawyer, 167
Ware, Robert, 4
Ware, Robert Bonham, New Jersey chairmaker, 167
Ware, Samuel Fithian, New Jersey chairmaker: account books, 169, 170; undertaking services, 169
Ware, Samuel Sloan, New Jersey chairmaker, 164; chair front stretchers of, 168ʳ
Ware, Theodore, New Jersey chairmaker, 169
Ware, Thomas, New Jersey chairmaker, 162–63, 165
Ware, Thomas Henry (Harry), New Jersey chair-seat maker, 168
Ware, Warren, New Jersey chairmaker, 167
Ware, William, New Jersey chairmaker, 164, 170, 171; production, 167ᵗ
Ware, William Frederick, New Jersey chairmaker, 166
Ware, William H., New Jersey chairmaker, 164–66
Ware, Wilmon, New Jersey chairmaker, 169
Ware, Wilmon W., 169
Ware family, furniture manufacturers, 161–73, 167ᵗ; genealogy, 163ʳ; manufactory advertisement, 164, 165ʳ, 170, 171
War of Independence, City Tavern, Philadelphia, during, 141–42
Washington, George, Society of Cincinnati and, 159
Waters, Deborah Dependahl, 161–73
Wayside Inn, 59
Webster, John, upholstery for John Cadwalader, 205
Weil, Martin Eli, 175–92
Wells, William, desk box, 28
Welsh, Samuel and William, Philadelphia furniture merchants, 82
Whitaker & Newcomb, New Jersey furniture manufacturers, 172; production, 167ᵗ
White, Charles H., Philadelphia cabinetmaker, 82
White, George W., shipmaster, 86
White, John F., Philadelphia cabinetmaker, 82
Whitley, Robert C., music stand, 155ʳ
Whitpaine, Zechiah, desk, 75
William and Mary style, in furniture, 73, 79, 80
Wills, Joseph, Philadelphia clockmaker, 78
Wilson, James K., Cincinnati architect, Mitchell & Rammelsberg retail store, 219–20
Wilson, John, Jr., colonial clergyman, 46
Windmill, Scituate, Massachusetts, 44
Window decoration: City Tavern, Philadelphia, 150, 158; by Mitchell & Rammelsberg, 229; tavern, 150, 151
Windsor furniture, 155; armchair by Saybolt & Cleland, 153ʳ; chair in Wallace Nutting collection, 59; chair, Wallace Nutting reproduction, 50ʳ; by Saybolt & Cleland, 155ʳ; side chair by Wallace Nutting, 51; South Jersey industry, 172
Wintersteen, Mrs. John, colonial Philadelphia desk-and-bookcase, 77ʳ
Winterthur Museum: chest by John Thurston, 18ʳ, 19, 26;

colonial Philadelphia armchair, 66[r]; colonial Philadelphia desk, 75[r]; colonial Philadelphia desk-on-frame, 75[r]; colonial Philadelphia easy chair, 67[r]; colonial Philadelphia gateleg folding table, 68[r]; colonial Philadelphia side chair, 67[r]; drapery model for City Tavern, Philadelphia, 158; saddle seat chair, 193, 194[r], 196[r], 200, 204; straight-front side chair, 196, 197[r], 201, 202[r]; straight-sided card table, 199[r], 200
Wood, N. F., Philadelphia chairmaker, 171
Wood, Richard, Jr., New Jersey store owner, 162
Woodcarvers, Philadelphia (checklist), 91–138
Woodcarving: in artifact study, 199, 200, 206–7, 208; City Tavern, Philadelphia, frontispiece, 143; Hadley style, 5, 11; *see also* Furniture carving; *specific objects*
Woodhouse, Samuel W., Jr., antiquarian, saddle seat chair identification and, 193, 194, 197, 203–4
Woodstown, New Jersey, furniture manufacture, 166, 167
Woodwork, City Tavern, Philadelphia, 154
Worktable, by Mitchell & Rammelsberg, 214, 215[r]
Wrentham, Massachusetts, sawmill, 46
Wright's furniture machinery, 213

Youth Attacked by a Shark, A (Copley), 158

Zimmerman, Philip D., 193–208